*International Review of*
*Industrial*
*and Organizational*
*Psychology*
*2000   Volume 15*

# International Review of Industrial and Organizational Psychology
## 2000 Volume 15

Edited by

Cary L. Cooper
*and*
Ivan T. Robertson

*University of Manchester*
*Institute of Science & Technology, UK*

JOHN WILEY & SONS, LTD
Chichester · New York · Weinheim · Brisbane · Singapore · Toronto

*The Library of Congress has cataloged this serial publication as follows:*

International review of industrial and organizational psychology.
   —1986—Chichester; New York; Wiley, c1986—
   v.: ill.; 24cm.
   Annual.
   ISSN 0886-1528 = International review of industrial and organizational psychology

   1. Psychology, Industrial—Periodicals.   2. Personnel management—Periodicals.
   [DNLM: 1. Organization and Administration—periodicals.   2. Psychology,
Industrial—periodicals. W1IN832UJ]
HF5548.7.157   158.7'05—dc 19 86-643874
                        AACR 2 MARC-S
Library of Congress [8709]


ISBN 0-471-85855-2

Typeset in 10/12pt Plantin by Dorwyn Ltd, Rowlands Castle, Hants
Printed and bound in Great Britain by Antony Rowe Ltd, Chippenham, Wilts
This book is printed on acid-free paper responsibly manufactured from sustainable forestry, in
which at least two trees are planted for each one used for paper production.

# CONTENTS

# ABOUT THE EDITORS

**Cary L. Cooper**
**Ivan T. Robertson**

*Manchester School of Management, University of Manchester Institute of Science and Technology, PO Box 88, Manchester, M60 1QD, UK.*

*Cary L. Cooper* received his BS and MBA degrees from the University of California, Los Angeles, his PhD from the University of Leeds, UK, and an honorary MSc from the University of Manchester, UK. He is currently Professor of Organizational Psychology and Pro Vice Chancellor of UMIST. Professor Cooper was founding President of the *British Academy of Management* and is a Fellow of the British Psychological Society, Royal Society of Arts, Royal Society of Medicine and Royal Society of Health. He is also founding editor of the *Journal of Organizational Behavior* and co-editor of *Stress Medicine*, serves on the editorial board of a number of other scholarly journals, and is the author of over 80 books and 400 journal articles.

*Ivan Robertson* is Professor of Occupational Psychology in the Manchester School of Management, UMIST. He is a Fellow of the British Psychological Society and a Chartered Psychologist. Professor Robertson received his BSc degree from the University of Exeter. His career includes several years experience working as an applied psychologist on a wide range of projects for a variety of different organizations. His PhD was awarded by the Open University in 1976. Professor Robertson's research and teaching interests focus on individual differences and organizational factors related to human performance. His other publications include 15 books and over 100 scientific articles and conference papers.

# CONTRIBUTORS

Paul M. Brewerton — *Department of Psychology, University of Surrey, Guildford, Surrey, GU2 5XH, UK*

David Chan — *Department of Social Work & Psychology, National University of Singapore, 10 Kent Ridge Crescent, Singapore 0511*

Timothy Coombs — *Department of Psychology, Baruch College, 17 Lexington Avenue, Box 6-112, NY 10010, USA*

Cary L. Cooper — *University of Manchester Institute of Science & Technology (UMIST), PO Box 88, Manchester, M60 1QD, UK*

Michael Frese — *Faculty of Psychology, University of Amsterdam, Roetersstraat 15, NL-1018 WB Amsterdam, The Netherlands*

Gary R. Henderson — *Graduate School of Management, University of California, Irvine, California 92717, USA*

Judith L. Komaki — *Department of Psychology, Baruch College, 17 Lexington Avenue, Box 6-112, NY 10010, USA*

Udo Konradt — *Christian-Albrechts-Universität zu Kiel, Institut für Psychologie, Universität Kiel, Olshausenstr. 40, D-24098 Kiel, Germany*

Mike Mälecke — *Christian-Albrechts-Universität zu Kiel, Institut für Psychologie, Universität Kiel, Olshausenstr. 40, D-24098 Kiel, Germany*

Lynne J. Millward — *Department of Psychology, University of Surrey, Guildford, Surrey, GU2 5XH, UK*

Jone L. Pearce — *Graduate School of Management, University of California, Irvine, California 92717, USA*

Andreas Rauch — *Faculty of Psychology, University of Amsterdam, Roetersstraat 15, NL-1018 WB Amsterdam, The Netherlands*

Thomas P. Redding, Jr — *Department of Psychology, Baruch College, 17 Lexington Avenue, Box 6-112, NY 10010, USA*

Renate Schmook — *Christian-Albrechts-Universität zu Kiel, Institut für Psychologie, Universität Kiel, Olshausenstr. 40, D-24098 Kiel, Germany*

Stephen Schepman — *Department of Psychology, Baruch College, 17 Lexington Avenue, Box 6-112, NY 10010, USA*

Sabine Sonnentag — *Faculty of Psychology, University of Amsterdam, Roetersstraat 15, NL-1018 WB Amsterdam, The Netherlands*

Anne Spurgeon — *Institute of Occupational Health, University of Birmingham, Edgbaston, Birmingham, B15, 2TT, UK*

# EDITORIAL FOREWORD

This is the fifteenth and new millennium edition of the now well established and internationally successful annual volume of the *International Review of Industrial and Organizational Psychology*. It has been our enormous privilege to be the editors of this *Review*, which has seen a topical range of chapters on all the substantive and seminal areas of industrial, occupational, work and organizational psychology. We have striven to bring together the highest quality reviews, by inviting some of the leading scholars in their subjects, and some of their disciples, to cover, critique and explore the future of the current and emerging topics in the field.

In this issue, we attempt to carry the mantle forward with topics that are new millennium or new issue driven. If the nature of work and organizations is, as Cooper and Jackson (1997) suggest in their book *Creating Tomorrow's Organizations*, 'changing as a consequence of globalization, cross-national alliances, privatizations, outsourcing, information technology and the contingent workforce', then as we enter the new millennium 'the challenge for those of us working in the field of organizational behaviour is to change as rapidly as the organizations and people we study'. This means that we need to explore topics of the beginning of this millennium, themes that look at the psychological contract in the twenty-first century; working time, health and performance (as we work longer and harder); psychological approaches to entrepreneurial success (if the trend is away from larger to small organizations); the impacts of teleworking on individuals, organizations and families; and how individuals adapt to work and change and understanding acts of betrayal in a contingent world of work. These are just some of the topical themes that we will explore in this volume, together with how we should approach a more rich and vigorous approach to behavioural research in the world of work in the future, and the role of expertise at work.

We hope you will find these topics of interest and that they will stimulate more high-quality I/O psychological research in the years ahead.

CLC
ITR
May 1999

# Chapter 1

# PSYCHOLOGICAL CONTRACTS: EMPLOYEE RELATIONS FOR THE TWENTY-FIRST CENTURY?

Lynne J. Millward and Paul M. Brewerton
*University of Surrey, UK*

> the most complex organizational issue since the industrial revolution: the funda-
> mental and irrevocable shift in the psychological contract between employee and
> organization. (Noer, 1993)

The employment contract is basic to organizational membership. It constitutes the mainstay of employment relations, establishing an exchange of
promises and contributions between two parties: employer and employee
(Rousseau, 1989, p. 121). Whilst the employment contract can be viewed
from many angles—psychological, political, economic, organizational, sociological and legal—none of these provides a complete picture. Moreover
there is often difficulty in defining disciplinary boundaries due to much conceptual and empirical overlap. In this review, we are concerned with what
Rousseau (1995, p. 1) calls the 'organizational, social and psychological
meaning of contracts'.

It has long been recognized that 'subjectivity is inherent in all contracts'
(Rousseau, 1989, p. 121), whether in written or unwritten form. This concerns the way the contract of employment is lived and breathed; the way it is
interpreted, understood and enacted on a daily basis as employees interface
with their workplace. Argyris (1960) was the first to undertake a formal
study of the subjective aspects of contracts and the first to introduce the term
'psychological contract'. He described the psychological contract as an *un-
derwritten agreement* that exists between an individual and the organization
when undertaking terms of employment (Argyris, 1960). Others followed
suit (e.g. Kotter, 1973; Levinson, 1962) but it was not until the 1980s that
the concept began to enter the vocabulary of writers on organizational life
and behaviour (Schein, 1980; Farnsworth, 1982; MacNeil, 1985).
Farnsworth (1982) for example, used the term psychological contract to

denote issues of exchange and of mutual expectation in the link between individuals and their employing organization. Thus, the concept of psychological contract emerged as a tool for describing and explaining what was *implicit* to the agreements made between employee and employer, and in particular the role played by *reciprocity and exchange* in the process of forming such agreements.

Until the last decade, the term psychological contract was used mainly as a framework or backdrop (rather than a scientific construct) in which to talk about what is 'implicit' to the exchange relationship between employee and employer. Little formal research had been undertaken at this stage. Since the early 1990s, however, the psychological contract has acquired construct status and in so doing has taken a major conceptual and empirical turn. It has been transposed from being a term used to refer to what is nebulous and difficult to access in connection with the *quality of the exchange relationship*, into a *cognitive-perceptual entity*. In this form it has been deemed to be *measurable* and *owned solely by the individual*, as opposed to being a property of the relationship between two parties. This was facilitated in part by the publication of a thesis by Rousseau (1989) on the distinction between psychological and implied contracts, which was later to form part of a more formal system of thinking about the psychology of the employment contract.

This thinking is presented in Rousseau's 1995 book *Psychological Contracts in Organizations* in which she defines the psychological contract as 'an individual's belief in paid for promises, or a reciprocal obligation between the individual and the organization' (pp. 16–17). An implicit contract however, is described as one that can be inferred by others as pertaining to the unwritten aspects of the employment contract. The psychological contract then became a reference to the 'beliefs' held by individuals pertaining to reciprocal obligations (not the reciprocal obligations themselves), and might be implicit or explicit to the agreements the individual perceives that he or she is party to. It became something specific and internal to the individual and the way they perceived the world. Beliefs in reciprocal obligations, notes Rousseau (1995), can arise from overt promises (e.g. bonus systems discussed in the recruitment process), interpretations of patterns of past exchange, vicarious learning (e.g. witnessing other employees' experiences), as well as through various factors which each party may take for granted (e.g. good faith or fairness). By contrast, the implicit contract (which used to pertain to what was 'psychological' about contracts) became instead the property of an observer, looking in from the outside (i.e. using behaviour as the basis through which to infer the unwritten aspects of contracts).

Since then, the psychological contract literature has grown in complexity, with some writers operating ostensibly in the cognitive-perceptual field, while others try to retain some of the more dynamic and relational aspects of the interface between individuals and organizations, as intimated by people like Barnard (1938), Argyris (1960) and also Levinson (1962) and Schein (1980).

Confusing the picture even further is the use of the term psychological contract as a metaphor for describing the current state of employment relations. In particular, the term has been harnessed by researchers and practitioners alike, as a means of analysing the nature and impact of transformation in the character of the contemporary workplace. It took the breakdown in traditional contracts of employment (which guaranteed a job-for-life and career prospects in return for loyalty and hard work), in parallel with a major increase in the centrality of contracting (i.e. short-term, task-specific, monetary contracts), to bring the psychological side of contracts and contracting into stark relief.

Changes in economic and political life, with the attendant collapse of traditional organizational designs and structures (through mass downsizing, streamlining and the contracting-out of peripheral functions) severely undermined conventional forms of employee-employer exchange (e.g. job security and career prospects offered in exchange for loyalty and commitment). Thus, organizational behaviour researchers began to concern themselves with the violation of 'old' contracts of employment, and its consequences for employee performance and morale. More general questions were also being asked about the character of the psychological contract, its conceptualization, measurement and more recently, and perhaps more urgently, its management (e.g. Herriot, Hirsch & Reilly, 1998; Sparrow, 1998, in the UK; Rousseau, 1995, in the US).

The concept of psychological contract is now of worldwide interest and significance (Schalk & Rousseau, 1999, in press) though it has as yet generated perhaps more questions than answers (see for example, Guest, 1999). This, coupled with multiple conceptualizations and measurement attempts, has generated an abundant literature. To some this is merely 'old wine in new bottles' (i.e. subjective regulation of employees by another name, or organizational commitment in a more fashionable guise); to others it offers a valuable means of reauthoring our old ways of construing the employee–employer interface. Reauthoring affords new insights and as such may provide the impetus and vision required to pull the employment world, and our understanding and management of it, into the new millennium.

This review assumes that the psychological contract pertains to a construct with theoretical substance, empirical validity and practical significance. Whilst the term has been used by some writers and practitioners as mere rhetoric, this review aims to separate the hyperbole from the researched reality of the construct. It is undoubtedly true that the psychological contract is a metaphor (at least one of many other potential metaphors) for describing the employee relations scene in the 1990s, given the burgeoning interest in the language and ideology of contracts among the British and American workforces. This, however, does not necessarily undermine the viability of the term 'psychological contract' as a scientific construct. The question is one of being able to agree on a definition, and making a case for the added value of the construct as a means of conceptualizing, investigating and managing employee relations. It is to this end that the current review is geared.

## CHANGING NATURE OF EMPLOYMENT AND EMPLOYEE RELATIONS

For a period following World War II, there was stability, predictability and growth in both the US and the UK economies. Since the 1970s, however, an increase in the magnitude and frequency of economic booms and busts (Herriot & Pemberton, 1995b) has meant that it is harder for organizations to predict and survive change. Globalization and deregulation of emerging markets has increased competition, forcing US and UK organizations to compete against cheaper labour costs and large economies of scale. Organizations have thus reacted by becoming 'leaner and meaner', operating as smaller, semi-autonomous businesses, better equipped to be responsive and flexible to change. Enforced redundancies have resulted, with a corresponding growth in part-time and contracted-in labour markets to keep labour costs down. Organizations have delayered, with originally bureaucratic, hierarchical structures undergoing flattening through the stripping out of executive layers. The Royal Bank of Scotland, for example, has compressed its corporate structure from twenty grades to five (Hiltrop, 1995). In many organizations, this has reduced the opportunity for promotion with movement now being primarily lateral, or even downward. Performance-related pay schemes have been introduced and roles and responsibilities are no longer well defined. Employees are expected to be multi-skilled and willing to relocate at the employer's whim. Many factors contributing to work-related psychological well-being such as job security, opportunity for promotion, status and increased salary are now no longer guaranteed. Organizations have tried to justify these changes but employees have not been fooled (Herriot & Pemberton, 1995b).

### New Ways of Working

The changing context of the workplace in the 1990s derives from a variety of economic, technological and sociological phenomena, too complex to be fully explored here. The point is that these changes have had significant implications for the majority of the full-time workforce within the industrialized world. Handy (1990) in *The Age of Unreason*, summarizes the implications of such changes for workers: 'many will work temporary or part-time— sometimes because that's the way they want it, sometimes because that's all that's available'. Pritchett (1994) opines, 'less than half the workforce in the industrial world will be holding conventional full-time jobs in organizations by the beginning of the 21st century. Those full-timers or insiders will be the new minority.' Other workplace commentators have suggested that 'constant training, retraining, job-hopping and even career-hopping will become the norm' (O'Hara-Devereux & Johansen, in Pritchett, 1994).

In mid-1996, demand for temporary staff in the UK had risen by 23% on the previous year and stood at its highest level since 1982 (Tooher, 1996). Companies now outsource many of their non-core, peripheral activities to external agencies, with many workers consequently employed on short-term or part-time contracts, with resultant reduced job security and continuously changing work environments. In the Survey of Long Term Employment Strategies 1996, one company executive was quoted as saying:

> Increasing rationalisation and economies of scale will lead to narrower margins and a considerable reduction in the number of providers in the world-wide market. Only the fittest, most innovative and flexible employers will survive.

It is clear from these comments that the world of work is fast becoming a very different one from that familiar a few decades ago. Management experts are now predicting a shift from traditional working patterns to a core/complementary structure by the turn of the century; that is organizations employing core long-term contract based and complementary short-term contract based employees. This has major implications for 'core' staff within organizations who are likely to become employed on fixed-term, rather than permanent, contracts and will become increasingly required to contemplate alternative forms of working, including teleworking, part-time working and job sharing (Millward & Hopkins, 1998). Short-term complementary staff must accept even more fully the change in contractual terms with employing organizations, and will be obliged to become proactive in seeking and retaining work while expecting little in return from employers other than financial recompense.

## The New Deal

So, the trend away from the 'traditional' working relationship with the employee offering loyalty, conformity, commitment and trust to the employing organization in return for job security, promotional prospects, training and development opportunities and support (see Table 1.1) is becoming increasingly evident. The contractual norm is shifting increasingly towards the individual accepting long hours, more responsibility, a requirement for a broader rang of skills and tolerance of change and role ambiguity, with the organization providing returns of high pay, rewards for performance and, in the simplest terms, a job (Arnold, 1996).

These changes are having, and will continue to have, wide-ranging implications for the workforce, regardless of the forms of work adopted in the future. Long-established organizational, professional and occupational identities are being eroded in order that organizations may multi-skill, rebrand, downsize,

**Table 1.1**  Old to new deals

| Old deal | New deal |
| --- | --- |
| ● Long-term security | ● No security |
| ● Fair pay for good performance | ● High pay for high performance |
| ● Structured, predictable employment scenario | ● Flexible and ambiguous employment scenario |
| ● Career managed by organization | ● Career managed by individual |
| ● Time and effort rewarded | ● Performance/results expected |
| ● Income related to experience/status | ● Income related to performance—performance-related pay |
| ● Offered promotion prospects and supported in return for 'going the extra mile' | ● Transactional attitudes 'tit for tat' mentality |
| ● Mutual trust and investment | ● Little trust, much cynicism |

delayer and refocus. The potential impact on the individual worker is immense. Employees will be required to adopt multiple coping strategies in order to deal with this fast-moving and demanding new environment, with their various identities coming under fire from all directions, as new ways of working are introduced, mass redundancies and restructuring into teams erode the established social network, the focus of work shifts from production to service and stable 'jobs for life' are replaced with self-managed regular career 'hops' (Herriot, Hirsch & Reilly, 1998).

### Diversity and the Mutlicultural Working World

Recognition of diversity and its systematic management is, according to many scholars of organizations, the key to future organizational survival and success (e.g. Herriot, 1992). Diversity is introduced into organizations insofar as:

- An increasing number of females are entering the employment world with different value priorities and many varied orientations to work.
- An increasing number of 'older' workers are represented in the workforce, meaning that there are intergenerational differences in value priority and orientation to work.
- An increasingly multicultured employment world is appearing as more and more organizations are operating on a global scale (i.e. multinational or even transnational).
- The practice of equal opportunity is becoming more prevalent with more minority group members entering the employment world (although some would say, not enough!).

- The proliferation of different types of employment contracts (e.g. part-time, flexi-time, job-share, annual hours, temporary, fixed-term) is increasing within a flexible, core/peripheral employment structure. In addition, many organizations are moving towards outsourcing and strategic alliance (with employees working alongside people from different organizations with differing business cultures and skill sets).

Diversity has major implications for how people work together and in particular for what work means to them, and thus provides an essential backdrop against which to investigate contractual issues. However, in undertaking the review which follows, it is important to point out that no direct correspondence between economic or structural and psychological realities is assumed (see for example, Herriot, Hirsch & Reilly, 1998; Millward & Herriot, 1999).

## THE ORGANIZATION AS A 'COOPERATIVE SYSTEM' OF EXCHANGE

Whilst often regarded as a relatively fresh concept in the literature, the psychological contract can be said to have originated from the work of Barnard (1938), in his 'Cooperative Systems View' of organizational behaviour. Barnard argued that the 'natural cooperation' inherent in human nature was largely responsible for the success or failure of business ventures. He argued that an investment or input by both employee and employer was crucial to an organization's success—in return for good treatment, he suggested, employees could be persuaded to 'pledge allegiance' to a common organizational goal or purpose, placing this above all else in organizational life, and leading to increased productivity within the workplace.

Barnard (1938, p. 139) argues that 'the individual is always the basic strategic factor in organizations. Regardless of his history or his obligations he must be induced to cooperate or there will be no cooperation . . . inadequate incentives mean dissolution'. This thesis is based on a conceptualization of the organization as 'a system of cooperation' (p. 3) and that its survival depends on individual 'cooperative' contributions. These contributions, he argues, are not automatically afforded; instead, the organization has to actively 'elicit' them. Whilst organizational effectiveness is defined as the extent to which the organization achieves its goals, this depends, he says, very heavily on organizational efficiency. Efficiency in turn can only be ensured to the extent that individual motives are satisfied. The test of efficiency then is the ability to 'elicit sufficient individual wills to cooperate' (Barnard, 1938, p. 60). Without cooperation the organization will fail in its purpose.

Barnard (1938, p. 141) points out that an organization can secure the efforts necessary to its existence by either providing objective inducements and/or 'changing states of mind'. The provision of objective inducement may involve: material inducements such as money or other financial compensation; personal non-material opportunity such as status or power; communion (e.g. social support, comradeship); increased participation; fulfilment of personal ideals; associational attractiveness (e.g. desire to belong); and desirable physical conditions. By contrast, changing states of mind in the workforce may require the 'method of persuasion' (Barnard, 1938, p. 149) either by rationalization (e.g. propaganda, rhetoric/argument) and/or the 'inculcation of motives', in addition to occasional coercion. Barnard (1938, p. 158) argues that 'every type of organization, for whatever purpose' will need to provide 'several incentives' and 'some degree of persuasion . . . in order to maintain the contributions required.

Barnard (1938, p. 230) describes the critical function of the executive as one of 'eliciting . . . the quantity and quality of efforts' required of organizational contributors. In his description of what exactly the executive can do to 'elicit' effort, it is clear that the executive role is about managing the 'exchange of utilities' (p. 240). Barnard also reminds us that the nature of the exchange will need to undergo continual adjustment and change due to changing individual requirements and states of mind (including employees' appraisal and reappraisal of existing exchange utilities).

Barnard's view of the 'exchange' process between individuals and organizations is echoed in various historical definitions of the psychological contract, and continues to form the backbone of psychological contract research and debate in the 1990s as the following examples illustrate:

An implicit contract between individual and organization which specifies *what each expects to give and receive from each other in their relationship.* (Kotter, 1973)

An unwritten set of *expectations operating at all times between every member of an organization* and the various managers and others in that organization. (Schein, 1980)

An individual's beliefs regarding the terms and conditions of a *reciprocal exchange agreement* between that person and another party. (Robinson & Rousseau, 1994).

This cooperative systems view of organizational life assumes that the interface between employer and employee cannot be taken for granted; it must be conceptualized, studied and more importantly, systematically managed. The notion of *interface* can thus be considered crucial to our understanding of the psychological contract, since it:

- Signals a *process of exchange* between the individual and the organization.
- Requires that questions are asked about the *character* of the interface (*i.e. content or type of contractual deal*) as well as its *dynamics* (*i.e. the process of contracting*).
- Requires consideration of the *needs of both individual and organization.*

- Presents questions about the nature of the exchange at *individual, group and intergroup levels of analysis.*

Until recently however, the focus of interest has been less in what the organization can offer the employee in exchange for their loyalty and commitment, and more in terms of what the employee can offer (or be made or persuaded to offer) the organization. Moreover, it would seem that what the employee might offer in terms of performance potential, has typically been regarded as something that can be conceptualized and measured independently of what is afforded them in return by the organization. Pet constructs such as commitment and satisfaction, which have generated volumes of research over the last century, are prime examples of the *single-sided employee-only* stance adopted by researchers on workplace motivation. This may in part be attributable to the reductionist nature of much psychological research on organizational life, insofar as the organizational side of the equation might be deemed the jurisdiction of management science and/or sociological analysis. Here is not the place to enter into a debate about levels of analysis or into philosophical discussion about the dialectic at work in connecting individuals with organizational entities. Such complexities are currently being addressed in postmodernist debates on the nature and workings of organizational life (see, for example, Alvesson, 1998). It is clear nonetheless that the behaviour of individuals in organizations cannot be understood in a social vacuum. The topic of motivation, for instance, pertains to a regulatory issue that is inextricably linked with how the individual is located within the organization as a whole.

Psychological contracts, then, can be described in terms of both content (the perceived terms of the employment contract) and process (how the contract was arrived at) (Millward & Herriot, 1999). To date, the majority of research on the psychological contract has been conducted in the 'content' rather than 'process' vein, and until recently, has been investigated somewhat single-sidedly as something owned and held by the individual, consistent with the conceptualization offered by Rousseau (1989).

## THE CONTENT AND CHARACTER OF THE PSYCHOLOGICAL CONTRACT

### The Psychological Contract as a Cognitive-perceptual Entity

As indicated earlier, Rousseau and colleagues have adopted a primarily cognitive-perceptual stance on the psychological contract. In the words of Rousseau (1995, p. 6), 'contracts are stable and enduring mental models', and accessing the model used by people will reveal how they come to understand the employment contract as it evolves through experience. The notion of 'belief' is pivotal to the particular way in which Rousseau conceptualizes and investigates the interface between employer and employee. In particular, this perspective holds that the psychological contract is characterized by *beliefs pertaining to reciprocal obligations* (i.e. beliefs about what each party in the relationship is 'obliged' to contribute to that relationship) (Rousseau, 1995, pp. 20–22), and 'promissory exchange' (i.e. beliefs about the exact nature of the exchange agreement) (Rousseau, 1995, pp. 16–18) as formed by individuals upon undertaking terms of employment (Argyris, 1960; Kaufman & Stern, 1988; Levinson, 1962; MacNeil, 1985; Schein, 1980). More formally stipulated, Rousseau (1995) defines the psychological contract as follows:

1. An individual's belief(s) in reciprocal obligations between that individual and another party.
2. Where one party has paid for, or offered consideration in exchange for, a promise that the other party will reciprocate (i.e. fulfil the promise).
3. Where both the promise and the consideration are highly subjective (i.e. exist 'in the eye of the beholder'). Parties to a contract, whether written or unwritten, can hold different perceptions regarding its terms (e.g. different people might focus on different elements of the contract in creating their understanding of it, depending on cognitive limits and frames of reference).
4. The individual holding the belief in a psychological contract attaches to that belief assumptions of good faith, fair dealing and trust, which results in the contract becoming part of the mainstay of the relationship between the parties.

## The Psychological Contract as an Implicit, Relationship-based Agreement

Drawing on the work of MacNeil (1985), Rousseau (1989) argues that the employment contract signals far more than simple economic forms of exchange (i.e. market-oriented, monetary, competitive). It can involve relationship-based agreements which denote the commitment of parties to maintaining the relationship (i.e. to stay together, continuing employment), providing some form of exchange (such as loyalty and hard work) indefinitely. Where interactions occur over time, and continued interaction is expected, beliefs about what is owed can arise from overt promises and other factors more likely to be taken for granted (e.g. assumptions of fairness and of good faith). Relationship-based agreements compensate for the inability to draw up economic contracts of sufficient coverage and scope to frame the employment relationship over the long term. The more taken for granted the 'considerations' exchanged, the greater the potential for *personal idiosyncrasies in the way the employment contract is interpreted and enacted* (Rousseau, 1989, p. 124)— that is people 'fill in the blanks . . . in somewhat unpredictable ways' (Rousseau, 1995, p. 1).

Even agreements in writing are open to different interpretations, which often only become evident when the contract is violated. The longer the reiationship endures, the broader the array of considerations involved in the exchange and the deeper the relationship becomes. The psychological contract then, pertains to the subjectivity inherent to all employment contracts. 'When an individual perceives that contributions he or she makes obligate the organization to reciprocity (or vice versa), a psychological contract emerges' (Rousseau, 1989, p. 124). To this extent, contracts are 'constructions' created by the interpretation of what a promise or obligation means to each individual.

## The Psychological Contract as Perceived 'Obligations of Reciprocity'

Psychological contracts are distinct from norms of reciprocity (i.e. they denote more than simply the endorsement of a norm, they involve *'obligations* of reciprocity' established a priori and also from what Rousseau (1989) terms *implied contracts*, that is those that can be inferred by an observer as to the patterns of obligation arising from the interaction between the two parties in an exchange relationship. An example of this might be an organization's reputation as a 'good employer' (e.g. affording job security and career prospects in exchange for loyalty and hard work) (Kiriakodou & Millward, 1999). Psychological contracts also denote more than simple considerations of equity (i.e. whether expectations have been met); they involve *socio-emotional considerations of trust and identification* and it is these which are not so easily restored when contracts are violated. In the words of Rousseau (1989, p. 127) psychological contracts 'interject a deeper emotional component to the experience of inequity' within a relationship.

Failed expectations can result in disappointment, whereas contract violation (i.e. perceived failure to meet contractual terms) can induce feelings of betrayal, anger, outrage, injustice and so on. Whilst all psychological contracts entail expectations, not all expectations are in themselves invested with a promissory interpretation. It is this promissory element that differentiates expectations from psychological contracts (see e.g., research by Robinson, 1995). Violation can fundamentally change the way the relationship is viewed (e.g. because of damage to self-respect as well as the basic sense of entitlement). The longer the duration of the psychological contract, the higher the investment and promissory element of both parties.

Robinson (1995) measured seven features of employment (e.g. pay, promotion, etc.) in two ways: as obligations (beliefs regarding extent of each specific obligation) and as expectations (descriptions of relative presence or absence of each feature). Psychological contract (promissory) beliefs contributed independently and more substantially to the prediction of trust, commitment and satisfaction than non-promissory expectations. Beliefs formed in the context of the psychological contract entail a special subset of expectations based on one party conveying a promise to another. The distinction between psychological contracts and expectations is of great practical significance since failure to meet contract-based expectations can engender more intense and emotionally salient reactions than failure to meet non-contract-based expectations (Rousseau, 1989; Robinson, 1995).

## 'Individuals Hold Psychological Contracts, Organizations Do Not'

It is important to point out that within this conceptualization, *the psychological contract is held unilaterally by the employee*: 'individuals have psychological contracts, organizations do not' (Rousseau, 1989, p. 126). The organization provides the 'context' for the creation of psychological contracts. However, psychological contracts can also be shared. Whilst individual contract holders may rely on their own experience to understand the contract, group members may 'share' a contract and to this extent can develop a reality about it. To this extent, psychological contracts become 'normative' where members 'identify themselves in similar ways with it' and believe they are party to the same contract (e.g. part-timers) (Rousseau, 1995, pp. 10–11). Normative contracts can create pressures to adhere to commitments (e.g. absence contracts which denote entitlement to use up sick leave) (Nicholson & Johns, 1985), and thus create a degree of homogeneity in values and behaviours (which then become self-perpetuating through selection, adaptation and attrition processes) (Herriot, 1989).

## The Psychological Contract as a Driver of Behaviour

How individual employees each view their contract is assumed to have a powerful effect on their behaviour. Rousseau (1995) argues that we can predict behaviour from the creation, change, or violation of contracts. Contracts operate like goals and to this extent are both self-organizing and self-fulfilling. They are promissory to the extent that they are formed on the basis of warranties and communications of future intent. Thinking contractually means believing one has made a commitment and is therefore bound to some future action in return for the promise (which is believed, accepted and relied upon) of future benefits. It should be noted, however, that promise-keeping per se is not the central theme of contracting, it is instead the reduced likelihood of loss that is fundamental.

The fuzziness and ambiguity that is such an integral part of the psychological contract might well afford flexibility in the way the contractual relationship is enacted by an individual, but it also means that conflict over the kinds of agreements and promises made is inevitable. It is also important to point out that several psychological contracts can occur simultaneously (e.g. with the team, with the department or division, with the profession or occupation of which one is a part, and with organization) (see Millward & Hopkins, 1998, for more on this), affording multiple contractual possibilities and realities lived and breathed by each and every employee. The prediction of behaviour is thus a complex issue, that requires simultaneous consideration of organizational, social (normative) and personal (idiosyncratic) factors, and assumes that the psychological contract is a precisely quantifiable entity, a point on which some might disagree (e.g. Guest, 1998; Herriot & Pemberton, 1997).

## The Process of Contract-making or Psychological Contracting

Rousseau (1995, pp. 34–44) outlines a model of psychological contracting in which she presents two sets of factors as critical to the formation of promissory contracts: *external messages* which may be in the form of overt statements (e.g. during the recruitment and/or organizational induction process), observations of the treatment and behaviour of others with the same kind of deal, and expressions of organizational policy and *personal interpretations and dispositions* (e.g. career motives and aspirations). Contracts can be formed by anyone who conveys (and is perceived to have the authority to convey) some form of future commitment to another, that is organizational representatives such as managers and recruiters (Rousseau, 1995, p. 60). Contracts are not imposed on people; they are made voluntarily. This requires acknowledgement of the active role that employees have in the contracting process (which is part and parcel of managing one's own socialization).

Rousseau (1990) conducted a survey on newly recruited MBAs to an organization, examining the development of psychological contracts. She found that employees developed their contractual orientation to the organization during the recruitment process. In particular, it was found that the content of the contract—that is transactional or relational orientation—was related to the *type of relationship the employee sought with the employer*. It was discovered that those individuals perceiving their current position as a stepping stone to another, and who emphasized short-term monetizable benefits in exchange for hard work, demonstrated a more transactionally oriented short-term view of their commitment to the organization. By contrast, those seeking a long-term relationship with their employer felt party to a contract exchanging job security for their loyalty, indicative of a more relational contractual orientation.

## Types of Psychological Contract

Whilst it is clear that psychological contracts can take on a potentially infinite number of cognitive-perceptual forms (Rousseau, 1995, pp. 91–97), certain contractual terms (e.g. an attractive benefits package, pay tied to performance, relatively secure job, good opportunities for promotion, competitive salary versus fair treatment, career development, support, open communication, collaborative work environment) are assumed to cluster together along dimensions of focus (economic, relational), inclusion (scope and flexibility), time-frame (duration of the relationship), formalization (specification of performance requirements), and tangibility (implicit, explicit). At the most aggregated level, Rousseau conceptualizes (and has also operationalized) the psychological contract in two forms, defined by the type of relationship perceived to predominate between employee and employer: 'transactional' and 'relational' (Robinson, Kraatz & Rousseau, 1994; Robinson & Rousseau, 1994; Rousseau, 1990, 1995; Rousseau & Parks, 1993; see also Herriot, Manning & Kidd, 1997; Millward & Hopkins, 1998; Stiles, Gratton, Truss, Hope-Hailey & McGovern, 1996). These two types of contractual relationship have been described as follows (Rousseau, 1995, pp. 90–95):

*Transactional*
- Short-term monetizable exchanges
- Specific economic conditions as primary incentive (wage rate)
- Limited personal involvement in job
- Specified time-frame
- Commitments limited to well-specified conditions
- Limited flexibility
- Use of existing skills
- Unambiguous terms

*Relational*
- Open-ended relationship and time-frame
- Considerable investment by employees (company skills, career development) and employers (training)
- High degree of mutual interdependence and barriers to exit
- Emotional involvement as well as economic exchange
- Whole-person relations
- Dynamic and subject to change
- Pervasive conditions (affects personal life)
- Subjective and implicitly understood

In short, the relational psychological contract can be regarded as being akin to the traditional working 'partnership' between employee and employer. A relational-type employee–employer relationship can engender feelings of affective involvement or attachment in the employee, and can commit the employer to providing more than purely remunerative support to the individual with investments such as training, personal and career development, and provision of job security. In contrast, the transactional contract denotes an attitude of 'money comes first': employees are more concerned with remuneration and personal benefit than with being good 'organizational citizens', or 'going the extra mile'. This type of contract may also include employees bending organizational rules to meet personal ends.

Rousseau (1995, p. 97) argues that 'transactional and relational terms are basic elements in most employment contracts', but that how long the relationship is expected to last will usually differentiate contracts that are largely transactional from more relational ones. In practice, however, this is not quite as simple as it sounds. Many short-term contractual relationships can be highly relational (e.g. student/mentor). Also specific performance requirements (which are most typical of transactional contracts) can be built into long-term contracts through appraisal and performance-related pay systems. Thus, transactional and relational terms are not mutually exclusive, although of course, extreme scenarios can be presented (e.g. employment agencies mostly operate with purely 'transactional' contracts). Transactional type psychological contracts may be sought out by those who prefer low-investment roles, perhaps because they have investments elsewhere (e.g. family and home, activities and interests outside the workplace), or because they have personal goals and agendas to fulfil (e.g. developing a career portfolio, the desire to simply earn some money) (Hall, 1993). Rousseau (1995, p. 104) does point out however that 'over a period of time . . . relational elements can drift into the contract' that might otherwise have been purely transactional at the outset (e.g. contractors whose short-term contracts are continually renewed over time) (for evidence that this can indeed be the case, see Williamson, 1991; Millward & Brewerton, 1999).

Evidence from both US (Robinson, Kraatz & Rousseau, 1994) and UK research (e.g. Millward & Hopkins, 1998; Millward & Brewerton, 1999) has confirmed the viability of the transactional and relational distinction. For example, using a 50-item bank derived from focus group discussion with employees, Millward and Hopkins (1998) constructed a 32-item scale to measure 'relational' and 'transactional' aspects of the contractual relationship. Scale construction was informed by the conceptualization provided by Rousseau (1995, pp. 91–97) using the following analytical dimensions: focus (emotional/economic); inclusion (extent of individual integration in an organization); time-frame (short term/long term); formalization (degree of performance specification); stability (stasis/dynamic); scope (job-specific versus whole-person implications); and tangibility (subjective/objective). Factor analysis yielded a two-factor solution which was then used to produce two reliable subscales.

Millward and Hopkins (1998) also obtained substantial preliminary evidence for the construct validity of these subscales. Specifically, the 'relational' subscale was significantly more strongly linked with permanent than temporary contracts, with full-time than with part-time working patterns, and with long-term than short-term employment relationships (as indicated by organizational and job tenure). In contrast, the transactional subscale was significantly more strongly associated with a temporary workplace relationship (i.e. temporary employment contracts, short-term organizational and job tenure). Moreover, the relational subscale was significantly positively correlated with job and organizational commitment, and also with the expressed willingness to work overtime without pay (i.e. go the extra mile for the organization). The transactional subscale, on the other hand, was significantly negatively correlated with each of these three measures.

Taken together, these findings indicate the validity of considering a relational psychological contract that comprises a tendency towards a promissory contract based on trust for the exchange party, a high degree of affective commitment, a high degree of integration and identification with the exchange partner, expectations of stability and long-term commitment, and a self-reported contribution to reciprocal exchange with the employing organization (Rousseau, 1995). Likewise, the findings add support to the idea of a transactional psychological contract characterized by a short time-frame and an attitude of limited organizational contribution, low commitment, weak organizational integration/identification, attitudes of limited flexibility, and easy exit.

Although current wisdom contends that the psychological contract should be conceptualized in terms of a bipolar continuum, ranging from relational (emotional involvement and 'extra mile' behaviours) to transactional (emotional distance, and contractually defined behaviours) (Herriot, Manning & Kidd, 1997; Millward & Hopkins, 1998; Robinson, Kraatz & Rousseau, 1994; Robinson & Rousseau, 1994; Rousseau, 1990, 1995; Rousseau & Parks, 1993; Stiles et al. 1996), researchers such as Arnold (1996) have pointed out that in order for this conceptualization to be robust, the various elements of transactional and relational contracts should be identified.

Robinson, Kraatz and Rousseau (1994) were the first researchers to attempt this, developing a series of items which study respondents were asked to report whether they believed *their employing organization* was obliged to provide (employer obligations) and another series of items which they were asked to report whether they believed *they* were obliged to provide (employee obligations). Their findings provided suggestive evidence for subcomponents of relational and transactional contracts, although some confused factor structures, a sample-specific result and no other forms of validation suggest that their conclusions were based more on intuitive reasoning than on psychometric or experimental rigour.

Current research by Millward and Brewerton (1998), building on work undertaken by Millward and Hopkins (1998) in developing and validating the Psychological Contract Scale (PCS), found evidence for a number of distinct subcomponents for each of the transactional and relational subscales contained within the instrument. These are listed below:

*Transactional Subscale*

| | |
|---|---|
| Transactional orientation | Focus on financial gain, and on sole fulfilment of contractual and job requirements |
| Long-term future | Not envisaging the organization as a long-term employer |
| Absence of extra mile | Lack of involvement in work; unwillingness to exceed specified work requirements |

*Relational Subscale*

| | |
|---|---|
| Emotional affinity | Feelings of organizational membership, identification with the organization's stated goals |
| Professional development | Opportunities and expectations for training, promotion and professional growth |
| Equitability | Perceptions of fair and just reward from the organization for employee inputs |

Each of these subfactors has been shown to achieve simple structure using a forced-factor oblique rotation under principal components factor analysis, with internal consistency reliability of alpha = 0.70 and above obtained for each subfactor ($n > 2000$). However, it should be noted that these factors and subfactors were derived from the clustering of attitudes concerning contract terms as opposed to perception of contract terms per se (which is the focus of the work conducted by Robinson, Kraatz & Rousseau, 1994) and are thus not directly comparable (see the section below on Operationalizing the Psychological Contract which focuses more specifically on measurement issues).

## Are Relational and Transactional Contracts Independently or Inversely Related?

It has been proposed by Rousseau (1995) that transactional and relational components of the psychological contract denote opposite ends of a bipolar continuum linked respectively to the notions of economic and social exchange. These contractual 'types' are seen as extremes, anchoring either end of a single continuum, describing the full range of both organizational types, and individual contracts, perceived by employees. Transactional, or 'buy', organizations (according to the definition offered by Miles & Snow, 1980) include contract and recruitment agencies whose approach to employment in many cases epitomises the transactional contractual orientation—employees expect nothing more than monetary reward for their efforts at work, and organizations expect little commitment or emotional involvement in return. Alternatively, relational, or 'make' organizations will continue to provide support for employees, and expect commitment and good citizenship in return.

Individuals expected to fall along the proposed contractual continuum in terms of their *beliefs* or orientations are said to range from purely temporary workers who tend to adopt transactional psychological contracts, through to core staff with secure 'jobs for life' whose contracts tend to be more relational in nature. Indeed, there is some evidence that this is the case (Millward & Hopkins, 1998). However, as pointed out above, temporary staff continuously assigned to the same company on relatively long-term contracts *may* begin to develop a relational contract with the long-term host organization even though the nature of their job demands a transactional relationship with the employer (see e.g. Millward & Brewerton, 1999). Moreover, as Arnold (1996) points out in his concise and critical review of the psychological contract construct, it is yet to be made clear which specific aspects of the workplace are related to which type of contract and whether each aspect is exclusive to one or other of the contract types.

If we are to assume that the relational-transactional continuum is, indeed, bipolar, that is those employees displaying highly relational contracts fall at one end of a spectrum and those employees displaying highly transactional contracts fall at the other end, we would expect to find a strong inverse relationship between measures of the two components. On examination of data from well over 2000 employees across various organizations (where respondents have completed the Psychological Contract Scale as presented in Millward & Hopkins, 1998) it becomes apparent, however, that the *moderate* inverse relationship (generally −0.2 to −0.3) between relational and transactional orientation may be masking some more complex responses (Millward & Brewerton, 1998). Some respondents report both relatively high relational *and* transactional orientation and some respondents show the opposite pattern, in addition to the recognized high relational-low transactionals and low relational-high transactionals. Is this pattern describing something more than simply high relational or high transactional individuals? If we conceptualize high-highs as 'careerists' and low-lows as 'indifferent', we may unmask some of the apparent anomalies in response.

Some further pilot work on this topic has identified that the incidence of careerists and indifferent employees may differ according to sociological or organizational group membership (Brewerton, 1999). For example, careerists are more often to be found among younger age groups, and among those groups who have only been with the organization for a short period. As age and organizational tenure increase, so the incidence of careerism decreases and employees become more relationally oriented towards their employer. Of course, this makes sense intuitively—young, dynamic, recently acculturated organizational members will retain a drive and ambition which may lead to a self-managed career, or these employees may develop a less transactional relationship over time, as they become comfortable with their employer and lose the desire to move on in order to further their careers elsewhere.

Rousseau (1995, pp. 104–105) likewise describes a slightly more complex model than that suggested by the bipolar relational-transactional continuum, based on a four-way conceptualization of contract duration and on the level of stated specificity of employee performance. This model and its essential features are described below in Figure 1.1.

## Summary, Conclusions and Outstanding Issues

It has been the cognitive-perceptual view of the psychological contract that has underpinned most of the research pursued to date. However, various criticisms have also been levelled. Arnold (1996) for instance, closely scrutinized the concept, pointing out areas of confusion (e.g. concerning the role

**PERFORMANCE TERMS**

| DURATION | Specified | Not specified |
|---|---|---|
| Short-term | **Transactional**<br>(e.g. shop assistants hired during Christmas season):<br>• Low ambiguity<br>• Easy exit/high turnover<br>• Low member commitment<br>• Freedom to enter new contracts<br>• Little learning<br>• Weak integration/ identification | **Transitional**<br>(e.g. employee experiences during organizational retrenchment or following merger or acquisition)<br>• Ambiguity/uncertainty<br>• High turnover/termination<br>• Instability |
| Long-term | **Balanced**<br>(e.g. high-involvement team):<br>• High member commitment<br>• High integration/ identification<br>• Ongoing development<br>• Mutual support<br>• Dynamic | **Relational**<br>(e.g. family business members)<br>• High member commitment<br>• High affective commitment<br>• High integration/ identification<br>• Stability |

**Figure 1.1** Rousseau's (1995) psychological contract typology

Adapted from D.M. Rosseau (1995). *Psychological Contracts in Organizations: Understanding Written and Unwritten Agreements.* London & New York: Sage Publications

of promises versus expectations in contract formation and operationalization, and also the validity of the distinction between transactional and relational terms) and inconsistency in the way it has been modelled (e.g. as an employee-only psychological construct as opposed to a relationship of exchange and its relationship with other psychological constructs such as commitment) and operationalized (e.g. lack of close attention to psychometric considerations).

Guest (1999) has also pointed out inconsistencies and confusions in the conceptualization and use of the term psychological contract. He notes the lack of precision in the conceptualization, and how too much attention has been paid to 'types' of contract (transactional, relational) with little consideration for other dimensions such as implicit/explicit, time-span, scope and so on. Such dimensions (as originally proposed by MacNeil, 1985, and since taken up by Rousseau, 1995) are theoretical rather than empirical, and so far, says Guest (1999) no one has questioned their validity or utility. Guest also highlights the confusion over the use of terms 'implicit/explicit' in connection with the psychological contract. In early definitions, the psychological contract was synonymous with all that was implicit (i.e. unwritten) about contracts. In subsequent work, the psychological contract has taken on both explicit (transactional, usually in written form) and implicit (relational, usually in unwritten form) aspects, which has clouded the issue somewhat, particularly given the use by Rousseau (1989, 1995) of the term 'implicit contract' to refer to what others (i.e. observers) might infer about the psychological contract.

Herriot and Pemberton (1997) have pointed out the limitations of the content-focused approach to psychological contract research. They note that the concept has become reified into something fixed and substantive, as if it exists other than in a hypothetical or analytical form. They point to the term's original use as a backdrop for discussing the employee–employer exchange process, and argue that a process view on the psychological contract may be more fruitfully adopted in exploring this operationalization, particularly in terms of perceived breaches in the employment relationship.

Finally, the question of 'who is the other party in the contractual exchange?' has been raised by several commentators. In the words of Guest (1999) 'Who is the nebulous "other party" called the "organization"?' Until recently, the 'other party' was taken for granted as the anthropomorphized organization. However, it has since been realized that this is not satisfactory: even if we were to hold onto the single-sided view of the psychological contract as a cognitive-perceptual idiographic entity we still need to reckon with the issue of with whom the individual sees him or herself as holding the contract. In the next section—the process of contracting—the question of 'with whom the contract is held' is addressed as a central issue.

## THE PROCESS OF CONTRACTING

### 'Contracting' versus 'Contracts'

In light of criticisms of single-sided research approaches to the psychological contract, it has been argued (e.g. by Herriot & Pemberton, 1997) that rather than address the question of the psychological contract as content, it may be more fruitful to recapture what was originally quite distinctive about the construct, as defined by Argyris (1960) and others (e.g. Schein, 1980). This distinctiveness concerns the potential of the construct to describe and explain the *exchange relationship* between employer and employee. It has been argued above that the term psychological contract has its roots in the notion of cooperative contribution described by Barnard (1938), whereby the individual is persuaded to pledge allegiance to an organization (to cooperate with it) in exchange for appropriate incentives. To this extent, the psychological contract can be said to be *located in the relationship between two parties*—the organization and the individual. To facilitate the analysis of the 'exchange relationship', it is perhaps useful to think in terms of a *process* of contracting.

The process or dialectical perspective on the psychological contract takes the view that content can only be examined in a snapshot fashion. This view is best exemplified in the work of Herriot and his colleagues (Herriot & Pemberton, 1997; Herriot, Hirsch & Reilly, 1998; Millward & Herriot, 1999). Questions about content, Herriot and Pemberton (1997) argue, enable us to describe a current relationship between employer and employee, and hence can point us to the product of the contractual process. Central to the ideas of those in the process tradition is the fundamentally two-way nature of the employer–employee exchange relationship. This is a critical consideration: as a mere snapshot of what the employment deal consists of, the content of the psychological contract can pertain to something so uniquely personal, context-bound, and fluid as to render it impossible to envisage making statements of any generic kind (Herriot, Hirsch & Reilly, 1998). Taking the contract as a process, however, questions arise such as 'With whom is the contract made?', 'How is the contract made?', 'What constitutes a breach in the contract?' and 'What are the consequences of such a breach?' (Millward & Herriot, 1999).

## With Whom is the Contract Made?

It is often assumed within the psychological contract literature that a psychological contract is held by individuals and that questions about the other party to the exchange are either irrelevant or non-problematic (Coyle-Shapiro & Kessler, 1998; Sparrow, 1998). But who is the employer? In a small organization, there is likely to be little doubt. In a large and highly complex multinational or transnational organization, however, the question is less likely to be so straightforward. With the devolution of responsibility to divisions, departments or even teams, the employer may be more appropriately construed in local day-to-day terms (e.g. Divisional Manager, Department Manager, Team Leader).

In the contracted-out employment scenario now becoming increasingly prevalent in the UK, in legal and technical terms at least, the employer is the recruitment or contracts agency. At a more psychological level though, the employer is likely to be more meaningfully located in the host organization or division in which an employee actually works. Many contractors also belong to professional institutions to which they feel first and foremost obligated, and in which they strongly invest their identify and self-esteem. It is even feasible to contemplate multiple exchange scenarios in operation at any one moment in time (e.g. with the agency and with the host organization, with the profession, with the division, department or team in which one also invests time and energy) (Millward & Hopkins, 1998). There is indeed some evidence to show that 'deals' can be forged at all these levels (Millward & Brewerton, 1998).

The complexity of the contemporary workplace, in its devolved and deregulated state, coupled with its increasingly matrix-managed and 'virtual' form, strongly suggests the need for caution in assuming that the employer side of the exchange relationship can be neatly sewn up in terms of one homogeneous category of 'employer'. If we take the term 'employer' to mean organization, thus denoting the need to adopt an 'organizational' level of analysis, it becomes equally clear that what the organization constitutes is not obvious either. To equate the employer with the organization as a whole, is to anthropomorphize the latter. As Rousseau (1995) stipulates, organizations cannot hold psychological contracts. Rather, she says, we need to think in terms of 'organizational representatives'.

Despite the heterogeneous character of large and also of many medium-sized enterprises within the UK workplace, and despite the large number of potential 'representatives' who might take on the persona of 'employer', research has nonetheless tended to be pursued largely without questioning who, exactly, the 'other party' might be in the exchange relationship. Millward and Hopkins (1998) found that *commitment to the job* was a far stronger mediator of the psychological contract than *commitment to the organization*. They took this to suggest that contracting is more appropriately construed at a more concrete and day-to-day level of reality than that signalled by the abstract term 'organization'. In many cases, 'organization' is little more than an umbrella term to denote a bundle of activities all pursued in its name but with little substantive meaning beyond that comprised by the activities themselves. This is increasingly the case in today's economic climate of outsourcing and the devolution of project management to small-scale teams. Very little is actually known about who the employer is, in the eyes of employees, or at what level of analysis it is appropriate to talk about the kinds of contracts that are made (Millward & Herriot, 1999).

## The Organization as a Framework for Contracting—the Drive to Develop 'New Deals'

The analysis above perhaps takes a rather extreme view on the 'organization', construing it in terms of Handy's (1994) empty raincoat image. The distinction made earlier between 'make' and 'buy' organizations (Miles & Snow, 1980) may be useful to revisit at this stage. A 'buy' organization is one that literally buys in labour on a just-in-time basis and as such is highly cost-driven. Employee regulation strategies in such organizations are largely economic in flavour. A 'make' organization on the other hand, is one that seeks to forge a lasting relationship with an employee; one that provides the employee with an important source of social identification and self-esteem as well as developing their skills and knowledge. Employee regulation strategies in this kind of organization are likely to be more concerned with winning over the hearts and minds of the employee. That is, subjective regulation strategies strive to harness a deeper social and emotional level of investment of the employee in the organization and its interests, than that possible within a purely economic exchange relationship. Handy (1994), however, predicted an employment scenario whereby organizations would transform from 'make' into 'buy' strategies.

It is indeed the case that in recent years both the US and the UK have witnessed a major growth in the contracts industry. Cost/economy driven restructuring of the workplace has not only involved mass downsizing but also the introduction of contractualization as the primary means by which to enhance numerical and financial flexibility (IES, 1998). In mid-1996, demand for temporary staff in the UK had risen by 23% on the previous year and stood at its highest level since 1982 (Tooher, 1996). Underpinning this movement is a shift from traditional working patterns to a core/complementary employment structure—that is organizations employing core long-term contract-based and complementary short-term contract-based employees (IES, 1998).

Large organizations now outsource many of their non-core, peripheral activities to external agencies, with many workers consequently employed on short-term or part-time contracts, with resultant reduced job security and continuously changing work environments (Brown, 1997). In the UK, it is estimated that the average number of functions outsourced by organizations has risen 225% (from 1.2 to 3.9 functions) in the last five years, an area set to show continued growth into the new millennium. As part of this growth, it is anticipated that core activities will also be strategically put out to tender as a means of in-house value creation (Brown, 1997). Where 'employment relations' at one time prevailed over 'labour contracting' the opposite is now increasingly the case (Williamson, 1991).

This move to 'externalization' of employees reflects a shift by organizations away from a reliance on social exchange considerations to a reliance on economic exchange considerations, with employees taken on as calculated risks (i.e. a 'buy' employment model) rather than as people with needs, concerns and interests of their own. The Human Resource metaphor is a prime example of how employees are construed as 'resources' to be harnessed in pursuit of economic ends. Whilst it is undoubtedly clear that economic concerns do reign supreme, and that cost-cutting has been pursued in the majority of cases with little regard for its human costs, evidence suggests that many organizations are now urgently trying to remake themselves, along with other 'survivors' of the storm.

There have always been those organizations in which both 'make' and 'buy' strategies comfortably coexist. This is still very much the case even in organizations that have contracted out most of their more peripheral functions to agency regulation and control (Millward & Brewerton, 1999), a UK finding consistent with that obtained by Pearce (1993) in the US. There is also a major increase in Human Resource Management (HRM) interest in organizational culture, culture change and culture management, partly due to the fear of potential cultural dilution or confusion resulting from merger, acquisition, or major reorganization. All of this suggests that organizations are still very much intent on 'making' rather than simply 'buying' at least some of their employees, whilst adopting a more transactional approach with others (Hirsh & Jackson, 1996).

Yet we must question whether employees can be 'remade' in the image of the new organization. This may have been feasible in the days when the employment deal comprised an organizational guarantee of a job-for-life in return for employee loyalty and commitment. The flexible, amoebic organization of the cost-conscious 1990s is no longer the entity it once was for the employee. Security of tenure—with its concomitant predictability of payment for services rendered, life/workplace routine and sense of belonging—has been largely replaced with insecurity over employment prospects, concern over promotional prospects, and hesitation in taking on long-term financial burdens such as mortgages, loans, and so on. The substitution of fixed-term for permanent contracts even for 'core' employees (i.e. employees with primary organizational responsibilities), coupled with mass redundancy of friends and colleagues, has exacerbated the feelings of insecurity felt by otherwise 'secure' employees in the contemporary marketplace.

This picture of widespread employee insecurity is the context in which organizations are attempting to reconstitute themselves and prepare themselves for the future. It is commonly noted that whilst clearly the 'old' employment deal is dead, 'new' deals through which the time, energy and commitment of employees can be harnessed have yet to be coherently formulated and articulated within organizational contexts. The 'deal' that exists at the social level of analysis (i.e. the social contract) is primarily economic in character. This makes for an insecure anchorage of the individual within the organization, one that does not bode well for organizations in the long term.

Herriot, Hirsch and Reilly (1998) note that those organizations which now seek to reanchor and reintegrate employees on a more 'make' than 'buy' basis, may face the fundamental challenge of rebuilding lost trust. Breach of the 'old' employment deal or social contract, it is argued, has undermined trust to the point where social capital (denoting the willingness of people to trust in and collaborate with others) within organizations is at an all time low and is being further undermined by management rhetoric which, more often than not, does not tally with the realities of organizational life. The absence of reserve social capital within the stock of UK society generally (due to the large-scale disintegration of institutions like the family and the education system), has made it less and less likely that 'trust' will be effectively secured.

Thus, organizations face the immediate challenge of rebuilding social capital on the basis of which more integrative deals can be forged with employees. This is the context within which new psychological contracts can emerge. It may therefore be appropriate to construe the organization as affording a normative framework in which shared psychological contracts (Rousseau, 1995) can be developed between the organization and its employees. It is feasible to contemplate a process of contracting at a normative level, which in turn provides the interpretative backdrop within which contracting can be pursued at the more psychological level.

Most organizations, it seems, have not yet reinvented themselves at the normative level, let alone at the more individuated level of the psychological contract. Many employees have turned to their professions or occupations as suitable vehicles within which to anchor their identity and self-esteem (Millward & Hopkins, 1998). Many perceive organizations as merely employment zones rather than as meaningful institutions in which to carve themselves out a viable niche in society. Many organizations are still fumbling about with 'buy' and 'make' considerations in a disorganized fashion, having yet to articulate any basis for the employment relationship beyond the purely financial.

It is important however, in thinking about the normative context in which deals are forged, not to lapse into advocating that one new deal will provide the ultimate collaborative solution. As stipulated by the process view on the psychological contract, a deal is a two-way affair that by definition has to be negotiated before it can be said to truly exist. Whilst many different types of deal scenarios are currently being envisaged (Sparrow, 1998), many organizations have been inclined to *impose* new 'deals' on their employees (Noon & Blyton, 1997). In their simultaneous efforts to change structurally and culturally, and also to enhance performance, organizations may encourage employees to accept new 'deals' that do not address their personal interests and needs. For the sake of anchorage, and of sheer survival on a financial level, many employees may find it difficult to resist the offer of a deal that provides them with the promise of a secure footage at least in the short term.

### The Dynamics of Contracting—the Need for Individuated Deals

Herriot, Hirsch and Reilly (1998) describe the dynamics of psychological contracting as an interplay of 'wants' and 'offers' on the part of both employees and organization alike. A psychological contract is said to be afforded by a match between what is wanted and what is on offer, for both parties in the exchange. It is unlikely that a perfect match will simply occur naturally. The process of contracting requires negotiation of wants and offers, and as such cannot take either for granted. Potentially, what an employee wants from a relationship with the organization is much more variable than what the organization wants in return (e.g. Guest, 1998). In the contemporary economic climate, the organization is likely to want investment in optimal performance, flexibility and the ability to adapt quickly and effectively to rapid change. On the other hand, each employee's wants are likely to be as idiosyncratic and subjective as ever.

Because the types of things that individuals might want from an organization are potentially infinite, the idea is obviously too unwieldy to contemplate without some means of organizing needs and wants into viable categories. To this end, Schein's (1993) model of 'career anchors' (or work value) is used by Herriot, Hirsch and Reilly (1998) as a way of unpacking individual differences in the kinds of things that an employee might be looking for in their relationship with an employer. According to Schein there are eight different categories of work value: security; autonomy/independence; technical/functional; managerial; entrepreneurship; service/dedication; challenge; and lifestyle integration. It should be noted that there are many sections of the UK workforce for whom security needs are so predominant (because of financial crisis), that anything beyond this basic transactional requirement is purely academic (Herriot, Manning & Kidd, 1997). There are also those for whom work is not the 'lived in' reality that it is for those who live to work. Some employees work to live. Yet research has tended to focus primarily on the former: employees who seek relational contracts with their employing organization rather than transactional ones.

It would be tempting at this stage to attempt segmentation of the workforce in terms of predominant work values. It is likely, for instance, that professionals will be looking primarily for autonomy and independence in their relationship with an employer, and that female employees with families will be more interested in lifestyle integration. However, such simplistic divisions must be avoided for risk of stereotyping particular groups of employees—such a practice would not be consistent with the process of contracting which addresses *individual* needs and interests. Moreover, conventional divisions such as age, sex and occupation for instance, are no longer viable ways of segmenting the UK workforce; diversity has been reconfigured and is potentially infinitely variable (Sparrow, 1998).

It is generally agreed by HRM experts that the diverse character of the workforce, coupled with the demand on organizations for innovation and adaptation to change in order to survive, requires highly individuated strategies of psychological contract management (Guest 1998; Herriot, Hirsch & Reilly, 1998; Sparrow, 1998). Organizations tend to underestimate the diversity of their employees' needs, assuming homogeneity of cultural values and thus personal values therein. Thus, norm structures can obscure individual needs and interests to the point of neglect. This is particularly true of employees lower down the organizational hierarchy and/or in peripheral roles.

There is evidence for some attempts by organizations in the UK to establish individuated deals with employees in all types of jobs and at all levels of status. Vauxhall Motors, for instance (as cited by Parsons & Strickland, 1996), has established a development scheme in which all employees are afforded the opportunity to identify and pursue their personal development needs both within and outside the employing organization. Since its introduction, there has been a 60% take up of the 'offer' of personal development, and a notable reduction in employee turnover. Other examples in the UK include First Direct and also Lloyds TSB, both of whom afford supervisors the autonomy to offer their telesales staff work patterns to suit their individual lifestyle needs (Herriot, Hirsch & Reilly, 1998).

## VIOLATION OF THE CONTRACT: PROMISES OR EXPECTATIONS?

The old psychological contract is dead! (Hall, 1993)

As the above statement illustrates, a major theme to be found within the literature is that of contract violation. It is this, it is argued, which is most likely to result in negative outcomes for the organization and for the individual (Herriot, Manning & Kidd, 1997; McLean Parks & Kidder, 1994; Robinson & Rousseau, 1994). It has been stipulated that in order for a breach to constitute a violation of a contract, the contract must comprise a promissory element, as opposed to merely carrying the expectations of *both parties*. According to Rousseau (1995, p. 111) contract violation can range from subtle misperceptions to stark breaches of good faith. She says that violation is commonplace (e.g. due to unfamiliarity with the job), often inadvertent (e.g. 'over-promise', say one thing—do another) and difficult to articulate, although this need not be fatal. Not all discrepancies are noticed and not all that are noticed are perceived as violations. Often, inadvertent contract violation occurs because of failure to communicate (see also Herriot, Hirsch & Reilly, 1998). Strongly felt experiences of violation, however, tend to occur when a failure to keep a commitment injures or causes damages that the contract was designed to avoid (Rousseau, 1995, pp. 112–113). Such outright failure can arise from opportunism (i.e. self-serving at the expense of other) or sheer negligence (i.e. non-fulfilment) (see also Robinson & Rousseau, 1994).

As already pointed out, Rousseau (1990), in one of the first major empirical studies of the psychological contract, emphasized that violated promises were at the core of the construct, arguing that this differentiated the psychological contract from the concept of unmet expectations (Wanous, Poland, Premack & Davis, 1992). She also suggested that this lent more weight (in terms of accounting for increased variance) to the prediction of work-related outcomes such as satisfaction and intention to leave. Violation, then, is a failure to comply with the promissory terms of a contract: how people interpret the circumstances of this failure determines whether they experience a violation (Rousseau, 1995, p. 112). Robinson and Rousseau (1994) addressed the contract violation theme with a longitudinal study of graduates over their first two years of employment. They found that over this period, 55% of the sample reported that reciprocal obligations had been violated by the employing organization and that reported occurrence of violation correlated positively with turnover and negatively with trust, satisfaction and intention to stay with the organization.

However, in practice, contract violation has not always been conceptualized solely in terms of this promissory element. Guzzo, Noonan and Elron (1994), for example, questioned expatriate managers about the support they felt they *should* receive from their employing organization, compared with the support they did receive, thereby eliminating the promissory element from the manager–organization contract. Similarly, Baker (1985) cites work role, social, economic and cultural employee *expectations* as underpinning the psychological contract with an employing organization, suggesting that violation of these expectations alone, whether or not they contain a promissory element, will ultimately result in dissatisfaction and be instrumental in a decision to quit.

Other researchers have focused on potential mediators of perceived contract violation, including Shore and Tetrick (1994), who discussed causal attribution in this context, arguing that reactions to violation may depend in part on the *type* of violation and the *extent to which the organization is perceived as being responsible* for it. They suggest that 'action-oriented' individuals (Kuhl, 1992) may be most likely to attempt to reinstate or renegotiate the contract, whereas 'state-oriented' individuals may be more inclined to avoid/withdraw from the situation. This assertion clearly has implications for individual-level management of the psychological contract by the employing organization. It has also been suggested that the relational-transactional contract distinction may be fundamental in predicting worker reaction to perceived violation. For example, McLean Parks and Kidder (1994) linked the psychological contract concept with that of procedural versus distributive justice. They argued that perceptions of procedural justice following a violation may be most salient to employees holding a relational contract, whereas distributive justice may be most significant to those with a transactional one. Intuitively, and as has been suggested by other researchers (e.g. Robinson & Rousseau, 1994), it could be argued that violation of a relational contract is likely to have more significant *affective* outcomes for the individual holding the contract, since the relationship between individual and organization is based more on trust, loyalty and commitment than a transactional contract. In short, relationship strength is likely to mediate perceived violation. Transactional employees may adopt a more pragmatic stance to a perceived violation, and are perhaps less likely to experience personal disillusionment and other affective responses (feeling 'cheated', becoming less trusting of the organization, etc.).

Noer (1993) describes the effects of downsizing on organizations' remaining employees, and the importance of negotiating new contracts with these staff. Goffee and Scase (1992) and Brockner, Grover, Reed and DeWitt (1992) have also provided evidence of alienated 'shell-shocked' survivors of organizational trauma, responding by either 'getting out', 'getting safe' (keeping their heads down) or 'getting even' (by psychological withdrawal or sabotage) (Arnold, 1996). Clearly, any of these outcomes will impact negatively on the organization. Evidence suggests that violation can promote distrust, anger, attrition (Robinson & Rousseau, 1994), can change behaviour (Rousseau et al, 1992) engineer declines in loyalty (Griffin, O'Leary-Kelly & Collins, 1998) and prompt an increase in litigation (Tyler & Bies, 1979).

It is clear that in many cases 'violation is a trauma for a relationship and undermines good faith'—once lost it is not easily restored. In the words of Rousseau (1995, p. 120), 'troubled relationships often go from bad to worse'. This is because the experience of violation can make people more alert to future potential violations, which can be self-fulfilling. Violation is said to be most likely to occur when there is:

- A history of conflict and low trust
- Social distance—parties do not understand the perspective of the other
- External pattern of violation (e.g. during an era of business retrenchment)
- Incentives to breach contracts are high
- One party perceives little value in the relationship

In summary, the issue of contract violation is a fashionable one given the change in contractual tone within the contemporary marketplace. However, some are wondering whether the issue simply rejuvenates (in the language of contracts) long-standing, almost century-old concerns about job dissatisfaction and its impact on workforce morale and performance (Guest, 1999). Until we know more about what the psychological contract is and how it can be most appropriately investigated, the notion of violation begs the question of what exactly it is that is being breached and in particular, on what basis can a breach be said to have occurred?

## OPERATIONALIZING THE PSYCHOLOGICAL CONTRACT

### Types of Contract Measurement

Early research on the psychological contract was primarily interview-driven (e.g. Argyris, 1962; Levinson, 1962). Attempts to quantify the psychological contract have only been fairly recently developed, although there is now a plethora of different approaches. Most of these measurement attempts are underpinned by the assumption that psychological contracts are cognitive-perceptual constructs, as espoused by Rousseau (1989, 1995) which means that (a) the self-report method is deemed the most valid way of accessing them (see for example, Pearce, 1997) and (b) that they are held by employees (not the employer) which means that they can be investigated form one viewpoint alone. As will be demonstrated, there are exceptions to the second of these principles, particularly in contemporary ways of exploring psychological contracts.

Measurement attempts can be divided into two main approaches: *content* (identifying the obligations and terms that employees hold themselves to be party to in the employment relationship, describing the types of relationship which predominate) (e.g. Robinson, Kraatz & Rousseau, 1994; Hutton & Cummins, 1997), and *process measures* (pertaining to the dynamic aspects of contract fulfilment and violation, such as whether an obligation has or has not been met) (e.g. Robinson & Rousseau, 1994; Robinson, 1996). The majority of published research is content-oriented, focusing on contractual obligations, although process research is on the increase. It should be noted, however, that process research is concerned with contract violation and not the psychological contract per se, which means that questions concerning the contracting process itself have yet to be formally addressed.

## Content-focused Measures

Content-focused research can be divided into studies which have attempted to elicit idiosyncratic information and those which aim at psychometric standardization (Robinson & Wolfe-Morrison, 1995). If, as it can be argued, psychological contracts comprise both idiosyncratic (usually obtained in qualitative form) and generalizable (usually obtained in quantitative form) aspects, then both types of measurement are likely to be viable (Rousseau, 1990).

### Efforts at standardization

Standardization was first attempted by Robinson, Kraatz and Rousseau (1994) who developed a psychometric tool to measure the psychological contract from the employee's perspective. On the basis of extensive pilot work, they developed a series of items which respondents were asked to report whether they believed *their employing organization* was obliged to provide (employer obligations) and another series of items which they were asked to report whether they believed *they* were obliged to provide (employee obligations). The aim of the tool was not only to ascertain contract content but to enable the tracking of contracts over time. Robinson, Kraatz and Rousseau (1994) reported a test-retest reliability item mean of 0.80 across a two-week time gap. However, some differences in the factor structure between administrations of the items suggested instability of some items, leading some researchers to suggest the need for further work to confirm the most appropriate scale for each work aspect (e.g. Arnold, 1996).

The vast number of obligation terms that could be potentially incorporated in a tool like this (with different obligations relevant for particular populations of respondent) can undermine the scope for generalization (e.g. what the employer is obliged to offer may cover working conditions, benefits, intrinsic job characteristics, good faith and so on, and what the employee is obliged to offer in return may cover things such as professionalism, loyalty and commitment, hard work, etc.). In a longitudinal study of MBA students (Rousseau, 1990; Robinson & Rousseau, 1994), the relational and transactional dimensions identified at time 1, also revealed themselves at time 2, suggesting relative stability across a period of 2½ years (see also Robinson & Wolfe-Morrison, 1995 and 1997). Although the factor structures derived from research on MBA students have not been replicated across other samples (Barksdale & McFarlane Shore, in press; Freese & Schalk, 1996), some obligation terms appear to be relatively valid and stable indicators of the relational psychological contract (i.e. the provision of job security and development opportunity in exchange for loyalty and commitment) and likewise the transactional contract (i.e. high monetary reward in exchange for efficient and effective performance).

Two other psychometric instruments geared to eliciting data on the psychological contract are worthy of note, both of which take an employee-only stance on the issue. Hutton and Cummins (1997) published a measure termed the Psychological Contract Inventory (PsyCon) in the *Australian Journal of Career Development*. Drawing on the qualitative work of Herriot, Manning and Kidd (1997) (as described below) coupled with the quantitative work of Robinson and Wolfe-Morrison (1995), Hutton and Cummins (1997) derived 44 items for inclusion in their scale. The response options ranged across a five-point scale from 1 (not at all obligated) through to 5 (completely obligated). Employee obligations were defined as 'anything you believe you owe your employer or workplace even though there may be no written or clearly spoken agreement between you'. Employer obligations were defined as 'anything you believe your employer should provide even though . . .' Responses were derived from a sample of 114 employees (in technical and professional jobs), both male and female in approximately equal numbers.

Factor analysis of employee obligations yielded three factors:

- 'Good will towards work including positive presence, effort, involvement and personal integrity'
- 'Doing more than required including intention to stay and flexibility'
- 'Loyalty including protecting the interests of the organization'

Factor analysis of perceived employer obligations yielded two factors:

- 'Support for the individual including opportunities for advancement and development, and recognition for needs and circumstances'
- 'Respect and fair practice including appropriate rewards, justice, resources and training'

The scale demonstrates potential but has as yet only been investigated on a limited sample. The scale was evolved on exploratory grounds, although as indicated above it was informed by previous research. The authors argue that the construct is in need of theoretical development, and agree that much more theoretical and empirical work is needed before the PsyCon Inventory can be considered to be the tool of choice in this regard.

In 1998, Millward and Hopkins published the Psychological Contract Scale (PCS), which was evolved on a priori grounds (to enable the identification of relational and transactional psychological contracts) (see also Millward & Brewerton, 1999). A 50-item bank initially derived from focus group discussions was subsequently reduced to a 37-item questionnaire, comprising 22 'relational' and 15 'transactional' items (reporting stable factor structure and internal consistency reliability). This tool has subsequently been validated on a sample of over 5000 employees across a wide range of industries and organizations, and has also been slightly shortened (Millward & Brewerton, 1998). The PCS now comprises 20 items for the transactional subscale and 12 items for the relational subscale, with the following internal consistency reliabilities: transactional (alpha = 0.79); and relational (alpha = 0.80). Consistent with the advice of Arnold (1996) in his incisive critique of the psychological contract, the possibility of subfactors within contractual types was explored and these results were discussed in an earlier section of this chapter. Interestingly, there is overlap with these factors and those identified by Hutton and Cummins (1997) described above, suggesting that through triangulation of methods it may be possible to identify some generic components of the psychological contract. However, as they themselves stipulated, much more work is needed before any definitive conclusions can be drawn.

Moving on from the employee-only stance on the psychological contract, Barksdale and McFarlane Shore (in press) used Robinson, Kraatz and Rousseau's (1994) 15-item measure to look at whether particular types of inter-relations between employer and employee obligations could be identified. To this end, they cluster analysed the obligation terms to identify people with different kinds of contracts. From this, four types of interrelation were identified and defined in terms of scope (i.e. covering a broad or limited array of contract terms) and the balance of the exchange of obligations (high-high, low-low, high-low, low-high). This approach is consistent with the definition of a psychological contract as a process involving reciprocal exchanges and agreements (Herriot & Pemberton, 1997; Herriot, Hirsch & Reilly, 1998). The findings showed that where mutual obligations are perceived to be high, and where the contracts are of broad rather than limited scope, there was significantly higher employee commitment, and intention to stay. The findings also demonstrate the potential of investigating the relevance of the notion of exchange to the way that psychological contracts operate.

Using a different approach altogether, Wade-Benzoni and Rousseau (1997) tested out the viability of using a very simple classification task involving doctoral students and faculty members in choosing 'the description which most closely fits the collaborative research relationship':

- *Transactional*—structured project with specified time-frame; clear and explicit performance terms
- *Relational*—mentoring relationship; open-ended time-frame, implicit performance standards
- *Balanced/Hybrid*—involved a mentoring relationship and at least one structured project; long-term time-frame, well-specified performance terms
- *Transitional/Uncertain*—no specified time-frame or performance requirements

Findings confirmed the viability of using typologies of this kind to elicit data on psychological contracts as a relationship of reciprocity and exchange. In this research, there was much agreement between students and faculty members on the contract types they saw as relevant to them.

## *The qualitative approach*

Attempts to explore the idiosyncratic nature of the psychological contract construct have been pursued in several ways, one of which is psychodynamic. Rousseau and Tijoriwala (1996) found that the psychological contract may be underpinned by a parent–child dynamic—for example nurses in relation to their seniors. On a different note, Herriot and Pemberton (1995b) looked at divergence in how the employment relationship was construed by managers and employees, divergence of the kind that can generate overt conflict. They used the focus group method to elicit both management's and employees' views of the 'new' psychological contract (following years of escalating competitiveness and pressures created by mass downsizing). In a similar vein, Herriot, Manning and Kidd (1997) utilised Critical Incidents technique to explore the psychological contract construct, deriving data from two samples: representatives from management, and employees. Both samples were asked to report specific instances when:

1. The organization offered more than it was obligated to.
2. An employee/employees offered more than they were obligated to.
3. The organization offered less than it was obligated to.
4. An employee/employees offered less than obligated to.

The elicited themes derived from content analysis of over 1000 incidents elicited from participants are summarized below:

| Organizational obligations | Employee obligations |
| --- | --- |
| • Training | • Hours |
| • Fairness | • Work |

| Organizational obligations | Employee obligations |
|---|---|
| • Needs | • Honesty |
| • Consultation | • Loyalty |
| • Discretion | • Property |
| • Humanity | • Self-presentation |
| • Recognition | • Flexibility |
| • Environment | |
| • Justice | |
| • Pay | |
| • Benefits | |
| • Security | |

By content and chi-square analysing these contractual themes within each group of participants, it was found that in terms of organizational obligations, management representatives focused on relational aspects of the workplace, and employees more on 'hygiene' aspects. In terms of employee obligations, again, a relational view was adopted by management (e.g. loyalty), with a more transactional view taken by employees (e.g. self-presentation, property). No group differences appeared, however, for the themes 'hours', 'work' and 'honesty'.

The principal rationale for using idiosyncratic measurement is that in times of radical change, structural features of one organization may not carry the same meaning in another (nor indeed within the same organization over time). In such circumstances, it could be argued that idiosyncratic measures are not only appropriate but are the only realistic source of information on psychological contracts (Herriot, Hirsch & Reilly, 1998). Moreover, given that employment relations are undergoing dramatic change, the particular practices that once characterized relational or transactional type contracts may also change (e.g. some employers may no longer offer career advancement but may instead offer more lifestyle type contracts with built-in flexibility to suit both parties and/or alternative types of development opportunities). It is feasible that many different combinations of 'offers' might nonetheless produce a similar employment relationship (e.g. for some employees, a relational contract is forged by offering them flexible contracts in exchange for their loyalty and commitment). In addition, it is becoming evident that a hybrid form of psychological contract is emerging which reconciles the precisely specified performance requirements of the conventional transactional contract with traditional relational agreements between employee and employer (Rousseau & Tijoriwala, 1996). The idiosyncratic approach to measurement is also characterized by an assumption of the psychological contract as a two-way rather than a one-way affair, thereby taking the construct out of the head of the individual and into the relationship characterized by a two-party exchange.

In summary, there is as yet little evidence for stable composites of obligation characterizing the employment relationship in the way predicted by the cognitive-perceptual model of the psychological contract. However, investigated in the form of an attitude, there is growing evidence for the viability of the relational and transactional distinction within the psychological contract model. The distinction holds strong across different organizational settings and samples. Whether the elements of which these 'types of relationship' are comprised will remain stable over time is yet to be ascertained, although this seems highly unlikely due to changes in the meaning of particular contractual terms with time. Moreover, this approach locates the psychological contract still very firmly in the head of the employee, thereby neglecting the two-party nature of the contractual exchange. To investigate the dynamics of contracting, its two-way nature as well as changes in meaning, a more idiosyncratic qualitative approach might be appropriate, although some attempts have already been made to quantify the relationship using classification as well as adapted versions of existing questionnaire methods. The use of employee-only measures of the psychological contract do not preclude the possibility of investigating the employer side of the equation, though the viability of this has yet to be systematically ascertained.

## Process-focused Measures

Process-focused measures aim to assess how well or otherwise a party to the contract has performed against promises and obligations—that is they aim to measure contract violation, rather than the psychological contract per se. Process measures can be divided into two main types: *direct* and *indirect*. Of the direct measures that have been used, the two most commonly cited are: (a) contract fulfilment (1–5 'not at all' to a 'very great extent') and (b) a dichotomous index of violation (yes/no) (see, for example, Robinson & Rousseau, 1994).

Using the continuous index, fulfilment and violation are found to be negatively related (−0.53). However, in reality, argues Rousseau (1995) violation and fulfilment can coexist within the same psychological contract—that is people can perceive some aspects of their contract to be fulfilled and other aspects to be violated. To this extent, she advocates that the dichotomous 'yes'/'no' measure is a more valid indicator of contract fulfilment/violation, enabling particular domains of fulfilment or violation to be more discretely ascertained. Likewise, Robinson and Wolfe-Morrison (1997) investigated obligation fulfilment using 25 obligation terms at time 1 and then traced how well each obligation had been fulfilled at time 2. These 25 obligation fulfilment items fell into 6 factors: enriched job; fair pay; opportunity for growth and advancement; sufficient tools and resources; supportive work environment; and attractive benefits.

An example of a more *indirect* measure of contract fulfilment is 'perceived organizational support' (POS) (which measures the perceived quality of support (Eisenberger et al, 1986) as used by Barksdale and Renn (in press), and

Barksdale and McFarlane-Shore (in press), Barksdale and Renn (in press) confirmed the validity of using the POS to investigate contract violation in the context of an organization in which radical changes in compensation policy had been experienced (i.e. from annual merit increases to lump sum bonuses). Existing employees tended to be low on POS and were especially prone to absenteeism whereas employees contracted in under the new scheme were largely unaffected.

One of the problems with the notion of contract violation is that it assumes that we know exactly what it is that has been violated (or fulfilled), when in fact (as the above discussion reveals) we are still not really sure what the psychological contract is or how in itself it should be measured. Moreover, some have pondered whether contract violation is no more than simply a surrogate term for job dissatisfaction particularly insofar as it is defined as a primarily affective construct (Guest, 1999).

In summary, contract fulfilment appears to be conceptually and empirically distinct from contract violation, thus confirming the inclination to measure these as discrete constructs rather than via a continuous scale. Surrogate variables of contract fulfilment such as perceived organizational support also appear to have some viability. In general, considerable caution is needed in the use of indicators of both contract violation and fulfilment, insofar as (a) it is not clear what exactly it is that is being violated or fulfilled and (b) it is not clear that the terms contract fulfilment and contract violation add any conceptual or empirical value over and above the more straightforward concepts of satisfaction and dissatisfaction, respectively.

## Performance Implications

Whilst affective outcomes to contract violation, such as commitment levels and job satisfaction, have been well documented (Robinson & Rousseau, 1994; Rousseau, 1990; Wanous et al. 1992), behavioural implications of contract violation and contract type are also of interest in that it is these behaviours which are most likely to impact *directly* on an organization's performance. A variety of behavioural indicators have been studied within the literature, most notably organizational citizenship behaviour (OCB), absenteeism, staff turnover and intent, and workplace violence. Robinson and Wolfe-Morrison (1995), in a longitudinal study of MBA alumni, found that if employees perceived organizational obligations to have been unfulfilled after 18 months within the company, they were significantly less likely to engage in organizational citizenship behaviour at 30 months tenure (although they noted that this relationship was mediated, in part, by trust). McLean Parks and Kidder (1994) also discussed the relationship between contract violation and employee engagement in anti-OCB behaviours, including theft and sabotage.

Nicholson and Johns (1985) attempted to link the psychological contract construct with the concept of 'absence cultures', arguing the contract to be the surface manifestation of communicated corporate values which may result in the production of one of four absence cultural 'types'. Geurts (1995) also suggested that absence from work may derive in part from the nature of an employee's psychological contract with the workplace. Work by Brewerton and Millward (1997) confirmed this assertion, reporting a significant relationship between relational psychological contractual orientation (as quantified using an abridged version of Millward and Hopkins' 1998 'Psychological Contract Scale') and worker absenteeism over a three-month period within a UK-based telemarketing call centre.

Staff turnover and intention to stay with or leave an organization has been explored by various researchers. Robinson and Rousseau (1994) found that perceived contract violation correlated positively with staff turnover and negatively with intention to remain. Guzzo, Noonan and Elron (1994) developed a model which maintained that the psychological contract held by expatriate managers could act as a mediator of organizational practices in predicting retention-relevant outcomes, including intention to leave the organization, and intention to return early to a domestic assignment. Research by Millward and Brewerton (1998) reports the following highly significant relationships between the psychological contract (as quantified by the Psychological Contract Scale) and intention to leave, across three major UK-based organizations: relational with intent to leave ($r = -0.31$, $n = 1561$) and transactional with intent to leave ($r = 0.20$, $n = 1542$).

## Evaluation

Research on the psychological contract which until recently has been largely content-focused, is becoming attuned to the need to investigate the two-party nature of contracting. In the early 1990s, the focus was principally on the employee as the holder of the psychological contract. More recently, however, the reciprocal nature of the exchange agreements involved in the process of contracting has been acknowledged and taken up. To this extent, it is now being argued that it is critical to look at the *interplay between employer and employee* terms as the definitive characteristic of the psychological contract in an organizational setting (Barksdale & McFarlane Shore, in press; Herriot, Hirsch & Reilly, 1998; Millward & Herriot, 1999). Reciprocity cannot be investigated solely from employee-derived data.

It is also clear from the above review that there is a strong case for using a combination of measures: content-focused as well as process-focused, qualitative (idiosyncratic) and quantitative (standardized, generic). There is evidence that the psychological contract comprises both stable and dynamic (i.e. continually in transition) elements (see Herriot, Hirsch & Reilly, 1998), as well as both generic and idiosyncratic aspects (which in turn are a function of person-specific, organization-specific, economic and political factors). To this extent, there is unlikely to be such a thing as a 'pure' contract in the absolute and substantive sense, and we are perhaps in danger of reifying the concept if we assume that there is. This criticism extends to research on contract fulfilment and violation which assumes that there is something fixed and stable to fulfil and violate, which masks the reality of a dynamic process of negotiation and adaptation to circumstances denoting a breach of contract (Sparrow, 1998). The discussion below on contemporary contracts takes up the issue of adaptation in connection with breached or changing contracts in more detail.

## RELATIONSHIPS WITH OTHER PSYCHOLOGICAL CONSTRUCTS: OLD WINE IN NEW BOTTLES?

Arnold (1996) has argued that if the psychological contract construct is to be of use, at least in its employee-only, idiosyncratic form, then it needs to be systematically differentiated (conceptually and empirically) from closely related constructs such as commitment. Many of the pet constructs researched by organizational psychologists, for example, report alarmingly strong relationships with supposedly conceptually and empirically distinct concepts, for example organizational commitment, job satisfaction, job involvement, and so on. Many conflated relationships are believed to exist due to method covariance and other statistical biases. It is possible however, one one level, to argue that such relationships are also descriptive of the complex and interdependent nature of workplace reactions. It is with these caveats in mind that we can explore the relationships found between the psychological contract and other measures of workplace perception and reaction, thereby attempting to identify or clarify what is distinct about the psychological contract.

### Organizational Commitment

It might be argued that the psychological contract as a cognitive-perceptual construct holds little explanatory or predictive significance over and above the concept of organizational commitment (e.g. Somers, 1995). Argyle (1989), citing Etzioni (1961), proposed that commitment can be thought of in two ways: calculative and affective. Calculative commitment corresponds to Etzioni's notion of 'utilitarian exchange', signalling an instrumental attachment to an organization, whilst affective commitment corresponds to Etzioni's notion of 'moral involvement', signalling a non-instrumental 'emotional' attachment to the organization through internalizing its values. This conceptualization of commitment echoes with the idea of a 'transactional' (i.e. calculative) and 'relational' (i.e. affective) organizational orientation.

Likewise, Becker's (1960) 'side-bet' *behavioural* theory of commitment pictures an individual bound to the organization through instrumental interests (e.g. salary, benefits, seniority/status) (also underpinning the work of McGee

& Ford, 1987) indicating, perhaps, a kind of transactional organizational orientation. Similarly, the affective/attitudinal view of commitment parallels the idea of a relational organizational orientation insofar as it is defined as 'the strength of an individual's identification and involvement with an organization' (Porter, Steers, Mowday & Boullian, 1974, p. 12; see also Mowday, Steers & Porter, 1979).[1] It might be argued, then, that the psychological contract is merely another way of operationalizing organizational commitment: the transactional orientation is similar to the calculative type of commitment proposed by Etzioni (1961) with the relational orientation corresponding to Etzioni's idea of an affective/attitudinal type of commitment.

Unlike the psychological contract, however, organizational commitment is construed to comprise employee attitudes towards an entire organization, rather than specific aspects or facets of that organization. As such, the commitment construct is believed to be less influenced by daily events (Angle & Perry, 1981; Dipboye, Smith & Howell, 1994), and to be more indicative of a relatively stable employee attribute (Porter et al., 1974; Koch & Steers, 1978). However, the conceptual and empirical overlap between the two models is difficult to ascertain from the existing literature. The concept of organizational commitment used by contemporary researchers is anchored one-sidedly in the affective/attitudinal tradition of Porter et al. (1974).

As pointed out by Rousseau (1995), the concept of the psychological contract is most definitely tied to that of organizational commitment; however, it does not address beliefs about reciprocity and obligation. Together, findings show that, even as a cognitive-perceptual employee-only construct, the psychological contract (operationalized in transactional and relational terms) explains substantially more variance than either organizational or job commitment, in organizational behaviour including extra-role activity, intention to stay or leave, and absenteeism (Millward & Hopkins, 1998; Millward & Brewerton, 1999; Coyle-Shapiro & Kessler, 1998). The added value of the psychological contract construct as an explanatory tool is also illustrated by evidence (to be described below in the section on the links with organized culture) demonstrating its fundamentally two-way, as opposed to one-way, character. Whereas organizational commitment pertains to the degree of emotional investment in, and identification with, an organization and its goals, the psychological contract can be said to operate in a more multifaceted and dynamic fashion. Organizational commitment can thus be said to denote an 'input', whereas the psychological contract distinctly denotes a 'relationship of exchange' (Millward & Hopkins, 1998; Millward & Herriot, 1999).

## Links with Organizational Culture

The potential relationship between the psychological contract and concepts such as organizational culture are clearly largely reliant on the way in which these concepts are conceptualized and measured. Rousseau (1995) has noted how psychological contracts are informed by social contracts in the form of particular cultural norms and values (e.g. assumptions of good faith, fair dealing and trust). In short, she says that the psychological contract is a product of culture not a cause, and to this extent will reflect it without being synonymous with it.

Taking a distinctly psychometric line on the topic of organizational culture, Millward and Brewerton's (1998) research into the measurement of organizational culture has identified 12 distinct dimensions of the construct which may be rated by employees within any organization. In order to explore the relationship between employees' perceptions of their organization's culture and their own psychological contracts, regression models were built for both relational and transactional psychological contract ratings, regressing each of the 12 dimensions onto transactional/relational contract rating in order to identify which cultural dimensions were most closely related to the psychological contract. Utilizing a sample size of over 5000, which comprised employees from a wide range of different organizations, both common (cross-organization) and distinguishing (organization-specific) patterns emerged from the data.

Specifically, it was found that perceptions of opportunity to develop, to belong, and to obtain recognition were cultural dimensions that predicted a high score on the relational subscale. It is the perceived absence of development opportunity, of organizational coherence and direction, and of loyalty and commitment demonstrated by employee and employer alike, that predicted a heightened score on the transactional subscale. Whilst causal links should not be assumed between what the organization is perceived to 'offer' and what the employee might then 'offer' in return, the evidence does suggest that the psychological contract is inextricably bound up with considerations of *employer–employee exchange*. Importantly, the findings also show clearly that relational and transactional contracts are unlikely to be part of a single bipolar construct (since different elements of culture were found to differentially predict relational and transactional contract formation).

Similar findings are reported by Coyle-Shapiro and Kessler (1998) for whom exchange was operationalized as the extent to which various obligations (on the part of the organization) of both a relational and transactional kind, were deemed fulfilled (Robinson & Rousseau, 1994). Their evidence, derived from public sector employees such as teachers and firefighters, demonstrated that the character of the exchange relationship is driven by the extent to which employees perceive themselves to be valued and supported.

Other researchers have also attempted to link the psychological contract and organizational culture constructs. Nicholson and Johns (1985) suggest that since the psychological contract is said to emerge from employee interaction and communication, it thereby effectively dictates how culture is 'acted out' at the *behavioural* level of analysis. The researchers go on to discuss the transmission of culture through the social context, reinforcing the social order of the organization via this medium and leading to formation of an appropriate psychological contract.

Borrill and Kidd (1994) discussed the experience of return to work following the birth of a child for samples of men and women, suggesting that for women at least, who were generally shown to shift from full-time to part-time work following pregnancy, the renegotiation of the psychological contract with their employing organization was problematic, if not impossible, if a truly mutually acceptable contract was to be arrived at. The researchers pointed to the alteration and change of various cultural practices and values within the organization as a possible mediator of this negotiation problem. Stiles et al. (1996) focus on the potential problems of renegotiating employee contracts following major organizational change programmes. Cultural changes within the workplace were found to result in violations of the old psychological contract for employees of three major UK-based firms, resulting in lowered morale, commitment and satisfaction at work. Finally, Rousseau (1995), in her introductory text concerning the psychological contract paradigm, links her conceptualization of the psychological contract with a Schein-esque (1980) 'layered' view of organizational culture.

## CONTEMPORARY CONTRACTS

### A Shift from Relational to Transactional Contracts?

It is commonly argued by commentators on organizational life that employees (in the US and UK alike) are experiencing a breach in the psychological contracts which they have evolved with their employers (e.g. Handy, 1994). In particular, breaches are said to have occurred in the 'relational' aspects of the psychological contract, to the point where an exchange relationship based on mutual loyalty and commitment can no longer be guaranteed (Herriot & Pemberton, 1995b). Economic pressures have created a workplace characterized by transactional forms of dealing. This, it is argued, will fashion a calculating, self-interested and opportunistic workforce, working within the 'limits' of the contract and no more, in return for high compensation or remuneration.

This analysis, however, presupposes a direct correspondence between economic and psychological reality. It also assumes that transactional contracts are intrinsically bad. There is, as yet, little actual evidence (at least within the UK) for a greater prevalence of 'transactional' than 'relational' psychological contracts (Millward & Hopkins, 1998; Millward & Brewerton, 1999). So, although many employees may feel that their psychological contracts have been breached (Herriot, Hirsch & Reilly, 1998; Coyle-Shapiro & Kessler, 1998), this has not necessarily led them into becoming more transactional in their exchange relationships with organizations (Guest & Conway, 1997; Guest,

1998). Whilst there is some suggestion that many employees have been forced into a situation whereby short-term survival or 'hygiene' needs do prevail, this does not necessarily equate with transactional contractual orientation. Instead, the issue may be a rather more complex one of employees seeking assurances that basic transactional requirements are met, before relational aspects of the contract can be considered (Herriot, Manning & Kidd, 1997, p. 161).

Herriot and Pemberton (1997) point out that 'transactional' deals may be appropriate, in some instances, for both parties in the exchange. More crucially, it can be argued that transactional deals need not preclude loyalty. Defined in terms of content, it might be difficult to reconcile transactional deals with relational-type content. However, defined in terms of process, transactional deals denote a strictly defined exchange of goods (i.e. one good is exchanged for another), indicating nothing about the actual content of the exchange (such as short-termism or preoccupation with pay and benefits). Instead, an employee operating primarily within a transactional deal is likely to value distributive equity (i.e. fair exchange of goods). Likewise, what differentiates the relational contract is not its content (of long-term loyalty, commitment, identification and so on) but reciprocity on a broader scale and over a longer time-frame. In this case, an employee is more likely to value procedural equity (i.e. fair decision-making procedures). An employee operating primarily within a relational deal is thus more likely to tolerate distributive inequity at one point in time, with view to justice in the long term.

It would seem from UK evidence that the exchange relationship is much more appropriately characterized as comprising both relational and transactional aspects in uniquely complex combinations (Millward & Brewerton, 1999a). Evidence from the US suggests that a similar pattern is emerging in the form of so-called 'hybrid contracts' (Rousseau, 1997). As such, an employee may choose to invest a great deal of effort or trust in a company with a view to obtaining a high personal return (financial, developmental) whilst retaining a practical (i.e. circumscribed) transactional attitude should their contract be terminated. This picture in fact may describe the classic 'entrepreneur', highly motivated to obtain the highest return for their input. In this sense, loyalty and commitment may result from fulfilment of transactional needs and interests (i.e. commitment of a calculative kind) (Meyer, Allen & Smith, 1993).

It is in the notion that relational deals signal reciprocity of a general (i.e. organizational level) rather than job or task-specific kind that the term 'social capital', used earlier in this review, can be most readily understood. If social capital describes the build-up of trust and willingness to collaborate in the long term (i.e. general reciprocity), then it is a short step to realizing that a breach of reciprocity at this level could have serious costs in terms of organizational survival (Herriot, Hirsch & Reilly, 1998). When it is perceived by employees that their long-term expectations for personal growth, increased pay and/or autonomy, for example, have not been honoured, they may react with anger, exit or withdrawal of organizational-level investment (Goffee & Scase, 1992; Robinson, Kraatz & Rousseau, 1994). For many employees, compulsory relocation, demotion or job change, threats of redundancy, and intensified workloads will have been construed as fundamental violations of long-term reciprocity deals (i.e. contractual elements encapsulated by the term relational contract).

## Self-correcting Contracts

We must be careful, however, not to assume that it is all doom and gloom with the contemporary psychological contract. Some UK commentators within the HRM field have suggested that we have overstated the case for the violation of relational contracts (e.g. Guest, 1998; Sparrow, 1998), with similar findings being documented in the US (Rousseau, 1997). Guest (1998) reports on findings from a recent telephone survey of 1000 UK employees (Guest & Conway, 1997) which indicate that feelings of security and trust in the employer are much higher than had been forecast, and that in the main, employees seem to hold a fairly optimistic view of their future. Levels of trust, commitment and satisfaction are reported to be slowly recovering, with 79% of employees saying they trust their management 'a lot'. Although 25% of the sample had experienced redundancy, expectations of future redundancy are low. Whilst 53% say they are working harder, most of these (42%) say it is because they want to. Moreover, those on temporary/fixed-term contracts are on average more satisfied than those on full-time contracts. It could be argued, then, that there is only limited evidence of any overt employee reaction to contractual violation within the UK (at least within this sample).

Whilst media stories in the UK document mass insecurity and opinion polls suggest universal reduction in job security, more detailed investigation shows that deterioration in the psychological contract is restricted to around 20% of employees, of whom most are less well-educated employees in peripheral jobs (Guest, Conway, Briner & Dickmann, 1996).

This, it is argued, may constitute evidence for 'self-correction' (i.e. an adjustment process) amongst those who have survived structural changes and job dislocation. On the other hand, it may be that HRM strategies designed to re-engage employees and rebuild their commitment have paid off. Moreover, many young employees will be entering the labour market today with expectations moderated by encounters with the increasing individualization of the employment experience and by their awareness of uncertain employment futures with a diminishing likelihood of full-time employment. For such employees, little other than this experience will be known or anticipated.

Thus, young employees will have entered the current situation as the only employment reality they know. What are perceived as 'new rules of the game' by older employees are merely accepted as the norm by younger ones. This would suggest a change in the psychological make-up of employees (e.g. a heightened importance of personal rather than organizational identity), and thus an imperative to evolve new strategies for HRM. Moreover, many older employees for whom the job-for-life scenario was their reality in the past, may have nonetheless adapted to the new employment scene (Sparrow, 1998). Many may find satisfaction in the autonomy and flexibility of transactional deals; others may simply have reinvested, but on new, more explicit and highly circumscribed contractual terms (i.e. more transactionally oriented commitment and trust). It is in the explicit nature of contractual terms that many may have derived satisfaction from new deals. The old employment deal was largely implicit and unquestioned, assuming homogeneity of employee requirements (i.e. a job-for-life, a prescribed career and so on). The new deal, however, affords opportunity for a diversity of different psychological deals to be made, within an employment world in which the language and ideology of 'contracts' and 'contracting' are becoming the norm.

There is of course, the likelihood that some employees will have little capacity or resilience for change, and will have found adjustment difficult (Sparrow, 1998). It is these employees for whom violation of old relational contracts may have hit the hardest. Such employees are unlikely to respond to conventional attempts to raise their levels of organizational trust and commitment to previous levels. These are the employees whose identity and self-esteem have been profoundly threatened or undermined by organizational change, and for whom the language of contract negotiation is not yet meaningful.

In short, the evidence strongly suggests that there is much more dynamism within the contracting and recontracting process than has hitherto been assumed. It is clear that there are likely to be some aspects of psychological contracts that resist change: some individuals will invest in their particular contract more than others and to this extent we can say that the individual is the 'holder' of the contract. However, there are aspects of the psychological contract that exist in the relationship or interface itself which are perhaps rather more nebulous and daunting to grapple with but which can be fruitfully explored by focusing on the contracting *process*. Perhaps the stability attributed to the psychological contract is era-specific. The old contract or deal may well have been fixed for a time, but now we are clearly moving into an era of continual adjustment and change, and to this extent the language of process is more appropriate. As researchers, we should also be mindful that the language we ourselves use to define and measure the psychological contract is also a product of the age.

## DE-GENDERING THE PSYCHOLOGICAL CONTRACT

It is commonly assumed that women are fundamentally different from men in their interface with the workplace (e.g. Gallos, 1989). Traditional assumptions hold that if women interface with the 'market world' they do so in largely 'transactional' terms (i.e. to short-term, temporary, secondary or supplementary ends) deriving their social identity from other, more primary, sectors of their lives (e.g. motherhood). They are also often construed as 'employment liabilities' whose priorities lie elsewhere, and who in the main do not depend on the organization as a source of identity or primary income. Whereas the relational contract can be taken as an indicator of the extent to which an individual identifies with the goals of the organization and the degree to which they intend to work to attain those goals (Mowday, Steers & Porter, 1979), a transactional contractual orientation on the other hand is predictive of turnover, absenteeism, and the pre-eminence of personal over social identity considerations (Millward & Hopkins, 1998; Millward & Brewerton, 1999). It is indeed the case that until recently, work and organizational life has—in the main—been more central to male than female identity (e.g. Hearn & Parkin, 1992; Wilson, 1996).

These predictions, however, are derived from traditional assumptions about male and female identity and their differential routes to social validation and self-worth. Whilst it cannot be denied that males and females interface 'from different directions and with recognition of opposite truths' (Gallos, 1989), this does not preclude the possibility that females may seek to fulfil their identity needs primarily through employment (Breakwell, 1985). Indeed, the 'male breadwinner' understanding of gender location and identity has been criticized as 'becoming increasingly less viable in the face of new employment realities' (Bradley, 1997, p. 89). The European employment scene is said to have undergone feminization[2] (Jensen, Hagen & Reddy, 1988; se ealso Furedi, 1995), referring to the increasing presence of women (i.e. the distribution of women in employment) and also 'women's work' (i.e. service work) in contemporary Western society. The notion of part-time, low paid, low status, semi-skilled 'secondary' work is increasingly confined to older women (e.g. 52% of 55–59 year olds versus 13% of 21–24 year olds) (Waldby, 1997). Likewise, rapid changes in educational policy and practice mean that young educated women are benefiting in relation to the careers they are entering, being much more likely than their female seniors to have a profile in skilled, professional work (Bradley, 1997; Waldby, 1997). Moreover, the blurring of boundaries between home and work (e.g. with the widespread introduction of teleworking), between economic and non-economic spheres, and between male and female roles generally, seriously calls into question 'old' assumptions about the relative insignificance (or peripheral significance) of 'market work' for the identity of adult women.

There is as yet scant research in the area of gender and the psychological contract. Mathieu and Zajac (1990) purport nonetheless that gender considerations are highly likely to interact with the way employees construe their interface with the workplace (see also Scandura & Lankau, 1997). Thus despite evidence for fundamental agreement between males and females in beliefs about employee–employer obligations (Herriot, Manning & Kidd, 1997), differences in the salience and importance of these 'obligations' are likely to arise as a function of whether work is an important source of identification and self-worth. Although women generally retain a primary responsibility for family and domestic duties, in addition to being full-time employed (Bielby & Bielby, 1984), this does not mean to say that work is not also important to their identity.

Research conducted by Millward and Brewerton (1999), demonstrates variation between males and females particularly in terms of their transactional orientation. Specifically, females ($n = 906$) came across as significantly more transactional than males ($n = 1635$) on all relevant components within the subscale—that is less inclined to be willing to go the extra mile, less oriented to a future within the company, and more oriented to financial gain. Crucially, however, it was also found that these differences were in part an artefact of the differing hierarchical levels and disciplines taken up by men and women in the organizations sampled. Moreover, the sample comprised a mix of both part-time and full-time working women, populations which can be extremely 'polarized' in the way they interface with the workplace (Hakim, 1996).

In a more focused investigation, Millward and Brewerton (in press) explored differences in full-time male and female contractual beliefs and orientations, as a function of their status in the organizational hierarchy. The findings clearly demonstrated that there is no such thing as the 'average' female employee. Whilst various predictable patterns were discernible in the way full-time female employees interface with their workplace, they demonstrated more in common with their male counterparts than ordinarily given credit for. Popular assumption fuelled by lack of knowledge about full-time (as opposed to part-time) female employees, perhaps leads us to expect that females will be largely 'transactional' in the way they connect with the workplace—that is maintaining a certain 'emotional distance from it and oriented to short-term financial gain. However, females ($n = 666$) were found to be no more 'transactional' in their interface with the workplace than their male counterparts. This finding held true within each of five different organizations (representing five different professional disciplines/occupations): two male-dominated (numerically more male than female employees), two female-dominated (numerically more female than male employees) and one in which males and females were fairly equally represented. In absolute terms, both male and female employees were found to be more 'relational' than 'transactional' in their contractual beliefs overall (again, across all five organizations and professional/occupational disciplines), despite the increasingly transactional nature of working life (see for example, Herriot & Pemberton, 1995a). Males and females reportedly felt equally strong in terms of their degree of emotional connection with the organization and in terms of how equitably they felt they were treated by it. Moreover, full-time female employees were actually significantly more oriented to professional development than males.

These preliminary findings throw into question commonly held assumptions and beliefs about differences in males' and females' interfaces with the workplace. In many cases, male and female employees, when matched for grade, age and industry, were found to exhibit almost identical orientations towards the workplace, with women demonstrating 'relational' investment comparable to that of their counterparts, while at the same time showing a suppressed 'transactional' orientation inconsistent with the traditional view of women at work. Whilst the findings pertain to full-time employees and cannot be generalized to other subpopulations within the female community, they do present an interesting picture of sex differences (and similarities) in the contemporary workplace. Full-time male and female employees in lower grade organizational positions were found to be almost identical in the way they interface with the workplace. Differentials—in instances where they did emerge—were only evident higher up the organizational scale and were largely context-specific. This calls into question the viability of studying sex differences in contextual isolation (Aries, 1996; Osterberg, 1996). Whilst clearly there remains a need for issues of gender 'to figure more loudly in organizational analysis' (Wilson, 1996), the study of sex differences should not be pursued to the point of clouding over the common features of the male and female work experience.

## CONCLUSIONS: CONSENSUAL AND CONTENTIOUS ASPECTS

### Areas of Agreement and Debate

In summary, then, the literature presents a number of elements of the psychological contract construct which have gained wide agreement and consensus, whilst others remain open to considerable discussion and debate. Areas that have gained consensual agreement include the following:

- The psychological contract comprises promises made and held by individuals and organizations. These promises are not necessarily mutual but can be understood to be reciprocal in nature.
- Understanding of the same contract may differ between individuals and between parties.
- Contract violations are significantly related to job performance, organizational commitment, job satisfaction, intent to leave, staff turnover and organizational citizenship behaviours.
- Psychological contracts can, and do, change over time.
- Contracts are shifting wholesale from traditional to dynamic and, in some cases, from relational to transactional in nature and content.
- Shifts such as these are resulting in mixed signals being transmitted from organizations to employees, with a consequent need for the negotiation of 'new' contracts.

- Contracts can be managed by both employees and employers.
- Multiple methods of measurement (generic, idiosyncratic, qualitative, quantitative) are required to investigate the psychological contracts and in particular the dynamics of contracting.

Areas touched on in the literature requiring further exploration and which continue to attract debate and contention include the following:

- Debate as to the precise content of the psychological contract, and the level of commonality of this content across organizations.
- Whether the construct incorporates only promises which may be violated, or expectations, which may be unmet, and whether contract violation simply denotes job dissatisfaction by another name. The frequency of contract violation may be overstated and hence also the dynamic aspects of contract negotiation and renegotiation (and repair) risk being understated.
- Whether the construct exists from an organization's perspective, or should be regarded at individual-level only—that is whether it exists only 'in the head' of the employee or whether it is more appropriately located within the employer–employee relationship.
- Whether transactional and relational contracts lie at opposite ends of a single continuum or whether they form discrete constructs which are conceptually and empirically distinct, and which can produce 'hybrid' forms.
- Whether the psychological contract is a valid analytic or scientific construct or simply a metaphor for describing contemporary organizational life.
- With whom the deal is made. Is this the organization, the division, the team, or the profession? To whom are breaches in the contract attributed? How are organizational responsibilities construed or represented? If the psychological contract is a two-way affair, who constitutes the nebulous 'other' (Guest, 1999)?
- The extent to which psychological contracts form normative contracts, and the ways in which these might be conceptualized and measured. Preliminary research involving nurses by Rousseau and Tijoriwala (1996) on this issue suggests that contracts are individual-level phenomena with little in common with coworkers, even within the same hospital subunit. What might be the conditions under which individuals share common elements in their psychological contract?
- The impact of cross-cultural differences in psychological contract formation and maintenance. Contracts may emerge differently across cultures with differential importance associated with facets of contracts themselves, especially explicitness and stability (Rousseau & Tinsley, 1997).

- Conceptualization and measurement of the *dynamics of contracting* including issues of contract formation, mutuality/reciprocity and contract negotiation and renegotiation, in the strict sense of the concept of psychological contract as pertaining to a relationship of exchange.
- Different ways in which individuals actively cope with, and adapt to, contract violation and change (e.g. Sparrow, 1998).

## Exploding Assumptions

It should be noted that, as the body of psychological contract literature grows, the concept is becoming increasingly widely used in a variety of organizational contexts as a neat and useful explicator or metaphor for understanding organizational changes and their impact on employees (Millward & Herriot, 1999). Whilst this widespread acceptance and adoption of the construct is to be encouraged, researchers should be vigilant that the term does not become an 'umbrella' descriptor of all to do with organizations. It seems that the construct is salient to so many areas of organizational behaviour, including career development and management, organizational performance, the political nature of downsizing and restructuring decisions, the changing relationship between employee and employer, and the management of that changing relationship, that it is at risk of becoming diluted in meaning and in its explicative power.

Many recent papers have been keen to incorporate the idea of organizations' 'short run myopic focus', resulting in 'a decade of downsizing and layoffs, more palatably termed "rightsizing" (McLean Parks & Kidder, 1994), which has supposedly led directly to the development of a transactional relationship between employees and employers. Whilst the metaphorical use of the psychological contract construct in this way seems appealing, it is clear that substantially more research is required into the content and meaning of the construct before such politicized comment can be lent any conceptual (or empirical) weight. Unfortunately, many organizations have latched onto the term psychological contract as useful rhetoric, one that hides the reality of imposed deals and ill-thought out attempts to reharmonize an insecure workforce.

The assumption is commonly made that 'commitment' is good for an organization: the more the better. Similarly, an implicit assumption is often made in the literature that the loss of the old relational contract is unfortunate and that we should aim to recreate new ones. Like commitment however, the issue of relational contracts is a two-edged sword. For instance, high relational contracts can lead to insufficient turnover (and thus organizational stagnancy) and also to too much conformity/rigidity and inability to either innovate or adapt, as personal considerations are sacrificed for organizational ones (Randall, 1988). On the other side of the coin, transactional contracts might in some instances be good for an organization, insofar as they afford the opportunity for personal contributions of the creative and innovative kind. Moreover, such a climate could perpetuate a 'natural' system for the turnover of disruptive/poor performers.

From the individual point of view, relational contracts might well afford career advancement and compensation opportunities but may also foster resistance to change, stress and tension with employees having to juggle family/ personal responsibilities with work and limited time for non-work activity. In a fast changing workforce, Meyer (1997) wonders whether a highly committed workforce might be a 'liability'. Alternatively, as organizations become leaner, they may rely more heavily on the commitment of just the core workers. Likewise, Rousseau (1995, p. 106) is eager to emphasize that the relational contract is by no means the 'best' or most 'appropriate'. Transactional contracts (as held by many 'careerists', for example) can afford 'flexibility' to an organization in which the dominant contract is relational. Moreover, transactional contracts increase the lifestyle options for individuals.

## Conclusions

In conclusion, this review has illustrated that the term psychological contract has potential utility as a scientific and analytic construct over and above constructs such as commitment. However, much work remains to be done in clarifying our use of the term, both theoretically and empirically. We need to decide whether a content- or process-focused view of the construct is likely to bear more analytical fruit or whether it is possible to integrate the content and process literature into a single analytical framework. The latter is a possibility that is already being contemplated by researchers in the UK (e.g. Guest, 1998; Herriot & Pemberton, 1997), and it is clear that many US writers on the topic are beginning to introduce 'process' considerations into their research efforts.

It is agreed by most researchers and commentators, that the term psychological contract is in need of a theory. Some have suggested that Equity Theory is the most obvious candidate here (e.g. Herriot & Pemberton, 1997; Hutton & Cummins, 1997) but others have argued that this itself is in need of theoretical clarification and elaboration (e.g. Guest, 1999). Perhaps an attempt to integrate considerations of equity with those pertaining to the psychological contract would aid the task of theoretical clarification on both fronts. Terms such as procedural and distributive justice, which are in the process of being knitted into Equity Theory may also help to provide some theoretical substance to the notion of contract violation (see, e.g., Herriot & Pemberton, 1997).

There are always problems in keeping analytic concepts that are taken up and used as management rhetoric and metaphor, within scientific bounds. Whilst the scientific nature of a construct should not preclude its application to real issues, there are dangers in the construct becoming reified. There is a sense in which the concept is being used to dress up established issues and constructs—that is to address the issue of subjective regulation of employee behaviour. Employee relations began its life in the form of a preoccupation with increasing job satisfaction. Later, the focus changed to one of how to heighten organizational commitment. Most recently, this has been replaced by the language of psychological contracts. All of these constructs have been used with a view to understanding how to alter the 'inputs' of an individual to the organization, in ways which optimize their performance contributions. However, the difference with the psychological contract construct is that it has the potential to be conceptualized and applied in a genuinely two-way fashion, taking into consideration the wants and offers of both individual and organization (Herriot, Hirsch & Reilly, 1998) in the way originally envisaged by Barnard in 1938.

## NOTES

1. It should be noted that this brief tour of commitment concepts is a simplified version of what is truly a very complex and multifaceted area (Meyer, Allen & Smith, 1993). Morrow (1983) for example, noted that there are more than 25 different commitment related-concepts in the literature.
2. Some have argued that 'feminization' of the workplace is more of a vision of the way things should be (i.e. equality of work distribution and reward in paid and unpaid working environments) as opposed to what they actually are (i.e. largely segregated from men in low-paid, low-status, insecure part-time or temporary jobs with few career prospects) (Bradley, 1997; Crompton, 1997; ILO, 1993). For instance, the ILO (1993) noted that women's earnings had only risen 2% since 1985 and were still only 71% of those of men. Others have since pointed to the persistence of male dominance and positional power in the contemporary workplace operating at both macro- (e.g. employment strategy) and micro-levels (e.g. masculine cultures of exclusion, discourses of masculinity and femininity) (Crompton, 1997). Most would agree however with the description of the contemporary employment scene as 'feminized' at least in the *numerical sense* (i.e. increased numbers of women in paid employment, new job creation particularly in fields traditionally described as 'women's work') (Bradley, 1997, p. 87).

## REFERENCES

Abramson, J. & Franklin, B. (1986). *Where Are They Now?*. New York: Doubleday.
Acker, J. (1992). Gendering organizational theory. In A. J. Mills & P. Tancred (Eds), *Gendering Organizational Analysis* (pp. 248–260). London: Sage.
Alvesson, M. (1998). Gender relations and identity at work: A case study of masculinities and femininities in an advertising agency. *Human Relations*, 51(8), 969–1005.
Angle, H. L. & Perry, J. L. (1981). An empirical assessment of organizational commitment and organizational effectiveness. *Administrative Science Quarterly*, 26, 1–14.
Argyle, M. (1989) *The Social Psychology of Work*. London: Penguin.
Argyris, C. (1960). *Understanding Organizational Behavior*. Homewood, Ill: Dorsey.

Aries, E. (1996). *Men and Women in Interaction: Reconsidering the Differences*. New York: Oxford University Press.

Arnold, J. (1996). The psychological contract: A concept in need of close scrutiny? *European Journal of Work and Organizational Psychology*, 5(4), 511–520.

Astin, H. S. (1984). The meaning of work in women's lives: A socio-psychological model of career choice and work behaviour. *Counselling Psychologist*, 12, 117–126.

Bakan, D. (1966). *The Duality of Human Existence*. Chicago: Rand McNally.

Baker, H. G. (1985). The unwritten contract: Job perceptions. *Personnel Journal*, 64(7), 37–41.

Baker, H. G. & Berry, V. M. (1987). Processes and advantages of entry-level career-counselling. *Personnel Journal*, 66(4), 111–121.

Bardwick, J. (1980). The seasons of a woman's life. In D. McGuigan (Ed.), *Women's Lives: New Theory, Research and Policy*. Ann Arbor: University of Michigan Center for Continuing Education for Women.

Barksdale, K. & McFarlane Shore, L. (in press). A typological approach to examine psychological contracts. *Journal of Orgnaizational Behavior*.

Barksdale, K. & Renn, R. W. (in press). A field study of the effects of a new pay-for-performance compensation plan on perceived organizational support and attendance: a psychological contract and justice perspective. *Group and Organizational Management*.

Barnard, C. (1938). *The Functions of the Executive*. Cambridge, MA: Harvard University Press.

Becker, G. S. (1960). Notes on the concept of commitment. *American Journal of Sociology*, 66, 32–40.

Becker, G. S. (1985). Human capital, effort and the sexual division of labour. *Journal of Labour Economics*, 3, S33–S38.

Becker, G. S. (1991). *A Treatise on the Family*. Cambridge MA: Harvard University Press.

Bell, C. S. & Chase, S. E. (1996). The gendered character of women superintendent's professional relationships. In Arnold, K. D. et al. (Eds), *Remarkable Women: Perspectives on Female Talent Development*. New Jersey: Cresskill.

Betz, N. (1993). Women's career development. In F. L. Denmark & M. A. Paludi (Eds), *The Psychology of Women: Handbook of Issues/Theory*, pp. 627–684, Westport, CT: Greenwood Press.

Beutel, A. M. & Marini, M. M. (1995). Gender and values. *American Sociological Review*, 60, 436–448.

Bielby, D. D. & Baron, J. N. (1984). A woman's place is with other women: Sex segregation within organisations. In G. F. Reskin (Ed.), *Sex Segregation in the Workplace: Trends, Explanations, Remedies*, pp. 27–55. Washington DC: National Academy Press.

Bielby, D. D. & Bielby, W. T. (1984). Work commitment, sex-role attitudes and women's employment. *American Sociological Review*, 49, 234–247.

Bierema, L. L. (1996). How executive women learn corporate culture. *Human Resource Development Quarterly*, 7(2), 145–164.

Blau, P. M. (1964). *On the Nature of Organizations*. New York: Wiley.

Bochner, S. & Hesketh, B. (1994). Power distance, individualism/collectivism, and job-related attitudes in a culturally-diverse work group. *Journal of Cross Cultural Psychology*, 25(2), 233–257.

Borrill, C. & Kidd, J. M. (1994). New parents at work: Jobs, families and the psychological contract. *British Journal of Guidance and Counselling*, 22(2), 219–231.

Boss, R. W. (1985). The psychological contract: A key to effective organization development consultation. *Consultation—An International Journal*, 4(4), 284–304.

Bradley, H. (1989). *Men's Work. Women's Work: A Sociological History of the Sexual Division of Labour in Employment*. Cambridge: Polity Press.

Bradley, H. (1997). Gender and change in employment: Feminization and its effects. In R. Brown (Ed.), *The Changing Shape of Work* (pp. 87–102). Macmillan: Basingstoke.

Breakwell, G. (1985). *The Quiet Rebel: Women at Work in a Man's World*. London: Century Publishing.

Brett, J. M. & Stroh, L. K. (1997). Jumping ship: Who benefits from an external labour market career strategy? *Journal of Applied Psychology*, **82**(3), 331–341.

Brewerton, P. M. (1999). Exploring the Psychological Contract: Combining relational and transactional. Unpublished Phd Thesis, University of Surrey, UK.

Brewerton, P. M. & Millward, L. J. (1997). Predicting performance at work: Orgnaizational culture, person–culture 'misfit' and affective workplace attitudes. Unpublished MSc thesis, University of Surrey, UK.

Brockner, J., Grover, M. S., Reed, T. S. & DeWitt, R. L. (1992). Layoffs, job insecurity and survivor work effort: Evidence of an inverted U relationship. *Academy of Management Journal*, **35**, 413–425.

Brown, M. (1997). Outsourcery. *Management Today*, January, 56–58.

Burack, E. (1993). *Corporate Resurgence and the New Employment Relationship*. Westport, CT: Quorum.

Carrier, S. (1995). Family status and career situation for professional women. *Work, Employment and Society*, **9**, 343–358.

Carsten, J. M. & Spector, P. E. (1987). Unemployment, job satisfaction and employee turnover: A meta-analytic test of the Muchinsky model. *Journal of Applied Psychology*, **72**, 374–381.

Cassell, C. & Walsh, S. (1997). Organisational cultures, gender management strategies and women's experience of work. *Feminism and Psychology*, 7(2), 224–230.

Chodorow, N. (1978). *The Reproduction of Mothering*. Berkeley, CA: University of California Press.

Cook, C. (1996). Gender differences in commitment. In A. L. Kalleberg, D. Knoke, P. V. Masden & J. L. Spaeth (Eds), *Organizations in America: Analysing their Structures and Human Resource Practices*. Beverly Hills, CA: Sage.

Coyle-Shapiro, J. & Kessler, I. (1998). Consequences of the psychological contract for the employment relationship: A large scale survey. Paper presented at the Academy of Management Conference.

Crompton, R. (1997). *Women and Work in Modern Britain*. Oxford: Oxford University Press.

Davidow, W. & Malone, M. (1992). *The Virtual Corporation*. New York: Harper.

De Meuse, K. P. & Tornow, W. W. (1997). Leadership and the changing psychological contract between employee and employer. Available from http://deming.eng.clemson.edu/pub/tqmbbs/prin.pract/psycon.txt. [accessed 6 June 1997].

de Vaus, D. & McAllister, I. (1991). Gender and work orientation: Values and satisfaction in Western Europe. *Work and Occupations*, **18**, 72–93.

Deaux, K. & Kite, M. (1993). Gender stereotypes. In F. L. Denmark & M. A. Paludi (Eds), *The Psychology of Women: Handbook of Issues/Theory* (pp. 107–140). Westpoint, CT: Greenwood Press.

Derr, C. B. (1986). *Managing the new Careerists: The Diverse Career Success Orientations of Today's Workers*. San Francisco: Jossey-Bass.

Diamond, E. E. (1987). Theories of career development and the reality of women at work. In B. A. Gutek & L. Larwood (Eds), *Women's Career Development*. Beverly Hills, CA: Sage.

Dipboye, R. L., Smith, C. S. & Howell, W. C. (1994). *Understanding Industrial and Organizational Psychology: An Integrated Approach*. Fort Worth, TX: Harcourt Brace.

Dodd-McCue, D. & Wright, G. B. (1996). Men, women, and commitment: The effects of workplace experiences and socialization. *Human Relations*, **49**(8), 1065–1091.

Doise, W., Clement, A. & Lorenzi-Cioldi, F. (1993). *The Quantitative Analysis of Social Representations.* European Monographs in Social Psychology. London & New York: Harvester Wheatsheaf.

Dunahee, M. H. & Wangler, L. A. (1974). The psychological contract: A conceptual structure for management/employee relations. *Personnel Journal,* **53**(7), 518–526.

Eichenbaum, L. & Orbach, S. (1988). *Between Women.* New York: Viking.

Eisenberger, R., Huntington, R., Hutchinson, S. & Sowa, D. (1986). Perceived organizational support. *Journal of Applied Psychology,* **71**, 500–507.

Etzioni, A. (1961). *A Comparative Analysis of Complex Organizations.* New York: Free Press.

Evatts, J. (1996). *Gender and Career in Science and Engineering.* London: Taylor & Francis.

Farmer, H. S. (1997a). Women's motivation related to mastery, career salience and career aspirations: a multivariate model focusing on the effects of sex role socialisation. *Journal of Career Assessment.* 5(4) 355–381.

Farmer, H. S. (1997b). Gender differences in career development. In H. S. Farmer et al. (Eds), *Diversity and Women's Career Development: From Adolescence to Adulthood,* Vol. 2 (pp. 127–158). Thousand Oaks, CA: Sage.

Farnsworth, E. A. (1982). *Contracts.* Boston, MA: Little Brown.

Feller, R. W. (1995). Action Planning for personal competitiveness in the 'Broken Workplace'. Special Issue: Action Planning. *Journal of Employment Counselling,* **32**(4), 254–263.

Fitzgerald, L. F. & Crites, J. O. (1980). Toward a career psychology of women: What do we know? What do we need to know? *Journal of Counselling Psychology,* **27**, 44–62.

Freese, C. & Schalk, R. M. (1996). The dynamics of psychological contracts. Paper presented at Changes in Psychological Contracts Conference, University of Tilberg, December.

Furedi, F. (1995). Is it a girls' world? *Living Marxism,* **79**, 10–13.

Gallos, J. V. (1989). Exploring women's development: Implications for career theory, practice and research. In M. B. Arthur, D. T. Hall & B. S. Lawrence (Eds), *Handbook of Career Theory* (pp. 110–132). Cambridge: Cambridge University Press.

Gilbert, L. A. (1984). Comments on the meaning of work in women's lives. *Counselling Psychologist,* **12**, 129–130.

Gilligan, C. (1977). In a different voice: Women's conceptions of self and of morality. *Harvard Education Review,* **47**, 4.

Gilligan, C. (1980). Restoring the missing text of women's developments to life-cycle theories. In D. McGuigan (Ed.), *Women's Lives: New Theory, Research and Policy.* Ann Arbor: University of Michigan Center for Continuing Education for Women.

Gilligan, C. (1982). *In a Different Voice: Psychological Theory and Women's Development.* Cambridge, MA: Harvard University Press.

Goffee, R. & Scase, R. (1992). Organizational change and the corporate career: The restructuring of managers' job aspirations. *Human Relations,* **45**, 363–385.

Golembiewsky, R., Billingsley, K. & Yeager, S. (1976). Measuring change and persistence in human affairs: Types of change generated by OD designs. *Journal of Applied Behavioural Science,* **12**, 133–157.

Granrose, C. S. & Skromme, E. E. (1996). *Work-Family Role Choices of Women in their 20–30s: From College Plans to Life Experiences.* New York: Greenwood.

Griffin, R., O'Leary-Kelly, A. & Collins, J. (1998). Dysfunctional work behaviours in organizations. In Cooper, C. L. & Rousseau, D. (Eds), *Trends in Organizational Behaviour,* Vol. 5 (pp. 65–82). Chichester: Wiley.

Guerts, S. A. (1995). Employee absenteeism: In defense of theory-based studies: Development in occupational psychology and organizational psychology. *Psychology,* **30**(9), 363–368.

Guest, D. (1998). The role of the psychological contract. In S. Perkins & St John Sandringham (Eds), *Trust, Commitment & Motivation*. Oxford: Strategic Remuneration Research Centre.

Guest, D. (1999) Is the psychological contract worth taking seriously? *Journal of Organizational Behaviour*, **19**, 649–664.

Guest, D. & Conway, N. (1997). *Employee Motivation and the Psychological Contract*. Issues in People Management. Institute of Personnel Directors, London, Report No. 21.

Guest, D. E., Conway, R., Briner, R. & Dickmann, M. (1996). *The State of the Psychological Contract in Employment*. Issues in People Management. Institute of Personnel Directors, London, Report No. 16.

Guzzo, R. A. & Berman, L. M. (1995). At what level of generality is psychological contract fulfillment best measured? Paper presented at the Academy of Management meetings, Vancouver.

Guzzo, R. A. & Noonan, K. (1994). Human resource practices as communications and the psychological contract. *Human Resource Management*, **33**, 447–462.

Guzzo, R. A., Noonan, K. A. & Elron, E. (1994). Expatriate managers and the psychological contract. *Journal of Applied Psychology*, **79**(4), 617–626.

Hakim, C. (1991). Grateful slaves and self-made women: Fact and fantasy in women's work orientations. *European Sociological Review*, 7, 101–121.

Hakim, C. (1993). The myth of rising female employment. *Work, Employment and Society*, 7, 97–120.

Hakim, C. (1995). Five feminist myths about women's employment. *British Journal of Sociology*, **46**, 429–455.

Hakim, C. (1996). *Key Issues in Women's Work: Female Heterogeneity and the Polarisation of Women's Employment*. London: Athlone Press.

Hall, D. T. (1993). *The new career contract: Alternative career paths*. Paper presented at the Fourth German Bsuiness Conference on Human Resources, Cologne.

Hall, D. T. & Mirvis, P. H. (1995). Careers as lifelong learning. In A. Howeard (Ed.), *The Changing Nature of Work*. The Jossey-Bass social and behavioral science series. San Francisco, CA: Jossey-Bass.

Handy, C. B. (1990). *The Age of Unreason*. London: Business Books.

Handy, C. B. (1994). *The Empty Raincoat*. London: Hutchinson.

Hardesty, S. & Jacobs, N. (1986). *Success and Betrayal: The Crisis of Women in Corporate America*. New York: Franklin Watts.

Hartley, J. & Mackenzie-Davey, K. (1997). The gender agenda in organisations: A review of research about women and organisational psychology. *Feminism and Psychology*, 7(2), 214–223.

Hearn, J. & Parkin, P. W. (1992). Gender and organizations: A selective review and critique of a neglected area. In A. J. Mills & P. Tancred (Eds), *Gendering Organizational Analysis* (pp. 46–66). London: Sage.

Hennig, M. & Jardim, A. (1978). *The Managerial Woman*. New York: Pocket.

Herriot, P. (1989). Selection as a social process. In M. Smith & I. Robertson (Eds), *Advances in Selection and Assessment*. London: Wiley.

Herriot, P. (1992). *The Career Management Challenge. Balancing Individual and Organizational Needs*, London: Sage.

Herriot, P. & Pemberton, C. (1995a). Contracting Careers. *Human Relations*, **49**(6), 757–790.

Herriot, P. & Pemberton, C. (1995b). *New Deals*. Chichester: Wiley.

Herriot, P. & Pemberton, C. (1997). Facilitating new deals. *Human Resource Management*, 7(1), 45–56.

Herriot, P., Hirsch, W. & Reilly, P. (1998). *Trust and Transition: Managing Today's Employment Relationship*. Chichester: Wiley.

Herriot, P., Manning, W. E. G. & Kidd, J. M. (1997). The content of the psychological contract. *British Journal of Management*, **8**, 151–162.

Hiltrop, J.-M. (1995). The changing psychological contract: The human resource challenge of the 1990s. *European Management Journal*, **13**, 286–294.

Hirsch, W. & Jackson, C. (1996). Strategies for career development: Promise, practice, and pretence. Brighton: Institute of Employment Studies, Report 280.

Hofstede, G. (1980, 1994). *Cultures Consequences: International Differences in Work Related Values*. Beverly Hills and New York: Sage.

Hunt, A. (1968). A survey of women's employemnt. London: HMSO.

Hutton, D. & Cummins, R. (1997). Development of the Psychological Inventory. *Australian Journal of Career Development*, **6**(3), 35–41.

Institute of Employment Studies (IES) (1998). Long Term Survey of Employment Trends. Report.

ILO (International Labour Office) (1993). *Job Evaluation*. Geneva: Author.

Irving, P. G. & Meyer, J. P. (1994). Reexamination of the Met-Expectations Hypothesis: A longitudinal analysis. *Journal of Applied Psychology*, **79**(6), 937–949.

Jackson, S. E. & Schuler, R. S. (1985). A meta-analysis and conceptual critique of research on role ambiguity and role conflict in work settings. *Organizational Behavior and Human Decision Processes*, **36**, 16–28.

Jensen, J., Hagen, E. & Reddy, C. (Eds) (1988). *Feminization of the Labour Force: Paradoxes and Promises*. New York: Oxford University Press.

Johnson, P. R. & Indvik, J. (1994). Workplace violence: An issue of the nineties. *Public Personnel Management*, **23**(4), 515–523.

Josselson, R. (1987). *Finding Herself: Pathways to Identify Development in Women*. San Francisco: Jossey-Bass.

Kanfer, F. H., Cox, L. E., Griner, J. M. & Karoly, P. (1974). Contracts, demand characteristics and self-control. *Journal of Personality and Social Psychology*, **30**, 605–619.

Katz, D. & Kahn, R. I. (1966). *The Social Psychology of Organizations*. New York: Wiley.

Kaufman, P. J. & Stern, L. W. (1988). Relational exchange norms, perceptions of unfairness, and retained hostility in commercial litigation. *Journal of Conflict Resolution*, **32**, 534–552.

Klenke, K. (1996). *Women and Leadership: A Contextual Perspective*. New York: Springer.

Kiriakodou, O. & Millward, L. (1999). The nature of corporate identity: Relations between culture, identitiy and image. Sixth European Congress of Psychology, 4–9 July 1999, Rome.

Koch, J. L. & Steers, R. M. (1978). Job attachment, satisfaction and turnover among public sector employees. *Journal of Vocational Behavior*, **12**, 119–128.

Kobasa, S. C. (1979). Stressful life events, personality and health: An inquiry into hardiness. *Journal of Personality and Soical Psychology*, **37**, 1–11.

Kolb, J. A. (1997). Are we still stereotyping leadership: A look at gender and other predictors of leader emergence. *Small Group Research*, **28**(3), 370–393.

Kotter, J. P. (1973). The psychological contract: Managing the joining-up process. *California Management Review*, **15**, 91–99.

Kuhl, J. (1992). A theory of self-regulation: Action versus state orientation, self-discrimination and some applications. *Applied Psychology: An International Review*, **10**, 397–407.

Larwood, L. & Gutek, B. A. (1987). Working towards a theory of women's career development. In B. A. Gutek & L. Larwood (Eds), *Women's Career Development*. Beverly Hills, CA: Sage.

Levinson, D. (1978). *The Seasons of a Man's Life*. New York: Knopf.

Levinson, H. (1962). *Organizational Diagnosis*. Cambridge, MA: Harvard University Press.

Levinson, H., Price, C. R., Munden, K. J. & Solley, C. M. (1962) *Men Management and Mental Health*. Cambridge, MA: Harvard University Press.

Lind, E. A. & Tyler, T. R. (1988). *The Social Psychology of Procedural Justice*. New York: Plenum.

Loden, M. (1985). *Feminine Leadership or How to Succeed in Business Without Becoming One of the Boys*. New York: Times Books.

London, M. & Stumpf, S. (1986). Individual and organizational career development in changing times. In D. Hall & Associates, *Career Development in Organizations*. San Francisco: Jossey-Bass.

Lucero, M. A. & Allen, R. E. (1994). Employee benefits: A growing source of psychological contract violations. *Human Resource Management*, **33**, 425–446.

Lynn, S. A., Cao, L. T. & Horn, B. C. (1996). The influence of career stage on the work attitudes of male and female accounting professionals. *Journal of Organizational Behaviour*, **17**(2), 135–149.

Macaulay, S. (1963). Noncontractual relations in business: A preliminary study. *American Sociological Review*, **28**, 55–69.

MacNeil, I. R. (1985). Relational Contract: What we do and do not know. *Wisconsin Law Review*, pp. 483–525.

Maddock, S. & Parkin, D. (1996). Gender cultures: Women's choices and strategies at work. Billsbury, J. et al. (Eds), *The Effective Manager: Perspectives and Illustrations*. London: Sage.

Marini, M. M. & Fan, P. L. (1997). The gender gap in earnings at career entry. *American Sociological Review*, **62**(4), 588–604.

Marshall, J. (1984). *Women Managers: Travellers in a Male World*. Chichester: Wiley.

Marshall, J. (1989). Revisioning career concepts: A feminist invitation. In M. B. Arthur, D. T. Hall & B. S. Lawrence (Eds), *Handbook of Career Theory* (pp. 275–291). Cambridge: Cambridge University Press.

Mathieu, J. E. & Zajac, D. M. (1990). A review and meta-analysis of the antecedents, correlates and consequences of organizational commitment. *Psychological Bulletin*, **108**(2), 171–194.

McFarlane Shore, L. & Tetrick, L. E. (1994). The psychological contract as an exploratory framework in the employment relationship. In C. L. Cooper & D. M. Rousseau (Eds), *Trends in Organizational Behavior*, Vol. 1. Chichester: Wiley.

McGee, G. W. & Ford, R. C. (1987). Two (or more?) dimensions of organizational commitment: Reexamination of the effective and continuance commitment scales. *Journal of Applied Psychology*, **72**, 638–642.

McLean Parks, J. & Kidder, D. L. (1994). 'Till death us do part . . .': Changing work relationships in the 1990s. In C. L. Cooper and D. M. Rousseau (Eds), *Trends in Organizational Behavior*, Vol. 1. Chichester: Wiley.

Melamed, T. (1996). Career success: An assessment of a gender specific model. *Journal of Occupational and Organizational Psychology*, **69**(3), 217–242.

Meyer, J. P. (1997). Organizational commitment. In C. L. Cooper & I. T. Robertson (Eds), *International Review of Industrial and Organizational Psychology*, Vol. 12. Chichester: Wiley.

Meyer, J. P., Allen, N. & Smith, C. A. (1993). Commitment to organisations and occupations: Extension and test of the three-component conceptualisation. *Journal of Applied Psychology*, **78**, 538–551.

Miles, R. E. & Snow, C. C. (1980). Designing strategic human resource systems. *Organizational Dynamics*, **8**, 36–52.

Mills, A. J. (1992). Organization, gender and culture. In A. J. Mills & P. Tancred (Eds), *Gendering Organizational Analysis* (pp. 93–111). London: Sage.

Millward, L. J. (1995). Contextualizing social identity in considerations of what it means to be a nurse. *European Journal of Social Psychology*, **25**, 303–324.

Millward, L. J. & Brewerton, P. (1998) Validation of the Psychological Contract Scale in an organisational context. SPERI Publication, University of Surrey, Guildford, UK.

Millward, L. J. & Brewerton, P. (1999). Contractors and their Psychological Contract. *British Journal of Management*, **10**, 253–274.

Millward, L. J. & Brewerton, P. M. Gender and exchange stance: a psychological contract approach. *Journal of Organizational Behavior*.

Millward, L. J. & Hopkins, L. J. (1998). Psychological contracts, organizational and job commitment. *Journal of Applied Social Psychology*, **28**(16), 16–31.

Millward, L. J. & Herriot, P. (1999). Psychological contracts in the UK. In R. Schalk & D. Rousseau (Eds), *International Psychological Contracts*. London: Sage.

Morey, N. C. & Luthans, F. (1984). An emic perspective and ethnoscience methods for organizational research. *Academy of Management Review*, **9**, 27–36.

Moray, N. (1997). Models of models of . . . mental models. In T. B. Sheridan & T. Van Luntern (Eds), *Perspectives on the Human Controller: Essays in Honor of Henk G. Stassen* (pp. 271–285). Mahwah, NJ: Lawrence Erlbaum.

Morris, L. (1990). The workings of the household. Cambridge: Polity Press.

Morris, L. (1997). Economic change and domestic work. In R. Brown (Ed.), *The Changing Shape of Work* (pp. 125–149). Basingstoke Macmillan.

Morrow, P. C. (1983). Concept redundancy in organizational research: The case of work commitment. *Academy of Management Review*, **8**, 486–500.

Mowday, R. T., Steers, R. M. & Porter, L. W. (1979). The measurement of organizational commitment. *Journal of Vocational Behavior*, **14**, 224–247.

Murrell, A. J., Frieze, I.-H. & Olson, J. E. (1996). Mobility strategies and career outcomes: A longitudinal study of MBAs. *Journal of Vocational Behaviour*, **49**(3), 324–335.

Nelson, D. L., Quick, J. C. & Joplin, J. R. (1991). Psychological contracting and newcomer socialization: An attachment theory foundation. Special Issue: Handbook on job stress. *Journal of Social Behavior and Personality*, **6**(7), 55–72.

Nicholson, N. & Johns, G. (1985). The absence culture and the psychological contract: Who's in control of absence? *Academy of Management Review*, **10**(3), 397–407.

Nicholson, N. & West, M. (1996). Men and women in transition. In Billsbury, J. et al. (Eds), *The Effective Manager: Perspectives and Illustrations*. London: Sage.

Nicolson, P. (1996). *Gender, Power and Organisation*. London: Routledge.

Noer, D. M. (1993). *Healing the Wounds: Overcoming the Trauma of Layoffs and Revitalizing Downsized Organizations*. San Francisco, CA: Jossey-Bass.

Noon, M. & Blyton, P. (1997). *The Realities of Work*. London: Macmillan.

Nordhaug, O. (1989). Reward functions of personnel training. *Human Relations*, **42**, 373–388.

Northouse, P. G. (1997). *Leadership: Theory and Practice*. Thousand Oaks, CA: Sage.

O'Hara-Devereux, M. & Johansen, R. (1994). Global Work: Bridging Distance, Culture and Time. In P. Pritchett (Ed.), *New Work Habits for a Radically Changing World*. Dallas, TX: Pritchett & Associates.

Osterberg, M. J. (1996). Gender in supervision: Exaggerating the differences between men and women. *Clinical Supervisor*, **14**(2), 69–83.

Parks, J. & Van Dyne, L. (1995). An idiosyncratic measure of contracts. Paper presented at the Academy of Management meetings. Vancouver.

Parsons, G. & Strickland, E. (1996). How Vauxhall Motors is getting its employees on the road to life-long learning. *European Journal of Work and Organizational Psychology*, **5**(4), 597–608.

Payne, K. E. & Cangemi, J. (1997). Gender differences in leadership. *IFE Psychologia. An International Journal*, **5**(1), 22–43.

Pearce, J. L. (1993). Towards an organisational behavior of contract laborers: Their psychological involvement and effects on employee co-workers. *Academy of Management Review*, **36**, 1082–1096.

Poole, M-E. & Langan-Fox, J. (1997). Australian women and careers: Psychological and contextual influences over the life course. Melbourne (longitudinal study). Cambridge University Press.

Porter, L. W., Pearce, J. L., Tripoli, A. & Lewis, K. (1996). The psychological contract: An empirical assessment. Paper presented at Changes in Psychological Contracts Conference, University of Tilberg, December.

Porter, L. W., Steers, R. M., Mowday, R. T. & Boullian, P. V. (1974). Organizational commitment, job satisfaction and turnover among psychiatric technicians. *Journal of Applied Psychology*, **59**(5), 603–609.

Post, P., Williams, M. & Brubaker, L. (1996). Career and life-style expectations of rural eighth grade students: A second look. *Career Development Quarterly*, **44**(3), 250–257.

Prasad, P., Mills, A. J., Elmes, M. & Prasad, A. (Eds) (1997). *Managing the Organizational Melting Pot*. Thousand Oaks, CA: Sage.

Pratch, L. & Jacobowitz, J. (1996). Gender, motivation and coping in the evaluation of leadership effectiveness. *Consulting Psychology Journal: Practice and Research*, **48**(4), 203–220.

Pritchard (1969). Equity theory: A review and critique. *Organizational Behavior and Human Performance*, **4**, 176–211.

Pritchett, P. (1994). *New Work Habits for a Radically Changing World*. Dallas, TX: Pritchett & Associates.

Radford, L. M. & Larwood, L. (1982). A field study of conflict in psychological exchange: The California taxpayers' revolt. *Journal of Applied Social Psychology*, **12**(1), 60–69.

Ragins, B. R. & Sundstrom, E. (1989). Gender and power in organisations: A longitudinal perspective. *Psychological Bulletin*, **105**, 52–88.

Randall, D. M. (1988). Multiple roles and organizational commitment. *Journal of Organizational Behavior*, **9**(4), 309–317.

Rawls, J. (1971). *A Theory of Justice*. Cambridge, MA: Bleknap.

Rizzo, J. R., House, R. & Lirtzman, S. (1970). Role conflict and role ambiguity in complex organizations. *Administrative Science Quarterly*, **15**, 150–163.

Robinson, S. L. (1995). Violation of PC: Impact on employee attitudes. In L. E. Tetrick & J. Barling (Eds), *Changing Employment Relations: Behavior and Social Perspectives*. Washington, DC: American Psychiatric Association.

Robinson, S. L. (1996). Trust and breach of the psychological contract. *Administrative Science Quarterly*, **41**, 574–599.

Robinson, S. L., Kraatz, M. S. & Rousseau, D. M. (1994). Changing obligations and the psychological contract: A longitudinal study. *Academy of Management Journal*, **37**, 137–152.

Robinson, S. L. & Rousseau, D. M. (1994). Violating the psychological contract: Not the exception but the norm. *Journal of Organizational Behaviour*, **15**, 245–259.

Robinson, S. L. & Wolfe-Morrison, E. (1995). Psychological contracts and OCB: The effect of unfulfilled obligations on civic virtue behaviour. *Journal of Organizational Behavior*, **16**, 289–298.

Robinson, S. L. & Wolfe-Morrison, E. (1997). The development of psychological contract breach and violation: A longitudinal study. *Academy of Management Review* (under review).

Roehling, M. (1996). The origins and early development of the psychological contract construct. Paper presented at the Academy of Management meetings, Cincinnati.

Rosin, H. M. & Korabik, K. (1991). Workplace variables, effective responses and intention to leave among women managers. *Journal of Occupational Psychology*, **64**, 317–330.

Rousseau, D. M. (1989). Psychological and implied contracts in organizations. *Employee Rights & Responsibilities Journal*, **2**, 121–139.

Rousseau, D. M. (1990). New hire perception of their own and their employees' obligations: A study of psychological contracts. *Journal of Organizational Behaviour*, **11**, 389–400.

Rousseau, D. M. (1995). *Psychological Contracts in Organizations: Understanding Written and Unwritten Agreements*. London & New York: Sage.

Rousseau, D. M. (1996). Changing the deal while keeping the people. *Academy of Management Executive*, **10**, 50–61.

Rousseau, D. (1997). Organizational behaviour in the new organizational era. *Annual Review of Psychology*, **48**, 515–546.

Rousseau, D. M. & Parks, J. M. (1993). The contracts of individuals and organizations. In L. L. Cummings & B. M. Staw (Eds), *Research in Organizational Behavior*. Greenwich, CT: JAI Press.

Rousseau, D. M., Robinson, S. L. & Kraatz, M. S. (1992). Renegotiating the psychological contract. Paper presented at the Society for Industrial/Organizational Psychology meeting, Montreal.

Rousseau, D. M. & Tijoriwala, S. (1996). It takes a good reason to change a psychological contract. Presented at Society for Industrial Organizational Psychology, April, San Diego.

Rousseau, D. M. & Tinsley, K. (1997). Human Resources are local: Society and social contracts in a global economy. In N. Anderson & P. Herriot (Eds), *Handbook of Selection and Appraisal*. London: Wiley.

Rousseau, D. M. & Wade-Benzoni, K. A. (1995). Changing individual–organization attachments: A two-way street. In A. Howard (Ed.), *The Changing Nature of Work*. The Jossey-Bass social and behavioral science series. San Francisco, CA: Jossey-Bass.

Sackmann, S. A. (1997). *Cultural Complexity in Organizations: Inherent Contrasts and Contradictions*. Thousand Oaks, CA: Sage.

Salminen, E. O. (1994). Career development anchors: A follow-up study of managerial success form the point of view of the individual and the organization. *Psykologica*, **29**(3), 173–175.

Scandura, T. A. & Lankau, M. J. (1997). Relationships of gender, family responsibility and flexible hours to organizational commitment and job satisfaction. *Journal of Organizational Behaviour*, **18**(4), 377–391.

Schalk, R. & Rousseau, D. (Eds) (1999). *International Psychological Contracts*. New York: Sage.

Schein, E. H. (1980). *Organizational Psychology*. Englewood Cliffs, NJ: Prentice-Hall.

Schein, E. H. (1993). *Career Anchors: Discovering your Real Values*. Revised Edn. London: Pfeiffer.

Sheppard, D. (1992). Women managers' perceptions of gender and organizational life. In A. J. Mills & P. Tancred (Eds), *Gendering Organizational Analysis* (pp. 151–166). London: Sage.

Shore, L. & Tetrick, L. E. (1994). The psychological contract as an exploratory framework in the employment relationship. In C. L. Cooper and D. M. Rousseau (Eds), *Trends in Organizational Behavior*, Vol. 1. Chichester: Wiley.

Shortell, S. M. & Zajac, E. J. (1990). Perceived and archival measures of Miles & Snow's strategic types: A comprehensive assessment of reliability and validity. *Academy of Management Journal*, **33**, 817–832.

Sims, R. R. (1992). Developing the learning climate in public sector training programs. *Public Personnel Management*, **21**(3), 335–346.

Smith, C. A., Organ, D. W. & Near, J. P. (1983). Organizational citizenship behaviour: Its nature and antecedents. *Journal of Applied Psychology*, **68**, 653–663.

Snow, C. C., Miles, R. E. & Coleman, H. J. (1992). Managing 21st century network organisations. *Organizational Dynamics*, Winter, 5–21.

Somers, M. J. (1995) Organizational commitment, turnover and absenteeism: An examination of direct and interaction effects. *Journal of Organizational Behavior*, **16**, 49–58.

Sparrow, P. R. (1996). Careers and the psychological contract: Understanding the European context. *European Journal of Work and Organizational Psychology*, **5**(4), 479–500.

Sparrow, P. R. (1998). New organisational forms, processes, jobs and psychological contracts: resolving the issues. In P. Sparrow & M. Marchington (Eds), *Human Resource Management: the New Agenda*. London: Pitman.

Spence, J. T. (1984). Masculinity, femininity, and gender-related traits: A conceptual analysis and critique of current research. *Progress in Experimental Personality Research*, **13**, 1–97.

Stiles, P., Gratton, L., Truss, C., Hope-Hailey, V. & McGovern, P. (1996). Performance management and the psychological contract. *Human Resource Management Journal*, 7(1), 57–66.

Stroh, L. K., Brett, J. M. & Reilly, A. H. (1996). Family structure, glass ceiling and traditional explanations for the differential rate of turnover of female and male managers. *Journal of Vocational Behaviour*, **49**(1), 99–118.

Stroh, L. K. & Reilly, A. H. (1997). Rekindling organizational loyalty: The role of career mobility. *Journal of Career Development*, 24(1), 39–54.

Tooher, P. (1996). Temps take over the British workplace. *The Independent*, 15/7/96.

Tornow, W. W. & De Meuse, K. P. (1994). 'New paradigm approaches in strategic human resource management': Comment. *Group and Organization Management*, 19(2), 165–170.

Tyler, T. R. & Bies, R. J. (1990). Interpersonal aspects of procedural justice. In J.S. Carroll (Ed.), *Applied Social Psychology and Organizational Settings* (pp. 77–98). Hillsdale, NJ: Erlbaum.

Wade-Benzoni, K. A. & Rousseau, D. M. (1997). Psychological contracts in the faculty-doctoral student relationship (under review).

Waldby, S. (1997). *Gender Transformations*. London: Routledge.

Wanous, J. P., Poland, T., Premack, S. L. and Davis, K. S. (1992). The effects of met expectations on newcomer attitudes and behaviors: A review and meta-analysis. *Journal of Applied Psychology*, 77(3), 288–297.

Wanous, J. P. & Reichers, A. E. (1996). Estimating the reliability of a single-item measure. *Psychologiucal Reports*, 78, 631–634.

Wickwire, K. S. & Kruper, J. C. (1996). The glass ceiling effect: An approach to assessment. *Consulting Psychology Journal: Practice and Research*, **49**(1), 32–39.

Williamson, O. E. (1991). Comparative economic organization. The analysis of discrete structural alternatives. *Administrative Science Quarterly*, **36**, 269–296.

Wilson, F. (1996). Organizational theory: blind and deaf to gender? *Organization Studies*, **17**(5), 825–842.

# Chapter 2

## IMPACTS OF TELEWORK ON INDIVIDUALS, ORGANIZATIONS AND FAMILIES—A CRITICAL REVIEW

Udo Konradt, Renate Schmook and Mike Mälecke
*University of Kiel*

### INTRODUCTION

Telework is defined as a form of work organization where the work is done partially or completely outside the conventional company workplace with the aid of information and telecommunication services. Although originally designed to overcome long distances (Olson, 1983; Pratt, 1984; Nilles, 1985), telework today offers more flexibility and agility for organizations beside telemanagement (coordination and management of distributed work) and teleservices (service as a product of geographically distributed work) (Hiltz & Turoff, 1987).

In the context of telework different forms have evolved. Besides home-based telework, where work is done exclusively at home, various forms of alternating or mobile telework can be differentiated. Home-based telework is most similar to classical home-based work where teleworkers work only at home either with a regular contract of employment (according to statutes of domestic work) or as self-employed. Alternating telework is nowadays the most common type of telework. Apart from their workplace at home, teleworkers usually still have a workplace at their organization. Location and timing of their work are determined by changing job requirements. In most cases the transition to this form of work is happening stepwise so that social ties with the organization remain.

Employees who do centre-based telework usually work in offices close to their home. These workplaces are used as so-called satellite offices by the main organization or, less often, are jointly used as neighbourhood offices by different organizations. However, coordination in this work setting can be difficult. Centre-based telework is well suited to foster employment in structurally

*International Review of Industrial and Organizational Psychology, 2000 Volume 15*
Edited by C.L. Cooper and I.T. Robertson. © 2000 John Wiley & Sons, Ltd

weak regions (PATRA, 1992–1994; Crellin, Graham & Powell, 1996). The demand for centre-based telework consequently varies strongly between different countries.

Finally, mobile telework can be considered as a further form of telework. Executives and employees who work outside the office, and also craftsmen and building companies, already make wide use of this type of telework. People who work directly with customers can link up via computer with the database of their organizations from a hotel, a construction site, a car or public transport to professionally prepare for a next meeting or respond to short notice requests from customers.

The transition to other forms of on-site telework is fluid. This term describes telework that is situated at the site of the customer or contractor. In a lot of professional areas, for example management consulting and software development, this kind of on-site telework has already been established. Teleworkers can work face to face with the client and at the same time have constant access to their organization via telecommunication. We will return to this issue in the context of the distribution of telework.

Besides providing the potential for more flexibility within organizations, structures underlying telework can support the evolution of virtual enterprises and cooperative joint ventures. Virtual enterprises are legally independent and geographically separated organizations, mainly self-employed entrepreneurs, that in general only connect to conduct a defined project. The communication within the enterprise is exclusively carried out through telecommunication technologies (Davidow & Malone, 1992). Thus a project manager can assemble the best and financially most advantageous organizations within a virtual enterprise or workgroup even when those organizations are located in a different region or country.

Because of its grand potential, telework has gained importance in industry, administration and science. It is estimated that at present 1.25–17.5 million positions in telework have been implemented throughout the EC (European Community) (EITO, 1997; Kordey & Korte, 1997). In the US, 3–20 million people are estimated to engage in telework (summarized in Büssing, 1997). Studies that incorporate the interest of employees and employers in telework as well as the feasibility of telework calculate a potential of 10 million positions in telework throughout the whole of Europe, including 2.5 million in Germany (DG XIII-B, 1996; summarized in Pollmann, 1997; Table 2.1). Giving an outlook on the year 2000, the EC expects a total of 2 million people to be employed in telework in the states of the EC. For Germany, national estimates assume several hundred thousand positions in telework around the year 2000 (ZVEI/VDMA, 1995). In a Delphi-based study on the use of the inter- and intranet, experts conclude that within the time-frame from 2005 to 2012, 30% of all employees working in offices will work at home on two to five days a week (State Department for Research and Technology, 1998).

**Table 2.1**  Potential of telework in Europe (Empirica, 1995)

|  | Germany (%) | France (%) | UK (%) | Italy (%) | Spain (%) |
|---|---|---|---|---|---|
| Interest among gainfully employed | 42.4 | 52.6 | 48.4 | 48.1 | 61.4 |
| Interest among executives within the organization | 40.4 | 39.3 | 34.4 | 41.8 | 29.6 |
| Potential interest in telework | 17.1 | 20.6 | 16.6 | 20.1 | 18.2 |
| Realistic potential of telework | 6.8 | 8.2 | 6.6 | 8.0 | 7.3 |
| Realistic number of potential teleworkers (millions) | 2.48 | 1.81 | 1.69 | 1.68 | 0.91 |

Reasons for the strongly deviating estimates can be found in the broad and rather unclear definition of telework. In a review on the definitions of telework Di Martino and Wirth (1990) isolate three basic concepts that give rise to most definitions: organization, location and technology. Assuming a relatively broad definition, telework can be done either online or offline, it can be organized either individually or collectively, it can cover either all working hours or a part of the working hours of a person, and it can be done either by an employee or a self-employed person. Within the European study, all decentralized or domestic workplaces that at least had an offline PC and a telephone are denoted as telework places (Empirica, 1994). A second reason lies in the fact that hidden forms of telework such as working outside the office or freelance work are also included. It is presently unresolved how narrow a definition would be useful. A too narrow definition could be counterproductive, as new forms of telecooperative work could then possibly not be integrated formally and in terms of research.

In an attempt to differentiate various forms of telework, Watson Fritz, Higa and Narasimhan (1994) chose a two-dimensional scheme of classification with the dimensions 'level of coordination' and 'traditional vs non-traditional organization'. According to this scheme traditional forms of organization employing methods of telecooperation exist, when features such as physical proximity to customers and contractors as well as availability of coworkers are given. This differentiation reveals that the extent of applied telecommunication technology does not suffice to discriminate selectively between telework and office-based computer work. Rather, the technical prerequisites have to be complemented by new forms of organization.

Figure 2.1 shows a taxonomy of telecooperative forms of work and organizations expanding the above mentioned reflections. Depending on the level of cooperation, isolated workers, non-interactive, interactive intra- and inter-working groups are taken into account. The second dimension represents to what degree telework is integrated (level of integration) within an organization (intra-organizational) or between a network of different organizations (inter-organizational). Virtual enterprises, as a form of telecooperative work, are based on inter-group relations between different organizations. Telework, in the sense of alternating telework, is in general understood as isolated work within an organization. The empty fields in this taxonomy illustrate further possible forms of telecooperative work.

The impacts of telework on people and organizations have been discussed (see Olson, 1989; Mehlmann, 1988; Kraut, 1988). Table 2.2 lists some of the impacts usually considered in early reviews. It is undeniable that telecooperation can lead to direct economic opportunities and a competitive chance (see the section below on profitability of telework). Moreover, closer commuting distances represent an important element of environmental planning. Finally, telecooperation also entails desirable aspects of social politics, as groups of the population suffering from reduced mobility such as disabled people or imprisoned persons can be, at least partially, integrated into working structures (Godehardt, 1994a; Cullen & Robinson, 1997).

A survey of 60 organizations that had already implemented telework showed that the major motivations to do so were cost reduction, keeping or recruiting qualified personnel, planned organizational restructuring,

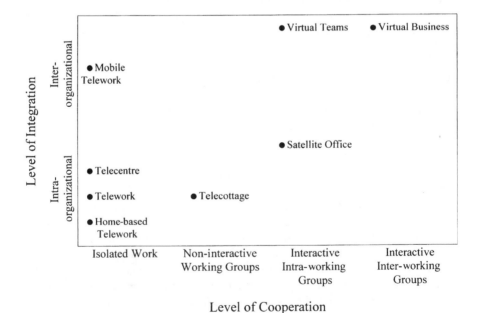

**Figure 2.1**   Taxonomy of telecooperative forms of work

**Table 2.2**  Chances and risks of telework regarding the interests of different groups (according to Kern & Wawrzinek, 1985)

| Effects | Employees | Organization | Society |
|---|---|---|---|
| Positive | • work comfort<br>• work opportunities<br>• commuting time<br>• individual organization<br>• residence<br>• being more independent from the organization<br>• flexible working hours | • productivity<br>• additional wage costs (e.g. social contributions)<br>• securing of location<br>• rationalization<br>• room costs<br>• compensation of work overload<br>• flexibility<br>• workforce potential | • global competitiveness<br>• energy conservation<br>• protection of the environment<br>• problematic issues<br>• conurbation<br>• structural measures<br>• traffic situation |
| Ambiguously | • family situation<br>• social security contributions<br>• wage<br>• qualifications<br>• work contents | • wage costs<br>• fluctuation | • self-employed/ employed<br>• women's situation<br>• demand behaviour |
| Negative | • contacts (social isolation)<br>• work safety<br>• career opportunities<br>• control | • overheads<br>• control<br>• opportunities to obtain information<br>• organizational effort<br>• selection of personnel<br>• identification with the organization | • occupational situation<br>• data protection<br>• parties involved in wage settlements |

increasing the motivation and productivity of the employees and more efficient coping with increased workloads (TELDET-Projekt, see also Wheeler & Zackin, 1994). Employees valued the easier coordination of professional and private life, particularly the quieter work situation and the decrease of commuting time. Employees' reasons for engaging in telework can be separated into three major fields:

1.  Financial-economic reasons: e.g. in the context of an increased financial burden (acquisition of real estate, birth, divorce, maintenance) or aiming for a higher standard of living (weekend house, leisure goods, travelling).
2.  Status and professional reasons such as maintenance and enrichment of professional qualifications, social contacts, financial independence, approved social status.

3.  Reasons related to specific life situations or life plans such as health problems or disability, minimizing commuting distance, lack of child-care options, reintegration after maternity leave.

The growing interest in telework is reflected in the increasing number of books as much in the German (e.g. Reichwald, Möslein & Oldenburg, 1998; Wedde, 1994; Weissbach, Lampe & Späker, 1997; Büssing & Aumann, 1999) as in the Anglo-American literature (e.g. Jackson & van der Wielen, 1998; Bertin & Denbigh, 1996; Hodson, 1992). At the same time a great number of guides on how to install telework have been developed (Gordon & Kelly, 1986; Kugelmass, 1995; Nilles, 1994; Reid, 1994; Kordey & Korte, 1996; Godehardt, 1994a; Godehardt, Kork, Michelsen & Quadt, 1997; Johanning, 1997). In light of this background the present review intends to pursue two lines of reasoning. First, the results of research on the effects of telework will be systematically reviewed. The effects of telework will be scrutinized using a broad set of criteria, including the influence on work, family and profitability. Second, special attention will be directed towards the underlying methodical standards of the studies. It will be shown that in the majority of investigations the opportunities and risks of telework were only summed up by those in management positions without any direct assessment of the effects with personnel. Furthermore, it has seldom been tried to explain theoretically the results of the respective investigations. This review is therefore meant to concentrate the discussion of the development and evaluation of telework once more on scientifically sound findings and to take a new look at the often quoted opportunities and risks of telework in light of these findings. In doing this, deficits in current research will be delineated and guidelines for prospect investigations will be developed.

The review is structured as follows: in the next section a model for the investigation of the effects of telework will be introduced. Opportunities and risks of telework that have been frequently mentioned in the literature will be discussed in the third section. In the fourth section the procedure of the literature research is described, followed by the results on the effects of telework in the fifth section. Finally, an outlook on further research needs and goals is given.

## A MODEL FOR THE INVESTIGATION OF THE EFFECTS OF TELEWORK

In the discussion of the opportunities and risks of telework a model for the explanation and prediction of the effects of telework has been repeatedly called for (Van Sell & Jacobs, 1994; Watson Fritz, Higa & Narashiman, 1994). In our view, this model should satisfy the following criteria:

1. A broad number of physical, spatio-temporal, personal and organizational aspects of the work situation should be taken into account.
2. Effects of telework on individual experience and behaviour should also be investigated beside performance.
3. Positive as well as negative consequences need to be considered.
4. Individual features of a person such as coping strategies, motivational and emotional resources, should be integrated.
5. Beside factors that cause work-related stress, stress and strain experienced during housework and leisure time should also be included.

Despite considerable efforts, neither research in industrial and organizational psychology nor stress research in the social sciences has succeeded in providing a model covering all the above issues. We therefore propose a two-step procedure to develop an adequate model. In the first step factors will be determined that are designed to modulate the generation of stress responses. In this context objective stimulus-oriented factors and subjective response-oriented features are discriminated. In the second step, objectively and subjectively stressing aspects of telework can be consequently used within a model of structural equations to predict actual stress during telework.

An expanded strain-stress model is proposed as the base for this model (Schönpflug, 1987; Wieland-Eckelmann, 1992; Richter & Hacker, 1998). In the field of professional work all factors externally affecting the individual and requiring his or her effort will be termed strains. Strain is defined as the sum of all influences that affect the individual within the work system. Stress is caused by strains and is expressed in respective changes in physiological and psychological functioning and subjective well-being during work performance. The consequences of stress, following the strain-stress process, are evident in work output or work performance as well as in short-, middle- and long-term changes in physical and mental power and energetic, emotional and motivational well-being.

As the type and magnitude of work-related strain are not independent of the working individual, strain needs to be understood as a relational term. This means that strains and demands (e.g. work tasks, equipment, organizational and procedural regulations, spatio-temporal and physical conditions) should be put in relation to the individual resources (e.g. physical, performance, motivational and emotional). Figure 2.2 shows a relevant model.

Strains that can arise in free time are, for example, the extent and temporal distribution of different kinds of housework. Studies investigating the participation of employees in telework projects have repeatedly shown that in particular the compatibility of housework and childcare with professional work is an important motivating factor. But equally other activities during leisure time such as cultural, social or sporting events can be pursued in a more flexible way by teleworkers (Burke, 1986). If this is not possible, then participation in telework projects can be seriously endangered. Burke shows that strains

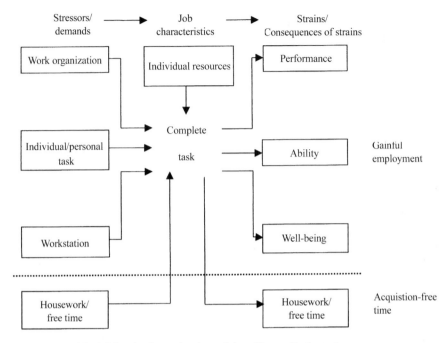

**Figure 2.2**    Model for the investigation of the effects of telework

experienced during leisure time can also contribute to the overall sum of strains in the context of telework.

## HYPOTHESES REGARDING THE EFFECTS OF TELEWORK

In the discussion of the effects and the future shaping of telework, far-reaching personal and organizational changes have been repeatedly stressed beside technical opportunities within this field. Benefits of telework such as the improvement of women's situation due to an improved compatibility of occupational and family duties, autonomy in the choice of working hours, increase of spare time because no commuting is needed, have been contrasted with costs such as perpetuating the discrimination of disadvantaged groups of employees, disruption of family life, lack of career opportunities, social isolation, increase of work demands and personal exploitation. Because theoretical models are lacking, benefits and costs are in general not linked.

In recent years, several reviews have been published on the consequences of telework on communication (Andriessen, 1991), organization (Watson Fritz, Higa & Narashimhan, 1994; Chapman, Sheehy, Heywood et al., 1995) and quality of life and work (Büssing, 1997; Van Sell & Jacobs, 1994; Mundorf, Meyer, Schulze & Zoche, 1994; Shamir & Salomon, 1985).

Although the planned and systematic introduction of telework in the context of measures of organizational and personnel development is of fundamental importance, only very few empirical studies, and these suffering from severe methodical flaws, have focused on this particular aspect. Current representative surveys throughout the EC emphasize this point: major obstacles to the dissemination of telework can be found in the lack of information about ways of organizing telework, potentials and risks on the one hand and anticipated problems in leading and instructing the 'invisible employees' (Reichwald & Möslein, 1996) on the other hand. These results have been confirmed in other international studies (see also Wheeler & Zackin, 1994).

The following possible effects of telework will be dealt with more thoroughly:

1.  What effects does telework have on social contacts? To answer this question , social contacts, personality traits and consequences for training and career are investigated.
2.  What effects does telework have on family and leisure time? This question will be discussed in the light of time autonomy, attitudes towards the mixing of work and leisure time, the structure of the social surroundings and the perceived use.
3.  How do communication within the organization, concepts of management and management behaviour change? Furthermore, effects on the whole organization are looked at.
4.  Which economic benefits does telework provide? Costs and benefits will be discussed.

## IDENTIFICATION AND SELECTION OF EMPIRICAL STUDIES

A literature search was conducted to identify all relevant empirical studies. The search included articles published between 1982 and mid-1997 using various databases[1] relevant to the field. The aim of the literature search was to identify only empirical, independent research investigating the effects of telework. The studies should focus on the effects of actually implemented telework places on teleworkers. Studies dealing with speculations, claims or projections concerning future telework projects were not included. The empirical character of a study was deduced from specific information about the size and composition of the sample and about the type of telework investigated as well as from the description of the applied measures.

Out of the 665 references gained in the second step, 215 empirical papers were selected based on the content of the abstract. After eliminating articles which dealt with the prognoses or projections of managers concerning the opportunities and risks of telework, 27 original empirical papers remained. After careful evaluation, studies investigating the potential of telework were also excluded, so that the present literature review on the effects of telework is based on 20 empirical studies.

The studies were categorized according to the following aspects: (a) type of study (personal report, case study, quasi-experimental field study); (b) sample size; (c) type of telework investigated; (d) trade; (e) type of work; and (f) applied methods. According to Nullmeier (1988) four basic types of telework were distinguished (see Table 2.3): executive tasks, high-profile professional tasks, low-profile professional tasks, supporting tasks. These tasks can be discriminated according to the central dimension of the task, to what extent work can be planned and structured ahead, the need for information, the cooperating partners and how problems are solved.

The papers that were selected are predominantly case or field studies with sample sizes of less than 50 people (approx. 80%). In 40% of the studies even

**Table 2.3**  Basic types of office work (modified according to Nullmeier, 1988)

| Tasks | Task characteristics | Examples |
|---|---|---|
| Executive tasks | Leading and motivation of employees, representative duties, development of communicational structures, gathering and dissemination of information, problem-solving and decision-making in the case of uncertainty/risk, finding consensus | Members of the board, managers on different hierarchical levels of the organization |
| High-profile professional task | Mastering of tasks that involve a great deal of expertise, independent organization of low-structured work, development of initiative, task-oriented | Qualified buyers and sellers, scientists and engineers in R&D as well as in production and DV, attorneys, judges, organizers, tax consultants, advertising specialists, publicists, accountants |
| Low-profile professional tasks | Mastering of tasks that involve only little expertise and are rather structured and repetitive, process- and result-oriented | Officials in charge of purchase and sale, officials working for insurance companies, banks, shipping agencies; book-keepers, administrative employees, counter clerks |
| Supporting tasks | Support of the other professional groups, processing, transcription and storage of information | Typists and secretaries, distributor of mail, operators |

fewer than 15 individuals are investigated. In some cases information about the sample size is based on whole organizational units (e.g. department, firms, neighbourhood offices) so that the actual sample size is actually higher. The number of organizational units within a study usually lies below 20. In the majority of studies interviews or questionnaires are the predominant measures. The content and procedure are, however, often not specified. The studies cover all four types of telework that are mentioned above, although most studies focus on alternating telework, home-based telework and telecentres. Only very few studies looked at the effects of mobile telework. Virtual enterprises were not considered in any study.

The samples cover all trades, although electronic data processing, service, banks and insurance companies are represented more strongly. The tasks mainly belong to the low-profile professional domain, followed by supporting and high-profile professional functions; executive functions can be found less often. This result corresponds with the finding that typical tasks and functions pursued by teleworkers can be generally assigned to office and administrative functions (Gray, Hodson & Gordon, 1993). Telework is especially suited for tasks that do not require a great deal of personal communication or the continual presence of the employee within the organization.

Finally, the effects of telework on social contracts, family and leisure time, management and communication and profitability were determined. Table 2.4 gives an overview of the empirical studies on the effects of telework that were taken into account.

## EFFECTS OF TELEWORK

In the following the results concerning the effects of telework on social contacts, family and leisure time, management and communication and profitability will be described in detail.

### Effects of Telework on Social Contacts

Negative effects of telework have been suspected to exist to a large extent in the area of social contacts. The relevant hypothesis is that telework leads to social isolation and in consequence to social alienation as it is generally pursued without direct contact with colleagues or superiors. This is supposed to be even more true for telehomeworkers exclusively working at home. Important variables in this context are not only the quantity but also the quality of social contacts, as well as the subjective importance teleworkers ascribe to social bonds. This importance depends not only on personal needs but also on a person's degree of extraversion and their job demands. Furthermore, a certain number of contacts is seen as an important prerequisite for a career within the organization. Of the 20 studies 11 analysed the effects of telework on social contacts.

**Table 2.4** Studies on the effects of telework

| No. | Author(s), year | Type of study | Sample | Methods | Form of telework | Trades |
|---|---|---|---|---|---|---|
| 1 | Aichholzer & Kirschner, 1995 (AUS, GB, G) | Personal report | $N^1=7$ $N^2_1=6, n_2=15,$ $n_3=4, n_4=3$ | Not mentioned | Neighbourhood offices ATW[3] | Electronic data processing, Training, Public administration, Agrar |
| 2 | Baylin, 1989 (GB) | Case study | $N_1=49, n_2=40$ CG[4] | Questionnaire | THW[5] | Electronic data processing |
| 3 | Büssing & Aumann, 1997 (G) | Field study | $N=5$ | Questionnaire | Centre-based telework, ATW | Electronic data processing Service |
| 4 | Büssing, Kunst & Michel, 1996 (G) | Field study | $N_1=11$ $n_2=9$ CG $n_3=10$ CG | Questionnaire, Interview | THW | Insurance |
| 5 | Euler, Froschle & Klein, 1987 (G) | Case studies | $N=14$ $N=17$ | Intervew, Group discussion | THW, Neighbourhood-, Satellite offices | Public administration, not mentioned |
| 6 | Fisher, Späker & Weissbach, 1987 (G) | Case studies | $N=6$ $N_1=180, n_2=15,$ $n_3=$ ca. 30, $n_4=$ ca. 300 | Not mentioned | ATW, Satellite offices | Electronic data processing, Service, Advertising |
| 7 | Glaser & Glaser, 1995 (G) | Field study | $N_1=38, n_2=33$ M[6] | Interview, Questionnaire | ATW | Electronic data processing |
| 8 | Godehardt, 1994b (G) | Case studies | $N=22$ | Interview, Expert dialogue, Group questioning | ATW, THW, Satellite offices | Service |
| 9 | Goldmann & Richter, 1991 (G) | Case studies | $N1=5$ $n_1=4, n_2=3,$ $n_3=4, n_4=12,$ $n_5=3$ (not mentioned for printing trade) $N2=15$ $n_1=11, n_2=90$ Experts $N3=3, n_3=16$ (electronic data processing, service) | Questionnaire, Interview | ATW, mobile TW, THW | Printing trade, Electronic data processing, Service |
| 10 | Grantham & Paul, 1995 (USA) | Case studies | $N=3$ $n_1=35+25$ M, $n_2=34$ $n_3=88$ M | Questionnaire | ATW | Public administration, Electronic data processing, not mentioned |
| 11 | Hartman, Stoner & Arora, 1991 (USA) | Field study | $N=11$ $n=97$ | Questionnaire | ATW | Telecommunication, Banks, Insurance, Printing trade, Public administration |
| 12 | Kreibich, Drüke, Dunkelmainn & Feverstein, 1990 (G) | Field study, Case studies | $N1=105,$ $N2=208, N3=20$ | Questionnaire, Interview | THW, mobile TW, ATW, Satellite offices and others | Industry Banks, Insurance, Public administration, Service, others |
| 13 | Morgan, 1985 (GB) | Field study | $n=78$ | Questionnaire | THW | Electronic data processing |
| 14 | Müller & Reuschenbach, 1992 (G) | Field study | $n=25$ M | Questionnaire, Interview | THW, ATW, mobile TW | Electronic data processing, Insurance |
| 15 | Olson, 1983 (USA) | Field study | $n=32$ | Interview | THW, ATW | Electronic data processing, not mentioned |

| No. | Author(s), year | Type of work at telework | Effect on | | | | Comments |
|---|---|---|---|---|---|---|---|
| | | | Social contact | Family & leisure time | Management & communication | Profitability | |
| 1 | Aichholzer & Kirschner, 1995 (AUS, GB, G) | High-profile functions, Low-profile functions, Supporting functions | Yes | Yes | Yes | Yes | Pilot projects |
| 2 | Baylin, 1989 (GB) | High-profile functions, Low-profile functions | – | Yes | – | – | |
| 3 | Büssing & Aumann, 1997 (G) | Low-profile functions, Supporting functions | – | – | Yes | Yes | |
| 4 | Büssing, Kunst & Michel, 1996 (G) | Low-profile functions, Supporting functions | Yes | Yes | Yes | – | Pilot projects |
| 5 | Euler, Froschle & Klein, 1987 (G) | Supporting functions | – | Yes | Yes | Yes | Model study |
| 6 | Fisher, Späker & Weissbach, 1997 (G) | High-profile functions, Low-profile functions | Yes | Yes | Yes | Yes | Model studies |
| 7 | Glaser & Glaser, 1995 (G) | High-profile functions, Low-profile functions | Yes | Yes | Yes | Yes | |
| 8 | Godehardt, 1994b (G) | Executive functions, High-profile functions, Low-profile functions, Supporting functions | Yes | Yes | Yes | Yes | |
| 9 | Goldmann & Richter, 1991 (G) | High-profile functions, Low-profile functions, Supporting functions | Yes | Yes | Yes | Yes | |
| 10 | Grantham & Paul, 1995 (USA) | Executive functions, Low-profile functions | Yes | Yes | Yes | Yes | Pilot project |
| 11 | Hartman, Stoner & Arora, 1991 (USA) | Executive functions, Low-profile functions | – | Yes | – | Yes | |
| 12 | Kreibich, Drüke, Dunkelmainn & Feverstein, 1999 (G) | Executive functions, High-profile functions, Low-profile functions, Supporting functions | – | Yes | – | Yes | |
| 13 | Morgan, 1985 (GB) | High-profile functions, Low-profile functions, Supporting funcions | Yes | Yes | Yes | Yes | |
| 14 | Müller & Reuschenbach, 1992 (G) | Executive functions, High-profile functions, Low-profile functions | – | – | Yes | Yes | |
| 15 | Olson, 1983 (USA) | Executive functions, Low-profile functions, Supporting functions | Yes | Yes | Yes | Yes | Pilot project |

(Continued over)

**Table 2.4**    *(Continued)*

| No. | Author(s), year | Type of study | Sample | Methods | Form of telework | Trades |
|---|---|---|---|---|---|---|
| 16 | Pupke, 1994 (Japan) | Field study | n=21 | Interview | THW | Construction, Commerce, Transport, Manufacturing industry, Service |
| 17 | Rüttinger, Grünebaum & Jost, 1995 (G) | Field study | N=29 n=87 M | Interview | ATW, THW, mobile TW | Industry, Commerce, Banks, Insurance, Service |
| 18 | Soares & Vargas, 1992 (Brazil) | Case study | $n_1$=12, $n_2$= 3 M | Interview | Centre based telework | Electronic data processing |
| 19 | Strauf & Nagele, 1996 (G) | Case studies | N=11 n=69 | Interview, Questionnaire | THW, ATW, Centre based telework, Satellite offices | Service, Construction, Manufacturing industry |
| 20 | Ulich, 1988 (Japan) | Case study | N=10 | Interview, Questionnaire | Satellite offices | Electronic data processing |

[1]Number of organizational units.
[2]Number of persons (teleworkers if not mentioned otherwise).
[3]Alternating telework.
[4]Control group.
[5]Telehomework.
[6]Managers.

## Social contacts

In most studies social contacts include contacts with colleagues at the workplace as well as contacts with family members, friends, and acquaintances. The latter occur in private activities, whereas social contacts with colleagues refer to goal-oriented meetings.

Exclusively looking at the quantity of social contacts, eight studies (Büssing, Kunst, & Michel, 1996; Godehardt, 1994b; Goldmann & Richter, 1991; Hartman, Stoner & Arora, 1991; Morgan, 1985; Olson, 1983; Rüttinger, Grünebaum & Jost, 1995; Soares & Vargas, 1992) found a decrease in contacts, characteristic social isolation due to telework. However, employees regard this phenomenon according to their professional and private situation. Telework, especially home-based telework, can lead to social isolation. However, this need not be the case. An important modulating variable in this context is the perceived quality of the actual social contacts, which is experienced very differently among teleworkers.

Three studies (Goehardt, 1994b; Grantham & Paul, 1995; Rüttinger, Grünebaum & Jost, 1995) merely mention that social isolation is a problem that can occur temporarily especially during extended periods of home-based telework. A more detailed analysis of the development of social contacts can be found in Büssing, Kunst and Michel (1996). This study shows that changes

| No. | Author(s), year | Type of work at telework | Effect on | | | | |
| --- | --- | --- | --- | --- | --- | --- | --- |
| | | | Social contact | Family & leisure time | Management & communication | Profitability | Comments |
| 16 | Pupke, 1994 (Japan) | High-profile functions Low-profile functions Supporting functions | – | Yes | – | Yes | |
| 17 | Rüttinger, Grünebaum & Jost, 1995 (G) | Executive functions, High-profile functions, Low-profile functions, Supporting functions | Yes | Yes | Yes | – | |
| 18 | Soares & Vargas, 1992 (Brazil) | Supporting functions | Yes | – | Yes | Yes | |
| 19 | Strauf & Nagele, 1996 (G) | Executive functions, Low-profile functions, High-profile functions, Supporting functions | – | Yes | – | Yes | |
| 20 | Ulich, 1988 (Japan) | Low-profile functions, Supporting functions | – | – | Yes | Yes | Pilot project |

take place in various forms. Of the teleworkers questioned, 80% reported they had less contact with colleagues whereas 20% experienced no difference. While 46% said that they had less contact with friends, 36% actually reported an increase in contacts and 18% of the teleworkers noticed no change in the number of contacts with friends. The evaluation of social contacts depends to a large degree on the type of work teleworkers engage in. In different case studies (Goldmann & Richter, 1991) generally half of the participants view social isolation as the major problem whereas the remainder do not experience it as a problem. If routine jobs are to be carried out, contact between teleworkers is considered unnecessary. Tasks that require regular team communication as, for example, in the software business can be most efficiently pursued by alternating telework, as this mode of telework offers the opportunity to work on problems in the privacy of one's own home (Goldmann & Richter, 1991). Working at home is experienced and judged as very effective in this context, because one's attention is not distracted by colleagues (Glaser & Glaser, 1995; Goldmann & Richter, 1991). These people evaluate their social contacts with family members, friends and acquaintances as positive and do not feel 'caged in' at home. At the same time, however, the lack of contact with colleagues is viewed as a potential danger fostering the development of social isolation (Goldmann & Richter, 1991; Morgan, 1985; Olson, 1983; Soares & Vargas, 1992). This situation is particularly problematic when participants miss informal exchanges with their colleagues and the opportunity of aiming for mutual goals. Occasional gatherings to meet these demands can be initiated by teleworkers themselves or by the management (Büssing, Kunst, & Michel, 1996; Goldman & Richter, 1991). Consequently social isolation is not perceived as a problem when institutionalized meetings are held and when their frequency can be adjusted according to the needs of the employees.

### Personality traits

In the discussion of social contacts in the context of telework, attention is also drawn to the suitability of certain personality types to carry out telework. This personality type is described as rather introverted with little need for social contact and exchange. Extraverted employees, having a stronger need for social relations, are in contrast expected to suffer more strongly from the feeling of alienation that is anticipated as a consequence of telework. However, this hypothesis could not be confirmed empirically (Glaser & Glaser, 1995). Interviews provided evidence that extraverted employees were actually more likely to cope with the social consequences of home-based work. They have in general enough self-confidence to adjust the intensity of their social relations according to their personal needs. They can therefore compensate their limited occupational contacts with private social activities.

### Training and career

Changing organization-bound workplaces into telework places can result in a loss of integration and might therefore cause isolation. However, for a freelance, telework can actually lead to a gain of integration. The integration of freelances through telework has not been explicitly examined in any of the studies, therefore no empirically based findings exist on this topic. The investigations of employees holding permanent positions in telework have mainly focused on social contact or social isolation respectively. Apart from a few exceptions, statements are made on the training and career opportunities of teleworkers (Glaser & Glaser, 1995).

The few studies on this topic emphasize that teleworkers can participate as much in training measures as organization-bound employees do and that they have the same career opportunities. Concerning career progress, teleworkers are actually thought to have a greater chance as their motivation and performance were positively valued by the management (Fischer, Späker & Weissbach, 1994).

### Conclusion

When teleworkers are looked at as a general group, no clear trends regarding changes in social contacts can be identified. Whereas one section of the teleworkers perceived a decline of contacts, the other section either judged the number of contacts with colleagues as still sufficient or they compensated for limited occuptional contacts with an increase of private contacts. When teleworkers are differentiated according to the main task they carry out, it becomes clear that especially routine tasks which are typically done by tele-homeworkers lead to feelings of social isolation. This finding is also confirmed in international comparison (Goldmann & Richter, 1991; Morgan, 1985; Olson, 1983; Soares & Vargas, 1992). The situation, however, differs for teleworkers who have at least the status of officials in different fields of exper-tise. They are especially more likely to perceive their social contacts as suffi-cient or to make up for fewer occupational contacts with more private contacts. Furthermore, this group of employees, according to personal estima-tion, works more efficiently at home, as they are not disturbed by colleagues.

Alternating telework seems to offer the benefits of undisturbed, efficient work at home without the risk of social isolation, Kraut (1988) concludes that alter-nating teleworkers use their workplace within the organization for social and interactive tasks whereas the workplace at home is preferred for mental tasks.

Empirical studies could provide no evidence that a specific personality type is better suited for telework. Watson, Fritz, Higa and Narasimhan (1994), review-ing the literature, come to the conclusion that certain key qualifications are necessary for the successful pursuit of telework such as the ability for time management, self-monitoring and self-motivation, a lower need for social con-tacts as well as a higher need for autonomy (see also Büssing & Aumann, 1996).

The present review suggests that teleworkers in comparison to organization-bound employees are not disadvantaged in terms of career opportunities if they make use of the training opportunities within the organization. Although it has frequently been stated in the literature that the lack of daily contact within the organization might endanger the chances of being promoted, the current studies could not confirm this fear (see also Di Martino & Wirth, 1990; Olson & Primps, 1984).

## Effects of Telework on Leisure Time and Family

The importance of telework lies not only in the possibility of organizing work hours more flexibly, but also in the resulting opportunity to combine pre-viously separated spheres of life more easily: gainful employment, housework and leisure time. If and to what degree these goals can be accomplished is dealt with in 13 of the 20 studies. The studies show that the compatibility of these spheres depends on a variety of occupational, personal and family condi-tions. Important factors are sovereignty over work hours, type and extent of household duties, attitudes towards the separation of work and private mat-ters, social support from the family, and the perceived use of opportunities to re-enter or continue work.

*Flexible use of time during work and within the family*

Flexible use of time is only possible in telework if the employer agrees to this flexibility. It does not suffice to restrict flexibility to the rims of the daily working hours, that is translating the already widespread flextime with stable core hours to telework jobs or demanding—taking the extreme case—fixed work hours for teleworkers that cover the complete regular working hours. However, the flexible use of working hours can be restricted when specific task and work demands arise through job demands. This can, for example, be the case when clients can only be reached at certain times or when the workload varies depending on the season. Working hours of qualified employees with fairly algorithmic or plannable tasks should not be linked to specific times of the day. In a current study, however, only one fifth of alternating teleworkers engaging in high- and low-profile professional tasks could make flexible use of their working hours (Glaser & Glaser, 1995).

Even when flexible working hours have been officially agreed upon, family demands can lead to a determination and condensation of the working hours, similar to or even stricter than at conventional workplaces. Furthermore, household and family tasks that follow a fixed circadian rhythm inevitably create a working rhythm adjusted to family and personal conditions (Glaser & Glaser, 1995). Working hours are therefore typically in the early morning and/or the late evening (Büssing, Kunst & Michel, 1996; Euler, Fröschle & Klein, 1987; Pupke, 1994). In many cases this leads to a reciprocal adjustment between occupational demands and the needs of the family, which implies that working hours are generally placed respective to the working hours of the spouse and to the times spent on childcare (Büssing, Kunst & Michel, 1996; Glaser & Glaser, 1995). A so-called 'fictitious flexibility' most often occurs when children or other relatives need to be taken care of. However, it cannot be assumed that paid work and housework cause a permanent overburdening. Just one study reported that this problem occurred sporadically, but that it was not experienced as particularly burdensome (Glaser & Glaser, 1995). Teleworkers generally appreciate that they have more time for family members or their partner (Glaser & Glaser, 1995; Grantham & Paul, 1995), and that they are available in the event of unpredictable events (Büssing, Kunst & Michel, 1996), and emergencies (Euler, Fröschle & Klein, B., 1987), as well as for occasional errands and administrative tasks (Glaser & Glaser, 1995).

*Attitude towards the separation of work and private sphere*

Telework requires the acceptance of a workplace within the domestic environment and consequently giving up, at least partly, the separation of private and work spheres. In individual cases, the separation of work and family spheres was not successful even under advantageous spatial conditions, such as the existence of a separate room (Euler, Fröschle & Klein, 1987). Results from a pilot project (Fischer, Späker & Weissbach, 1994) could show that around every tenth employee perceived the superposition of work and private spheres as unpleasant and therefore cancelled telework. This finding gives an idea of the importance of this problem.

A further survey found a close connection between satisfaction with telework and disturbances by the family, with an increase in satisfaction with telework corresponding to a decrease of disturbances and interruptions by members of the family (Hartman, Stoner & Arora, 1991). Environmental factors have consequently proven to be important determinants for the satisfaction of teleworkers with this specific way of work. When it is not possible to create an appropriate social environment and to adjust individual role definitions, job satisfaction declines and can lead to the termination of telework. Quite often changes in the distribution of family roles and consequently 'periods of intensified family adjustment' become necessary (Euler, Fröschle & Klein, 1987; Glaser & Glaser, 1995; Grantham & Paul, 1995).

*Social surroundings*

Aspects of the social surroundings are closely connected with the distribution of roles within the family. In households with pre-schoolers undisturbed home-based work can be assured by other caretakers. Relatives, friends and acquaintances, neighbours, but also paid helpers (e.g. day mother, daycare centre, au pairs) can take charge of the children and/or the household (Goldmann & Richter, 1991). So far, however, there have been only very few relevant findings on this topic in the context of telework.

*Perceived benefit*

According to the re-entry hypothesis telework is supposed to offer employees a convenient opportunity to re-enter the work process. The current results do not support this hypothesis. The resumption of professional activity is more likely to be motivated by local changes, new and extended social relations and the opportunity to be mobile (Fischer, Späker & Weissbach, 1994). It is additionally reported that telehomeworkers would not have chosen this way of working if they did not have children to take care of (Euler, Fröschle & Klein, 1987; Morgan, 1985). Specifically telehomeworkers see a major importance in the 'intrinsic character' of family duties that temporarily arise (Bailyn, 1989). However, this is only valid for those employees who do not live in areas with poor infrastructures and who have a sufficient amount of professional alternatives in acceptable commuting distance (Euler, Fröschle & Klein, 1987; Strauf & Nägele, 1996). For long-term employees telework can provide an increase in motivation and self-esteem: there are indications that this group of employees views working outside the organization as a privilege reflecting the confidence of the management (Glaser & Glaser, 1995). An increased sense of responsibility and a better identification with the organization were mentioned as a consequence.

The decision to take up telework is predominantly judged as a decision for the family. The possibility of taking care of the children is therefore specified as the major benefit of home-based telework (Morgan, 1985; Olson, 1983), limited, at least during the planning phase, to the time of the children's education (Euler, Fröschle & Klein, 1987) to facilitate re-entry into the organization after maternity leave (Goldmann & Richter, 1991; Rüttinger, Grünebaum & Jost, 1995). When the motivations and reasons of employees and employers to start telework are put into focus, the major motive is to maintain employment during changes within the family. Women taking their maternity leave often use home-based telework as a transient solution in order to be able to continue employment in the legally defined way. When these situations do not exist, home-based telework is often found to be less attractive, indicating that the evaluation of telework can be primarily influenced by the current life situation (see also Gutscher, 1988).

Overall, it is evident that the compatibility model of paid work and housework can only be applied to women (Goldmann & Richter, 1991). The feasibility is evaluated differently depending on the organization, the qualification of the employee and other circumstances. It has been found to be limited to bad for employees with highly qualified jobs in an organization with a strong team orientation (Goldmann & Richter, 1991). In addition executive functions or jobs involving high mobility are viewed as less compatible with home-based telework.

*Conclusion*

To actually make use of one of the major benefits of telework—the opportunity to have more sovereignty of time—the distribution of work hours should be prescribed as little as possible by the organization. Home-based telework is most often undertaken by women taking their educational leave. The flexible use of time and the success of an individually structured timetable are nevertheless determined by professional demands as well as by family demands. Problems can be expected to arise when full-time employment in combination with specific constellations within the family (children, taking care of relatives) leads to an ongoing double stressor (see also Shamir & Salomon, 1985). However, this was a theoretical assumption that could not be supported empirically. Instead it could be shown that telework is often viewed as a transitional solution, for example during periods of childcare. This implies that changes within the life situation (when the children grow more independent) also lead to a reconsideration of the current work situation causing a new decision for or against telework.

The consequences of the superposition of work and private spheres are also important. Teleworkers need to be aware to what degree they wish for or reject a mingling of both spheres. In the latter case, measures should be taken that allow a separation of work and private space, for example by setting up a separate study or arranging external childcare.

## Effects of Telework on Management and Communication within the Organization

One of the major obstacles in the implementation of telework can be found in the attitudes of executive personnel (Korte & Wynne, 1996; Wheeler & Zackin, 1994). Executives often reject telework because they anticipate losing control over their subordinates. They do not feel capable of supervising 'invisible' coworkers. It should be therefore investigated whether superiors supervise teleworkers significantly differently than employees working within the organization.

As communication is a fundamental supervising task, the question arises whether the executive's style of communication is particularly affected. As telework inevitably requires computer-based forms of communication instead of personal contact, changes in formal aspects and content of communication are expected. Work in computer-based cooperative groups appears to be related (Andriessen, 1991).

The issue of management, especially leadership, is mentioned in 10 of the 20 studies; work-related communication is covered in 15 studies. Four studies do not deal with either topic. Altogether managerial and communicational issues are an important topic, they are treated very generally in all investigations. Differentiating the results according to type of study, method, type of telework or type of job is hardly possible.

*Management*

Management in telework cannot be accomplished with conventional measures such as detailed control. Furthermore, executives must get rid of the idea that employees only work when they are closely supervised. Management should instead focus on result-orientation or goal-orientation respectively (see e.g. Guzzo, Jette & Katzell, 1985). Out of the 10 studies that covered management, 9 stress the necessity of this principle (Büssing & Aumann, 1997; Euler, Fröschle & Klein, 1987; Fischer, Späker & Weissbach, 1994; Glaser & Glaser, 1995; Godehardt, 1994b; Grantham & Paul, 1995; Müller & Reuschenbach, 1992; Olson, 1983; Rüttinger, Grünebaum & Jost, 1995). At the same time it is emphasized that this form of management requires a certain amount of trust (Rüttinger, Grünebaum & Jost, 1995). The basis for truse lies in the assumption that someone who strives for space and autonomy in his or her work, knows that he or she needs to work reliably (Fischer, Späker & Weissbach, 1994). Prerequisites on the side of the employee are maturity, organizational abilities, good time management and responsibility. Adequate management, however, cannot be considered to be a sufficient condition for the success of telework (Olson, 1983). A further important component is the appropriate selection of jobs and employees in telework. Moreover, executives should possess particular management qualities (Fischer, Späker & Weissbach, 1994) or should be trained in the handling of teleworkers (Grantham & Paul, 1995).

The concept of management by objectives (MbO) is evaluated positive both for telework places and for conventional workplaces (Fischer, Späker & Weissbach, 1994; Glaser & Glaser, 1995; Godehardt, 1994b; Grantham & Paul, 1995). Thus MbO does not constitute a specific way of leading in the context of telework, even though it is often regarded as a necessary prerequisite for the successful establishment of telecooperative work. Problems of MbO are not brought up. Just one study points out that when goal-oriented management, especially control, is applied, an objective comparison of the work results of different teleworkers is sometimes not possible because of specific influences during the work progress (Euler, Fröschle & Klein, 1987). Further analyses regarding positive and negative effects of goal-oriented management are not reported.

The attitudes of executives towards telework were assessed in only one study (Glaser & Glaser, 1995), that found the attitudes were in general positive. In the study by Fischer, Späker and Weissbach (1994) it is implicitly assumed that a positive attitude on the part of the executives is essential for the success of telework. It is stressed that an agreement between executive and subordinate is necessary for the implementation of a telework place. A further important task of executives is to function as a link between teleworkers and the organization (Fischer, Späker & Weissbach, 1994).

In summary, none of the reviewed studies focused on the possible effects of telework on management. Rather it is assumed without scrutinizing it that an adequate style of management is a prerequisite for the success of telework.

*Communication within the organization*

Because of the increasing delinkage of location and time of communication between sender and receiver, communication has changed. Compared to other forms of communication, messages within electronic mail systems clearly contain less personal and social information. Furthermore, norms of communication are more often transitioned as during direct communication. It can therefore be expected that the social competence of group members will decline as electronic communication substitutes for conventional forms of communication (see also Kiesler & Sproull, 1986; Kiesler, Siegel & McGuire, 1984). As the exchange of information with the teleworkers increasingly needs to take place over longer distances and as the greater flexibility of working hours leads to a more intensive use of the respective media, the communication of and with teleworkers becomes particularly significant.

The analyses of teleworkers' communicative behaviour are most often restricted to a description of the media used for communication (Büssing & Aumann, 1997; Fischer, Späker & Weissbach, 1994; Godehardt, 1994b; Goldmann & Richter, 1991; Morgan, 1985; Olson, 1983; Rüttinger, Grünebaum & Jost, 1995; Ulich, 1988). In this connection the improved possibilities in computer-aided communication arising from continuing technical development should also be considered. Thus e-mail is mentioned in only one of the studies conducted in the eighties, whereas newer studies all report the use of electronic mail. As the studies cover a time range from 1982 to 1997 in which significant technological innovations have taken place, a detailed analysis of the communication media described in the studies is not useful as the studies are not compatible in this regard.

Beside a mere description of the media used the importance of functioning structures of communication (Aichholzer & Kirschner, 1995; Grantham & Paul, 1995), according to the communicative skills of the involved personnel, is stressed in several studies, as well as the training of these skills (Goldmann & Richter, 1991; Grantham & Paul, 1995). The need for communication, however, is at the same time viewed as a limiting factor of telework. When the need for communication and/or cooperation increases, the expenses (for the organization) are perceived as unacceptable and telework, accordingly, does not seem to be justified as a way of organizing work (Fischer, Späker & Weissbach, 1994; Goldmann & Richter, 1991; Pupke, 1994).

If and how communicative and/or informative behaviour concerning work-related information is changed because of the implementation of telework or is different from other forms of work organization, has been investigated sporadically (Büssing & Aumann, 1997; Büssing, Kunst & Michel, 1996). In these studies a restriction in the supply of information as well as in the active search for information has been reported for teleworkers.

The importance of informal communication is emphasized in studies by Glaser and Glaser (1995), Goldmann and Richter (1991), Grantham and Paul (1995) and Soares and Vargas (1992). The study by Glaser and Glaser (1995) assesses the importance of informal communication. Employees judge the opportunity to ask colleagues for help as important. Getting to know the latest rumour, however, was considered unimportant. The studies by Goldmann and Richter (1991), Grantham and Paul (1995) and Soares and Vargas (1992) simply state the lack of informal communication in telework that in return leads to social isolation. These studies stress the negative consequences of telework.

One of the case studies (Fischer, Späker & Weissbach, 1994), however, observes a change in communication due to the introduction of technical aids. This leads to the conclusion that altered communicative behaviour is not the result of the new way of organizing work, but can be caused by the general changes in communication inherent to computer workplaces. Negative consequences such as social isolation that might arise from altered communicative behaviour might therefore be better explained by the introduction of new techniques of information and communication.

## The organization

It is repeatedly emphasized that the implementation of telework requires extensive measures of reorganization within the organization. The studies by

Fischer, Späker and Weissbach (1994) and Soares and Vargas (1992) take a closer look at some far-reaching effects of telework on the total organization. In the study by Fischer, Späker and Weissbach (1994), a case study, it is not expected that telework can stimulate a reduction of hierarchies or can democratize decisional structures. Soares and Vargas (1992), however, fear that the introduction of telework will lead to clearly negative consequences such as a more rigid or static organizational structure.

*Conclusion*

Concerning management in telework, there is consensus that a delegative, goal-oriented concept of management is the most adequate for the successful implementation of telework (see also Di Martino & Wirth, 1990; Van Sell & Jacobs, 1994). Beside these rather general and unvalidated statements no specific study investigated topics such as the effect of telework on management behaviour, the influence of management style on different areas of telework or the interaction of management behaviour and teleworkers.

It can be further stated that telework alters the communicative behaviour of the people involved in it, although it cannot be clearly decided against the background of the current studies whether this effect can be directly attributed to telework or to the overall use of new techniques. Communicative behaviour may also be different in employees who work within the organization. However, studies employing control group designs that are able to reliably answer this question are lacking. The application of new media requires certain communicative skills on the part of teleworkers as well as of their counterparts within the organization (e.g. executives and colleagues) that possibly need to be conveyed in training.

## Profitability of telework

Although Reichwald and Möslein (1996) portray the anticipation of problems in management as the main obstacle to the installation of telework, Kordey and Gareis (1997) state that profitability, at least from the perspective of the organization, is the essential argument for introducing and maintaining telework. IBM Germany, for example, only installs telework places when the potential increase of productivity justifies the costs of investment. They deviate from this principle only in specific cases, for example when urgent family problems force an employee to take up telework.

Costs and benefits of telework depend on the type of the workplace as well as on the technical equipment and the general economic conditions (Kordey & Gareis, 1997). Consequently, on the one hand, high costs were named as a negative consequence of telework (12% of the questioned organizations), but on the other hand, a decrease of costs was mentioned as a benefit (19%) (Strauf & Nägele, 1996). A cost-benefit calculation is further complicated by the large number of factors that need to be considered, for example also qualitative factors that are not clearly quantifiable (Kordey & Gareis, 1997). Of the 20 studies, 16 concentrated on the profitability of telework.

*Costs*

Kordey and Gareis (1997) divide potential costs into four categories: decentralized infrastructure, central infrastructure, communication, as well as organization and coordination. Investments into the decentralized infrastructure represent the largest portion in this context. Beside single costs arising from the investment into hard- and software, telecommunication and further auxiliary devices, the running costs for maintenance and insurance need to be included as well. Energy consumption and rent are usually proportionally covered by a monthly flat rate by the employer. The furniture at the workplace most often consists of the employee's property; ergonomic aspects in the arrangement of the telework place, however, are only considered in individual cases. Adequate technical conditions for communication with teleworkers also need to be created within the organization. Moreover, premises for regular meetings should be available. The costs of telecommunication strongly depend on the distance between the central organization and the workplace, the time of day and the duration of the on-line connection (Kordey & Gareis, 1997).

The costs for the technical infrastructure and telecommunication depend on the type of job and the required amount of communication with the central organization. It is therefore difficult to generalize the respective costs (Kordey & Gareis, 1997). Furthermore they are quickly outdated as prices fall consequent to technical development and the demand situation (Fischer, Späker & Weissbach, 1994; Goldmann & Richter, 1991). Although the installation of a telework place is in general regarded as more cost-effective than that of a conventional office place (Godehardt, 1994b) it needs to be considered to what extent the already implemented decentralized infrastructure is used. Thus home-based telework places that are only used half-time are less profitable for the organization (Euler, Fröschle & Klein, 1987).

Costs for organization and coordination entail, for example, planning and conducting the preparation, development of a security concept and selection of project participants. The expenses per teleworker are the higher the fewer telework places are planned. After the implementation further costs needed for training, supervision and coordination should be taken into account (Kordey & Gareis, 1997). The necessary extra expenditure for the organization and the coordination involved in the introduction of telework are not considered in any of the studies on the profitability of telework. Only studies that have scientifically monitored the implementation of neighbourhood offices and telecentres point out that problems with the acquisition of clients and the like are often underestimated in the beginning (Aichholzer & Kirschner, 1995; Euler, Fröschle & Klein, 1987; Fischer, Späker & Weissbach, 1994).

*Benefits*

The economic benefits of telework can be summed up in two points: increased work performance and work quality as well as saving of work and running costs (Kordey & Gareis, 1997).

The literature reports on differently sized increases in productivity. However, it is rarely evident which aspects were actually included in the calculations. The discussion on the conditions of eventual increases in productivity often appears speculative due to the lack of empirical data. The decisive factor is seen in the undisturbed atmosphere of the own home (Glaser & Glaser, 1995; Strauf & Nägele, 1996). However, teleworkers who were often contacted by their colleagues at home report a smaller improvement in efficiency (Glaser & Glaser, 1995). Jobs involving contact with customers use the benefits of closer proximity (Aichholzer & Kirschner, 1995) and temporal flexibility, working outside regular business hours (Strauf & Nägele, 1996), to contribute to the profitability of telework. In one study, teleworkers reported that customers were more content (Grantham & Paul, 1995). Quantifications or statements by the customers themselves or independent observers, however, are not available.

In some cases, the increase in productivity cannot be attributed to the specifics of telework but to factors closely connected to the innovative character of its implementation. Thus the improvement in efficiency and productivity in a satellite office was due not to the undisturbed atmosphere but to the ergonomic design of the workplace and the excellent technical equipment (Ulich, 1988).

Several studies look at the potential for increases in performance in the context of qualification. The latter is closely linked to personnel costs which vary considerably depending on the region and country. In Germany, the outsourcing of low-level, monotonous jobs does not appear to be profitable despite low wages (Fischer, Späker & Weissbach, 1994). Thus in the mid-eighties a project in Baden-Württemberg in which paperwork was transferred to a satellite office failed (Euler, Fröschle & Klein, 1987). The lack of the anticipated performance improvement is ascribed to the scattering of office work inherent to decentralization. This leads to an increase in coordinating effort while at the same time the motivation and satisfaction of the employees decreases.

The productivity shown in creative, high-level jobs, however, is more likely to improve as these jobs are more vulnerable to interference and disturbances (Fischer, Späker & Weissbach, 1994). This is supported by results gained by the telework initiative of IBM Germany, as only highly qualified employees profited from telework. Teleworkers as well as superiors judged working at home as being more productive and efficient, although the latter were more reserved in their evaluation (Glaser & Glaser, 1995).

Investigations outside Europe obtained different results regarding the importance of qualification. A North American study stresses that the observed increase in productivity of 16% can be found for jobs with different demands. The actual level of qualification of the persons investigated, however, was not specified (Grantham & Paul, 1995). The outsourcing of low-level data entry jobs leads to more productivity in Brazil, although the 'decentralization' is carried out from the suburbs to the town centre, causing higher costs for rent (Soares & Vargas, 1992). Examples showing that the outsourcing of low-level jobs is profitable for the organization due to low wages also exist in Japan (Pupke, 1994).

In introducing telework it is possible to establish a lower wage level. On the one hand additional wage costs such as pension scheme payments do not arise when people work freelance or are self-employed, on the other hand organizations can recruit cost-effective employees from structurally weak regions. Transferring regular employees to a freelance basis is said to yield potential savings of 30–40% (Christensen, 1987). Although decentralization of work places is cost-effective for the organization, it sometimes entails a deterioration of the employees' financial situation. German and British mothers who try to combine childcare and professional re-entry with the aid of telework, receive wages below average in respect to their qualification (Bailyn, 1989; Büssing, Kunst & Michel, 1996). In Great Britain women are the dominant group in the electronic telework which spread rapidly at the beginning of the eighties. They work in pseudo self-employment and have to face an unsteady order situation (Morgan, 1985). Their wages are way below average in comparison to those that are obtained in comparable areas of business, social security is insufficient, and they are sometimes even burdened with the costs for the technical equipment (Morgan, 1985).

Kordey and Gareis (1997) see further benefits in the opportunity to retain an employment in the event of moving and to stay with family members who are in need of constant care. Organizations are apparently interested in keeping their personnel, especially in the case of highly qualified employees, to reduce costs due to fluctuation. This aspect, however, is not emphasized in any of the studies.

Costs are further reduced by the discontinuation of voluntary social benefits (subsidies for fares and meals) and financial compensation of overtime (Morgan, 1985). In this context it should be pointed out that widespread informal homework is promoted by large number of enterprises (Fischer, Späker & Weissbach, 1994; Müller & Reuschenbach, 1992). While working at home, outside office hours, employees probably do more overtime without causing additional costs for the organization. Moreover, because of insufficient legal background problems concerning data protection as well as obligations to provide welfare for employees and liability of the organization occur.

*Conclusion*

It seems to be very difficult to make general statements concerning the profitability of telework. Costs and benefits need to be evaluated in the context of the respective situation and condition. When examining the profitability of telework the organization-based workplaces should be included in the analysis as an increase in performance at telework places could be due to a disadvantageous distribution of work, leaving the organization-based employee with less efficient jobs. The technical costs and the organizational expenditure depend on the demands of the workplace and the original structures within the organization. The personal costs vary with the qualification, the form of contract and the local region. Cost reduction results from the cancellation of additional financial benefits and overall from the free resources within the central infrastructure. Concerning productivity, telework influences quantity and quality of products and services not only directly, but also indirectly by reducing absenteeism, improved customer service and maybe a more efficient work organization. The level of qualification, flexible use of time, being undisturbed and technical equipment are also of importance. The significance of factors that are hard to quantify is judged by the persons involved. For example, work within a telecentre is cited because of good results and a higher job satisfaction despite lacking cost reduction (Fischer, Späker & Weissbach, 1994). Overall, it seems to be highly possible that telework can be realized as either cost-neutral or even bearing financial profit, especially as technical, organizational and economic impediments tend to be on the decline.

## CONCLUSIONS AND PERSPECTIVES

The review has shown that the research on the effects of telework is still fragmentary. Central topics such as management and self-leadership, models of flexible working time and ergonomics of the work setting are not or just barely covered. Classical elements of organizational development such as individual training, special team training and quality circles are rarely applied. The need to consider a wide range of various factors that could explain success and failure of telework is met by only very few methodically sound empirical studies. The attempt to develop a model explaining the effects of telework has not yet been made (see also Van Sell & Jacobs, 1994).

In content there are hardly any homogeneous findings within the reviewed research on family, social contacts, communication and management as well as profitability. Looking at profitability, for example, it could be shown that a general statement on the efficiency of telework cannot be made but that a multitude of organizational, personal and task-related factors influence its profitability. But the review shows a lot of prevailing conditions leading to positive consequences.

Due to the spatial and organizational proximity of telecooperative forms of paid work and housework the rigid separation of paid work and 'non-work' in the sense of housework, family duties and leisure time becomes more and more obsolete. There are good reasons to deliver the assumption of neutrality assuming no interaction, for telework. Because of the demands on the future working society such as increasing flexibility, autonomy and responsibility as well as fusion of gainful employment, family and leisure time it will become inevitable that we abolish our traditional understanding of work focusing too narrowly on gainful employment.

## Problems in the Evaluation of the Effects of Telework

All studies investigating the effects of telework are subject to three basic problems denoted as the technology problem, the phase problem, and the intercultural problem. These problems make it difficult to draw a general evaluation of the impacts of telework. The technology problem is evident in the fact that due to increasingly powerful technology forms of cooperation and communication can now be realized that, years ago, were unthinkable. Evaluation studies from the mid-eighties, for example, do not mention the use of e-mail. Work-related problems, however, can also be solved with the aid of the technical infrastructure. Reactivity, being the basic problem of evaluation studies, weighs more heavily in the highly dynamic area of technical development than in other areas, as qualitatively new forms of computer-aided communication become available and comparisons between current and older studies can only be drawn to a very limited extent.

The second problem, the phase problem, can be found on the organizational as well as on the individual level. On the organizational level it must be taken into account that enterprises that implemented telework are within different project phases. Basing the implementation of telework on a simple phase model covering the initial taking up of the concept, the pilot or model phase and the optimization and consolidation (Chapman et al., 1995, see Qvortrup, 1992), each phase leads to inherent problems. In the first phase, the fragmentation, single, divisable jobs are subject to outsourcing. The focus is on the adequate selection and limiting of organizational options. In the second phase, the dispersion, expansion and dispersion of the respective jobs take place, questioning the importance of the central organization as a whole/as a unit. During this phase it is important to spot the specific opportunities and risks of the newly installed workplaces to obtain, beside a general evaluation, information for the optimization. The third phase, finally, is characterized by diffusion, creating specialized service centres and highly specialized individuals. In the phase of optimization and consolidation even informational and organizational adaptations that concern the whole organization are decisive. So far there are no investigations integrating the life-cycle of telework into the evaluation of telework.

On the individual level the phase problem can be described as follow: in the context of looking at the effects of home-based telework on the family it was obvious that duties within the family that depend on the current life phase play an important role in the decision to take up telework and in its evaluation.

When duties are discontinued, the valence of telework can change. The dynamic in individual valence and instrumentality consequently needs to be considered.

The inter-cultural problem is caused by differences in the understanding of paid work and leisure time that can be also seen in the differing national labour and social laws. In international comparison, Germany, Italy and Austria are 'highly regulating' countries whereas the US and Great Britain have far fewer respective regulations (see Späker & Weissbach, 1997). From the perspective of 'high regulators' a special danger could lie in the lack of adherence to work time control, regulations concerning breaks, work environment and the representation of employees. Therefore it ought to be positively stressed that special precautions are indeed guaranteed during the introduction of telework. Excluding freelances and employees working outside the office, taking up telework is in general done voluntarily. The preliminary character of telework is evident in the fact that, at least in Europe, telework is implemented within limited model projects. By modifying the existing work contract teleworkers can return to their previous work situation without having to fear negative consequences. However, if the perceptions of social effects of telework in Germany and North America are compared, it can be shown that the conflict of paid work and leisure time does not exist in North American samples, giving further evidence for inter-cultural differences (Garhammer, 1997).

### Critical Reflection of Evaluation Methods

The majority of the reviewed studies were carried out using relatively unsophisticated methods (see Van Sell & Jacobs, 1994). They were mostly case or field studies that often employed free, non-structured interviews or questionnaires. On the one hand precise pre-post measurements are also lacking that would allow us to state whether telework is actually the cause of observed changes in behaviour and experience. On the other hand control data from employees still working in conventional work settings rarely exist. Due to this lack it cannot be clarified whether problems named in the context of telework can be attributed to this new form of work organization or to a general increase of the workload. Finally, little is known about the long-term effects of telework because of the lack of longitudinal studies.

Beside these general methodical flaws, a large number of studies just give a recollection of diverse subjective impressions. Precise definitions and translations into experimental variables, however, as well as clear quantifications, are necessary to reliably measure constructs of individual behaviour and experience and to facilitate the compatibility of results. It was also not possible to integrate in our analysis how much of the complete working time was actually spent at the workplace at home, as only very few studies differentiated between home-based telework, home-based alternating telework, and office-based alternating telework. In some studies it was unclear whether a differentiation had been made. The review, however, shows that considerable differences exist between the motives to take up different types of telework and between the effects they exert. Andriessen (1991) for example, emphasizes the discrimination between clerical homeworkers who work freelance and are less well supported by legal regulations and professional homeworkers who are full-time employees. The importance of this discrimination is evident in differing effects on the individual, the family and the organization (see also Mehlmann, 1988). Our own studies illustrate that perceived stress and strain are dependent on the type of telework (Konradt & Schmook, 1999). Home-based telework and home-based alternating telework with a telework proportion over 50% is predominantly used by mothers during maternity leave in order to continue their current employment. Alternating teleworkers on the other hand, who spend less than 50% of their time engaging in telework, usually take up telework to work overtime. In future it will therefore be of major importance to differentiate more strongly between the various forms of telework. In this context the small sample size of most studies should be pointed out, which is not suited to adequately represent characteristics of the population.

Furthermore, the reviewed studies most often do not clearly separate between results stemming from empirical investigation and information or speculations obtained from other sources. Methodological problems of empirical studies on telecommuting are also discussed by McCloskey and Igbaria (1998). They mention small sample sizes, lack of control groups, heavy reliance on self-reports, failure to control extraneous factors and the entanglement of gender and employment status as factors which make it difficult to interpret the results.

### Consequences for the Modification of Telework—What Should be Done?

It still must be assumed that there is hardly any empirically based knowledge on the effects of telework so that recommendations on the modification of telework inevitably remain speculative. Therefore scientific research accompanying projects especially in multinational enterprises (e.g. IBM, BMW, SNI, HP) is much to be desired. However, the transfer of possible findings to the situation of small and middle-sized enterprises would still be difficult. A further problem could lie in the enormous diversity among different types of telework, as recommendations would need to be either very general or very specific, naturally limiting their applicability. Despite the lack of empirical research, the number of telework places is growing slowly but steadily. Because of the lack of appropriate research, however, one must fear that preventive and prospective forms of organizing work will be applied less often.

In the current review the theoretical, methodological and methodical problems and weaknesses of the studies that investigated the effects of telework were repeatedly stressed and numerous demands for future research were deduced. In the following, suggestions that could be directly translated into empirical research designs will be finally suggested.

1.  Further prognoses, projections and statements concerning the development of telework as well as the opportunities and risks involved are not necessary. The review of the literature has shown that only very few empirical studies could serve as a basis for a fruitful discussion of the impacts of telework.
2.  Investigations should be conducted with more sophisticated methodology. This means that standardized, reliable and valid measures should be employed, allowing a quantitative assessment of the effects of telework. Furthermore, studies are urgently needed that directly compare teleworkers with strictly organization-based employees, engaging in similar jobs.
3.  Longitudinal studies should be launched that investigate stress, strains and successful coping strategies in the course of ongoing telework. Evaluation studies could then not only offer summative evaluation but also formative evaluation which would provide a direct contribution to the preventive and prospective organization of work. In this connection the use of classical elements of organizational development such as health circles (for an example see Konradt, Schmook & Hertel, in press), participating in structuring of work and individually tailored training should be stressed as they could lead to a successive improvement of situational and organizational work conditions of teleworkers.
4.  The management views leading and supervising teleworkers as the major obstacle in the context of introducing telecooperative forms of work. Although this concern has been identified, the literature does not provide usable empirical information. Therefore research is clearly needed in this area.

These demands could be directly integrated into the planning and conducting of studies investigating the effects of telework, thereby providing definite progress in the discussion on the evaluation and development of telework.

## NOTE

1.  PsycLIT, PSYNDEX, WISO III, Bildung, ADG (Archiv der Gegenwart—politics and economy), APS (ABC Political Science—politics, sociology and economy), CAB ABSTRACTS and CAB International (agricultural sciences), DISS (dissertations and habilitations), DNB (Deutsche Nationalbibliogrpahic—all areas), IBZ (Internationale Bibliographie der Zeitschriftenliteratur—all areas), ISTP (Index to Scientific & Technical Proceedings), ISSHP (Index to Social Sciences & Humanities Proceedings), MEDLINE and SERLINE. Most hits were found within data

banks on psychology, pedagogy, business administration and social sciences. Technical and medical databases as well as databases for political science contributed only few references.

## ACKNOWLEDGEMENTS

The preparation of this chapter was supported by a grant from the Technology Foundation Schleswig-Holstein. We are grateful to Silke Sorgenfrey and Kerstin Krauel for their assistance on the preparation and comments on an earlier version of the manuscript.

Correspondence should be addressed to Udo Konradt, University of Kiel, Institute for Psychology, Olshausenstr. 40, 24 098 Kiel, Germany. E-mail: *konradt@PSychologie.uni-kiel.de*

## REFERENCES

(Studies included in the empirical review are marked with *)

*Aichholzer, G. & Kirschner, A. (1995). *An Evaluation of the Neighbourhood Office Model of Teleworking*. Projektbericht am Institut für Technikfolgenabschätzung der Österreichischen Akademie der Wissenschaften, Vienna.

Andriessen, J. H. E. (1991). Mediated communication and new organizational forms. In C. L. Cooper & I. T. Robertson (Eds), *International Review of Industrial and Organizational Psychology*, Vol. 6 (pp. 17–70) Chichester: Wiley.

*Bailyn, L. (1989). Toward the perfect workplace. *Communications of the ACM*, **32**(4), 460–471.

Bertin, I. & Denbigh, A. (1996). *The Teleworking Handbook. New Ways to Work in the Information Society*. Warwickshire: TCA.

Burke, R. J. (1986). Occupational and life stress and the family: Conceptual frameworks and research findings. *International Review of Applied Psychology*, **35**, 347–369.

Büssing, A. (1997). Telearbeit und Telekooperation—Interdisziplinäre Perspektiven. *Zeitschrift für Arbeitswissenschaft*, **51**, 194–196.

Büssing, A. (1998). Teleworking and quality of life. In P.J. Jackson & J.H. van der Wielen (Eds), *Teleworking: International Perspectives: From Telecommuting to the Virtual Organization* (pp. 144–165). London: Routledge.

Büssing, A. & Aumann, S. (1996). Telearbeit im Spannungsfeld der Interessen betrieblicher Aketure: Implikationen für das Personalmanagement. *Zeitschrift für Personalforschung*, **10**, 223–239.

*Büssing, A. & Aumann, S. (1997). Telezentren im bayerischen Raum. Organizationsanalyse von kollektiver Telearbeit in Telezentren. In A. Büssing (Ed.), *Berichte aus dem Lehrstuhl für Psychologie der TU München* (Nr. 38). München: Technische Universität München.

Büssing, A. & Aumann, S. (1999). *Telearbeit. Analyse, Bewertung und Gestaltung ortsungebundener Arbeit*. Göttingen: Verlag für Angewandt Psychologie.

*Büssing, A., Kunst, R. & Michel, S. (1996). Qualifikationsanforderungen, berufliche qualifizierung und Mehrfachbelastung unter Telearbeig. In A. Büssing (Ed.), *Berichte aus dem Lehrstuhl für Psychologie der TU München* (Nr. 31). München: Technische Universität München.

Chapman, A. J., Sheehy, N. P., Heywood, S., Dooley, B. & Collins, S. C. (1995). The organizational implications of teleworking. In C. L. Cooper & I. T. Robertson (Eds). *International Review of Industrial and Organizaitonal Psychology*, Vol. 10 (pp. 229–248). Chichester: Wiley.

Christensen, K. E. (1987). Impacts of computer-mediated home-based work on women and their families. *Office: Technology and People*, **3**, 211–230.

Crellin, J., Graham, J. & Powell, A.-P. (1996). The Australian telecentres program: Providing public access to information networks for people in rural and remote regions. *Quarterly Bulletin of IAALD*, **41**, 173–177.

Cullen, K. & Robinson, S. (Eds) (1997). *Telecoms for Older People and People with Disabilities in Euorope*. Amsterdam: IOS Press.

Davidow, W. H. & Malone, M. S. (1992). *The Virtual Corporation*. New York: Harper Collins.

DG XIII-B (1996). *Action for stimulation of transborder telework and research cooperation in Europe. Telework 1996. Final Report on Telework Stimulate Actions (1994–1995)*. European Commission, Brussels.

Di Martino, V. & Wirth, L. (1990). Telework: An overview. *Conditions of Work Digest*, **9**, 3–42.

Empirica (1994). *Pan-europiaische Befragung zur Telearbeit* (Vols. 1–6). Bonn.

Empirica (Ed.) (1995). *Telematik- und Teleservices. Entwicklungen in deutschen Städten in 1995 und 2005* (Internes Arbeitspapier). Bonn.

*Euler, H., Fröschle, H.-P. & Klein, B. (1987). Dezentrale Arbeitsplätze unter Einsatz von Teletex. In F. Gehrmann (Ed.), *Neue Informations- und Kommunikationstechnologien* (pp. 55–71). Frankfurt: Campus.

European Information Technology Observatory (EITO) (1997). *EITO Yearbook 1997*, Frankfurt/M. [see *http://www.fvit-eurobit.de/eito*].

*Fischer, U. L., Späker, G. & Weissbach, H. J. (1994). *Neue Entwicklungen bei der sozialen Gestaltung von Telearbeit* (Materialien und Berichte des IuK-Instituts. Dortmund: IUK-GmbH.

Garhammer, M. (1997). Teleheimarbeit und Telecommuting: ein deutsch-amerikanischer Vergleich über kulturelle Bedingungen und soziale Auswirkungen einer neuen Arbeitsform. *Zeitschrift für Arbeitswissenschaft*, **23**, 232–239.

*Glaser, W. R. & Glaser, M. O. (1995). *Telearbeit in der Praxis. Psychologische Erfahrungen mit außerbetrieblichen Arbeitsstätten bei der IBM Deutschland GmbH*. Berlin: Luchterhand.

Godehardt, B. (1994a). *Telearbeit. Rahmenbedingungen und Potentiale*. Opladen: Westdeutscher Verlag.

*Godehardt, B. (1994b). *Telearbeit: Rahmenbedingungen und Potentiale* (ISDN-Forschungskommission des Landes ordrhein-Westfalen, Materialien und Berichte Nr. 15). Düsseldorf: Ministerium für Wirtschaft, Mittelstand und Technologie des Landes Nordrhein-Westfalen.

Godehardt, B., Kork, W. B., Michelsen, U. & Quadt, H. P. (Eds) (1997). *Management Handbuch Telearbeit*. Heidelberg: Hüthig/HVS.

*Goldmann, M. & Richter, G. (1991). *Beruf und Familie: Endlich vereinbar? Teleheimarbeit von Frauen*. Dortmund: Montania Druck- und Verlagsgesellschaft mbH.

Gordon, G. E. & Kelly, M. M. (1986). *Telecommuting: How to Make it Work for You and your Company*. Englewood Cliffs, NJ: Prentice-Hall.

*Grantham, C. E. & Paul, E. D. (1995). The 'Greening' of organizational change: A case study. *Innovation*, **8**, 221–233.

Gray, M., Hodson, N. & Gordon, G. (1993). *Teleworking Explained*. Chichester: Wiley.

Gutscher, H. (1988). Telearbeit: Neue Arbeitsformen, neue Risiken, neue Chancen. *Report Psychologie*, **13**, 10–17.

Guzzo, R. A., Jette, R. D. & Katzell, R. A. (1985). The effects of psychologically based intervention programs on worker productivity. *Personnel Psychology*, **38**, 275–291.

*Hartman, R. I., Stoner, C. R. & Arora, R. (1991). An investigation of selected variables affecting telecommuting productivity and satisfaction. *Journal of Business and Psychology*, **6**, 207–225.

Hiltz, S. R. & Turoff, M. (1987). *The Network Nation: Human Communication via Computer*. Cambridge, MA: MIT Press.

Hodson, N. (1992). *The Economies of Teleworking*. London: British Telecom.

Jackson, P. J. & van der Wielen, J. H. (Eds) (1998). *Teleworking: International Perspectives: From Telecommuting to the Virtual Organization*. London: Routledge.

Johanning, D. (1997). *Telearbeit.Einführung und Leitfaden für Unternehmer und Mitarbeiter*. München: Hanser.

Kern, P. & Wawrzinek, S. (1985). Homework—dezentraler produktiver arbeiten? *Arbeitspapier des Fraunhofer Instituts für Arbeitswissenschaft und Organization*.

Kiesler, S., Siegel, J. & McGuire, T. (1984). Social psychological aspects of computer-mediated communication. *Ameircan Psychologist*, **39**, 1123–1134.

Kiesler, S. & Sproull, L. S. (1986). Response effects in the electronic survey, *Public Opinion Quarterly*, **50**, 402–413.

Konradt, U. & Schmook, R. (1999). Telearbeit—Belastungen und Beanspruchungen im Längsschnitt. *Zeitschrift für Arbeits-und Organizationspsychologie*, **43**, 142–150.

Konradt, U., Schmook, R. & Hertel, G. (in press). Health circles for teleworkers: Selective results on stress, strain, and coping strategies. *Health Education Research*.

Kordey, N. & Gareis, K. (1997). Wirtschaftlichkeitsbetrachtungen bei der Einführung von Telearbeit. In Ministerium für Wirtschaft und Mittelstand, Technologie und Verkehr (Ed.), *Telearbeit und Telekooperation* (Schriftenreihe des Landes NRW—media NRW), Vol. 4 (pp. 94–109). Dusseldorf: Ministerium für Wirtschaft und Mittelstand, Technologie und Verkehr.

Kordey, N. & Korte, W. B. (1996). *Telearbeit Erfolgreich Realisieren*. Wiesbaden: Vieweg.

Kordey, N. & Korte, W. B. (1997). Verbreitung und Potential der Telearbeit in Europea. In Ministerium für Wirtschaft und Mittelstand, Technologie und Verkehr (Ed.), *Telearbeit und Telekooperation* (Schriftenreihe des Landes NRW—media NRW). Vol. 4 (pp. 18–40). Düsseldorf: Ministerium für Wirtschaft und Mittelstand, Technologie und Verkehr.

Korte, W. B. & Wynne, R. (1996). *Telework, Penetration, Potential and Practice in Europe*. Amsterdam: IOS Press.

Kraut, R. E. (1988). Telework as a work-style innovation. In B. D. Ruben (Ed.), *Information and Behavior*, Vol. 2 (pp. 116–146). New Brunswick: Transaction Books.

*Kreibich, R., Drüke, H., Dunkelmann, H. & Feuerstein, G. (1990). *Zakunft der Telearbeit. Empirische Untersuchung zur Dezentralisierung und Flexibilisierung von Angestelltentätigkeiten mit Hilfe neuer Informations- und Kommunikations-technologien*. Eschborn: RKW-Verlag.

Kugelmass, J. (1995). *Telecommuting: A Manager Guide to Flexible Work Arrangements*. New York: Lexington Books.

McCloskey, D. W. & Igbaria, M. (1998). A review of the empirical resarch on telecommuting and directions for future research. In M. Igbaria & M. Tan (Eds), *The Virtual Workplace* (pp. 338–358). Hershey, PA: Idea Group Publishing.

Mehlmann, M. (1988). Social aspects of telework: Facts, hopes, fears, ideas. In W. B. Korte, S. Robinson & W. J. Steinle (Eds), *Telework: Present situation and Future Development of a New Form of Work Organization* (pp. 101–110). Amsterdam: Elsevier Science.

*Morgan, V. M. (1985). Die neue Heimarbeiterin. *Frauen und Arbeit*, **3**, 17–20.

*Müller, T. & Reuschenbach, T. (1992). *Dezentrale Organisiationsformen von re-chnergestützter Arbeit* (Unveröff. Projektbericht), Technische Universität Berlin, Berlin.

Mundorf, N., Meyer, S., Schulze, E. & Zoche, P. (1994). Families, information technologies, and the quality of life: German research findings. *Informatics and Telematics*, 11, 137–146.

Nilles, J. (1985). Teleworking from home. In T. Forester (Ed.), *The Information Technology Revolution*. Oxford: Blackwell.

Nilles, J. (1994). *Making Telecommuting Happen. A Guide for Telemanagers and Telecommuters*. New York: International Thomson Publ./van Nostrand Reinhold.

Nullmeier, E. (1988). Gestaltung rechnergestützter Arbeitsplätze in Büro und Verwaltung. In E. Nullmeier & K. H. Rödiger (Eds), *Dialogsysteme in der Arbeitswelt* (pp. 109–121). Mannheim: Wissenschaftsverlag.

*Olson, M. H. (1983). Remote office work: Changing work patterns in space and time. *Communications of the ACM*, 26, 182–187.

Olson, M. H. (1989). Work at home for computer professionals: Current attitudes and future prospects. *ACM Transactions on Office Information Systems*, 7, 317–338.

Olson, M. H. & Primps, S. B. (1984). Working at home with computers: Work and nonwork issues. *Journal of Social Issues*, 40(3), 97–112.

Psychological and Social Aspects of Teleworking in Rural Areas [PATRA] (1992–1994). CEC/DGXIII Contract Number 02004, Opportunities for Rural Areas (ORA Programme).

Pollmann, R. (1997). Entwicklung der Telearbeit in Europa—Eine Standortbestimmung. In B. Godehardt, W. B. Kork, U. Michelsen & H. P. Quadt (Eds), *Management Handbuch Telearbeit* (ch. 120.2), Heidelberg: Hüthig/HVS.

Pratt, J. (1984). Home Teleworking: A study of its pioneers. *Technological Forecasting and Social Change*, 25, 1–14.

*Pupke, H. (1994). *Tele-Heimarbeit in Japan. Berliner Beiträge zur sozial- und wirtschaftswissenschaftlichen Japan-Forschung* (Vol. 25). Bochum: Brockmeyer.

Qvortrup, L. (1992). Visions, definitions, realities, barriers. In OECD (Ed.), *Cities and New Technologies* (pp. 77–108). Paris: OECD.

Reichwald, R. & Möslein, K. (1996). Telearbeit und Telekooperation. In H.-J. Bullinger & H. J. Warnecke (Eds), *Neue Organizationsformen im Unternehmen*. (pp. 671–708). Berlin: Springer.

Reichwald, P., Möslein, K. & Oldenburg, S. (1998). *Telearbeit, Telekooperation und virtuelle Unternehmen*. Berlin: Springer.

Reid, A. (1994). *Teleworking: A Guide to Good Practice*. New York: Blackwell.

Richter, P. & Hacker, W. (1998). *Belastung und Beanspruchung*. Heidelberg: Asanger.

*Rüttinger, B., Grünebaum, B. & Jost, D. (1995). *Der Status der Telearbeit in der Bundesrepublik Deutschland 1994* (Institutsbericht). Darmstadt: Technische Hochschule Darmstadt.

Schönpflug, W. (1987). Beanspruchung und Belastung bei der Arbeit—Konzepte und Theorien. *Enzyklopädie der Psychologie* (1). Göttingen: Hogrefe.

Shamir, B. & Salomon, I. (1985). Work-at-home and the quality of work life. *Academy of Management Review*, 10, 455–464.

*Soares, A. S. & Vargas, F. G. (1992). Telework and communication in data processing centres in Brazil. In U. E. Gattiker (Ed.), *Studies in Technological Innovation and Human Resources*, Vol. 3 (pp. 117–149). Berlin: De Gruyter.

Späker, G. & Weissbach, H.-J. (1997). Regulationsmodelle für Telearbeit—ein europäischer Vergleich. *Zeitschrift für Arbeitswissenschaft*, 51, 214–223.

State Department for Research and Technology (BMBF) (1995). *Telearbeit—Definition, Potential und Probleme*. Bonn.

State Department for Research and Technology (BMBF) (1998). *Delphi '98. Studie zur globalen Entwicklung von Wissenschaft und Technik*. FhG-ISI, Karlsruhe.

*Stauf, S. & Nägele, B. (1996). *Möglichkeiten und Grenzen der Telearbeit*. Freiburg: Institut für Regionale Studeien in Europa.

*Ulich, E. (1988). Überlegungen zur Aufhebung der Ortsgebundenheit von Arbeit. *Psychosozial*, 11, 83–91.

Van Sell, M. & Jacobs, S.M. (1994). Telecommuting and quality of life: A review of the literature and a model for research. *Telematics and Informatics*, 11, 81–95.

Watson Fritz, M. E., Higa, K. & Narasimhan, S. (1994). Telework: Exploring the borderless office. *Proceedings of the Twenty-Seventh Annual Hawaii International Conference on System Sciences* (pp. 149–158).

Wedde, P. (1994). *Telearbeit. Handbuch für Arbeitnehmer, Betriebswirte und Anwender* (2nd edn). Köln: Bund-Verlag.

Weissbach, H.-J., Lampe, N. & Späker, G. (1997). *Telearbeit*. Marburg: Schüren.

Wheeler, M. & Zackin, D. (1994). Work–family roundtable: Telecommuting. *The Conference Board*, 4(1).

Wieland-Eckelmann, R. (1992). *Kognition, Emotion und Psychische Beanspruchung*. Göttingen: Hogrefe.

Zentralverband Elektrotechnik und Elkektronikindustrie e. V. (ZVEI)/Verband Deutscher Maschinen- und Anlagenbau e. V. (VDMA) (1995). *Informationsgesellschaft—Herauforderungen für Politik, Wirtschaft und Gesellschaft*. Frankfurt.

# Chapter 3

# PSYCHOLOGICAL APPROACHES TO ENTREPRENEURIAL SUCCESS: A GENERAL MODEL AND AN OVERVIEW OF FINDINGS

Andreas Rauch and Michael Frese
*University of Amsterdam*

Small and medium-sized enterprises are important for today's economy. They have become major agents of economic growth and employment (ECSB Newsletter, 1997). Drucker (1985) described this as a shift from a managerial to an entrepreneurial economy. About 99% of the European companies are small or medium-sized and the provide 66% of the working places (ECSB Newsletter, 1997). Twenty-five years ago, entrepreneurship research was still in its infancy. The number of small-scale enterprises decreased until 1979 (Bruederl, Preisendoerfer & Ziegler, 1992) and consequently, research focused on bigger companies. Since 1979 the founding rate of small and medium-sized enterprises has grown and particularly the number of smaller firms has increased disproportionally. At the same time, there has been an increase in research in this area (Low & McMillan, 1988).

Although there are some good reviews on psychological entrepreneurship research (cf. Chell, Haworth & Brearly, 1991; Cooper & Gimeno-Gascon, 1992; Furnham, 1992), our approach is different. First, we are looking at a much larger database; we do not just concentrate on one area (e.g. personality), but include all variables of psychological importance. Second, we start out with a general model of entrepreneurial success and attempt to coherently relate it to what we have found in the literature. Third, our contribution is a start in the direction of a quantitative review. Unfortunately, it is not possible to do a proper meta-analysis in this area (and with the exception of Schwenk and Shrader, 1993, it has never been done so far), because there are too few studies and the quality of the studies is often insufficient (e.g., standard deviations, exact $t$- or $F$-value, or exact correlations are often not reported). However, we think it is time to get away from purely verbal reviews and at

*International Review of Industrial and Organizational Psychology*, 2000 Volume 15
Edited by C.L. Cooper and I.T. Robertson. © 2000 John Wiley & Sons, Ltd

least to start with a quantitative approach in this area. Fourth, this review is about a psychological approach to entrepreneurship research. This approach is clearly controversial in the general entrepreneurship literature and, therefore, it is necessary to show that this approach is useful; we hope that the reader will be convinced of the importance of such an approach after looking at the evidence without biases. Finally, our conclusions should point out the areas that still demand further research and the methodological approaches that should be favored in future entrepreneurship research.

Entrepreneurship research concentrates on small firms. Compared to bigger companies, small-scale enterprises have their specific strengths and weaknesses. Over the last decade, enterprises with fewer than 10 employees provided more new jobs than bigger companies (Mullhern, 1995). On the other hand, small-scale enterprises do not only add jobs faster than bigger companies but they also eliminate them faster because of a higher failure rate (Ripsas, 1998). However, small enterprises contribute to a high extent to a net growth in jobs both in the developed as well as in the developing countries (Birch, 1987; Bruederl, Preisendoefer & Ziegler, 1992; Mead & Liedholm, 1998). Compared to bigger companies, small-scale firms are more flexible, they act more quickly, they adapt more easily to changing market conditions, they are more innovative and have a closer understanding with their customers. On the other hand, small-scale enterprises often have a weak financial basis, lower-than-average wages, lower labor productivity, lack of strategic marketing approaches, less international orientation and are restricted to operating in highly segmented markets (Mulhern, 1995). Whereas these weaknesses occur in most industries, there are spectacular counter-examples, in which small and medium-sized firms actually achieve 100% of a niche world market (e.g., in the production of theatre curtains, cf. Simon, 1996).

In summary, research on small-scale enterprises has been an almost neglected field in organization research. The field can be described as young, at a formative stage and still in its infancy (Cunningham & Lischeron, 1991). It is multi-disciplinary as various approaches (e.g., psychology, sociology, economics, management, anthropology, and regional sciences) provide different insights to entrepreneurship. For psychologists it provides an interesting area in which the individual psychology of the owner/manager meshes with organizational conditions and which allows them to study predictors and effects of economic success. Thus, the field of entrepreneurship is a challenging area for academic research.

Unfortunately, it is a difficult field to get a complete overview on. Relevant literature in this area is distributed in many outlets and can be found in diverse journals such as the *Journal of Applied Psychology, Acadamy of Management Journal and Review, Administrative Science Quarterly, Journal of Small Business Management, Journal of Business Venturing, Entrepreneurship Theory and Practice, Journal of Management, Small Business Economics, World Development, Strategic Management Journal, Organization Studies*, and there are many articles in conference procedures such as Frontiers of Entrepreneurship Research, International Council of Small Business Conference Proceedings, and Academy of Management Conference Proceedings. Our search has been guided by looking into PsychLit, SCCI, and EconLit. Unfortunately, not all psychological articles in this area are referenced in these databases, which makes it very probable that there are contributions to the field that we have overlooked.

## A GENERAL MODEL OF ENTREPRENEURIAL SUCCESS

Figure 3.1 presents the general model that is the starting point of our review (the Giessen–Amsterdam model of entrepreneurial success). It is interdisciplinary, taking into consideration most areas that have been studied in entrepreneurship research. As such, it helps us to organize this chapter as we will describe the literature referring to every single box. However, looking at the arrows one can see that it is a model that clearly has controversial implications. For example, there are no direct arrows from personality, human capital, or environment to success although such relationships have often been studied. The reasoning behind is rather simple: we assume that there is no success without actions. Actions are mainly determined by goals and by strategies. Thus, the concept of action is central to this model and the strategies and tactics of action is the bottleneck through which all entrepreneurial success is or is not accomplished. All strategies and tactics are goal-oriented and therefore, all entrepreneurial success has to start to look at these variables (obviously, most studies do not do that and therefore, show less power to predict success than is possible). Of course, both goals and strategies may turn out to be wrong, inefficient, or misplaced in a certain environment. Consequently, prior success and failure have an effect on modifying goals and strategies. However, we think that the market is made up of actors who have goals, at least rudimentary strategies, and ideas about how to proceed with their business. For this reason, all of the influences of personality, human capital, and environment on success have to be mediated by strategies and tactics of actions. This concept differs strongly from the theoretical stance of the ecological approach which assumes that essentially a random process of actions is shaped and selected by the environment, including the function of the environment to produce certain failure and success rates. We shall discuss this theory in more detail in the section about environment.

Our point of view will be taken up again in the conclusions at the end of this chapter. At the moment, the Giessen–Amsterdam model of entrepreneurial success will be used simply as a convenient way of guiding the subsections of the chapter. In principle, the Giessen–Amsterdam model can be used on different levels of analysis—the organizational level and the individual level of the firm owner. The level of analysis issue (cf. Klein & Sorra, 1996) has a slightly different function in the area of entrepreneurship because company

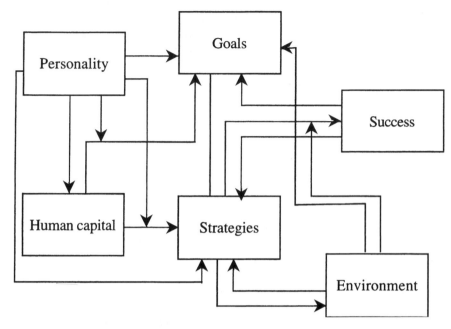

**Figure 3.1**   The Giessen–Amsterdam Model of small business owners' success

size determines which level is the adequate one. In large companies, the right level of analysis of variables that determines organizational success is the organizational level (an owner may have very different ideas of where this company should go from what it actually does); in small firms, the firm owner is typically the source of action of his firm. When there are only four or five employees in a firm, the owner usually has a much stronger impact on company policy, company culture and the company's actions than in larger firms. Thus, the potential differences between individual and organizational level variables are larger in bigger organizations and become increasingly smaller in small organizations. Consequently, an individual level of analysis—using the personality, human capital, goals, strategies and environment of the individual owner—can profitably be used to study success in these firms (Frese, Van Gelderen & Ombach, 2000). In middle-sized companies, the level of analysis issue is of major importance and it really needs to be empirically determined to which extent data from the owner/manager are useful predictors of success or not.

## DEFINITION ISSUES: ENTREPRENEURS, BUSINESS OWNERS AND OTHER CONCEPTS

As in any new field, there is no agreed upon definition of entrepreneurship, entrepreneurs, business owners, and so forth (Cunningham & Lischeron,

1991; Gartner, 1985). Furthermore, founders and owners/managers constitute a highly heterogeneous group that defies a common definition (Gartner, 1985).

The focus of this review is on small-scale enterprises, and on the founders and the owners of these firms. Some authors differentiate between entrepreneurs, small business owners, founders, and chief executive officers (CEOs). Carland, Hoy, Boulton and Carland (1984) distinguished entrepreneurs from small business owners. An entrepreneur is innovative, employs strategic management practices, and manages his business for the purpose of profit and growth (Carland et al., 1984, p. 358). A business owner establishes the enterprise to follow personal goals. Focusing on innovative behavior, this definition follows Schumpeter (1935) who emphasized the creative activities of the innovator. Other researchers consider risk-bearing as the key factor in entrepreneurship (Mill, 1984; Palmer, 1971; Liles, 1974).

However, if one restricts the concept of entrepreneur to innovative behavior (or risk-taking), one needs a clear definition of innovation. Since innovation research is also an area with vague boundaries and difficult conceptual arguments (cf. West & Farr, 1990), one does not really gain a lot of conceptual clarity with Carland et al.'s approach (Gartner, 1988, p. 60). Moreover, it restricts the definition to a very small group of people (e.g., is Bill Gates an innovator or is the only innovator the person who developed the first direct manipulation approach in software?).

For all of the definition problems, we agree with Gartner (1988) who used a descriptive and behavioral definition: 'Entrepreneurship is the creation of new organizations' (p. 62). Thus, entrepreneurs are the founders of new firms. This definition may again be too restrictive because it implies that once the company is established entrepreneurship ends. Therefore, founding, owning, and managing a firm are the important aspects of entrepreneurship. This comes close to Hisrich's (1990) definition of entrepreneurship: 'Entrepreneurship is the process of creating something different with value by devoting the necessary time and effort, assuming the accompanying financial, psychic, and social risks, and receiving the resulting rewards of monetary and personal satisfaction' (p. 209). In contract to Hisrich, one can argue that numerous non-profit organizations are created by entrepreneurs as well.

Often articles do not clearly describe their samples and even combine different groups into one sample without differentiating them. Consequently, it is difficult to compare results of different studies. Research projects should carefully select the sample appropriate to answer their research question. The following groups can be differentiated:

1. Entrepreneurs are founders, owners, and managers of organizations. Thus, to be simply an owner/manager is not enough to be included in this group (e.g., after having taken over the business from one's parents).

2.   Managers may be entrepreneurial to a certain extent but they typically work with other people's money and not with their own. Thus, they can leave the organization and organizational death does not have the same implications for them as it has for entrepreneurs. However, there is a discussion about corporate entrepreneurship in existing organizations looking at managers from an entrepreneurial point of view (cf. Hisrich, 1990).

3.   Size matters and should be taken into consideration. Firm owners without any employees are in a very different psychological situation than owners who employ at least one person. Closing down is obviously much more difficult if one has to fire employees than if one just packs up and takes a job somewhere else. One should have at least one employee to be included in the group of entrepreneurs. Size also matters in other ways. Is the organization still easy to lead and with only a few employees (e.g. up to 10), the psychological prerequisites are different than if one has to deal with a small-scale firm of up to 50 employees (1–50 employees constitutes the European Union definition of small-scale firms)? More delegation and management are needed in a firm above 10 employees. Starting with 50 employees, we should talk about mid-size firms.

4.   Finally, one needs to differentiate between studies which are based on representative samples of small-scale enterprises and those with selected business samples, for example high-tech firms, innovative firms, fast growing firms.

## CHARACTERISTICS OF THE ENTREPRENEUR

There are several approaches in describing the entrepreneur: trait, motivational, human capital, and typological approaches. Early approaches typically focused on personality characteristics of the entrepreneur. It is necessary to separate two issues in the following discussion: the emergence and the success of entrepreneurs. There should be different processes by which a person decides to become an entrepreneur and by which a person achieves entrepreneurial success (Utsch, Rauch, Rothfuss & Frese, 2000). It makes sense that personality characteristics may be more important for the decision to become a founder than for success (Begley & Boyd, 1987; Herron & Robinson, 1993). Leadership research has shown that leadership emergence is greatly affected by personality traits (Lord, DeVader & Alliger, 1986) while leadership success is less clearly related to personality factors (Landy, 1989). Thus, in the following, we shall differentiate between emergence of entrepreneurship and success of small-scale enterprises even though this differentiation is not always made in the literature our review is based on.

## Personality and Emergence of Entrepreneurship

Studies on the emergence of entrepreneurship often study differences in personality characteristics between entrepreneurs and other populations, in particular managers. McClelland's (1961) early work on need for achievement initiated many studies on characteristics of the entrepreneur. A high need for achievement leads to a preference for challenging tasks of moderate difficulty rather than routine or very difficult tasks, to take personal responsibility for one's performance, to seek feedback on performance, and to look for new and better ways to improve one's performance. As described in the introduction, we would like to provide a first quantitative review even though the literature does not really allow a proper meta-analysis. Whenever there were a minimum of five studies providing the necessary data, the results are presented quantitatively. In entrepreneurship research both independent and dependent variables are often operationalized in very different ways; therefore, such a quantitative review always carries the risk of comparing apples and oranges. However, it still gives the reader additional information that cannot be obtained from a purely verbal review. Table 3.1 presents a quantitative comparison of business owners with other groups, mostly managers. We converted all data into one correlation. A high correlation indicates a close relationship between entrepreneurs' personality characteristics and being an entrepreneur.

**Table 3.1**    Need for achievement of business owners compared to other samples

| Study | $N$ | $r$ | Comments |
|---|---|---|---|
| Begley & Boyd (1987) | 239 | 0.15* | Founders vs. non-founders |
| Cromie & Johns (1983) | 83 | 0.01 | Entrepreneurs vs. managers |
| Utsch et al. (2000) | 177 | 0.50** | Business owners vs. managers |
| Bonnett & Furnham (1991) | 190 | 0.09 | Founders vs. non-founders |
| Green, David & Dent (1996) | 207 | 0.22** | Entrepreneurs vs. managers |
| Weighted mean correlation | 896 | 0.21** | |

Note: *p<0.05 ** p<0.01

Table 3.1 indicates that three of the five studies reviewed found entrepreneurs to be significantly higher in need for achievement than the comparison group. Two studies reported non-significant results. The weighted mean correlation is positive and significant. Thus, there is empirical support that entrepreneurs are higher in need for achievement than other populations. McCelland's need for achievement theory was widely criticized, most notably his use of the projective Thematic Apperception Test to measure needs because it does not have high reliability. However, its validity is high (Spengler, 1992). Additionally, the theory was applied to whole countries. But, since the theory focuses on individual motives the theory is strongly influenced by Western culture and values (Triandis, 1994).

Locus of control, a concept from Rotter's (1966) social learning theory, was tested with regard to characteristics of entrepreneurs. People with an internal locus of control believe themselves to be in control of their destiny. People with an external locus of control believe themselves to be controlled by others or by chance events. One might expect that business owners have a higher internal locus of control than other populations. However, results here are less consistent than results on need for achievement (Table 3.2). While Green, David and Dent (1996) reported negative relationships ($r = 0.05$, ns.), Cromie and Johns (1983) found strong differences between entrepreneurs and managers (Table 3.2). The weighted mean correlation indicates that there is a small, but positive relationship between internal locus of control and being an entrepreneur. Given the huge differences in the results of different studies, there seems to be some other variable moderating the relationship between internal locus of control and becoming a small business owner.

**Table 3.2**    Locus of control of business compared to other samples

| Study | N | r | Comments |
|---|---|---|---|
| Begley & Boyd (1987) | 239 | 0.01 | Founders vs. non-founders |
| Cromie & Johns (1983) | 83 | 0.31** | Entrepreneurs vs. managers |
| Brockhaus & Nord (1979) | 93 | 0.02 | Entrepreneurs vs. moved and promoted managers |
| Bonnett & Furnham (1991) | 190 | 0.18* | Rotter's economic locus of control |
| Rahim (1996) | 526 | 0.22** | Entrepreneurs vs. managers |
| Green, David & Dent (1996) | 207 | –0.05 | Entrepreneurs vs. managers |
| Weighted mean correlation | 1338 | 0.13** | |

Note: *p<0.05 **p<0.01

Additional personality variables have been addressed in various studies. However, they do not allow a quantitative review because they are typically single studies that have not been replicated. Utsch et al. (in press) found entrepreneurs to be higher in innovativeness, competitive aggressiveness, and autonomy than managers. In Begley and Boyd's (1987) study, business founders were higher in risk-taking and had more tolerance to ambiguity than non-founders. Entrepreneurs were higher on a primacy of business scale (Cromie& Jones, 1983) and on intrinsic work motivation (Green, David & Dent, 1996). In contrast to Green, David and Dent (1996), Bonnett and Furnham (1991) reported that entrepreneurs scored higher on Protestant Work Ethic beliefs.

Business owners were frequently compared to managers, because managers are considered as a hard comparison group. There are good arguments for other contrasts as well. For example, when studying the emergence of entrepreneurship it is better to select people before they have become self-employed instead of comparing entrepreneurs and managers. Brandstaetter (1997) compared people interested in starting up their own company, entrepreneurs who had taken over a business, entrepreneurs who had set up their own business, and employed managers. The four samples were compared by using a 16PA adjective rating scale (Brandstaetter, (1987), a measure that is closely related to the 16-Personality-Factor-Questionnaire (Schneewind, Schroeder & Cattell, 1983). Personality characteristics of founders were similar to those of people who were interested in starting up their own company. However, founders were more stable and more independent than were entrepreneurs who had taken over a business or than managers. While such a design is strictly speaking not appropriate to detect causal relationships, it provides further insight into the issue of emergence. For example, since people who are interested in founding are quite similar to the founders, one can question the argument that founding an enterprise changes one's self-interpretation.

The literature about the emergence of entrepreneurship highlights that entrepreneurs are different from managers and other groups. However, the trait approach was widely criticized in entrepreneurship research because of the greater diversity among entrepreneurs themselves than between entrepreneurs and non-entrepreneurs. There is no average or typical venture creation (Gartner, 1985, p. 697). Gartner recommended a behavioristic approach to new venture creation. It is more important to ask what people do to enable venture creation rather than evaluating traits.

More recently, researchers have developed more sophisticated personality concepts. An attitude approach is concerned with a close match of an attitude and the behavioral requirements to be an entrepreneur (Fishbein & Ajzen, 1975). The Entrepreneurial Attitude Scale (EAO), which consists of achievement, self-esteem, personal control, and innovation is a fairly good instrument to distinguish entrepreneurs from non-entrepreneurs (Robinson, Stimpson, Huefner & Hunt, 1991). The task motivation theory is an additional example of studying entrepreneurs' characteristics on a more specified level (Miner, Smith & Bracker, 1989). Task motivation is a motivational pattern closely related to achievement motivation theory. The motivational pattern consists of five different roles: self-achievement, avoiding risks, feedback of results, personal innovation, and planning for the future. Task theory includes a look at the tasks to be performed, and thus represents the domain of entrepreneurship. Miner, Smith, and Bracker (1989) as well as Bellu (1988) could differentiate managers from entrepreneurs in their total task motivation, even though the five sub-scales distinguished between entrepreneurs and managers differentially in these two studies.

The trait theory and Gartner's (1988) position do not actually contradict each other; they just focus on different levels of specificity. Gartner recommended studying the entrepreneur on a very specific level of his or her behavior. Personality traits represent broad classes of behaviors, which are indeed weak predictors of specific behavior (Epstein & O'Brian, 1985). Task theory and attitude approaches come between the two positions because they focus on attributes representing classes of behavior without assuming them to be stable and situationally independent.

## Personality and Success

Personality characteristics of business owners were not only studied with respect to the emergence of entrepreneurship, but also with respect to the entrepreneurial success. A typical approach in this area is to ask business owners to fill in a general personality questionnaire and then correlate the personality scales with performance measures. Singh (1988) for example used five questionnaires that measured 29 scales. The author found that 8 personality scales were related positively to growth, 3 scales were negatively related, and 18 scales were unrelated to growth. A major problem of an approach like this is that the study is purely descriptive and lacks theory. Why should all the 16 personality factors (16PF) be related to small business success? Which factors are of particular importance? Researchers first have to identify a range of entrepreneurial characteristics, and then to apply these specific characteristics to the field (cf. Cromie & Johns, 1983). Timmons, Smollen and Dingee (1985) for example presented a list of 15 learnable and four not-so-learnable characteristics of entrepreneurship. The most frequently studied personality characteristics were need for achievement, risk-taking, and internal locus of control.

### Need for achievement

McClelland (1961) related the concept of achievement motivation to economic development and growth. Frey (1984) supported the result that need for achievement of nations leads to economic development. Cooper and Gimeno-Gascon (1992) reported that three out of four studies found a positive relationship between a need for achievement and the success of small-scale enterprises. One study showed that personality characteristics can change over time. It is possible to increase this motivation through training programs which then, in turn, increase business performance (Mirron & McClelland, 1979). Similarly, our review provided positive results in three out of six studies (Table 3.3). The weighted mean correlation provided significant positive results. However, the mean correlation is quite small. Possibly other variables moderate the need for an achievement–success relationship.

### Risk-taking

Chell, Haworth and Brearley (1991) described the risk-taker as someone 'who in the context of a business venture, pursues a business idea when the

**Table 3.3**  Need for achievement of business owners and its relationship with success

|  | N | r | Comments |
|---|---|---|---|
| Begley & Boyd (1987) | 147 | 0.05 | Mean correlation of 3 financial measures |
| Lorrain & Dussault (1988) | 64 | −0.04 | Successful/unsuccessful entrepreneurs |
| Rauch & Frese (1997)[1] | 71 | 0.27* | Achievement motivation was a second order factor consisting of higher order need strength, need for achievement, optimism, internal locus of control, self-efficacy |
| Miller & Toulouse (1986) | 97 | 0.01 | Mean correlation on 5 success measures |
| Goebel & Frese (1999) | 98 | 0.28** |  |
| Spencer & Spencer (1993) | 24 | 0.49* | Successful/unsuccessful entrepreneurs |
| Weighted mean correlation | 501 | 0.13** |  |

Note: *=p<0.05  **p<0.01
Only the Irish sample is presented because the West German sample is presented in Goebel & Frese (1999).

**Table 3.4**  Risk-taking of business owners and its relationship with success

| Study | N | r | Comments |
|---|---|---|---|
| Begley & Boyd (1987) | 147 | −0.06 | Mean correlation of 3 financial measures |
| Lorrain & Dussault (1988) | 64 | 0.00 | Successful/unsuccessful entrepreneurs |
| Brockhaus (1980) | 31 | −0.01 | N had to be estimated |
| Duchesnau & Gartner (1990) | 26 | −0.39* | Successful vs. unsuccessful entrepreneurs |
| Singh (1988) | 224 | −0.18* |  |
| Goebel & Fese (1999) | 97 | 0.11 |  |
| Weighted mean correlation | 589 | −0.08* |  |

Note: *p<0.05  **p<0.01

probability of succeeding is low' (p. 42). In general, people assume small business owners to be high risk-takers. However, the results of the quantitative review indicate that high risk-taking is negatively associated with business success (Table 3.4). The relationship is small.

However, according to Timmons, Smollen and Dingee (1985), successful entrepreneurs take calculated risks, a position which suggests a non-linear relationship between risk-taking and success. Similarly, Begley and Boyd (1987) found that risk-taking predicted success only up to a certain point beyond which risk-taking had a negative effect on success. Some inconsistencies about risk-taking and its relationship to success might be due to different perspectives of considering something as risky. From an observer's point of view a particular behavior might be viewed as highly risky while a business owner might see the same behavior as an attempt to minimize risk (Chell, Haworth & Brearley, 1991). Another issue is that to become an entrepreneur is risky but running a business in a risky way might be dangerous.

*Locus of control*

Rotter (1966) differentiated between internal and external locus of control. Since business owners with an external locus of control believe they are in the control of other people or chance events they are assumed to be less active in their daily work and thus, less successful. While only one study reported a significant positive relationship between internal locus of control and business success (Goebel & Frese, 1999), the weighted mean correlation of six studies was small but significantly positive (Table 3.5). Thus, there is empirical evidence for a relationship between internal locus of control and business success.

With regard to small business success other personality characteristics have been studied. Brandstaetter (1997, see above) showed that the same traits related to the decision of starting up a business were also related to business success. Emotional stability and independence correlated positively with

**Table 3.5**   Quantitative review of locus of control of business owners and its relationship with success

|  | $N$ | $r$ | Comments |
|---|---|---|---|
| Begley & Boyd (1987) | 147 | −0.08 | Mean correlation of 3 financial measures |
| Brockhaus (1980) | 31 | 0.29 | No $N$ of subgroups available |
| Duchesnau & Gartner (1990) | 26 | 0.37 | Success vs. failure |
| Lorrain & Dussault (1988) | 62 | −0.02 | Successful/unsuccessful entrepreneurs |
| Miller & Toulouse (1986) | 97 | 0.12 | |
| Goebel & Frese (1999) | 97 | 0.35** | |
| Weighted mean correlation | 460 | 0.11* | |

Note: *p<0.05  **p<0.01

subjective success measures. Miner, Smith and Bracker's (1994) task motivation theory is an example of measuring personality characteristics at a more specific level (see above). All five subscales were related to success, the total task motivation index explained 15–24% of variance in growth measures. However, Baum (1995) reported that general traits operate through more specific concepts of competencies, business strategies, and growth motivation. This result confirms the theoretical position of Herron and Robinson (1993) that motivation and behavior mediate the personality–success relationship.

### Personality Reconsidered

Personality factors have been criticized on both theoretical and empirical grounds. Gartner (1985) argued theoretically, that the diversity among entrepreneurs is much larger than differences between entrepreneurs and non-entrepreneurs. Since there is no average entrepreneur any personality description is found wanting. He therefore argues stopping looking for personality variables that have an impact on emergence and on success. Empirically, the overview of studies in this article shows that there are differences between entrepreneurs and managers, and that there is a relationship between personality and success, although the correlations found are not high.

However, both approaches—the personality proponents and their critics— have overlooked the significant advances that have been made in personality research during the last 20 years. We therefore think that there is good reason to be interested in personality again. However, one will have to use a more sophisticated theoretical approach, which is outlined in several points below.

1. A general trait can predict behavior (starting up a business) only through certain mediating processes (Epstein & O'Brian, 1985). The most important mediating processes are strongly related to actions (cf. the Giessen–Amsterdam model in Figure 3.1). Very similarly, Herron and Robinson (1993) argued that motivation is the mediator through which personality traits determine entrepreneurial behaviors. Baum (1995) showed that business strategies and growth motivation mediated the relationship between general traits and business outcomes. Rauch and Frese (1997) found that planning mediated the relationship between achievement orientations and success. Similarly, Goebel and Frese (1999) found that the relationship between personality and success is mediated by strategies. Thus, personality is related to business outcomes through more specific mediating processes.

2. Both the content of the personality variable and the level of specificity need to be defined carefully for the study. A general personality approach, such as when using the 16PF test (Cattell, Eber & Tatsouka, 1970) or the Big Five (Costa & McCrae, 1988) is not related to the content of entrepreneurship. Why should neuroticism, extroversion,

openness, agreeableness, and conscientiousness be strongly related to entrepreneurial success? Thus, such studies will definitely lead to questionable results. On the other hand, there is strong evidence that a more specific trait (such as the achievement motive) is related to the decision to start up a company, as our overview shows. Fishbein and Ajzen (1975) and Bandura (1997) have argued forcefully for specific measures of personality and attitude/belief processes and they show that prediction is much higher with such approaches. For this reason, entrepreneurial orientation is more closely related to the decision to become an entrepreneur and even to success than these general traits (we shall describe the studies on entrepreneurial orientation later). Baum (1995) found that predictors that are closely related to entrepreneurial behaviour have stronger effects than more general predictors. In any case, one needs to do at least a rudimentary task analysis to carefully select those personality characteristics that are potentially related to the entrepreneurial task domain.

3.  The discussion on entrepreneur's personality is very similar to the debate on leadership research. Early leadership research focused on the leader's personality (see reviews by Bass, 1990; Kirkpatrick & Locke, 1991). Later, the trait approach was criticized (Stodgill, 1948). The charismatic leadership theory reintroduced personality issues, but now these characteristics are specifically related to the domain of leading people (House, 1977). As in leadership research, entrepreneurship research should conceptualize entrepreneurs' characteristics in terms of more specific attributes instead of using broad trait measures. In the words of Robinson et al. (1991, p. 13): 'The problem is not the absence of psychological characteristics, but rather the theories and methods used to identify those characteristics.'

4.  Today's personality psychology would argue that the interaction between individuals' characteristics and situational conditions predicts entrepreneurial behavior better than any one of these factors alone (Magnusson & Endler, 1977). For example, only if the entrepreneur is active in an area where networks are important (e.g. consulting business), should extroversion play a role. Conscientiousness should play a role only in an area where there is a strong emphasis on quality control, and so on. Research on entrepreneurs should therefore take the situational demands into account.

5.  The impact of personality can vary depending on a situation being strong or weak (Mischel, 1968). In a strong situation there should be less impact of the personality than in a weak situation. When the entrepreneur is told that he has to develop a good business plan—otherwise he would not get money from the bank—it is unlikely that personality differences determine whether or not he will write a business plan. This is a strong situation. Craftspeople often work in strong situations and, therefore,

personality differences should play a smaller role in determining behavior in the crafts sector than in the new technology sector.

An example of a weak situation is when one has to decide whether one actually wants to start up a company. Thus, personality variables should be more important in the emergence of entrepreneurs than, for example, in a situation where the company has more than 200 employees (it is unlikely that one can escape the necessity to employ a professional manager at this point). Some authors argue that personality is more important for the emergence of entrepreneurship than for success (Herron & Robinson, 1993; Begley & Boyd, 1987; Utsch et al., 1999).

6. However, it should be clear that to a certain extent people actively select environments. Thus, the selection of a market niche is an influence on the environment. This depends on the goal-oriented strategy of an entrepreneur, which in turn is influenced by personality characteristics (Goebel & Frese, 1999). Obviously, it depends on the skills and abilities of entrepreneurs to perceive opportunities in the environment—again an area in which personality traits (e.g., intelligence) may play a role (Zempel, 1999).

7. Any single personality trait will never have a strong relationship with any outcome variables (such as making a decision to become an entrepreneur). The decision to start up a firm is probably due to a whole range of personality characteristics and not just to one. Thus, one should never expect a high correlation to appear and if it does, it may be an indicator of a badly designed study rather than an example of a 'smashing' empirical finding. Consequently, the multiple effects of several relevant personality characteristics rather than single traits should be analyzed.

8. Testing hypotheses at a given alpha level always implies the risk of rejecting a hypothesis even though the hypothesis is valid in reality (Beta-error). This risk is even higher when effects are small in general. Therefore, a non-significant result, such as a comparison of managers with a sample of only 31 business owners (Brockhaus & Nord, 1979) should not be overestimated.

Considering these arguments, it is obvious that one cannot expect strong main effects of personality on small business success. However, we have shown that personality is important, but we would expect small correlations since personality is related to success through mediating and moderating processes (see Figure 3.1).

## Typologies

Since small-scale business owners represent a highly heterogeneous group, it makes sense to attempt to classify them into types and sub-groups. These typologies differ in the extent to which they use different attributes, for example demographic characteristics, psychological characteristics, or business strategies. Crafts people and opportunists are often differentiated: Smith (1967) for example, carried out 52 interviews with owner/managers of manufacturing firms. 'Craftsman entrepreneurs' came from a blue-collar background, had a lower education and no management experience, and they restricted their source of finance to personal savings, money from relatives, or friends. Crafts people tended to have rigid firms. In contrast, 'opportunistic entrepreneurs' had a middle-class background, a broader education, management experience, they sought new opportunities, developed more innovative and more diverse strategies, delegated more, were proactive, and used many sources of finance. Opportunists tended to have adaptive firms. Firms of opportunistic entrepreneurs had higher growth rates than those of craftsmen (Smith & Miner, 1983). Woo, Cooper and Dunkelberg (1988) confirmed the two types of Smith's (1967) study. More recently, the inventor-entrepreneur was introduced as a third distinguishable type (Miner, Smith & Bracker, 1992). The inventor-entrepreneur had a certain craftsman-orientation with a high priority placed on product development and patent production.

Chell, Haworth and Brearley (1991) classified 31 firms by using personality characteristics, strategies, and demographic attributes. The prototypical entrepreneur is alert to business opportunities regardless of resources currently controlled, he is innovative, and he uses a variety of sources of finance. He is a high-profile image-maker and strives to be the best. He constantly tries to modify the environment and create situations which result in change. In contrast, the caretaker does not show any of these behaviors. Between the two extremes there are two other types which are less clearly defined. The quasi-entrepreneur is similar to the entrepreneur but does not have all of the characteristics of the entrepreneur, for example he is less innovative and less proactive. The administrator is more reactive and takes opportunities, but not regardless of current resources (Chell, Haworth & Brearley, 1991, p. 72).

By using psychological attributes, Miner (1996) categorized business owners into four different personality types. The 'personal achiever' is similar to the classical entrepreneur proposed by McClelland (1961). His characteristics are a need to achieve, a desire to get feedback, and to plan and to set goals, strong personal initiative, strong commitment to the venture, internal locus of control, and a belief in personal goals rather than those of others. The pattern of 'supersales persons' consists of five overlapping characteristics: a capacity to understand and to feel with another person, a desire to help others, a belief that social processes are very important, a need for positive relationships with others, and a belief that a sales force is crucial to carrying out company strategy. The 'real manager' possesses 13 characteristics that are similar to those of managers. Some of his characteristics are: a high supervisory ability, a need for occupational achievement, a need for self-actualization, positive attitudes towards authority, a desire to compete with others, directive in cognitive style and so on. The fourth type, the 'expert idea-generator', is characterized by a desire to personally innovate, a belief in new product development, high intelligence, a high conceptual cognitive style, and a desire to avoid risks. Miner (1997) showed that firms founded by personal achievers had grown more than those founded by other types. There was also evidence that business owners who were characterized by more than one pattern were more likely to be successful.

Typologies have improved our knowledge about small-scale enterprises not only because they contributed to the description of entrepreneurs and their behavior but also because they contributed to theory development (Woo, Cooper & Dunkelberg, 1988; Doty & Glick, 1994). But there are also important criticisms. First, different researchers used different samples and different attributes to categorize enterprises. Most typologies have not been replicated. As a matter of fact, most typologies have not been adequately tested (e.g. with cluster analysis). A second problem is the labelling of the types. Woo, Cooper and Dunkelberg (1988) as well as Smith and Miner (1983) identified two distinct types of business owners and both studies used the terms 'craftsmen' and 'opportunists' to describe them. Did both studies identify the same type of business owners? Probably not, because both studies used different attributes to describe their typology. Third, typologies are simplistic because they focus on extreme or proto-typical configurations and only a small part of business owners fit exactly in a certain type. Chell, Haworth and Brearley (1991) tried to reduce that problem by introducing two intermediate types (quasi-entrepreneur, administrator). In the fourth, and probably the most important, critique it is argued that typologies are rather descriptive and often do not pay enough attention to theory development.

## Human Capital

The human capital theory is concerned with the knowledge and experiences of small-scale business owners. The general assumption is that the human capital of the founder improves small firms' chances of survival (Brueder, Preisendoefer & Ziegler, 1992). Human capital acts as a resource. Human capital makes the founder more efficient in organizing processes or in attracting customers and investors. Different studies used various operationalizations of human capital. Brueder, Preisendoefer and Ziegler (1992) distinguished between general human capital—years of schooling and years of work experience—and specific human capital—industry-specific experience, self-employment experience, leadership experience, and having a self-employed father. In Table 3.6, we aggregated various measures of human capital to compare the results of different studies. The general trend indicates a small positive relationship between human capital and success.

In different studies that were conducted there appears to be a relatively consistent relationship between business owners' level of education, their

**Table 3.6**   Human capital of business owners and its relationship with success

|  | N | r | Comments |
|---|---|---|---|
| Chandler & Hanks (1996) | 102 | 0.15 | Same sample as in Chandler & Jansen (1992) |
| Chandler & Jansen (1992) | 134 | 0.07 | Founder's competencies |
| Duchesnau & Gartner (1990) | 26 | 0.42* | Successful vs. unsuccessful entrepreneurs |
| Goebel & Frese (1999) | 91 | 0.22* |  |
| Lussier (1995) | 216 | −0.11 | Successful vs. failed enterprises |
| Chandler & Hanks (1994) | 155 | 0.19* | Mean correlation of 2 success measures |
| Lorrain & Dussault (1988) | 69 | 0.14 | Successful/unsuccessful entrepreneurs |
| Weighted mean correlation | 793 | 0.09* |  |

Note: *p<0.05  **p<0.01

industry-specific experience, and their management experience on the one hand and success on the other hand (cf. Cooper, Dunkelberg & Woo, 1988; Dyke, Fischer & Reuber, 1992; Gimeno, Folta, Cooper & Woo, 1997; Bruederl, Preisendoefer & Ziegler, 1992). Goebel (1995) showed that a business owner's personality explained more variance in success than his or her human capital. Additionally, planning and leading style mediated the relationship between human capital of business owners and success.

The human capital theory has an important implication. Since it is concerned with knowledge and capacities, the theory implies processes as well: human capital can be trained and improved. Additionally, if human capital acts as a resource it might be interesting to study the human capital of employees in small-scale enterprises and its implications on success as well. In manufacturing settings it was shown that a human resource management (HRM) system was related to performance particularly when combined with a quality manufacturing strategy (Youndt, Snell, Dean & Lepak, 1996).

In summary there is some support for the human capital hypotheses. However, different studies point out different aspects of human capital to be important. Since our quantitative review showed a small relationship between human capital and success (Table 3.6), it may very well be that small improvements of performance are not worth the effect of human capital unless the firm is in a situation where small differences in performance affect its survival. Moreover, human capital only functions via concrete goals and behaviors. Therefore, the Giessen–Amsterdam framework includes the preposition that human capital is related to business success via goals and strategies (Figure 3.1).

## GOALS

Goals and objectives are often not separated from strategies in management theory (exceptions are Schendel & Hofer, 1979 and Venkatraman, 1989). A psychological concept would relate goal development and goal decision to a task. However, goals differ from strategies because strategies imply an action. Strategies (and tactics) are attempts to translate the goals into actions (Frese, 1995; Hacker, 1985).

Klandt (1984) distinguished between goals related to the start up of an enterprise and goals related to the existing enterprise. Goals or motives to become self-employed can be categorized into push and pull factors (Stoner & Fry, 1982). Push factors imply that a current situation is perceived as dissatisfying. By comparing enterprises in 10 different countries over a period of more than 30 years, Bögenhold and Staber (1990) found a positive relationship between self-employment rates and unemployment rates. The authors concluded that unemployment leads to self-employment. Similarly, Galais (1998) reported that in East Germany, 47% of business owners stated that unemployment had been a motive for becoming self-employed as compared to 8% in West Germany. The unemployment rate was three times higher in East Germany compared to West Germany (Statistisches Bundesamt, 1994). Brockhaus and Nord (1979) found that entrepreneurs were less satisfied with their previous work than promoted managers. Thus, there is support for the push hypothesis, even though there are regional differences. When self-employment is considered as a positive future option, pull factors might constitute the main reasons for becoming self-employed. By using factor-analysis, Scheinberg and McMillan (1988) identified six motives for becoming self-employed: need for approval, perceived instrunentality of wealth, degree of communitarianism, need for personal development, need for independence, need to escape. Only the last factor represented a push factor. Shane, Kolvereid and Westhead (1991) found a four-factor solution of reasons for founding a new firm: recognition, independence, learning, and roles. One can argue, however, that pull factors were underrepresented in this study because there were no items on unemployment or on previous jobs. Despite the fact that several studies have shown that different motives lead to business start ups, once the enterprise is established these motives have minimal influence on subsequent business success (Birley & Westhead, 1994; Galais, 1998).

With regard to the goals of existing enterprises, it is important to distinguish between growth targets and autonomy targets (Katz, 1994). Growth goals are related to growth expectations (Davidsson, 1989) as well as to business growth (Baum, 1995).

According to goal-setting theory, high and specific targets are main motivators in working organizational settings and predict performance (Locke & Latham, 1990). The theory also applies to small-scale enterprises (Baum, 1995; Frese, Krauss & Friedrich, 2000). Leadership theory has recently focused on visionary (or charismatic, transformational) leadership. The importance of visions is also discussed in the entrepreneurship literature. Collins and Porras (1994) indicated that visionary companies have a stronger organizational culture and they are more successful than non-visionary companies. Baum, Locke and Kirkpatrick (1998) found direct and indirect causal effects of vision attribute, vision content, and vision communication on small-venture performance. In entrepreneurial companies visions might be more important than in bigger organizations because of the relatively close contact between entrepreneur and employees, customers, and suppliers (Baum, Locke & Kirkpatrick, 1998). Therefore, goals and visions are important areas in entrepreneurship research.

## STRATEGIES (CONTENT, PROCESS, ENTREPRENEURIAL ORIENTATIONS)

Chandler (1962), Anshoff (1965), and Porter (1980) emphasized that strategies are particularly important for small-business success. Ten years ago, Low and McMillan (1988) criticized the fact that only a few good empirical studies had been done in the area of entrepreneurship strategies. Strategies can be studied on the firm and on the individual owner's level. It is important to distinguish between three dimensions of business strategies (Figure 3.2). Olson and Bokor (1995) distinguished between strategic processes and strategic content. Strategic content is concerned with the type of decision. The strategic process focuses on strategy formulation and implementation. More recently, researchers have focused on firm-level entrepreneurship. Entrepreneurial orientation refers to processes, practices, and decision-making activities that lead to new entries (Lumpkin & Dess, 1996). In our opinion entrepreneurial orientation can be conceptualized as a third strategic dimension. Whereas strategic content is concerned with a specific type of strategy, entrepreneurial orientation represents a general strategic orientation that is dependent on environmental and organizational factors. The framework in Figure 3.2 shows that each type of strategy is implemented through different categories of the strategic process, based on a certain entrepreneurial orientation. Thus, all the three strategy dimensions can be crossed with another. The following three paragraphs will discuss each dimension separately.

### Strategic Content

Strategic content is concerned with the type of business decisions. Porter's (1980) and Miles and Snow's (1978) typologies of strategies initiated some research on small-scale enterprises. Porter (1980) distinguished three generic strategies: focus, differentiation, and cost leadership. A focused strategy means concentrating on a particular product or market segment. A differentia-

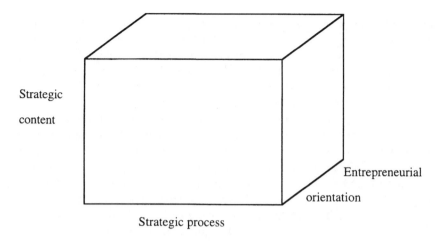

**Figure 3.2**   Three dimensions of business strategies

tion strategy means creating a product or service that customers see as unique. Cost leadership focuses on becoming a low-cost producer in an industry without sacrificing quality and service. With regard to new entries, focused strategies have several competitive advantages because they avoid heavy competition with established enterprises and are able to focus their limited resources on a narrow market segment. Thus, the theory would predict that focused strategies outperform broad strategies. With a small sample of 17 ventures, Sandberg and Hofer (1987) analyzed the relationship between Porter's (1980) generic strategies and success. In contrast to the theory, there was evidence that differentiated strategies outperformed focused strategies. Sandberg and Hofer (1987) found even stronger support for a contingent strategy–success relationship. They found that in an industry at an early stage of evolution, broad strategies outperformed focused strategies. In an industry at a late stage of evolution narrow strategies were better than broad strategies. Similar results were found in a survey of 491 independent bank formations over a 5-year period: broad strategies were better than focused strategies (Baumford, Dean & McDougall, 1997). Successful craft retailers used cost leadership and differentiation strategies more often, while they did not use focused strategies (Kean, Niemeyer & Miller, 1996). McNamee and McHugh (1989) found differentiated strategies to be related with profitability in the clothing industry but not focused strategies and cost leadership. These findings contradict Porter's (1980) assumptions and suggest that focused strategies are not better than broad strategies.

The Miles and Snow (1978) typology classifies firms according to four different strategic orientations: prospectors, defenders, analyzers, and reactors. Prospectors constantly seek new opportunities and focus on product development. In contrast, defenders try to control secure niches in their industries and do not engage in product or market development. Analyzers combine characteristics of both prospectors and defenders. Reactors do not follow a conscious strategy. The typology proposed that defenders, analyzers and prospectors will outperform reactors. Reviewing the empirical literature on the Miles and Snow typology, Zahra and Pearce II (1990) questioned the validity of the typology as well as the link between strategic types and performance. However, by comparing Miles and Snow's (1987) typology with Minzberg's (1983) theory, Miles and Snow's typology was confirmed, the configurational fit explained 24% in organizational effectiveness (Doty, Glick & Huber, 1993). Similarly, Conant, Mokwa and Varadarajan (1990) replicated the Miles and Snow typology successfully. Results suggest that prospector, analyzer and defender organizations outperform reactor organizations.

Olson and Bokor (1995) used a single dimension classification of strategies, namely product/service innovation. Schumpeter (1935) and Drucker (1985) argued that innovative behavior is a core characteristic of entrepreneurs. Moreover, innovative strategies were described to be successful particularly for small enterprises because they are seen as useful attempts to maintain market share, to produce below price level or to maintain flexibility (Heunks, 1996). Innovativeness can be defined as a characteristic of an individual person and innovation implementation effectiveness depends on a group of persons, and thus is a characteristic of an organization (Klein & Sorra, 1996). The literature on innovative strategies focused on the latter.

Several carefully conducted studies have shown a relationship between innovative strategies and success of small-scale enterprises (Brouwer & Kleinknecht, 1996; Roper, 1997; Heunks, 1998). However, there were nonsignificant results as well (Olson & Bokor, 1995). Since evidence of the innovativeness-success relationship is not really conclusive, some authors tested successfully moderating variables of the innovation-success relationship. They showed that innovations are more important for very small enterprises with less than 50 employees (Pfirmann, 1994; Brouwer & Kleinknecht, 1996; Heunks, 1996). Other moderator variables were formal planning (Olson & Bokor, 1995), environmental conditions (Miller & Frisen, 1983; Acs & Gifford, 1996), and competitive position (Brouwer & Kleinknecht, 1996).

A weakness of research on strategic content is its lack of sophisticated classification systems. Business strategy categorizations, such as described by Porter (1980), fall short because they are related towards product, markets, and competitors only. A firm's strategy can also be related to suppliers, customers, employees, and environmental conditions. Therefore, we need to develop strategy classifications that reflect the whole domain of actions initiated by small-scale enterprises.

## Strategic Process Research

The strategic process is concerned with the formulation and implementation of strategic decisions (Olson & Bokor, 1995). Schendel and Hofer (1979) identified six tasks that constitute the process of strategic management: goal formulation, environment analysis, strategy formulation, strategy evaluation, strategy implementation and strategic control. However, most research on strategic processes is concerned with planning and its impact on small-business success. In numerous books and articles it has been taken for granted that planning is of particular importance to small firms' performance (Ryans, 1997). Therefore, training programs for entrepreneurs usually include the development of start up plans. However, empirical investigation of the planning–success relationship did not lead to consistent results. While some carefully designed studies have shown that planning in the founding phase was related to success of small businesses (Ackelsberg & Arlow, 1985; Bracker, Keats & Pearson, 1988; Jungbauer-Gans & Preisendoerfer, 1991), there have been contradicting results as well (Lumpkin, Shrader & Hills, 1998; Lyles, Baird, Orris & Kuratko, 1995; Robinson & Pearce, 1983; Shuman, Shaw & Sussman, 1985). In an early review, Robinson and Pearce (1984) concluded that many small-scale enterprises do not plan at all. However, most studies indicated that enterprises that do plan are more successful. In a more recent meta-analysis Schwenk and Shrader (1993) compared 14 studies on the planning–success relationship in small-scale enterprises. They found a small, positive relationship between planning and performance (effect size $d=0.40$) and concluded that other variables might moderate the planning–success relationship.

Unfortunately, not many studies analyzed the conditions under which performance is enhanced by planning. In a cross-cultural study Rauch and Frese (1997) showed that planning is differentially important in different countries. Planning is valued and important in a culture with high values in uncertainty avoidance, because plans can be seen as an attempt to get control of an uncertain future (Thurston, 1983). In Ireland planning had a negative effect on success, most probably because the environment demanded flexibility rather than strict adherence to a plan. Ireland is one of the cultures with the lowest uncertainty avoidance in Europe (Hofstede, 1991). In Germany, a country with a high level of uncertainty avoidance, planning was positively related to success. In a longitudinal study, the planning–success relationship was moderated by environmental conditions (Rauch & Frese, 1998). Planning predicted success in a hostile or uncertain environment but not in a certain and non-hostile environment. Risseeuw and Masurel (1993) found that in high dynamic environments planning was negatively correlated with success. Thus, environmental conditions are moderating the planning–success relationship. In summary, there is some evidence that planning is related to small-business success, but further research is called for to clarify the conditions under which planning might be a powerful tool.

Frese, Van Gelderen and Ombach (1998) looked at planning and proactivity at the same time. They differentiated between complete planning, critical point strategy, opportunistic strategy, reactive strategy, and habits. The main finding was that a reactive strategy is negatively related to success. This could be shown to be a causal process and it was replicated in three studies in Africa (all of them reported in Frese, 2000). These results were confirmed by research on the Miles and Snow (1978) typology (see section above on strategic content). The reactor firm, which is not following a conscious strategy, was least successful. Thus, a reactive strategy has negative consequences for small-scale enterprises.

## Entrepreneurial Orientation

The empirical investigation of 'entrepreneurship' was a major topic in small-scale business research. But criticism of viewing entrepreneurship as an individual's psychological profile has led to the operationalization of entrepreneurship as a firm-level behavior (Covin & Slevin, 1986). We have already discussed the level-of-analysis issue earlier (see first section above).

According to Covin and Slevin (1986), entrepreneurial firms are those in which top managers employ entrepreneurial management styles and operating management philosophies. The entrepreneurial behavior of those firms focuses on risk-taking, innovation, and proactiveness. Lumpkin and Dess (1996) conceptualized entrepreneurial orientation to consist of five dimensions: innovation, proactiveness, risk-taking, autonomy and competitive aggressiveness. Venkatraman (1989) identified six dimensions of strategic orientation: aggressiveness, analysis, defensiveness, futurity, proactiveness, and riskiness. In Covins and Slevin's (1986) conceptualization of entrepreneurial orientation the dimensions covary, whereas Lumpkin and Dess (1996) suggested that the dimensions may vary independently, depending on the environmental and organizational context.

Since the concept of entrepreneurial orientation is relatively new, there is a limited body of empirical literature on that concept. Tan (1997) showed that the strategic orientation of small firms is related to the business environment. Innovativeness, proactiveness, and risk-taking were positively correlated with environmental dynamism and complexity. Entrepreneurial orientation was studied with respect to small-firm performance as well. Covin and Slevin (1986) showed that entrepreneurship was highly related with company performance ($r=0.39$, $p<0.01$). Similarly, Wicklund (1988) reported strong direct relationships between entrepreneurial orientation and performance. Significant, but smaller relations between entrepreneurial orientation and success were found by Venkatraman (1989) and by Brown and Davidsson (1998). Lumpkin and Dess (1996) pointed out that the relationship between entrepreneurial orientation and success is contingent on environmental and organizational factors. Dess, Lumpkin and Covin (1997) analyzed a sample of

32 firms and found that entrepreneurial strategy-making is most strongly related with success when combined with low-cost strategy and high environmental uncertainty.

The concept of entrepreneurial orientation is relatively new and therefore it may be too early to assess its implications for small-scale enterprises. However, it would be interesting to evaluate the relationship between individual- and organizational-level entrepreneurship. Koop, De Reu an Frese (2000) found, for example, that entrepreneurial orientation of African (Ugandan) micro-enterprise owners was highly related to success. Moreover, this study suggests that personal initiative by the owner/manager may be the psychological characteristic that is behind the concept of entrepreneurial orientation (Frese & Fay, 2000).

## ENVIRONMENTAL CONDITIONS

Each enterprise is rooted in a specific environment. Boulding (1978) defined environment in a broad way as everything else outside a particular organization. Environment can be conceptualized at different levels of specificity (Castrogiovanni, 1991). At a specific level, environment implies resources available to the organization. The geographical or cultural context of organizations represents a broad macro-environmental level. Within each environmental level there are different dimensions of the environment.

### The Ecological Perspective

Ecologists are concerned with changes in organizational populations (Aldrich & Wiedenmayer, 1993). A central theoretical assumption is that the environmental shapes rates of entry, mortality, or changes of organizations (Singh, 1990). The ecological model draws upon the natural selection paradigm: an organization is subjected to environmental forces that have an effect on survival rates. Thus, the environments select the 'fittest' organizations. The ecological approach is concerned with the aggregate- or macro-environmental level and, therefore, industrial-level data are typically used within this theory.

The concepts 'liability of newness' and 'liability of smallness' are of particular interest for small-scale enterprises. Businesses start up with the 'liability of newness'. This means that newly founded firms have a higher risk of failure than older organizations (Hannan & Freeman, 1984; Singh, Tucker & House, 1986). Enterprises that survived the initial risk have reduced mortality rates because the environment selected only the strongest organizations. However, some studies support a non-linear relationship between age and survival. Bruederl, Preisendoerfer and Ziegler (1992) found support for a liability of adolescence: small businesses have a low mortality rate immediately after starting up. Then, the mortality rate increases to a maximum (after approximately 10 months of existence). Thereafter, the mortality rate declines in accordance with the liability of newness hypothesis.

The concept 'liability of smallness' describes the higher risk of failing for smaller organizations compared to bigger organizations. Both concepts are confounded because most new organizations tend to be small. Many studies do not separate these two effects adequately (Singh, 1990). However, there is empirical support for an independent effect of liability of smallness (Bruederl, Preisendoerfer & Ziegler, 1992).

'Density dependence' refers to processes that depend on the number of organizations in a population (Aldrich & Wiedemayer, 1993). Density dependence should affect business survival because it increases competitive pressures and resourcee-scarcity. Carroll and Hannan (1989) found that density at the time of founding has a positive effect on mortality rates in five different populations.

Dean and Meyer (1996) related characteristics of the industry environment to the emergence of new ventures. One aspect of industry environment was industry dynamism, which included increasing demands, modification of demands, and technological development. A second measure was on entry barriers, which refers to factors that were erected against new entries. The third dimension was organizational inertia, which refers to factors that constrain existing firms from taking advantage of already existing opportunities. Industry dynamism organizational inertia were positively related to venture formations. Entry barriers constrained venture creation.

The ecological perspective is criticized because of its determinism. The only possible thing an entrepreneur can do is to start up the business at the right time. The concept ignores the fact that individuals behave actively in a certain environment. The entrepreneur may adapt to a certain environment, but he may also select a specific environment or may try to change the environment. A company, for example, that tries to satisfy the needs of customers with specific preferences changes the environment. According to Aldrich and Wiedenmayer (1993), the trait approach is complementary to the ecological approach: the first implies micro-level analysis whereas the latter involves a macro-level approach. In contrast to the ecologists' view, the strategic choice perspective assumes that organizations are able to shape their environment (Child, 1972).

## The Task Environment and Contingency Approaches

Research about the task environment is concerned with how the individual enterprise interacts with customers, competitors and suppliers. A relatively broad body of empirical literature already exists on this environmental level. Dess and Beard (1984) categorized task environment into three bipolar dimensions: complexity, dynamism, and munificence. Complexity describes the homogeneity versus the heterogeneity of an environment. In a complex environment it is more difficult to get and to consider all the necessary information than it is in an easy environment. Dynamism describes the variability and unpredictability of the environment. Munificence falls into two subconcepts: ease of getting customers and ease of getting capital.

Sharfman and Dean (1991) showed with industry-level data that munificence had a non-significant negative relationship with performance, but that complexity and dynamism were positively related to success. Dynamism explained 32% of the variance of company performance. Thus, an unfavorable environment has positive consequences on business outcomes. This sounds implausible but immediately becomes more plausible if one realizes that they studied surviving companies. However, we also know from stress inoculation research, that reinterpreting stressors as challenges helps people to deal with stressors. Thus, having mastered challenges in the past leads to higher competence to deal with stressors in the future (Meichenbaum, 1985). Similar results were found by Shane and Kolvereid (1995) who studied small-scale enterprises in three countries. Results indicated that firm performance was highest when the national environment was perceived as less favorable. According to Swaminathan (1996) environmental conditions are of particular importance for newly founded enterprises because they have long-term consequences for business strategy, structure, and success. He showed that organizations founded in adverse environments have a higher initial mortality rate. But beyond a certain age, the surviving organizations had a lower mortality rate than those of organizations founded in less adverse environments.

The contingency theory has already been discussed when reviewing literature about the personality–success relationship (see section above on personality reconsidered). In this section it is assumed that environmental conditions are moderating the relationship between business strategies and success. In contrast to ecological theories, the successful business owners are actively assessing a given situation and then choosing the strategies that are most appropriate in that situation.

Sandberg and Hofer (1987) analyzed the industry structure and its impact on the relationship between strategies and venture performance. They found that in an industry at an early evolutionary stage, broad strategies outperform focused strategies. If the industry is at a late evolutionary stage, focused strategies are better than broad strategies. Romanelli (1989) analyzed a sample of 108 firms that produced minicomputers. He found that when industry sales are increasing generalists have a higher likelihood of early survival than specialists. When sales are declining, efficient organizations have a greater chance of surviving than aggressive organizations. Thus, a change in industry sales is an important contingent factor.

Covin and Slevin (1989) analyzed performance implications of small businesses in hostile environments. In a hostile environment, an organic structure and an entrepreneurial strategic posture were related to high performance, while in a non-hostile environment, a mechanistic structure and a conservative strategic posture were related to success. Similarly, competitive aggressiveness was related to performance in hostile environments, while it had negative consequences in non-hostile environments (Covin & Covin, 1990). Zahra (1996) showed that environmental conditions moderated the form and the strength of the relationship between technology strategy and business success. Pioneering, for example, was strongest related to success in dynamic environments, while followership was better in hostile environments.

Through the contingency theory our knowledge in the field has improved. The entrepreneur or the business can act on a given situation. Success is not determined by the environment but by the strategy–environment fit. However, we need to develop a system to classify contingent factors.

## OTHER ISSUES OF PSYCHOLOGICAL ENTREPRENEURSHIP RESEARCH

While the literature review was focusing on areas which are frequently evaluated and which are relevant from a psychological point of view, there are other important approaches to entrepreneurship we want to summarize briefly in this section.

A network approach assumes that the entrepreneur's ability to organize and coordinate networks between individuals and organizations is critical both for starting up a company and for business success. One can differentiate between formal networks (banks, Chamber of Commerce) and informal networks (friends, previous employers). Birley (1985) showed that formal support sources were hardly used, the institutions mostly mentioned being banks. Informal networks were used more often and were considered to be most helpful. Bruederl and Preisendoerfer (1998) showed that network support is related to both survival and growth of newly founded enterprises. Support from friends and relatives was more important than support from business partners, former employers, and coworkers. Related to the network approach, some researchers focused on the central role of information-seeking activities. Small business owners deal with a wide range of issues and they often have to make decisions while facing time and resource constraints. However, small business owners hardly ever use external information sources such as expert advice (Pineda, Lerner, Miller & Phillips, 1998). Information-seeking activities appeared to be dependent on the type of decision. Product-related decisions were correlated with more information seeking compared to employee-related or technical decisions. Another study showed that information-seeking activities are related to environmental threats and opportunities (Lang, Calantone & Gudmundson, 1997). Welsch and Young (1982) found that entrepreneurs' personality was related to the use of specific sources of information. Internal locus of control was positively related to the use of all information sources categories, while risk-taking correlated only with the use of personal sources of information.

Organizational life-cycle models have also been tested in entrepreneurship research. It is assumed that small enterprises face different sets of critical variables, depending on their stage of development. Dodge and Robbins (1992) tested a four-stage model that differentiated between formation, early growth, later growth, and stability. Planning was an important problem area in early live stages, while management problems become more important in later live stages.

Leadership issues are also discussed in entrepreneurship literature. Eggers, Leahy and Churchill (1996) studied 112 entrepreneurial companies by using 20 behavioral scales that measure CEO's leadership and management skills. Visionary leadership, communication, delegating, and performance facilitation were positively related to success. A longitudinal study found that visions of small business owners affect company performance directly as well as indirectly through vision communication to employees (Baum, Locke & Kirkpatrick, 1998). Another longitudinal study showed that participation of employees predicts growth and size of enterprises in the long run (Rauch & Frese, 1999).

Cognitive factors were related to entrepreneurial outcomes as well. Different factors were evaluated, such as cultural values (McGrath, MacMillan & Scheinberg, 1992), attributional theory (Gatewood, Shaver & Gartner, 1995), and problem-solving styles (Buttner & Gryskiewicz, 1993). These are new strands of research that may become important in the future. Other issues of this type are concerned with learning, women and entrepreneurship, minorities and entrepreneurship, human resource management, learning and training, feedback processing, transition from business founder to manager, financing, organizational culture and others. Strangely enough, many issues that are of importance in social psychology have not yet been made useful for entrepreneurship research. We think particularly about feedback processing which has been shown to be influenced by success (e.g. more upward comparison—for example, with a stronger competitor—after one has had success. A downward comparison is preferred after a failure: Wills, 1981). Thus, feedback processing is related to keeping up one's self-esteem—again a topic not much studied in entrepreneurship literature.

Another fascinating area is where psychological approaches make small-scale entrepreneurs able to deal with banks and other capital providers effectively.

One fascinating topic is the issue of making psychological entrepreneurship research useful for developing countries. It has been shown that micro-business contributes more to employment growth in developing countries than larger companies do (Mead & Liedholm, 1998). Thus, the issues surrounding entrepreneurship are more important in developing countries than in the West. Issues such as the ones discussed in the Giessen–Amsterdam model have been researched recently involving micro-business. Strategies, goal-setting, self-efficacy towards solving problems and personal initiative have been shown to be important factors related to success (Frese, 2000). The practical usefulness of this research is particularly high if resources are scarce because both selection and training have to be applied with more care than in the affluent countries.

## CONCLUSION

We hope that we have shown that psychological approaches to entrepreneurship are fascinating both for entrepreneurship as well as for work and organizational psychology. Entrepreneurship can profit from this interface between business and psychology because psychological variables are clearly and often surprisingly consistently related to entrepreneurial entry and success. Moreover, psychological variables (most notably action-related concepts) function as necessary mediators in the process that leads to success (e.g. strategies).

For work and organizational psychology, entrepreneurship is interesting because it combines the following features. First, the level of analysis question becomes even more interesting because it relates to the dynamics of enterprise growth; in the very beginning, a small-scale enterprise is best described by looking at the owner. However, in somewhat more mature enterprises, the level of analysis has to change because more delegation, management and implementation are necessary. Moreover, innovation and innovation implementation need to be described on different levels of analysis. In short, this issue relates to both methodology and theory more strongly in this area than in large-scale organizations. Second, some interesting organizational hypotheses can better be studied with small-scale entrepreneurs than with larger organizations. A good example is the study of contingency theories. The description of large organizations is always fraught with a high degree of error because different subparts of the organizations may differ highly from each other. In contrast, small-scale enterprises are more coherent and, therefore, contingency models can be tested better. Third, even large organizations attempt to mimic small enterprises (e.g. Avery Brown and Bovery) and stress intrapreneurship, innovation, and personal initiative. Thus, the study of small-scale entrepreneurs is a field that allows for a high degree of transfer of knowledge to larger organizations and that makes it necessary to test certain models before they are applied in a larger organizational context. There is no doubt that future jobs will focus on innovation and personal initiative more strongly (Frese & Fay, 2000). Again, these issues may be more easily (and theoretically more fruitfully) studied with small-scale entrepreneurs. Fourth, there is no area in which the interface between business and psychology becomes more obvious than in small-scale entrepreneurship; interdisciplinary cross-fertilization can and does take place in this area.

What have we found? There are clear, albeit often small, relationships between need for achievement, locus of control and the emergence of entrepreneurship (start up). Additionally, these variables are also related to success. Factors related to success are need for achievement, locus of control, low risk-taking, human capital, planning and strategies, innovation, entrepreneurial orientation, and tough environmental conditions. All of these correlations are small, but significant. The small correlations together with the large variance between the different studies suggest that moderators should be included into future entrepreneurial success models. Environmental conditions proved to be such moderators (e.g. hostility and dynamism). Other potential moderators are life-cycle stages, typologies (such as the one by Miles & Snow), growth vs. lifestyle goals, and culture. Another factor that allows a higher degree of prediction is to take variables into consideration that are directly related to the tasks that have to be done by the entrepreneurs and to uses them as mediators. This also supports a process view of entrepreneurship. Finally, more than one predictor has to be incorporated into models and studies of entrepreneurship.

A number of recommendations follow for the future research:

1. The use of more sophisticated approaches in personality as well as task-domain analysis, moderators, mediators, specific personality factors, emphasizing processes (e.g. interactions with environment and changes of the environment), weak and strong situations.

2. Human capital studies have typically used proxy measures: thus, it is not really skills that have been studied but rather experience (even tough expertise research has shown that it is not the length of experience but rather the depth of experience that has any influence on expertise: Sonnentag, 1996). There is no specific knowledge test for entrepreneurs—often only educational rank is used as a variable. Intelligence is not usually controlled, so we do not know whether a personality variable (namely cognitive ability) is really the third variable producing the correlation between educational level and success. Therefore, it is not surprising that the relationships between human capital and success are by and large very small.

3. Researchers often do not ask whether entrepreneurs have subsistence, lifestyle, or growth goals. It is simply assumed that entrepreneurs have to have growth goals. Most owners do not and actually have clearly decided against growing too large. Still, their business provides stable employment and often interesting work to their employees. The bias for growth in entrepreneurship research is intellectually and empirically out of touch with reality for most entrepreneurs.

4. Strategies are not usually distinguished in their components and much of strategy research does not clearly differentiate goals from strategies (e.g. Porter, 1980). Moreover, many strategies have not been studied,

for example human resource development, which happens to be a rather effective strategy for larger companies (Youndt et al., 1996); we do not yet know enough about its usefulness for smaller companies even though first evidence also proves it to be positive (Goebel & Frese, 1999).

5. While there have been several approaches to develop a taxonomy of the entrepreneurial environment, they are still underdeveloped. While munificence, dynamism and complexity are certainly important variables, other issues are lacking, for example, network requirements, cultural requirements, support systems, government contacts in certain industries and countries, degree of corruption.

6. Typologies of entrepreneurs have been suggested but have not really been developed as yet. Empirical support is usually marginal (an exception being Miles and Snow's typology). In principle, it makes sense to look empirically at clusters of entrepreneurial characteristics and to develop an empirically supported taxonomy.

7. We have not discussed the measurement of success in this review because much of it is outside the realm of psychology (Schenk, 1998). Obviously, it is important to measure several different aspects of success, such as meeting goals, economic success, lifestyle success (e.g., prestige, satisfying work, contributing to a cause), growth, and others. Studies that look at only one dependent variable are by necessity restrictive and cannot really give a full picture of the processes involved. Moreover, the indicators are not always necessarily good indicators of success: for example, a large profit margin is a sign of bad planning and bad taxation consulting in most Western European countries.

Much more and much better research needs to be done in this area. Comparing the research on entrepreneurship with other areas of work and organizational psychology (e.g. leadership, selection, or stress research), one cannot but argue that the methodological quality of entrepreneurship research is still relatively weak. There are very few longitudinal studies, the analysis is often not up to date (e.g., often no or inadequate control variables are included), often reliabilities of scales (or interrater reliabilities) are not reported. Methodological misinterpretations (e.g., non-significant findings based on very few subjects are interpreted to null findings) are common. Conceptually, modern psychological reasoning is not incorporated (e.g. in much of the personality literature and also its critique). In short, much of what Low and McMillan (1988) have criticized in entrepreneurship literature in general is also true for its psychological approaches: the lack of a clear discussion of the purpose of research, the weak theoretical perspective, the underdeveloped focus on process, the simple assumptions about the correct level of analysis, the lack of taking the time-frame of developments explicitly into consideration, the lack of use of multiple methods and the little use of methodology that can test causal hypotheses (e.g., modern regression or LISREL analyses). We were surprised by the fact that many articles do not report the statistics necessary to include them into meta-analysis (e.g., intercorrelation matrixes, Ms and SDs, $t$- or $F$-statistics, and reliabilities are not reported). Editorial policies are clearly not yet as sophisticated as they are in the mainstream work and organizational psychology journals.

We have reported a number of different models in this review; they are often presented as being contradictory. For example, some people have pitted personality approaches against human capital approaches. As Figure 3.1 shows, we assume that they coexist and can influence each other (e.g. IQ has an influence on the development of skills and knowledge). Even ecological approaches may coexist with a personality theory (e.g., Aldrich & Wiedenmayer, 1993) even though these two approaches sound rather contradictory. But given the importance of personality–situation interactions, it makes sense that these approaches should be combined. Moreover, hypotheses on the interaction of environmental conditions and strategies have worked out well and increased the explained variance considerably. An integration of various approaches to make real headway towards understanding a societally important phenomenon—entrepreneurship—is called for and produces challenging research.

## REFERENCES

Ackelsberg, R. & Arlow, P. (1985). Small businesses do plan and it pays off. *Long Range Planning*, **18**(5), 61–67.

Acs, Z. J. & Gifford, S. (1996). Innovation of entrepreneurial firms. *Small Business Economics*, **8**, 203–218.

Aldrich, H. E. & Wiedenmayer, G. (1993). From traits to rates: An ecological perspective on organizational foundings. In J. A. Katz & R. H. Brockhaus (Eds), *Advances in Entrepreneurship, Firm Emergence, and Growth*, Vol. 1 (pp. 145–195). Greenwich, CT: JAI Press.

Ansoff, H. I. (1965). *Corporate Strategy*. New York: McGraw-Hill.

Bandura, A. (1997). *Self-efficacy: The Exercise of Control*. New York: Freeman.

Bass, B. M. (1990). *Bass and Stogdill's Handbook of Leadership: The Research and Managerial Implications* (3rd edn). New York: Free Press.

Baum, J. R. (1995). *The relation of traits, competencies, motivation, strategy and structure to venture growth*. Frontiers of Entrepreneurship Research.

Baum, J. R., Locke, E. A. & Kirkpatrick, S. A. (1998). A longitudinal study of vision and vision communication to venture growth in entrepreneurial firms. *Journal of Applied Psychology*, **83**(1), 43–54.

Baumford, C. E., Dean, T. J. & McDougall, P. P. (1997). Initial strategies and new venture growth: An examination of the effectiveness of broad vs. narrow breadth strategies. In P. D. Reynolds, W. D. Bygrave, N. M. Carter, C. M. Mason & P. P. McDougall (Eds), *Frontiers of Entrepreneurship Research*. Wellesley MA: Babson Park MA: Babson College.

Begley, T. M. & Boyd, D. B. (1987). Psychological characteristics associated with performance in entrepreneurial firms and small businesses. *Journal of Business Venturing*, **2**, 79–93.

Bellu, R. R. (1988). Entrepreneurs and managers: Are they different? In B. A. Kirchhoff, W. A. Long, W. E. D. McMullan, K. H. Vesper & W. E. Wetzel (Eds), *Forntiers of Entrepreneurship Research*, Vol. 2 (pp. 16–30). Wellesley, MA: Babson College.

Birch, D. L. (1987). *Job Creation in America*. New York: Free Press.

Birley, S. (1985). The role of networks in the entrepreneurial process. *Journal of Business Venturing*, 1, 107–117.

Birley, S. & Westhead, P. (1994). A taxonomy of business start up reasons and their impact on firm growth and size. *Journal of Business Venturing*, 9, 7–31.

Bögenhold, D. & Staber, U. (1990). Selbständigkeit als ein Reflex auf Arbeitslosigkeit? *Kölner Zeitschrift für Soziologie und Sozialpsychologie*, 42(2), 265–279.

Bonnett, C. & Furnham, A. (1991). Who wants to be an entrepreneur? A study of adolescents interested in a Young Enterprise scheme. *Journal of Economic Psychology*, 12, 465–478.

Boulding, K. E. (1978). *Ecodynamics*. Beverly Hills, CA: Sage.

Bracker, J. S., Keats, B. W. & Pearson, J. N. (1988). Planning and financial performance among small firms in a growth industry. *Strategic Management Journal*, 9, 591–603.

Brandstaetter, H. (1997). Becoming an entrepreneur—a question of personality structure? *Journal of Economic Psychology*, 18, 157–177.

Brockhaus, R. H. (1980). Psychological and environmental factors which distinguish the successful from the unsuccessful entrepreneur: A longitudinal study. *Academy of Management Proceedings* of the 40th annual meeting, pp. 368–372.

Brockhaus, R. H. & Nord, W. R. (1979). An exploration of factors affecting the entrepreneurial decision: Personal characteristics versus environmental characteristics. *Academy of Management Proceedings* of the 39th annual meeting.

Brouwer, E. & Kleinknecht, A. (1996). Firm size, small business presence and sales of innovative products: A micro-econometric analysis. *Small Business Economics*, 8, 189–201.

Brown, T. E. & Davidsson, P. (1988). Entrepreneurial orientation versus entrepreneurial management: Relating Miller/Covin & Slevin's conceptualization of entrepreneurship to Stevenson's. In P. D. Reynolds, W. D. Bygrave, N. M. Carter, S. Manigart, C. M. Mason, G. D. Meyer & K. G. Shaver (Eds). *Frontiers of Entrepreneurship Research* (pp. 352–353). Babson Park, MA: Babson College.

Bruederl, J., Preisendoerfer, P. & Ziegler, R. (1992). Survival chances of newly founded business organizations. *American Sociological Review*, 57, 227–242.

Bruederl, J. & Preisendoerfer, P. (1998). Network support and the success of newly founded businesses. *Small Business Economics*, 10, 213–225.

Buttner, E. H. & Gryskiewicz, N. (1993). Entrepreneurs' problem-solving styles: An empirical study using the Kirton adaption/innovation theory. *Journal of Small Business Management*, 31(1), 22–31.

Carland, J. W., Hoy, F., Boulton, W. R. & Carland, J. C. (1984). Differentiating entrepreneurs from small business owners: A conceptualization. *Academy of Management Review*, 9(2), 354–359.

Carroll, G. R. & Hannan, M. T. (1989). Density delay in the evolution of organizational populations: A model and five empirical tests. *Administrative Science Quarterly*, 34, 411–430.

Castrogiovanni, G. J. (1991). Environmental munificence: A theoretical assessment. *Academy of Management Review*, 16(3), 542–565.

Cattell, R. B., Eber, H. W. & Tatsouka, M. M. (1970). *Handbook for the Sixteen Personality Factors Questionnaire (16PF)*. Champian: IPAT.

Chandler, A. D. (1962). *Strategy and Structure*. Cambridge, MA: Massachusetts Institute of Technology Press.

Chandler, G. N. & Hanks, S. H. (1994). Founder competence, the environment, and venture performance. *Entrepreneurship Theory and Practice*, **18**(3), 77–89.

Chandler, G. N. & Hanks, S. H. (1996). An examination of the substitutability of founders' human and financial capital in emerging business ventures. *Journal of Business Venturing*, **11**, 353–369.

Chandler, G. N. & Jansen, E. (1992). The founder's self-assessed competence and venture performance. *Journal of Business Venturing*, 7, 223–236.

Chell, E., Haworth, J. & Brearley, S. (1991). *The Entrepreneurial Personality: Concepts, Cases and Categories*. London, New York: Routledge.

Child, J. (1972). Organizational structure, environment, and performance—the role of strategic choice. *Sociology*, **6**, 1–22.

Collins, J. C. & Porras, J. I. (1994). *Built to Last: Successful Habits of Visionary Companies*. New York: Harper.

Conant, J. S., Mokwa, M. P. & Varadarajan, P. R. (1990). Strategic types, distinctive marketing competencies and organizational performance: A multiple measures-based study. *Strategic Management Journal*, **11**, 365–383.

Cooper, A. C., Dunkelberg, W. C. & Woo, C. Y. (1988). Survival and failure: A longitudinal study. In B. A. Kirchhoff, W. A. Long, W. E. D. McMullan, K. H. Vesper & W. E. Wetzel (Eds), *Frontiers of Entrepreneurship Research*, Wellesley, MA: Babson College.

Cooper, A. C. & Gimeno-Gascon, F. J. (1992). Entrepreneurs, process of founding, and new-firm performance. In D. L. Sexton & J. D. Kasarda (Eds), *The State of the Art of Entrepreneurship* (pp. 301–340). Kent: PSW.

Costa, P. T. & McCrae, R. R. (1988). From catalog to classification: Murray's needs and the five-factor model. *Journal of Personality and Social Psychology*, **55**, 258–265.

Covin, J. G. & Covin, T.J. (1990). Competitive aggressiveness, environmental context, and small firm performance. *Entrepreneurship Theory and Practice*, **16**, 35–50.

Covin, J. G. & Slevin, D. P. (1986). The development and testing of an organizational-level entrepreneurship scale. In R. Ronstadt, J. A. Hornaday, R. Peterson & K. H. Vesper (Eds), *Frontiers of Entrepreneurship Research* (pp. 628–639). Wellesley, MA: Babson College.

Covin, J. G. & Slevin, D. P. (1989). Strategic management of small firms in hostile and benign enviornments. *Strategic Management Journal*, **10**, 75–87.

Cromie, S. & Johns, S. (1983). Irish entrepreneurs: Some personal characteristics. *Journal of Occupational Behavior*, **4**, 317–324.

Cunningham, B. J. & Lischeron, J. (1991). Defining entrepreneurship. *Journal of Small Business Management*, **29**(1), 45–61.

Davidsson, P. (1989). Entrepreneurship—and after? A study of growth willingness in small firms. *Journal of Small Business Venturing*, **4**, 211–226.

Dean, T. J. & Meyer, G. D. (1996). Industry environments and new venture formations in the US manufacturing: A conceptual and empirical analysis of demand determinants. *Journal of Business Venturing*, **11**, 107–132.

Dess, G. D. & Beard, D. W. (1984). Dimensions of organizational task environments. *Administrative Science Quarterly*, **29**, 52–73.

Dess, G. G., Lumpkin, G. T. & Covin, J. G. (1997). Entrepreneurial strategy making and firm performance: Tests of contingency and configuration models. *Strategic Management Journal*, **18**(9), 677–695.

Dodge, H. R. & Robbins, J. E. (1992). An empirical investigation of the organizational life cycle model for small business development and survival. *Journal of Small Business Management*, **30**(1), 27–37.

Doty, D. H., Glick, W. H. & Huber, G. P. (1993). Fit, equifinality, and organizational effectiveness: A test of two configural theories. *Academy of Management Journal*, **36**(6), 1196–1250.

Doty, D. H. & Glick, W. H. (1994). Typologies as a unique form of theory building: Toward improved understanding and modeling. *Academy of Management Review*, 19(2), 230–251.

Drucker, P. F. (1985). *Innovation and Entrepreneurship*. New York: Harper.

Duchesneau, D. A. & Gartner, W. B. (1990). A profile of new venture success and failure in an emerging industry. *Journal of Business Venturing*, 5, 297–312.

Dyke, L. S., Fischer, E. M. & Reuber, A. R. (1992). An inter-industry examination of the impact of owner experience on firm performance. *Journal of Small Business Management*, 30(4), 72–87.

Eggers, J. H., Leahy, K. T. & Churchill, N. C. (1996). Leadership, management, and culture in high-performance entrepreneurial companies. Ronstadt et al. (Eds), In *Frontiers of Entrepreneurship Research*, Wellesley, MA: Babson College.

Epstein, S., & O'Brian, E. J. (1985). The person–situation debate in historical and current perspective. *Psychological Bulletin*, 98, 513–537.

European Council for Small Business (ECSB) (1997). *Newsletter*, 4, 5.

Fishbein, M. & Ajzen, I. (1975). *Belief, Attitude, Intention and Behavior. An Introduction to Theory and Research*. Reading, MA: Addison-Wesley.

Frese, M. (1995). Entrepreneurship in East Europe: A general model and empirical findings. In C. L. Cooper & D. M. Rousseau (Eds). *Trends in Organizational Behavior*, 2, 69–81.

Frese, M. (2000). *Success and Failure of Microbusiness Owners in Africa: A Psychological Approach*. Westport, CT: Greenwood Publications.

Frese, M. & Fay, D. (2000). *Personal initiative (PI): A concept for work in the 21st century*. Submitted for publication.

Frese, M., Krauss, S. & Friedrich, S. (2000). Micro-business in Zimbabwe. In M. Frese (Eds). *Success and Failure of Microbusiness Owners in Africa: A Psychological Approach*. Westport, CT: Greenwood Publications.

Frese, M., Van Gelderen, M. & Ombach, M. (2000). *How to plan as a small scale business owner: Psychological process characteristics of action strategies and success. Journal of Small Business Management*, 38(2).

Frey, R. S. (1984). Does n-Achievement cause economic development? A cross-lagged panel analysis of the McClellant thesis. *Journal of Social Psychology*, 122, 67–70.

Furnham, A. (1992). *Personality and Productivity*. London: Routledge.

Galais, N. (1998). Motive und Beweggruende fuer die Selbstaendigkeit und ihre Bedeutung fuer den Erfolg. In M. Frese (Eds). *Erfolgreiche Unternehmensgruender* (pp. 89–98). Goettingen: Hofgrefe.

Gartner, W. B. (1985). A conceptual framework for describing the phenomenon of new venture creation. *Academy of Management Review*, 10(4), 696–706.

Gartner, W. B. (1988). 'Who is an entrepreneur?' is the wrong question. *Entrepreneurship Theory and Practice*, 12(2), 47–68.

Gatewood, E. J., Shaver, K. G. & Gartner, W. B. (1995). A longitudinal study of cognitive factors influencing start-up behaviors and success at venture creation. *Journal of Business Venturing*, 10, 371–391.

Gimeno, J., Folta, T. B., Cooper, A. C. & Woo, C. Y. (1997). Survival of the Fittest: Entrepreneurial human capital and the persistence of underperforming firms. *Administrative Science Quarterly*, 42, 750–783.

Goebel, S. (1995). Der Zusammenhang zwischen Personeneigenschaften, Strategien und Erfolg bei Kleinunternehmern. Unpublished master thesis, University of Giessen, Department of Psychology.

Goebel, S. & Frese, M. (1999). Persoenlichkeit, Strategien und Erfolg bei Kleinunternehmern. In K. Moser, B. Batinic & J. Zempel (Eds). *Unternehmerisch erfolgreiches Handeln*. Goettingen: Hogrefe.

Green, R., David, R. G. & Dent, M. (1996). The Russian entrepreneur: A study of psychological characteristics. *International Journal of Entrepreneurial Behavior*, 2(1), 49–58.

Hacker, W. (1985). Activity: A fruitful concept in industrial psychology. In M. Frese & J. Sabini (Eds), *Goal Directed Behavior: The Concept of Action in Psychology* (pp. 262–284). London: Erlbaum.

Hannan, M. T. & Freeman, J. (1984). Structural inertial and organizational change. *American Sociological Review*, 49, 149–164.

Herron, L. & Robinson, R. B. (1993). A structural model of the effects of entrepreneurial characteristics on venture performance. *Journal of Business Venturing*, 8, 281–294.

Heunks, F. J. (1996). Innovation, creativity, and success. *Small Business Economics*, 8, 263–272.

Hisrich, R. D. (1990). Entrepreneurship/Intrapreneurship. *American Psychologist*, 45(2), 209–222.

Hofstede, G. (1991). *Cultures and Organizations: Software of the Mind*. London: McGraw-Hill.

House, R. J. (1977). A 1976 theory of charismatic leadership. In J. G. Hunt & L. L. Larson (Eds), *Leadership: The Cutting Edge* (pp. 189–207). Southern Ill: Southern University Press.

Jungbauer-Gans, M. & Preisendoerfer, P. (1991). Verbessern eine gruendliche Vorbeitung und sorgfaeltige Planung die Erfolgschancen neugegruendeter Betriebe? *Zeitschrift fuer betriebswirtschaftliche Forschung*, 43, 987–996.

Katz, J. A. (1994). Modeling entrepreneurial career progressions: Concepts and considerations. *Entrepreneurship Theory and Practice*, 4, 23–39.

Kean, R. C., Niemeyer, S. & Miller, N. C. (1996). Competitive strategies in the craft product retailing industry. *Journal of Small Business Management*, 34(1), 13–23.

Kirkpatrick, S. A. & Locke, E. A. (1991). Leadership: Do traits matter? *Academy of Management Executive*, 5(2), 48–60.

Klandt, H. (1984). Aktivitaet und Erfolg des Unternehmensgruenders. Eine empirische Analyse unter Einbeziehung des mikrosozialen Umfeldes. Reihe Gruendung, Innovation und Beratung. Bergisch-Gladbach.

Klein, K. J. & Sorra, J. S. (1996). The challenge of innovation implementation. *Academy of Management Review*, 21(4), 1055–1080.

Koop, De Reu & Frese (1999). Entrepreneurial orientation, initiative, and environmental forces in Uganda. In M. Frese (Eds), *Success and Failure of Microbusiness Owners in Africa: A Psychological Approach*. Westport, CT: Greenwood Publications.

Landy, F. J. (1989). *Psychology of Work Behavior*. Belmont CA: Wadsworth.

Lang, J. R., Calantone, R. J. & Gudmundson, D. (1997). Small firm information seeking as a response to environmental threats and opportunities. *Journal of Small Business Management*, 35(1), 1–23.

Liles, P. R. (1974). Who are the entrepreneurs? *MSU Business Topics*, FB22(1), 5–14.

Locke, E. A. & Latham, G. P. (1990). *A Theory of goal Setting and Task Performance*, Englewood Cliffs, NY: Prentice-Hall.

Lord, R. G., DeVader, C. L. & Alliger, G. M. (1986). A meta-analysis of the relation between personality traits and leadership perceptions: An application of validity evaluation procedures. *Journal of Applied Psychology*, 71, 402–410.

Lorrain, J. & Dussault, L. (1988). Relation between psychological characteristics, administrative behaviors, and success of founder entrepreneurs at the start up stage. In B. A. Kirchhoff, W. A. Long, W. E. D. McMullan, K. H. Vesper & W. E. Wetzel (Eds), *Frontiers of Entrepreneurship Research* (pp. 150–164). Wellesley, MA: Babson College.

Low, B. M. & McMillan, B. C. (1988). Entrepreneurship: Past research and future challenges. *Journal of Management*, 14(2). 139–162.

Lumpkin, G. T. & Dess, G. D. (1996). Clarifying the entrepreneurial orientation construct and linking it to performance. *Academy of Management Review*, 21(1), 135–172.

Lumpkin, G. T., Shrader, R. C. & Hills, G. E. (1998). Does formal business planning enhance the performance of new ventures? In P. D. Reynolds, W. D. Bygrave, N. M. Carter, S. Manigart, C. M. Mason, G. D. Meyer & K. G. Shaver (Eds), *Frontiers of Entrepreneurship Research* (pp. 180–189). Babson Park MA: Babson College.

Lussier, R. N. (1995). A nonfinancial business success versus failure prediction model for young firms. *Journal of Small Business Management*, **1**, 8–20.

Lyles, M. A., Baird, I. S., Orris, B. & Kuratko, D. F. (1995). Formalized planning is small business: Increasing strategic choices. *Journal of Small Busines Management*, **33**(1), 38–50.

Magnusson, D. & Endler, N. S. (1977). Interactional psychology: Present status and future development. In D. Magnusson & N. S. Endler (Eds), *Personality at the Cross Roads: Current Issues and Interactional Psychology* (pp. 3–36). Hillsdale, NJ: Erlbaum.

McClelland, D. C. (1961). *The Achieving Society*. Princeton, NJ: Van Nostrand.

McGrath, R. G., MacMillan, I. C. & Scheinberg, S. (1992). Elitists, risk-takers, and rugged individualists? An exploratory analysis of cultural differences between entrepreneurs and non-entrepreneurs. *Journal of Business Venturing*, **2**, 115–135.

McNamee, P. & McHugh, M. (1989). Competitive strategies in the clothing industry. *Long Range Planning*, **22**(4), 63–71.

Mead, D. C. & Liedholm, C. (1998). The dynamics of micro and small enterprises in developing countries. *World Development*, **26**(1), 61–74.

Meichenbaum, D. H. (1985). *Stress Inoculation Training*. New York: Pergamon Press.

Miles, R. & Snow, C. (1978). *Organizational Strategy, Structure, and Process*. New York: McGraw-Hill.

Mill, J. S. (1984). *Principles of Political Economy with some Application to Social Philosophy*. London: John W. Parker.

Miller, D. & Friessen, P. H. (1983). Strategy-making and environment: The third link. *Strategic Management Journal*, **4**, 221–235.

Miller, D. & Toulouse, J. (1986). Chief executive personality and corporate strategy and structure in small firms. *Management Science*, **32**(11), 1389–1409.

Miner, J. B. (1996). *The 4 Routes to Entrepreneurial Success*. San Francisco: Berrett-Koehler.

Miner, J.B. (1997). A psychological typology and its relationship to entrepreneurial success. *Entrepreneurships and Regional Development*, **9**, 319–334.

Miner, J. B., Smith, N. R. & Bracker, J. S. (1989). Role of entrepreneurial task motivation in the growth of technologically innovative firms. *Journal of Applied Psychology*, **74**(4), 554–560.

Miner, J. B., Smith, N. R. & Bracker, J. S. (1992). Defining the inventor-entrepreneur in the context of established typologies. *Journal of Business Venturing*, **7**, 103–113.

Miner, J. B., Smith, N. R. & Bracker, J. S. (1994). Role of entrepreneur task motivation in the growth of technologically innovative firms. Interpretations from follow-up data. *Journal of Applied Psychology*, **79**(4), 627–630.

Minzberg, H. T. (1983) *Structure in Fives: Designing Effective Organizataions*. Englewood Cliffs, NY: Prentice-Hall.

Mirron, D. & McClelland, D. C. (1979). The impact of achievement motivation training on small businesses. *California Management Review*, **21**(4), 13–28.

Mischel, W. (1968). *Personality and Assessment*. New York: Wiley.

Mulhern, A. (1995). The SME sector in Europe: A broad perspective. *Journal of Small Business Management*, **33**(3), 83–87.

Olson, P. D. & Bokor, D. W. (1995). Strategy process–content interaction: Effects on growth performance in small, start up firms. *Journal of Small Business Management*, **33**(1), 34–44.

Palmer, M. (1971). The application of psychological testing to entrepreneurial potential. *California Management Review*, **13**, 32–38.

Pineda, R. C., Lerner, L. D., Miller, M. C. & Phillips, S. J. (1998). An investigation of factors affecting the information search activities of small business managers. *Journal of Small Business Management*, **30**, 60–71.

Pfirmann, O. (1994). The geography of innovation in small and medium sized firms in West Germany. *Small Business Economics*, **6**, 41–54.

Porter, M. (1980). *Competitive Strategy*. New York: Free Press.

Rahim, A. (1996). Stress, strain, and their moderators: An empirical comparison of entrepreneurs and managers. *Journal of Small Business Management*, **34**(1), 46–58.

Rauch, A. & Frese, M. (1997). Does planning matter? Relations between planning and success in small enterprises in Ireland and in Germany. Paper presented at the 42nd World Conference of the ICSB International Council for Small Business, San Francisco.

Rauch, A. & Frese, M. (1998). A contingency approach to small-scale business succes: A longitudinal study on the effects of enviornment hostility and uncertainty on the relationship of planning and success. In P. D. Reynolds, W. D. Bygrave, N. M. Carter, S. Manigart, C. M. Mason, G. D. Meyer & K. G. Shaver (Eds), *Frontiers of Entrepreneurship Research* (pp. 190–200). Babson Park, MA: Babson College.

Rauch, A. & Frese, M. (1999). Employees in small-scale enterprises. A longitudinal study on the relationship between employee's participation and small-scale enterprise success. Paper submitted for publication.

Ripsas, S. (1998). Towards an interdisciplinary theory of entrepreneurship. *Small Business Economics*, **10**, 103–115.

Risseeuw, P. & Masurel, E. (1993). The role of planning in small firms: Empirical evidence from the service industry. *Small Business Economics*, **6**, 313–322.

Robinson, P. B., Stimpson, D. V., Huefner, J. C. & Hunt, H. K. (1991). An attitude approach to the prediction of entrepreneurship. *Entrepreneurship Theory and Practice*, **15**(2), 13–31.

Robinson, R. B. & Pearce, J. A. (1983). The impact of formalized strategic planning on financial performance in small organizations. *Strategic Management Journal*, **4**, 197–207.

Robinson, R. B. & Pearce, J. A. (1984). Research thrusts in small firm strategic planning. *Academy of Management Review*, **9**(1), 128–137.

Romanelli, E. (1989). Environments and strategies of organization start up: Effects on early survival. *Administrative Science Quarterly*, **34**, 369–387.

Roper, S. (1997). Product innovation and small business growth: A comparison of the strategies of German, UK and Irish companies. *Small Business Economics*, **9**, 523–527.

Rotter, J. B. (1966). Generalized expectancies for internal versus external control of reinforcement. *Psychological Monographs*, **609**(80), 1.

Ryans, C. C. (1997). Resources: Writing a business plan. *Journal of Small Business Management*, **35**(2), 95–98.

Sandberg, W. R. & Hofer, C. W. (1987). Improving new venture performance: The role of strategy, industry structure, and the entrepreneur. *Journal of Business Venturing*, **2**, 5–28.

Scheinberg, S. & McMillan, I. C. (1988). An 11 country study of motivation to start a business. In B. A. Kirchhoff, W. A. Long, W. E. D. McMullan, K. H. Vesper & W. E. Wetzel (Eds), *Frontiers of Entrepreneurship Research* (pp. 669–687). Wellesley, MA: Babson College.

Schendel, D. E. & Hofer, C. W. (1979). *Strategic Management*. Boston: Little, Brown.

Schenk, R. (1998). Beurteilung des Unternehmenserfolges. In M. Frese (Eds), *Erfolgreiche Unternehmensgruender. Psychologische Analysen und praktische Anleitungen fuer Unternehmer in Ost-und Westdeutschland*, (pp. 59–82). Goettingen: Hofrefe.

Schneewind, K. A., Schroeder, G. & Cattell, R. B. (1983). *Der 16-Persoenlichkeits-Faktorentest-16PF*. Bern: Huber.

Schumpeter, J. (1935). *Theorie der wirtschaftlichen Entwicklung* (Theory of economic development), 4th edn. Munich, Leipzig: Von Duncker & Humbold.

Schwenk, C. R. & Shrader, C. B. (1993). Effects of formal strategic planning on financial performance in small firms: A meta-analysis. *Entrepreneurship Theory and Practice*, **17**, 48–53.

Shane, S., Kolvereid, L. & Westhead, P. (1991). An exploratory examination of reasons leading to new firm formations across country and gender. *Journal of Business Venturing*, **6**, 431–446.

Shane, S. & Kolvereid, L. (1995). National environment, strategy, and new venture performance: A three country study. *Journal of Small Business Management*, **33**(2), 37–50.

Sharfman, M. P. & Dean, J. W. (1991). Conceptualizing and measuring the organizational environment: A multidimensional approach. *Journal of Management*, **17**(4), 681–700.

Shuman, J. C., Shaw, J. J. & Sussman, G. (1985). Strategic planning in smaller rapid growth firms. *Long Range Planning*, **18**(6), 48–53.

Simon, H. (1996). *Die heimlichen Gewinner (The hidden champions)*. Frankfurt: Campus.

Singh, J. V. (1990). Organizational ecology and organizational evolution. In J.V. Singh (Ed.), *Organizational Evolution: New Directions* (pp. 11–20). London: Sage.

Singh, J. V., Tucker, D. J. & House, R. J. (1986). Organizational legitimacy and the liability of newness. *Administrative Science Quarterly*, **31**. 171–193.

Singh, S. (1988). Personality characteristics, work values, and live styles of fast and slow progressing small-scale industrial entrepreneurs. *Journal of Social Psychology*, **129**(6), 801–805.

Smith, N. R. (1967). *The Entrepreneur and his Firm: The Relationship between Type of Man and Type of Company*. East Lansing, MI: Michigan State Unviersity Press.

Smith, N. R. & Miner, J. B. (1983). Type of entrepreneur, type of firm, and managerial motivation: Implications for organizational life circle theory. *Strategic Management Journal*, **4**, 325–340.

Sonnentag, S. (1996). Planning and knowledge about strategies: Their relationship to work characteristics in software design. *Behavior & Information Technology*, **15**(4), 213–225.

Spencer, L. M. & Spencer, S. M. (1993). *Competence at Work: Models for Superior Performance*, New York: Wiley.

Spengler, W. D. (1992). Validity of questionnaire and TAT measures of need for achievement. Two meta-analyses. *Psychological Bulletin*, **112**, 140–154.

*Statistisches Jahrbuch fuer das Ausland* (1994). Statistisches Bundesamt (Eds). Metzler/Poerschel.

Stogdill, R. M. (1948). Personal factors associated with leadership. A survey of the literature. *Journal of Psychology*, **25**, 35–71.

Stoner, C. & Fry, F. F. (1982). The entrepreneurial decision: Dissatisfaction or opportunity. *Journal of Small Business Management*, April, 39–44.

Swaminathan, A. (1996). Environmental conditions at founding and organizational mortality: A trial-by-fire model. *Academy of Management Journal*, **39**(5), 1350–1377.

Tan, J. (1997). Regulatory environment and strategic orientations in a transitional economy: A study of Chinese private enterprise. *Entrepreneurship Theory and Practice*, **21**, 11–32.

Thurston, P. H. (1983). Should smaller companies make formal plans? *Harvard Business Review*, **9**, 162–188.

Timmons, J. A., Smollen, L. E. & Dingee, A. L. M. (1985). *New Venture Creation*. Homewood, Ill: Irvine.

Triandis, H. C. (1994). Cross-cultural industrial and organizational psychology. In M. D. Dunette & L. M. Hough. *Handbook of Industrial and Organizational Psychology*, Vol. 4 (ch. 2, pp. 103–172). Palo Alto, CA: Consulting Psychologists Press, Inc.

Utsch, A., Rauch, A., Rothfuss, R. & Frese, M. (1999). Who becomes a small scale entrepreneur in a post-socialist environment: On the differences between entrepreneurs and managers in East Germany. *Journal of Small Business Management*, 37(3), 31–43.

Venkatraman, N. (1989). Strategic orientation of business enterprises: The construct, dimensionality, and measurement. *Management Science*, 35(8), 942–962.

Wall, R. A. (1998). An empirical investigation of the production function of the family firm. *Journal of Small Business Management*, 36(2), 24–32.

Welsch, H. P. & Young, E. C. (1982). The information source selection decision: The role of entrepreneurial personality characteristics. *Journal of Small Business Management*, 14(4), 49–57.

West, M. A. & Farr, J. L. (1990). *Innovation and Creativity at Work: Psychological and Organizational Strategies*. Chichester: Wiley.

Wicklund, J. (1988). Entrepreneurial orientation as predictor of performance and entrepreneurial behavior in small firms. In P.D. Reynolds, W.D. Bygrave, N.M. Carter, S. Manigart, C. M. Mason, G. D. Meyer & K. G. Shaver (Eds), *Frontiers of Entrepreneurship Research* (pp. 281–296). Babson Park, MA: Babson College.

Wills, T. A. (1981). Downward comparison principles in social psychology. *Psychological Bulletin*, 90, 245–271.

Woo, C. Y., Cooper, A. C. & Dunkelberg, W. C. (1988). Entrepreneurial typologies: Definition and implicationa. In B. A. Kirchhoff, W. A. Long, W. E. D. McMullan, K. H. Vesper & W. E. Wetzel (Eds), *Frontiers of Entrepreneurship Research*. Wellesley, MA: Babson College.

Youndt, M. A., Snell, S. A., Dean, J. W. & Lepak, D. P. (1996). Human resource management, manufacturing strategy, and firm performance. *Academy of Management Journal*, 39(4), 836–866.

Zahra, S. A. (1996). Technology strategy and financial performance: Examining the moderating role of the firm's competitive environment. *Journal of Business Venturing*, 11, 189–219.

Zahra, S. A. & Pearce II, J. A. (1990). Research evidence on the Miles–Snow typology. *Journal of Management*, 16(4), 751–768.

Zempel, J. (1999). Selbstaendigkeit in den neuen Bundeslandern: Praediktoren, Erfolgsfaktoren und Folgen—Ergebnisse einer Laengsschnittuntersuchung. In K. Moser, B. Batinic & J. Zempel (Eds), *Unternehmerisch erfolgreiches Handeln*. Göttingen: Hogrefe.

# Chapter 4

# CONCEPTUAL AND EMPIRICAL GAPS IN RESEARCH ON INDIVIDUAL ADAPTATION AT WORK

David Chan
*National University of Singapore*

As we enter into the third millennium, many changes are occurring or have occurred at the workplace. Schmitt and Chan (1998) noted that changes such as advances in communications technology, the increasing use of teams to accomplish work, globalization of corporations, and the increased service orientation of organizations will almost certainly have implications for the ways in which job candidates are selected, what knowledge, skills, abilities, and other characteristics (KSAOs) are most related to performance in organizations, and the manner in which performance itself is defined. Indeed, I predict that changes such as those just described are likely to drive much of the research in industrial and organizational (I/O) psychology for the next few decades.

Despite the variety of changes that are occurring at the workplace, they do share something in common, namely the increased demands they will make on workers to adapt to constant change in the work they do. Hence, it is not surprising that the idea of *individual adaptation* in one form or another underlies many studies carried out in the last decade of I/O psychology. The purpose of this paper is to integrate the relevant but diverse studies in research on individual adaptation at work. I will highlight several conceptual and empirical gaps in the literature and offer some concrete suggestions on ways to bridge these gaps.

## LITERATURE ON INDIVIDUAL ADAPTATION

Individual adaptation refers to the process by which an individual achieves some degree of fit between his or her behaviors and the new work demands created by the novel and often ill-defined problems resulting from changing

*International Review of Industrial and Organizational Psychology, 2000 Volume 15*
Edited by C.L. Cooper and I.T. Robertson. © 2000 John Wiley & Sons, Ltd

and uncertain work situations (Chan, in press-a). Chan identified four elements that seem to characterize what researchers describe when they examine the need to be adaptive: (a) changes and uncertainty in the work situation create novel and ill-defined problems; (b) problems make new work demands on individuals; (c) established and routine behaviors that were successful in the previous work situations become irrelevant, suboptimal, or less useful in the new situations; and (d) adaptive behaviors that are in some way qualitatively different from established routines are successful in the new situation. Note that the essence in the description of individual adaptation is generic in the sense that neither the cause of adaptive behaviors (e.g., individual difference constructs or training) nor the nature of the change or demand created due to the change is specified. If we adopt this description of adaptation, then it is not difficult to see that diverse and sometimes apparently disparate areas of research are in fact investigating a similar process or phenomenon at work. What distinguishes the different research literatures are the assumptions or arguments (implicit or explicit) concerning the cause of adaptive behaviors and the types of substantive contexts of the research (e.g., individual versus team contexts). As argued later in this paper, the nature of the change or demand in the new situation is often not explicated in the different research literatures.

To organize the review, four distinct but related research literatures will be discussed. The four are literatures on (a) individual differences, (b) training, (c) teams, and (d) newcomer socialization. I will briefly review the current state of research in each of these areas. On the basis of the review, several issues constituting conceptual and empirical gaps in the research on individual adaptation at work will be explicated.

### Individual Differences Research

In the literature on individual differences, the research on individual adaptation is concerned with *who* are the individuals best suited for functioning in changing and uncertain environments. Adaptation is construed in terms of an individual's level of *adaptability*. That is, successful adaptation is largely a function of the individual's critical KSAOs which are viewed as stable individual difference attributes or traits (e.g., Judge, Thoresen & Pucik, 1996; Mumford, Baughman, Threfall, Uhlman & Costanza, 1993; Paulhus & Martin, 1988). From the individual differences perspective, some people are more adaptable than others, and the ranking of individuals on adaptability is relatively stable across time. The traditional selection paradigm that uses one or more measures of adaptability to predict some job-relevant criterion (e.g., job performance) is the archetype of individual differences research approach to the study of adaptation.

The literature on adaptability as an individual differences construct often treated the construct as unitary, but researchers' diverse operationalizations of adaptability strongly suggest that they have different aspects of adaptation in mind. The diverse measures of 'adaptability' include *cognitive measures* such as tests of fluid intelligence (Snow & Lohman, 1984) and practical intelligence (Wagner, 1986; Sternberg, 1994), *personality measures* such as scales assessing flexibility (Gough, 1987) and change orientation (Jackson, 1967), *structured interviews* focusing on either past experiences (Motowidlo, Carter, Dunnette et al., 1992) or hypothetical situations (Latham, Saari, Pursell & Campion, 1980), *assessment center* exercises such as interview simulations and leaderless group discussions (Chan, 1996), and *biodata* items written specifically to tap adaptability (Schmitt, Jennings & Toney, 1996). The diversity of operationalizations reflects the different aspects of adaptability emphasized by researchers. Schmitt and Chan (1998) suggested that the diversity is due to the different adaptive situations examined across studies, an important point which I will return to later. Suffice now to say that an adequate theory of adaptability is probably one that construes adaptability as a multidimensional construct and identifies the major types of situations or demands requiring adaptation.

### Training Research

Training researchers who studied individual adaptation are concerned with how trainees can acquire or learn the important skills required for functioning in changing and uncertain situations. Instead of construing successful adaptation as a function of individual differences in adaptability, the training literature emphasizes and focuses on how training interventions can enable individuals to learn to be adaptive. For example, Kozlowski, Gully, McHugh, Salas and Cannon-Bowers (1996) examined how sequenced mastery training goals can increase trainees' levels of adaptation.

Research on training adaptive expertise has focused on trainees' acquisition of appropriate knowledge structures and metacognitive or self-regulation skills. These cognitive representational and processual constructs pose important measurement and construct validation challenges and some promising advances have been made in the recent training literature (e.g., Ford & Kraiger, 1995; Goldsmith & Kraiger, 1997; Kraiger, Ford & Salas, 1993; Smith, Ford & Kozlowski, 1997). Many of these advances draw on earlier research on development of expertise (Anderson, 1983, 1993; Chi, Feltovich & Glaser, 1981; Holyoak, 1991) and measurement of structural knowledge (e.g., Schvaneveldt, Durso & Dearholt, 1985, 1989). Detailed discussions on training adaptive expertise are available in Chan (in press-a), Ford and Kraiger (1997), and Smith, Ford and Kozlowski (1997).

### Teams Research

With the increased use of teams in organizations to accomplish complex tasks and improve productivity, teams have become a hot topic in both research and practice in I/O psychology. The study of individual adaptation in teams research has to be understood in the context of the nature of the teams examined. As noted by Schmitt and Chan (1998), because information exchange and decision-making are primary reasons for the use of teams at the workplace, much of the recent research on teams has focused on the sharing and coordination of information among team members and on the team decision-making process. The exchange between multiple expert sources of information in attempts to effectively arrive at good decisions defines the boundary conditions for much of the recent research on teams, that is, team decision-making under conditions of distributed expertise. The types of teams studied are often those where members with different specialized skills operate together in a dynamic context of high stress and unpredictable events (e.g., military combat units, surgery teams, flight crews). Sophisticated team decision-making models such as the one proposed by Hollenbeck, Ilgen, Phillips and Hedlund (1994) have been developed and empirically tested. Given this framework of teams research, individual adaptation is important to the extent each team member is expected to effectively cope with new information provided by other members and demands created by the constantly changing and uncertain team task environment if he or she is to contribute to successful team decision-making and team performance.

Conceptually, the importance of individual adaptation in the context of naturalistic team decision-making is evident in the fact that most problem situations encountered by teams in organizations are ill-structured and they often involve incompatible or shifting goals (Kozlowski, 1998). But empirically there is little research that has directly examined individual adaptation in teams and established or demonstrated clear links between individual adaptation and team performance or other team functioning. One possible reason is that the understanding of naturalistic decision-making teams requires a conceptual and empirical research base quite different from traditional types of work teams found in business organizations such as quality circles, production teams, and planning committees. Social psychology and group dynamics, which focus on concepts such as group norms and morale as opposed to the notion of distributed expertise, constitute the conceptual and empirical base for many of the traditional team models. It is only recently that researchers examining naturalistic decision-making teams (e.g., Kozlowski et al., 1996) found the literature on adaptive expertise (Holyoak, 1991) to provide a useful conceptual and empirical research base for the study of adaptation in such teams.

The program of research by Kozlowski and his colleagues (Kozlowski, 1998; Kozlowski et al., 1996; Kozlowski, Gully, Nason, & Smith, in press) represents one of the few attempts in teams research to relate individual adaptation to team functioning. Drawing on Holyoak's (1991) characterization of adaptive expertise as a deep comprehension of the problem domain made possible by the individual's possession and application of organized and flexible knowledge structures, Kozlowski and his colleagues argued that adaptive experts in the team are those who are able to recognize changes in task priorities and modify their strategies and actions accordingly. Although the conceptual framework adopted by these authors by no means denies the role of stable individual differences, their focus on the individual team member follows the research on training adaptive expertise described in the preceding section. That is, the foundation for individual adaptation or adaptability is provided by the training or learning of metacognitive and self-regulation skills. The process of building of individual adaptive expertise through training is alluded to in the preceding section and described in detail in Smith, Ford and Kozlowski (1997).

The notion of individual adaptation underlies most of recent team studies that attempt to model team performance (e.g., Cannon-Bowers, Tannenbaum, Salas & Volpe, 1995; Kozlowski et al., 1996). However, the assessment of adaptation and performance both at the individual and team levels raises complex conceptual and measurement issues that are only beginning to be addressed (Chan, 1998a; Tesluk, Mathieu & Zaccaro, 1997). The study of teams provides an excellent context for research on individual adaptation because it often forces the researcher to address the complex but critical issues involving the construct validity and processual nature of adaptation. I will discuss these issues after reviewing the fourth area of research on individual adaptation.

## Newcomer Socialization Research

During the first few months in an organization, newcomers are continually trying to make sense of the uncertainties and adapt to the new and changing work environment (Louis, 1980). Thus, the newcomer's experience during organizational entry is often described in recent socialization literature as an individual adaptation process (Ashford & Black, 1996; Bauer & Green, 1994; Morrison, 1993a, b). This adaptation process is seen as critical to the development of attitudes and behaviors that enable the newcomer to function effectively during the transition period and adjust to the new work environment (Vandenberg & Self, 1993).

Early socialization research conceptualized and assessed adaptation outcomes in terms of traditional variables such as job performance, turnover, satisfaction, and organizational commitment (e.g., Feldman, 1981). As recent research construes the newcomer as proactive rather than reactive or passive, the focus of attention is turned to such variables as task mastery, role clarity, and social integration, which are more proximal adaptation outcomes of newcomer proactivities than the traditional outcomes. A detailed review of the literature on newcomer adaptation is provided in Bauer, Morrison and Callister (1998) and hence will not be repeated here.

The central interest in the newcomer individual adaptation process is the intra-individual change that occurs over time during organizational entry.

However, the assessment of intra-individual change has largely been inadequate in previous studies. For example, important individual adaptation questions such as the presence of individual differences in the rate of change in an adaptation outcome and the associations between initial levels of adaptation and rates of change have been neglected. Chan and Schmitt (in press) explicated the weaknesses of traditional approaches to intra-individual change and showed how a latent growth modeling approach can address these weaknesses and directly answers important individual adaptation questions. A more comprehensive version of the modeling approach is provided in Chan (1998b). As argued later, Chan's method provides a powerful and flexible framework for bridging many of the conceptual and empirical gaps in the assessment of intra-individual change and, more generally, the research on individual adaptation.

## BRIDGING GAPS IN RESEARCH ON INDIVIDUAL ADAPTATION

The above brief review indicates that diverse research literatures have adopted somewhat different research paradigms and often apparently disparate assumptions in the approach to individual adaptation. This section will argue that each of the four areas of research, however, has not paid sufficient attention to several critical issues. There are both conceptual and empirical gaps that need to be bridged if we are to gain a better understanding of the phenomenon of individual adaptation. These gaps relate to issues of (a) dimensionality, (b) malleability, (c) predictor–criterion relationships, (d) levels of analysis, and (e) change over time.

### Dimensionality

As noted in the above discussion on individual differences research, there is no agreement on what specific KSAOs constitute adaptability. With one researcher assessing adaptability using a personality measure and another assessing adaptability using a cognitive ability measure, findings on adaptability relationships across the two studies may not be directly comparable. When results of these studies are combined in a meta-analysis, the meta-analytic findings may not be meaningful and may even be misleading. Advances in the individual differences approach to adaptation are likely to be preceded by the explicit recognition, in terms of both conceptualization and measurement of the multidimensionality of the adaptability construct (Chan, in press-a). There is probably no single unitary individual difference construct (i.e., trait) of adaptability that is applicable to the diverse adaptive situations of interest.

To address the issue of dimensionality, both conceptual and empirical gaps need to be bridged. Conceptually, we have to begin by proceeding in a theory-driven manner to identify the relevant domains of individual difference constructs such as cognitive ability (e.g., fluid intelligence), cognitive style (e.g., field dependency), personality (e.g., openness to experience), and motivational styles (e.g. learning goal orientation) that could form the foundation for adaptability. These adaptability domains, within each of which specific attributes are defined, would constitute the core components of adaptability. As I will argue later, explicating this multidimensionality is important for meaningful theorizing and estimation of predictor–criterion relationships and it provides an important step towards the development of an adequate theory of adaptability.

Bridging the conceptual gap in the dimensionality issue provides the necessary basis for bridging the empirical gaps. A clear conceptual definition of the specific adaptability construct in question would allow precise and valid measures to be developed and potential differences across various adaptability constructs could be empirically assessed. When researchers are explicit in their conceptualization and measurement of their adaptability constructs, meaningful meta-analyses could be performed and primary studies could be coded according to construct to test for moderator effects.

## Malleability

The issue of malleability or trainability of an individual's level of adaptability has not received adequate attention in either the individual differences or training research. By construing adaptability in terms of trait-like attributes, individual differences researchers almost always assume that an individual level of adaptability is a given and is stable across time so that it is not susceptible to change (increase or decrease). Training researchers, on the other hand, tend to emphasize the efficacy of interventions or conditions to develop or increase adaptive expertise and have somewhat ignored or downplayed the role of individual differences. Within-group variance is more often treated as error variance than residual variance that may be of substantive interest. In short, while the individual differences researcher has not given sufficient attention to the search for contextual or situational moderators (i.e., training interventions), the training researcher should pay more attention to potential individual differences in trainability. The extent of malleability is likely to differ across different aspects of adaptation or adaptability components. For example, it may be the case that training individuals to adapt to changes in organizational policies is easier than training individuals to adapt to changes in emergency crisis situations. Likewise, it may be the case that adaptability levels are more malleable when they involve learning goal orientations than when they involve cognitive ability or personality traits. This underscores the importance of addressing the fundamental question of dimensionality discussed above.

To address the issue of malleability, an integrative person–situation approach that views the individual differences perspective and training or learning perspective as complementary is necessary (Chan, in press-a). This approach requires the traditional individual differences researcher and training researcher to reconceptualize the notion of residual variance. Instead of treating residual variance as entirely made of random measurement error, it should be treated as unexplained variance due to model mis-specification resulting from omission of important variables from 'the other perspective'. Hence, researchers should consider including both individual differences and training or situational variables when conceptualizing and measuring individual adaptation. Aptitude X Treatment study designs would have to be the rule rather than the exception so that we could assess how effects of individual differences may be dependent on context (i.e., training interventions or other situational variables) and vice versa. Finally, we should specify what demands related to adaptation exist, and measure outcomes focused on whether or not individuals meet these demands. In other words, the issue of malleability cannot be adequately addressed without a clear delineation of the aspects of adaptive situations and outcomes involved. This is essentially a criterion problem. The issue is discussed in more detail in the next section.

## Predictor–Criterion Relationships

Conceptual and empirical gaps also exist in the theorizing and estimation of predictor–criterion relationships in research on individual adaptation. The predictors studied are usually some individual difference constructs such as personality traits or other person variables such as job knowledge and work experience. The criteria are adaptive outcomes and are typically some measures of the individual's adaptive performance on some given task. The problem is that many studies appear to uncritically assume a simple linear positive bivariate association between predictor and criterion when they select predictors of adaptive performance and estimate the predictor–criterion relationship. Studies examining more complex predictor–criterion relationships involving curvilinear and interaction terms are virtually non-existent.

A primary reason for the failure to consider such complex relationships is the lack of a construct orientation in either the predictor or criterion space. In Chan (in press-a), I provided a detailed account of how complex predictor–criterion relationships could be revealed when the nature of work experience as a predictor construct is explicated. Using conceptual frameworks (Quinones, Ford & Teachout, 1995; Tesluk & Jacobs, 1998) that emphasize the multidimensional, multilevel, and dynamic nature of the work experience construct; I have argued that experience can either promote or inhibit adaptation. For example, having more experience (amount) of working on different task types which share the same underlying deep structure is likely to increase the probability of successfully abstracting the underlying principles in the structure. That is, for some task domains, work experience of different types at the task level may have a positive effect on the development of adaptive expertise. On the other hand, work experience may inhibit adaptation through the mechanism of routinization. Experience in terms of extensive repeated task practice may lead to compilation of declarative knowledge into procedural productions (condition-action rules). When task performance is proceduralized, the individual quickly or automatically applies well-practiced strategies or solutions to familiar and well-learned problem situations. However, in novel situations requiring new strategies or responses, similar but causally irrelevant (in terms of problem solution) features would match the condition in the individual's production, causing this *routine* (as opposed to adaptive) expert to automatically execute the action. The action executed would be inappropriate to meet the new demands in the novel situation. This would be an instance of a negative association between experience and adaptive performance. Alternatively, there could be a curvilinear (inverted-U shaped) relationship between amount of experience and adaptive performance such that performance increases with initial practice but, with more extensive practice, proceduralization occurs and performance decreases (see function for same task type in Figure 4.1).

The complexity of predictor–criterion relationships also calls for more complex ways of estimating the effects of interest. Consider again the two modes of experience (conceptualized at the task level)—amount and type. Figure 4.1 hypothesizes that (for some given task domain), based on some theory similar

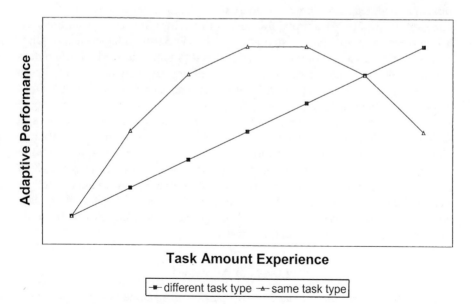

**Task Amount Experience**

| -■- different task type -▲- same task type |

**Figure 4.1**  A hypothetical polynomial interaction effect between task amount experience and task type on adaptive performance

to the arguments presented in the preceding paragraph, there is a complex interaction effect between task amount experience and task type on adaptive performance. The test of such a hypothesis would require performing a hierarchical regression analysis assessing the unique contribution of a polynomial interaction term. If one is exploring possible interaction effects without a theory of the predictor–criterion relationships, then one is likely to stop at the step where the simple amount X type interaction term is entered into the regression equation. Note that the presence of a polynomial interaction effect, depending on its nature, may or may not imply the presence of a simple interaction effect.

Clearly, the first step in bridging gaps in the theorizing and estimation of predictor–criterion constructs is developing comprehensive and useful conceptual models and valid measures in both the predictor and criterion space. On the predictor side, the literature in differential psychology provides relatively comprehensive models or taxonomies of individual differences variables that can be developed into models of adaptability constructs and relevant valid measures of many of these constructs are likely to be found in the personnel selection literature. In contrast, there is apparently little literature from which we can readily draw to develop conceptual models and valid measures on the criterion side. Campbell's (1990) theory of job performance which decomposes the multidimensional construct of performance into eight components may provide a useful starting point for developing a model of adaptive performance.

Modeling and assessing the criterion space in adaptation research has to go beyond the construct of job performance to develop theory-based and empirically validated taxonomies of adaptation demands and performance outcomes. Pulakos (1996) is probably the first to attempt the development of such a criterion taxonomy. She systematically abstracted the adaptability requirements of a wide variety of jobs and considered potential individual differences correlates of these requirements. She analyzed critical incidents related by job incumbents in a wide variety of military and civilian jobs and classified the types of situations that required adaptation. Her final list of adaptive behaviors ranged from 'handling crisis situations and work stress' to 'learning work tasks and technologies' and 'interpersonal and intercultural sensitivity and adaptability'. Taxonomic efforts as such (both in the predictor and criterion space) require substantial research resources but they are critical to advances in research in individual adaptation. Significant advances will be made if researchers could use these validated taxonomies to derive taxonomic or predictor–criterion linkages and elaborate them into specific models of individual adaptation, which can be further empirically tested (Chan, in press-a).

## Levels of Analysis

Organizational phenomena have the properties of dynamic systems, with critical antecedents, processes, and outcomes conceptualized and measured at multiple levels of organizational analysis such as the individual, group, and organization (Chan, 1998a). A number of authors have underscored the importance of adopting a multilevel approach to organizational phenomena and several theoretical frameworks for multilevel research have been proposed (e.g., Chan, 1998a; House, Rousseau & Thomas-Hunt, 1995; Klein, Dansereau & Hall, 1994; Rousseau, 1985). Discussion on important mathematical issues related to the analysis of multilevel data (e.g., Bliese, 1998; Bliese & Halverson, 1998; Ostroff, 1993) and analytical models for structuring multilevel data (e.g., Bryk & Raudenbush, 1987; McArdle & Epstein, 1987; Meredith & Tisak, 1990; Willett & Sayer, 1994) are also available. However, despite the existence of these theoretical frameworks and methodological advances, the fundamental conceptual and measurement issues related to levels are often neglected in substantive research in I/O psychology. Several conceptual and empirical gaps in the research in individual adaptation are results of insufficient attention paid to the multilevel issues raised by these authors. These gaps are most salient in the team and newcomer socialization literatures on adaptation.

A central issue in teams research is gaining a clear understanding of the nature of individual contributions to team effectiveness (Kozlowski et al., in press). Recall that in teams research individual adaptation is important to the extent each team member is expected to effectively cope with new information provided by other members and new demands created by the team task environment. On the surface, it appears that the issue is straightforward. To make a team high in adaptive performance, don't we simply staff the team with individuals who are high in adaptability? The problem is that interaction and coordination among team members are central in team functioning so that team performance is often not a straightforward result of the additive aggregate of individual team members. As noted by Kozlowski et al. (in press), teams research that focuses on identifying the KSAOs that individual team members should possess can only provide a limited gain in our understanding of team effectiveness. Kozlowski et al. presented an elaborate model of the development of adaptive teams. According to this model, the basis for the development of a team's adaptive expertise is the process of team compilation in which team members comprehend patterns of role exchange and relations of these patterns to task contingencies. Because team adaptive performance is the result of dynamic and complex interactions of these network patterns, adaptability at the team level is not simply an additive aggregate of adaptability at the individual level.

But whether the additive aggregate model or some other composition models should be employed is dependent on how the construct of team adaptability is conceptualized. In Chan (1998a), I argued that a fundamental problem in multilevel research is that the issue of construct validation has not been adequately addressed. Specifically, multilevel researchers often do not make explicit their *composition* model(s) when composing 'new' constructs from their lower-level counterparts. A composition model specifies the functional relationships between constructs at the two different levels of analysis. These relationships enable the explicit transformation from the lower-level construct (individual adaptability) to the higher-level construct (team adaptability) which in turn provides conceptual precision in the target construct (team adaptability) hence aiding the derivation of test implications for hypothesis testing. Using the typology of composition models provided in Chan (1998a), the teams' researcher can explicate the conceptual definition of the team-level construct of adaptability, as assumed in his or her study, and the appropriate model for composing the target construct from the lower-level construct of individual adaptability.

Consider the example where individual adaptation is construed essentially as individual self-regulation. The teams researcher proposes that a self-regulation functionally similar to individual self-regulation also exists at the team level (e.g., Kozlowski et al., 1996). At the individual level, self-regulation refers to the activities carried out by the individual to monitor and evaluate his or her own performance with respect to progress toward a goal. The critical parameters of self-regulation include understanding of the coordination of one's actions, error detection, balancing multiple tasks or workloads to stay on track towards goal achievement, and a knowledge of one's task environment (Kanfer & Ackerman, 1989). On the basis of these critical parameters, the teams researcher could employ the *process composition* model described in Chan (1998a) to compose the process of self-regulation from the individual level to the team level. Kozlowski et al. (1996) did just that when they described team self-regulation as team members gaining 'an understanding of how to coordinate member actions, engage in error detection, and monitor each other's performance, so the team can balance workloads and stay on track toward stated objectives' (p. 276). The authors provided the conceptual definition of team self-regulation (team adaptability) by explicating the team-level analogues for the critical parameters of self-regulation (adaptability) at the individual level (individual adaptability).

In practice, composing adaptation from the individual level to the team level is often not easy because the adaptation process of interest is often multifaceted or multidimensional with embedded subprocesses. Unlike the other models (e.g., additive composition, direct consensus composition) in Chan's (1998a) typology, process composition has no concrete empirical algorithm to compose the lower-level process(es) to the higher-level process(es). A challenge for researchers examining adaptive teams is to develop an adequate process composition model and derive explicit hypotheses to be tested as part of the validation of the model. The researcher may have to start by composing the less complex subprocesses of adaptation and systematically integrate these component processes into the complex and multidimensional process of team adaptation. Note also that because multiple constructs may be specified and interrelated in the description of a process, it may be the case that an adequate process composition model of team adaptation has to be preceded by specifying one or more composition forms in Chan's (1998a) typology for composing the relevant higher-level constructs. For example, the process composition may be preceded by an additive composition in which some team adaptability construct (e.g., team ability) is composed from the individual level adaptability construct (cognitive ability).

When we pay attention to issues of levels of analysis and composition models, we will be able to clarify the relationships between individual and team adaptability, both in the individual differences and training literatures. Chan (1998a) provided an example of how construct development of the notion of team adaptability can proceed from the individual differences and learning (training) approaches. In the individual differences approach, we can adopt a static approach of adaptability and begin with the individual-level construct of adaptability defined in terms of a stable individual difference attribute. We then specify an additive (or direct consensus, see Chan, 1998a) composition for composing the individual-level construct to the team level. Hypotheses concerning the new construct could then be formulated. For example, we could hypothesize that this static notion of team adaptability is positively associated with team morale. In the learning or training approach, we begin with the individual-level construct of adaptability defined in terms of a process in which the individual suppressed proceduralized actions and developed new productions when confronted with novel task demands. We then specify a process composition for composing the individual-level construct to the team level. Hypotheses concerning the new construct now could be formulated. For example, we could hypothesize that team mastery orientation is positively associated with this dynamic or process notion of team adaptability.

There are also conceptual and empirical gaps in the newcomer socialization literature on individual adaptation that may be construed as results of insufficient attention paid to levels of analysis. As described earlier, the assessment of intra-individual change over time in extant studies on newcomer adaptation has largely been inadequate. Intra-individual change is assessed using repeated measurements from the same individuals over time and it occurs at a level lower than the individual level of analysis. To put it another way, time is nested within individuals. Traditional approaches to newcomer adaptation research emphasized within-time inter-individual variability (i.e., at the individual level of analysis) and failed to consider across-time intra-individual variability (i.e., at the intra-individual level of analysis). Even when longitudinal studies are performed, the focus has almost always been on change at the aggregate level (typically in terms of mean differences) and thus does not provide an adequate conceptualization and analysis of intra-individual changes over time and inter-individual differences in these changes. Only when a distinction is made between individual and intra-individual levels of analysis are we able to directly address such questions as individual differences in the form of the intra-individual trajectory and the rate of intra-individual change, associations between individual differences at initial status and in rate of change, and associations between rate of change and external correlates. Chan and Schmitt (in press) argued for the importance of these questions to our understanding of the newcomer individual adaptation process. Using data collected from newcomers over four repeated measurements spaced equally at one-month intervals, the authors demonstrated how these and other adaptation questions can be directly addressed using a latent growth modeling approach that explicitly distinguishes between individual and intra-individual levels of analysis.

## Change over Time

Individual adaptation does not occur in a time vacuum. Thus, questions concerning different aspects of change over time are directly relevant. In Chan (1998b), I explicated nine fundamental questions on change over time and proposed an integrative analytical model to help conceptualize and assess the different facets of change over time corresponding to these questions. (The reader is referred to Chan, 1998b for the description of the analytical model including details on how aspects of the model are used to address the nine questions on change over time.) I will summarize these questions and relate them to research in individual adaptation. Addressing these questions would bridge many conceptual and empirical gaps relating to change over time as well as to the above discussions on dimensionality, malleability, predictor–criterion relationships, and levels of analysis.

Question 1 asks if the change is to be considered as *systematic differences* or *random fluctuations*. An adequate change assessment in the study of individual adaptation should account for measurement error and allow observed variance to be partitioned into true construct variance, nonrandom (systematic) error variance, and random error variance. When change over time is assessed, the notions of time-specific and time-related errors have to be incorporated in the change assessment. This is because measurement errors may not be homoscedastic and independent within individuals over time. Very often, we do not have a priori reasons to expect the precision with which an adaptation attribute can be measured to remain identical (i.e., homoscedastic) or change (i.e., heteroscedastic) over time. Even if we do, we need ways of testing the particular assumption. When consecutive measurements are closely spaced in time, errors may also be correlated, especially for identical measures. A failure to adequately model the error covariance structure could lead to biased estimates of the magnitude of true change and even mis-specification of the true change patterns. The model proposed by Chan (1998b) has the capability and flexibility to (a) model a variety of a priori specified error covariance structures and (b) assess the effects of mis-specification of the error to covariance structure on the estimates of true change.

Question 2 asks if the change is to be considered *reversible* or *irreversible*. Change can be unidirectional with no possibility of returning to or restoring previous states or levels, or it can be reversible. The trajectory representing the change over time may be monotonically increasing or decreasing (e.g., linear) so that change is construed as irreversible, or the trajectory may be one of several nonmonotonic functional forms (e.g., an 'inverted U') so that change over time is construed as reversible. Using the procedures described in Chan (1998b), the researcher can capture the form of the change trajectory representing the individual adaptation process by specifying a priori one or more functional forms and assessing the goodness-of-fit of each form and the incremental fit of one form over the other (e.g., the incremental fit of a quadratic over a linear trajectory).

Question 3 asks if the change is to be considered *unitary* or *multipath*. Change can be represented as proceeding in one single pathway or through multiple different pathways. Multiple paths occur when a detour from a single change trajectory is possible as individuals proceed from one point to another. Consider the example of changes in levels on an adaptation outcome as newcomers proceed from Time 1 to Time 4 (through Times 2 and 3). Even if all newcomers share the same level at Time 1 and at Time 4, some newcomers may follow a linear trajectory while others follow a quadratic trajectory. The multiple-group growth modeling procedures described in Chan (1998b) allow the researcher to identify subgroups of individuals that followed different change trajectories.

Question 4 asks if the change is to be considered as (a) a *continuous, gradual, quantitative* phenomenon; (b) *large magnitude shifts* on a *quantitative* variable; or (c) a progression through a series of *qualitatively distinctive* stages. When representing change with a linear trajectory, the change may be construed as (a) or (b) to the extent that the slope of the linear trajectory is gradual or steep. However, the trajectory, linear or otherwise, will be an inappropriate representation when the true nature of change over time is best characterized as (c) in which there is a qualitative shift in the conceptualization of the phenomenon between time points. When such qualitative changes occur, representing and interpreting change over time in terms of the parameters (e.g., slope) of a change trajectory is misleading and not meaningful because we would be comparing apples at one time point with oranges at another. Chan (1998b) argued that the researcher should assess if (c)-type changes occur prior to modeling (a)-type and (b)-type changes. In their study on newcomer adaptation, Chan and Schmitt (in press) demonstrated the absence of (c)-type changes prior to modeling the change trajectories of several adaptation variables. The notion of (c)-type change is described in more detail in Question 5.

Question 5 asks if the change is to be considered as differences in (a) magnitude in an absolute sense, (b) calibration of measurement, or (c) conceptualization. These three types of changes correspond to Golembiewski, Billingsley and Yeager's (1976) *alpha*, *beta*, and *gamma* change respectively. The issue described in Question 4 is a special instance of this more general and fundamental question concerning the type of change. Alpha change refers to changes in absolute levels given a constant conceptual domain and a constant measuring instrument. In research in individual adaptation, assessment of change over time is often directly based on absolute differences in responses on some measures, that is, true change is assumed to be alpha change. However, the reliance on absolute differences as a direct indicator of change over time assumes measurement invariance (equivalence) of responses across repeated measurements. We can meaningfully speak of alpha change only when there is measurement invariance of responses across time. Measurement invariance across time exists when the numerical values across time waves are on the same measurement scale (Drasgow, 1984, 1987).

Measurement invariance could be construed as absence of beta and gamma changes. Beta change refers to changes in absolute level complicated by changes in the measuring instrument given a constant conceptual domain. Beta change occurs when there is a recalibration of the measurement scale. That is, in beta change, the observed change results from an alteration in the respondent's subjective metric or evaluative scale rather from an actual change in the construct of interest. A difficulty in the training research approach to individual adaptation is that the training intervention may have caused beta change as much as alpha change so that direct comparisons between pre- and post-training may not necessarily be a good indication of changes in adaptation levels on the construct of interest. Sometimes beta change (as opposed to alpha change) may be the idea underlying adaptation in the sense that the recalibration of measurement is critical to adaptive performance. To my knowledge, no research has construed adaptation as such or attempted to separate alpha from possible beta change when examining changes in adaptation due to training. Chan's (in press-b) application of mean and covariance structures analysis to detect differences in item 'evocativeness' of a construct (i.e., uniform differential item functioning) may be used to assess beta change by treating pre- and post-training adaptation measures as different items assessing the same construct.

Gamma change refers to change in the conceptual domain. The change described in Question 4(c) is a gamma change. Gamma change can take a variety of forms. For example, in the language of factor analysis, the number of factors (a factor representing a construct) assessed by a given set of measures may change from one time point to another. Alternatively, the number of factors may remain constant across time, but a differentiation process occurs so that the factor intercorrelations decrease over time, or an integration process may occur so that the factor intercorrelations increase over time. When individuals adapt, their conceptual structures may be undergoing factorial differentiation as they acquire a more differentiated view of the knowledge domain. Or, their conceptual structures may be undergoing factorial integration as previously unrelated dimensions in the knowledge domain get integrated into global undifferentiated dimension. Given the emphasis on the qualitative change in conceptualization of the the task problem domain that purportedly occurs when individuals develop adaptive expertise, it is somewhat surprising that previous research has not explicitly discussed and assessed the various forms of gamma change as measures of individual adaptation. The literature on gamma change is directly relevant for bridging the conceptual and empirical gaps in research that construe adaptation as changes in conceptualization. More discussions on gamma change including measurement issues are available in Chan (1998b), Millsap and Hartog (1988), Schaubroeck and Green (1989), Schmitt (1982), and Vandenberg and Self (1993).

Question 6 asks if the change is to be considered as a shared characteristic of a *group of individuals* over time or to be referred to what occurs *within an individual* over time, or *both*. This issue has been discussed above in the section on levels of analysis. Suffice to say that researchers should be sensitive to the different aspects of change over time that may be occurring at different levels of analysis. Even if the researcher hypothesizes that change occurs at one but not the other level, it is important to collect data at both levels and employ analytical models that estimate effects at both levels so that the assumption of no change at the non-target level can be tested.

Question 7 asks if *individual differences in intra-individual change* in the focal variable are predictable from external variables. For example, in newcomer adaptation research, we may want to know if individual differences in the rate of change in an adaptation outcome are predictable from individual differences in cognitive ability or some individual difference adaptability construct.

Question 8 asks if there are *cross-domain relationships* in change over time. For example, are individual differences in rate of change in adaptive performance during training related to individual differences in rate of change in adaptive performance on the job? For the same set of predictor variables, is the pattern of predictive relationships (e.g., predictor-rate of change associations) invariant across different domains (i.e., training versus job)? Chan (1998b) described how a variety of these cross-domain relationships can be examined by relating predictors and change trajectories from different domains in a single multivariate model.

Question 9, the final question, asks if there is *invariance across groups* with respect to the specific facet of change over time under investigation. These groups could be experimental and control groups in research on training adaptive expertise or they could be natural occurring groups such as gender groups or groups which differ on some adaptability construct. The question of interest is whether a specific change pattern found in one group is equal to (invariant) or differs from (noninvariant), in either magnitude or form, the change pattern in a different group. For example, the trajectory representing changes in adaptive performance on a novel job task may differ in functional form between newcomers and veterans. Or, in training adaptive expertise, the experimental group may undergo a type of gamma change represented by factorial integration of performance measurement so that performance components (factors) become increasingly interrelated over time, whereas the control group may exhibit factorial invariance so that intercorrelations among performance components remain constant over time. Chan (1998b) demonstrated how specific facets of change in patterns in multiple groups can be modeled and compared to determine if invariance exists across groups.

The adequacy of the answers to the relevant questions enumerated above forms the basis for bridging the conceptual and empirical gaps in research on individual adaptation. As discussed, these questions on change over time are inextricably linked to the issues of dimensionality, malleability, predictor–criterion relationships, and levels of analysis.

## CONCLUDING REMARKS

There is an increased proliferation of new concepts and assessment technologies in the research on individual adaptation, whether it is in the literature on individual differences, training, team, or newcomer socialization. For example, concepts such as team mental models and team compilation and new assessment technologies or measurement techniques such as the Pathfinder algorithm for eliciting knowledge structures and various cognitive task analysis methods are increasingly employed in recent research. However, as discussed in this paper, several important conceptual and empirical gaps exist. Unless these gaps are satisfactorily addressed, we may end up with a multitude of labels, all of which purportedly refer to scientific constructs or valid measurements concerning individual adaptation but in reality have no incremental explanatory value.

## ACKNOWLEDGEMENTS

The author would like to thank Neal Schmitt, Elaine Pulakos, and Paul Tesluk for the fruitful discussions on some of the ideas contained in this paper. Correspondence concerning this paper should be directed to David Chan, Department of Social Work and Psychology, National University of Singapore, 10 Kent Ridge Crescent, Singapore 119260, Republic of Singapore. Electronic mail can be sent to *swkcct@nus.edu.sg*.

## REFERENCES

Anderson, J. R. (1983). *The Architecture of Cognition*. Cambridge, MA: Harvard University Press.
Anderson, J. R. (1993). Problem-solving and learning. *American Psychologist*, **48**, 35–44.

Ashford, S. J. & Black, J. S. (1996). Proactivity during organizational entry: The role of desire for control. *Journal of Applied Psychology*, **81**, 199–214.

Bauer, T. N. & Green, S. G. (1994). Effect of newcomer involvement in work-related activities: a longitudinal study of socialization. *Journal of Applied Psychology*, **79**, 219–223.

Bauer, T. N., Morrison, E. W. & Callister, R. B. (1998). Organizational socialization: A review and directions for future research. In G. R. Ferris (Ed.), *Research in Personnel and Human Resource Management*, Vol. 16 (pp. 149–214). Greenwich, CT: JAI Press.

Bliese, P. D. (1998). Group size, ICC values, and group-level correlations: A simulation. *Organizational Research Methods*, **1**, 355–373.

Bliese, P. D. & Halverson, R. R. (1998). Group size and measures of group-level properties: An examination of eta-squared and ICC values. *Journal of Management*, **24**, 157–172.

Bryk, A. S. & Raudenbush, S. W. (1987). Application of hierarchical linear models to assessing change. *Psychological Bulletin*, **101**, 147–158.

Campbell, J. P. (1990). Modeling the performance prediction problem in industrial and organizational psychology. In M. D. Dunnette and L. M. Hough (Eds), *Handbook of Industrial and Organizational Psychology*, Vol. 1, (pp. 687–732). Palo Alto, CA: Consulting Psychologists Press.

Cannon-Bowers, J. A., Tannenbaum, S. I., Salas, E. & Volpe, C. E. (1995). Defining competencies and establishing team training requirements. In R. A. Guzzo & E. Salas (Eds), *Team Effectiveness and Decision Making in Organizations* (pp. 333–380). San Francisco: Jossey-Bass.

Chan, D. (1996). Criterion and construct validation of an assessment center. *Journal of Occupational and Organizational Psychology*, **69**, 167–181.

Chan, D. (1998a). Functional relations among constructs in the same content domain from different levels of analysis. *Journal of Applied Psychology*, **83**, 234–246.

Chan, D. (1998b). The conceptualization and analysis of change over time: An integrative approach incorporating longitudinal means and covariance structures analysis (LMACS) and multiple indicator latent growth modeling (MLGM). *Organizational Research Methods*, **1**, 421–483.

Chan, D. (in press-a). Understanding adaptation to changes in the work environment: Integrating individual difference and learning perspectives. *Research in Personnel and Human Resources Management.*

Chan, D. (in press-b). Detection of differential item functioning on the Kirton Adaptation-Innovation Inventory using multiple-group mean and covariance structures analysis. *Multivariate Behavioral Research.*

Chan, D. & Schmitt, N. (in press). Interindividual differences in intraindividual changes in proactivity during organizational entry: A latent growth modeling approach to understanding newcomer adaptation. *Journal of Applied Psychology.*

Chi, M. T. H., Feltovich, P. J. & Glaser, R. (1981). Categorization and representation of physics problems by experts and novices. *Cognitive Science*, **5**, 121–152.

Drasgow, F. (1984). Scrutinizing psychological tests: Measurement equivalence and equiavalent relations with external variables are central issues. *Psychological Bulletin*, **95**, 134–135.

Drasgow, F. (1987). Study of measurement bias of two standardized psychological tests. *Journal of Applied Psychology*, **72**, 19–29.

Feldman, D. C. (1981). The multiple socialization of organization members. *Academy of Management Review*, **6**, 309–318.

Ford, J. K. & Kraiger, K. (1995). The application of cognitive constructs and principles to the instructional systems model of training: Implications for needs assessment, design, and transfer. In C. L. Cooper and I. T. Robertson (Eds), *Inter-*

*national Review of Industrial and Organizational Psychology*, Vol. 10 (pp. 1–48). Chichester: Wiley.

Goldsmith, T. E. & Kraiger, K. (1997). Structural knowledge assessment and training evaluation. In J. K. Ford and Associates (Eds), *Improving Training Effectiveness in Work Organizations* (pp. 73–96). Hillsdale, NJ: Erlbaum.

Golembiewski, R. T., Billingsley, K. & Yeager, S. (1976). Measuring change and persistence in human affairs: Types of change generated by OD designs. *Journal of Applied Behavioral Science*, **12**, 133–157.

Gough, H. G. (1987). *Manual for the California Psychological Inventory*. Palo Alto, CA: Consulting Psychologists Press.

Hollenbeck, J. R., Ilgen, D. R., Phillips, J. M. & Hedlund, J. (1994). Decision risk in dynamic two-stage contexts: Beyond the status quo. *Journal of Applied Psychology*, **79**, 592–598.

Holyoak, K. J. (1991). Symbolic connectionism: Toward third-generation theories of expertise. In K. A. Ericsson and J. Smith (Eds), *Toward a General Theory of Expertise* (pp. 301–336). Cambridge: Cambridge University Press.

House, R., Rousseau, D. M. & Thomas-Hunt, M. (1995). The meso paradigm: A framework for the integration of micro and macro organizational behavior. *Research in Organizational Behavior*, **17**, 71–114.

Jackson, D. N. (1967). *Personality Research Form Manual*. Goshen, NY: Research Psychologists Press.

Judge, T. K. A., Thoresen, C. J. & Pucik, V. (1996). Managerial coping with organizational change: A dispositional perspective. Paper presented at the Academy of Management Meetings, Cincinnati, Ohio.

Kanfer, R. & Ackerman, P. L. (1989). Motivation and cognitive abilities: An integrative-aptitude-treatment interaction approach to skill acquisition. *Journal of Applied Psychology*, **74**, 657–690.

Klein, K. J., Dansereau, R. G. & Hall, R. J. (1994). Levels issues in theory development, data collection, and analysis. *Academy of Management Review*, **19**, 195–229.

Kozlowski, S. W. J. (1998). Training and developing adaptive teams: Theory, principles, and research. In J. A. Cannon-Bowers & E. Salas (Eds), *Decision Making Under Stress: Implications for Training and Simulation* (pp. 115–153). Washington, DC: APA Books.

Kozlowski, S. W. J., Gully, S. M., McHugh, P. P., Salas, W. E. & Cannon-Bowers, J. A. (1996). A dynamic theory of leadership and team effectiveness: Developmental and task contingent leader roles. *Research in Personnel and Human Resources Management*, **14**, 253–305.

Kozlowski, S. W. J., Gully, S. M., Nason, E. R. & Smith, E. M. (in press). Developing adaptive teams: A theory of compilation and performance across levels and time. In D. R. Ilgen & E. D. Pulakos (Eds), *The Changing Nature of Work and Perfomance: Implications for Staffing, Personnel Actions, and Development*. San Francisco: Jossey-Bass.

Kraiger, K., Ford, J. K. & Salas, E. (1993). Application of cognitive, skill-based, and affective theories of learning outcomes to new methods of training evaluation. *Journal of Appled Psychology*, **78**, 311–328.

Latham, G. P., Saari, L. M., Pursell, M. A. & Campion, M. A. (1980). The situational interview. *Journal of Applied Psychology*, **69**, 569–573.

Louis, M. R. (1980). Surprise and sense-making: What newcomers experience in entering unfamiliar organizational settings. *Administrative Science Quarterly*, **25**, 226–251.

McArdle, J. J. & Epstein, D. (1987). Latent growth curves within developmental structural equation models. *Child Development*, **58**, 110–133.

Meredith, W. & Tisak, J. (1990). Latent curve analysis. *Psychometrika*, **55**, 107–122.

Millsap, R. E. & Hartog, S. B. (1988). Alpha, beta, and gamma change in evaluation research: A structural equation approach. *Journal of Applied Psychology*, 73, 574–584.

Morrison, E. W. (1993a). Longitudinal study of the effects of information seeking on newcomer socialization. *Journal of Applied Psychology*, 78, 173–183.

Morrison, E. W. (1993b). Newcomer information seeking: Exploring types, modes, sources, and outcomes. *Academy of Management Journal*, 36, 557–589.

Motowidlo, S. J., Carter, G. W., Dunnette, M. D., Tippins, N., Werner, S., Burnett, J. R. & Vaughn, M. J. (1992). Studies of the structured behavioral interview. *Journal of Applied Psychology*, 77, 571–587.

Mumford, M. D., Baughman, W. A., Threfall, K. V., Uhlman, C. E. & Costanza, D. P. (1993). Personality, adaptability, and performance: Performance on well-defined and ill-defined problem-solving tasks. *Human Performance*, 6, 241–285.

Ostroff, C. (1993). Comparing correlations based on individual level and aggregated data. *Journal of Applied Psychology*, 78, 569–582.

Paulhus, D. L. & Martin, C. L. (1988). Functional flexibility: A new conception of interpersonal flexibility. *Journal of Personality and Social Psychology*, 55, 88–101.

Pulakos, E. D. (1996). Proposal for the test of a model of adaptability. (Submitted to Department of Defense Small Business Innovation Research Program.) Washington, DC: Personnel Decisions Research Institutes.

Quinones, M. A., Ford, J. K. & Teachout, M. S. (1995). The relationship between work experience and job performance: A conceptual and meta-analytic review. *Personnel Psychology*, 48, 887–910.

Rousseau, D. M. (1985). Issues of level in organizational research: Multilevel and cross-level perspectives. In L. L. Cummings & B. Staw (Eds), *Research in Organizational Behavior*. Greenwich, CT: JAI Press.

Schaubroeck, J. & Green, S. G. (1989). Confirmatory factor analytic procedures for assessing change during organizational entry. *Journal of Applied Psychology*, 74, 892–900.

Schmitt, N. (1982). The use of analysis of covariance structures to assess beta and gamma change. *Multivariate Behavioral Research*, 17, 343–358.

Schmitt, N. & Chan, D. (1998). *Personnel Selection: A Theoretical Approach*. Thousand Oaks, CA: Sage.

Schmitt, N., Jennings, D. & Toney, R. (1996). Can we develop measures of hypothetical construct? Paper presented at the 1st Biannual Biodata Conference, Athens, GA.

Schvaneveldt, R. W., Durso, F. T. & Dearholt, D. W. (1985). *Pathfinder: Scaling with network structures* (Memoradum in Computer and Cognitive Science, MCCS-85-89, Computing Research Laboratory). Las Cruces: New Mexico State University.

Schvaneveldt, R. W., Durso, F. T. & Dearholt, D. W. (1989). Network structures in proximity data. In G. G. Bower (Ed.), *The Psychology of Learning and Motivation*, Vol. 24, (pp. 249–284). New York: Academic Press.

Smith, E. M., Ford, J. K. & Kozlowski, S. W. J. (1997). Building adaptive expertise: Implications for training design strategies. In M. A. Quinones & A. Ehrenstein (Eds), *Training for a Rapidly Changing Workplace*. American Psychological Association. Washington, DC.

Snow, R. E. & Lohman, D. L. (1984). Toward a theory of cognitive aptitude for learning from instruction. *Journal of Educational Psychology*, 76, 347–376.

Sternberg, R. J. (1994). The PRSVL model of person–context interaction in the study of human potential. In M. G. Rumsey, C. B. Walker & J. H. Harris (Eds), *Personnel Selection and Classification*. Hillsdale, NJ: Erlbaum.

Tesluk, P. & Jacogs, R. R. (1998) Toward an integrated model of work experience. *Personnel Psychology*, 51, 321–355.

Tesluk, P., Mathieu, J. E. & Zaccaro, S. J. (1997). Task and aggregation issues in the analysis and assessment of team performance. In M. T. Brannick, E. Salas & C.

Prince (Eds), *Team Performance Assessment and Measurement: Theory, Methods, and Applications*. Hillsdale, NJ: Erlbaum.

Vandenberg, R. J. & Self, R. M. (1993). Assessing newcomers' changing commitments to the organization during the first 6 months of work. *Journal of Applied Psychology*, **78**, 557–568.

Wagner, R. K. (1986). The search for intraterrestrial intelligence. In R. J. Sternberg & R. K. Wagner (Eds), *Practical Intelligence: Nature and Origins of Competence in the Everyday World*. Cambridge: Cambridge University Press.

Willett, J. B. & Sayer, A. B. (1994). Using covariance analysis to detect correlates and predictors of individual change over time *Psychological Bulletin*, **116**, 363–380.

# Chapter 5

# UNDERSTANDING ACTS OF BETRAYAL: IMPLICATIONS FOR INDUSTRIAL AND ORGANIZATIONAL PSYCHOLOGY

Jone L. Pearce and Gary R. Henderson
*University of California, Irvine*

Because it is an air of all-pervading bitterness that lingers over what has been one of Asia's most successful brokerage operations following the June departure of five of Morgan Grenfell Asia's (MGA's) top six Singaporean directors including Chairman NG Soo Peng and managing director Hsieh Fu Hua). Accusations of betrayal from the Singaporeans and counter-accusations from MGA's London-based parent Morgan Grenfell are still flying with stinging ferocity (Shale, *AsiaMoney*, 1993).

As interest has grown in complex organizational forms and contractual arrangements, industrial/organizational (I/O) psychologists throughout the world have directed their attention to interpersonal relations as the foundation for successful organization. As the above quotation illustrates, when these relationships flounder, feelings of betrayal often follow. In today's more fluid organizational environment trust has become both more important and more problematic. Trust is more important because it cannot rest on stable hierarchies and functional relationships among people who work together their entire careers. Trust is more difficult because the growth of international networked organizations, cross-cultural teams and new forms of contingent employment make building and sustaining such relationships more difficult. We believe that for a better understanding of interpersonal relations in complex forms of interdependent organizations we can better understand these relationships by knowing more about betrayal. Our own interest reflects others' growing interest: industrial and organizational psychologists increasingly talk of betrayal. Reflecting this burgeoning interest, betrayal appears in scattered subdisciplines, for example, betrayal has been mentioned by scholars of trust, workplace justice and by those studying violations of psychological contracts. We also find that betrayal is at the intersection of several important scholarly trends in I/O psychological research; yet it is an ill-lit crossing.

*International Review of Industrial and Organizational Psychology, 2000 Volume 15*
Edited by C.L. Cooper and I.T. Robertson. © 2000 John Wiley & Sons, Ltd

This is so for two reasons. First, the concept of betrayal is being used in a multitude of ways, most of them quite narrow, some of them implicit, and with differing implications for theory and practice. In part this reflects the study of betrayal in the larger world of behavioral and social science, where the term has many meanings and uses. The growth of interest in topics of networks, trust, justice and psychological contracts, matters in which a betrayal is a key feature, suggests that there is need to clarify and organize what we do know about betrayal in its workplace forms. Second, a closer examination of betrayal helps illuminate other contemporary concerns in the field of I/O psychology. These include questions about intra-psychic processes, assumptions that more explanation will mitigate unwelcome organizational acts, how emotions affect behavior at work, and cross-national differences in interpretations of others' actions. This chapter begins with a wide-ranging review of the social and behavioral science conceptualizations of betrayal. Then we discuss several contentious issues from the literature that are most relevant to workplace psychology. We conclude by summarizing the implications of our discussion for several of those contemporary conceptual issues in international I/O psychology.

## BETRAYAL IN INDUSTRIAL/ORGANIZATIONAL PSYCHOLOGY

Betrayal is a difficult topic to embrace adequately because it has been touched on in work as old as the I/O field itself. In Roethlisberger and Dickson's (1939) classic Hawthorne Studies, for example, the workers of the Bank Wiring Room attempted to restrain the high productivity of the Room's rate-buster; they saw his violation of their informal quota as a betrayal likely to lead to them all having to work harder for the same pay. This study of betrayal of a work group's own normative expectations formed the basis for several decades of research on workplace rewards, work-group norms, and interpersonal influence. More recently betrayal has been noted by those seeking to understand the role of trust in organizational settings, those studying workplace justice, and theorists of psychological contracts.

### Betrayal of Trust

Two sets of scholars seeking to understand workplace trust have discussed betrayal in depth. They see betrayal as integral to an understanding of trust (Elangovan & Shapiro, 1998; Morris & Moberg, 1994), and consider betrayal to be the risk one runs when trusting another, the inherent vulnerability people have when they must place their fortunes in the uncertain hands of others (cf., Bigley & Pearce, 1998). They note that workplace trust is necessary because tasks are ambiguous and changing, and others' actions and the outcomes of those actions are often difficult to observe. Both works distinguish personal betrayal from impersonal betrayal and focus on the former. As Morris and Moberg (1994) state their case, personal betrayal is situated in the relationship between two people and a betrayal occurs when the expectations of a specific person for the actions of another person are not met. For example, the Bank Wiring Room rate-buster described above personally betrayed his coworkers. In contrast, impersonal betrayal is when a normative expectation or expectations pertaining to an office or to membership in a group are violated. If a government official accepts a bribe for a favorable decision, this is a violation of impersonal trust pertaining to that person's membership in the organization and occupation of a particular office or role. Similarly, if a general sells his army's battle plans to the enemy that is impersonal betrayal. Morris and Moberg (1994) developed a theoretical framework of personal betrayal in work settings. They focused on conditions leading individuals to perceive that they have been betrayed by another, and suggested that betrayal will be felt if the act was perceived as intentional, and if it was 'personal' (intentionally directed at the victim), rather than accidental.

The second set of scholars is Elangovan and Shapiro (1998), who provide a comprehensive theoretical model of personal betrayal in organizations. In contrast to others in industrial/organizational psychology they focused on why the perpetrator betrays rather than on the circumstances under which a breach or transgression is interpreted as a betrayal by the victim. Elangovan and Shapiro took a utilitarian approach to explaining why someone would betray others at work. They suggested that a person at work is more likely to betray others if the act is likely to be personally beneficial, the penalties or possibility of detection are low, other principles supporting the betrayal can be evoked, and if the perpetrator has a personal propensity to betray. Morris and Moberg (1994) and Elangovan and Shapiro (1998) have contributed to our understanding of workplace trust by articulating the circumstances that would lead victims to classify a transgression as a betrayal and that might cause perpetrators to violate others' trust in them.

## Workplace Injustice

In much work on injustice the word betrayal is rarely mentioned but descriptions of reactions to felt injustice reflect many elements of betrayal. For example, Bies (1987) reported the results of programmatic research on how argumentation lessens others' perceived moral outrage. He examined how offending acts could be reframed so they no longer seemed morally culpable, eliciting moral outrage in the victim. Outrage at perceived injustice has also been examined by Bies and Tripp (1998) and Bies, Tripp & Kramer (1997). This work has helped to counterbalance the excessive emphasis on cognitive calculation in much justice research by highlighting that a perceived injustice can elicit very strong emotions. In these works 'moral outrage' appears to be a synonym for betrayal. If anything, one might assume that some offending acts might be relatively mild, provoking sorrow, perhaps, but not moral outrage. Yet in the injustice literature the examples provided (e.g. underpayment) include unmet expectations which can be merely inconvenient or irritating rather than the kind of morally outrageous acts characterized as betrayals. That is, those studying injustice appear to address a broad range of workplace unmet expectation, from the trivial to the most extreme. Yet, we would not expect perpetrators' attempts to mitigate with self-justifying explanation to apply equally to a wide range of transgressions. For example, argumentation may only be effective for ambiguous acts, or mild transgressions, ones that have little chance of evoking moral outrage in the first place. Certainly, the excuses of perpetrators of genuinely morally outrageous acts are likely to be greeted with scorn. Differences in degree do matter, and so a better understanding of betrayal can help in understanding the boundary conditions for social accounts in mitigating reactions to transgressions with the potential to outrage.

### Breach of Psychological Contract

The growing interest in reframing employees' relationships with their organizations as psychological contracts has led to inquiry into the consequences of a breach of the psychological contract. A psychological contract is a set of beliefs, held by the employee, about what the employee and employer are obliged to give and receive in the relationship (Morrison & Robinson, 1997; Robinson, Kraatz & Rousseau, 1994; Robinson, 1996; Rousseau, 1995). Sandra Robinson (Morrison & Robinson, 1997; Robinson, 1996) has developed a model of the circumstances under which a breach of the psychological contract leads employees to experience the emotion of violation. She noted that a perception of a breach of psychological contract does not necessarily lead to 'feelings of betrayal and psychological distress', what she called perceived violation. Robinson suggested that a breach will be experienced as a violation if it is of sufficient magnitude, has important implications, is purposeful, is unfair, and violates the prevailing social contract. Her theoretical and empirical work makes an important contribution by emphasizing that all breaches of expectations do not necessarily result in strong feelings of violation or betrayal. However, in contrast to Elangovan and Shapiro's suggestion that betrayal is experienced only in personal relationships, Robinson includes an impersonal partner—the organization.

Like Morris and Moberg (1994) and Bies (1987), Robinson's work provides a basis for a more comprehensive examination of issues they introduce. These include determining which expectations are important enough to evoke feelings of betrayal if violated, a re-examination of the exclusion of impersonal betrayal from I/O psychology, the necessity of perpetrator intent to betray, the role of third parties, and necessity of shared knowledge, among others. We hope to build on this work with a comprehensive examination of betrayal. It begins with a discussion of what betrayal is, with particular attention to what leads certain transgressions to be more likely to be perceived as betrayals. This is followed by an analysis of areas in which theorists differ in their description of betrayal or its consequences. The paper concludes with a discussion of the implications of this conceptualization of betrayal for research in I/O psychology.

## UNDERSTANDING ACTS OF BETRAYAL

There are widely differing definitions of betrayal depending on the focus of the scholar. It is necessary to gain clarity on two defining features of betrayal before proceeding. First, to some betrayal is an individual's perception of another's act since, following Robinson, any given act may be perceived to be a betrayal or not. Others view betrayal as the action itself. Here, the latter act-based focus is adopted. This is because it is the most widely adopted definition, avoids a potentially autistic focus solely on individuals' potentially idiosyncratic perceptions, and directs attention to the question of why an act may or may not be interpreted as a betrayal.

Second, once we understand betrayals as acts defined as transgressing important expectations, we are free to treat the acts of groups, organizations or other collective entities as having the potential to be perceived as betrayals. Individuals have expectations for collective groupings as well as for individuals. Psychological contracts, for example, involve an individual's expectations for organizations' obligations to them. Certainly, there is widespread agreement on the importance of trust in and trust created by institutions (e.g., North, 1990; Zucker, 1986), and where there is trust there is the potential to betray the trust. Yet, before examining the characteristics of acts of betrayal we begin with the point of widespread agreement.

### Betrayal Enrages

When a transgression is categorized as a betrayal, strong negative emotions are aroused (Bateson, 1977). Åkerström (1991) suggested that an act of betrayal arouses intense sentiments such as indignation, contempt, revenge, and rage that can continue long after the event took place. As an illustration, Hansson, Jones and Fletcher (1990) reported that adults over age 60 stated that half of the incidents of betrayal at work they recalled had occurred more than twenty years before. The perception of being betrayed can unleash powerful emotions and so can have severe and potentially lasting consequences. It is this potentially powerful emotional quality and motivating potential of felt betrayal that attracts the interest of industrial/organizational psychologists. In organizations not all transgressions will enrage, yet when individuals experience a transgression as a betrayal the effects are potentially grave.

## Transgressions that Betray

If a violation is perceived to be a betrayal when it transgresses important expectations, what makes some expectations important while others are not? As Shackelford (1997, p. 73) notes, 'The actions or events that constitute betrayal in one relationship context may not constitute a betrayal in another such context'. Robinson noted that to qualify as a betrayal the trust violated needs to be important—what Elangovan and Shapiro called 'pivotal expectations'. Yet labeling transgressions which evoked feelings of betrayal as important after the fact has little predictive value. It would be more useful to have some guidance regarding which expectations are likely to be important or pivotal. Fortunately, many researchers in social psychology, sociology and political science have sought to distinguish betraying transgressions from others. While there is much overlap in the ideas of these theorists from different disciplines, each perspective is worth exploring.

### Violations of a constitutive rule

Metts (1994) argued that a transgression is more likely to be perceived as a betrayal if it violates a 'constitutive rule'. These are rules about what actions must occur if the relationship is going to continue. If constitutive rules are seen to be violated the relationship becomes meaningless or incoherent. The relationship or group must cease to exist in its present form (cf., Jones & Burdette, 1994). Constitutive rules are contrasted with 'regulative rules' which govern how interdependence will be managed. Thus, a constitutive rule for physicians may be to recommend only those procedures and drugs they believe will help the patient, while a regulative rule might be to see patients at their appointed times. A perceived violation of the constitutive rule (only beneficial treatment) goes to the heart of the nature of the relationship and so its violation is more likely to be seen as a betrayal than is a 30-minute delay in seeing the doctor.

In organizations constitutive rules would be those necessary to the coherence of the relationship with another individual, group or organization. For organizations these would be role requirements necessary to the functioning of the organization, and would be expected to vary depending on the context. For example, we would consider a colleague's 'selling' a good grade to a student at our university to be a violation of a constitutive rule and thus a betrayal. However, we are familiar with universities elsewhere in which such acts have occurred and the transgressions were treated more as a regulative-rule violation than a betrayal. Doesn't the assignment of grades based solely on students' performance constitute a core function of a university? It did appear that grades in those settings did not have the same constitutive meaning as they do in ours. There students obtained jobs and other opportunities based on who they knew, and their intellectual prowess was judged from personal interaction. Grades had no use as signals of intelligence or conscientiousness or knowledge because they all knew one another in these small intellectual circles, and so selling university grades was not a constitutive rule transgression.

### Revelations of group-defining secrets

Another approach to identifying why certain transgressions constitute betrayals is offered by Åkerström (1991). While having many similarities to the above arguments on constitutive rules, he examines one kind of constitutive rule in some depth—secrecy. He argues that betrayal involves overstepping a 'We-boundary'. A 'We' consists of relations ranging from a pair of friends to a nation (Åkerström, 1991, p. 2). He suggests that secrets and confidences exchanged are the creators of social bonds, the necessary component to the creation of a We. Åkerström echoes Simmel's (1994) contention that without secrets many aspects of social life would be impossible. Secrets divide those who know from those who do not. Such We-groupings can vary in size and intimacy and may be quite unstable. Thus, betrayal is a dishonoring of the We.

Åkerström goes on to note that in times of conflict or when individuals or groups have invested a great deal in their secrecy the betrayal can become very threatening. He distinguishes 'telling' betrayals from 'leaving' betrayals. On the one hand, telling betrayals may divulge information which is harmful in the hands of the outsider (i.e., the planned product innovation in the hands of a competitor) or may simply be mundane information that symbolizes the 'specialness' of the relationship or group. Nevertheless, it violates the We bond. On the other hand, leaving the group, occupation or organization can be seen as betrayal, as is desertion during war. Sometimes there are instrumental reasons for treating leaving as a betrayal—as violent underworld association members are concerned that a deserter is a potential informer. Alternatively, leaving may simply be interpreted as a rejection of the values of the We.

Applying his ideas to organizational settings helps illustrate why it is often so difficult to determine which acts will be seen as betrayals there. Both telling and leaving are a normal part of many career patterns. The skills and practices one learns on the job become the person's own foundation for a successful career. Employees often occupy explicitly 'boundary spanning' roles in which information exchange with their counterparts in other organizations is encouraged, and employees are frequently hired from other companies so that the hiring firm can learn new practices. Thus, telling and leaving may be expected activities at work, and not viewed as betraying acts. However, whether an act of employee telling or leaving is an act of betrayal can be a matter of great dispute. Following Åkerström, we suggest this is when such telling and leaving threatens the group or organization's values or survival. The fact that such expectations can be very contentious is reflected in the numerous lawsuits regarding 'no compete' clauses in employment contracts which bind employees after they have left an employer. Certainly, we would expect tellings and leavings that threaten the organization, occupation, or group to be more likely to evoke feelings of betrayal. Thus, we might expect participants to develop normative expectations about which leavings and tellings are an expected part of work and which ones would be betrayals.

### Threats to security

Transgressions that threatens the relationship, group, occupation or organization's security are likely to be seen as betrayals (Shackelford, 1997). Different acts pose security threats to different relationships, so the same acts may be seen as a betrayal in one relationship or setting but not in another. Shackelford (1997) provides insights into distinguishing acts that are betraying transgressions in one relationship from the same acts which do not evoke that judgement in another. He suggests that over evolutionary history human beings have adapted to relationships with different specific functions, and that a betrayal will be perceived as a transgression that threatens the viability of that specific relationship. He uses the contrast between same-sex friendships with mateships, producing evidence that extra-relationship intimate involvement is more threatening to a security in mateships than friendships and so more likely to be perceived as a betrayal.

Certainly, organizations and work groups will differ in the acts which might threaten their security. For example, in some organizations trade secrets pose a real threat to the continued viability of the organization while in others there are no real trade secrets. Some organizations working at the leading edge of internet or other software technology will not even disclose the kind of projects they are developing, whereas teachers do not have any trade secrets from one another. So we would expect the internet product developer to be more likely to see a software writer's departure for a competitor as a betrayal, but the principal would host a party to wish the departing teacher good luck.

### Threats to identity

Finally, transgressions that threaten one's identity are more likely to be seen as betrayals (Jones & Burdette, 1994). In their discussion, Morris and Moberg (1994) argue that in order to be felt as a betrayal a transgression must be personalized such that 'the victim's sense of self-legitimacy or social identity' is threatened (p. 180). Likewise, Afifi and Metts (1998) suggest that 'many of the examples of betrayal provided by participants are directly related to identity attacks' (p. 386). For example, not receiving an expected promotion may threaten one person's self-image as an upwardly mobile, successful manager while for another it may be disappointment but poses no threat to self-identity.

In the former case the victim is more likely to see the non-promotion as a betrayal. Thus, personal relationships, groups and organizations will vary in the extent to which membership is important to an individual's identity and for those individuals transgressions of constitutive rules would strike at the core of one's self-image (Metts, 1994).

In summary, transgressions are more likely to lead to classification as betraying acts if the expectations transgressed are pivotal or important. What leads some transgressions to be important enough to be judged betrayals are violations of those rules or normative expectations that govern the very purpose of the relationship, or if they violate secrets that support the relationship, or if they threaten the victim's basic security or sense of identity. These are the sorts of transgressions that evoke feelings of betrayal in either personal or impersonal relationships. Further, such betrayals also reflect disruptions in what the victim had assumed or taken for granted, introducing uncertainty about one's security and sense of self. The foregoing discussion is summarized in Table 5.1.

**Table 5.1**  Understanding organizational betrayal

---

Betraying acts enrage those betrayed.

Transgressions will be classified as betrayals if they:

- violate expectations serving as constitutive rules for the relationship, or
- violate expectations protecting relationship-defining secrets, or
- threaten members' security, or
- threaten members' identities

Betrayals:

- may be transgressions of impersonal role obligations to groups or organizations as well as personal obligations to other individuals
- may be perceived whether or not the perpetrator intended to betray the victim or victims
- involve implicit or explicit third parties
- do not necessarily involve shared expectations
- may be situationally or dispositionally driven.

---

## DIFFERING PERSPECTIVES OF BETRAYAL

Despite general consensus on the characteristics of those acts likely to be seen as betrayals, there remain several equivocal issues. A discussion of these differences helps to highlight several current issues in I/O psychology, and so we briefly address questions such as: Can transgressions of impersonal role obligations be perceived as betrayals? Is it a necessary condition that an act of betrayal be intentionally harmful? Must all participants agree on the meaning and interpretation of acts of betrayal? What is the role of emotion in reactions to betrayals?

## Personal and Impersonal Betrayal

In I/O psychology theorists vary as to whether transgressions of expectations regarding impersonal relationships may be experienced as acts of betrayal. Recall that personal betrayal occurs when the expectations of a specific person for the actions of another person are not met, while impersonal betrayal is when a normative expectation or expectations pertaining to an office or to membership in a group are violated. Personal betrayals concern only the relationship between two people—their expectations for one another based on the relationship they have built—while impersonal betrayal is violation of role expectations as a member of a collective entity such as a group or organization. Morris and Moberg argue that individuals will seek to distinguish actions intended to harm them personally from accidental harm as a byproduct of something else in deciding whether or not they have been personally betrayed. This is because harmful events at work can happen for many reasons. Thus a focus on personal betrayal alone allows them to focus on the victims' search for intent in deciding how to classify a transgression.

Similarly, Elangovan and Shapiro (1998) argue that transgressions of obligations owed to impersonal entities such as groups or organizations would not be viewed as betrayals by employees. While Elangovan and Shapiro (1998) provide an articulate defense of their reason for considering violations of impersonal trust to be deviations rather than betrayals, we contend that a better understanding of why acts may be classified as betrayals makes the elimination of impersonal betrayal unnecessary. A deviation is a violation of a group's normative expectation for members. We contend that a betrayal may be a type of deviation, but it is a special type of deviance. Deviance can include such mild acts as wearing a suit on Casual Friday or eating at your desk. Clearly, some violations of collective norms are serious and threatening enough to be seen as betrayals, and therefore to enrage. While Elangovan and Shapiro's (1998) restriction to personal betrayals assists them in maintaining clarity in their discussion of why perpetrators betray, we believe that limiting I/O psychology solely to the study of personal betrayals in the workplace unnecessarily neglects an important aspect of work and forgoes insights that can be gained from understanding impersonal betrayal. This is so for several reasons.

First, other theorists include impersonal entities as parties to betrayal and trust. Robinson considers violations when the perpetrator is a collective (the organization) and so a strict focus on personal betrayals alone would exclude her work. Similarly, organizations, groups and institutional arrangements may be trusted in the course of conducting organizational work (cf., Bigley & Pearce, 1998) and where trust exists it can be betrayed.

Second, in practice, it may not be possible to clearly distinguish personal from impersonal transgressions in organizational settings. The general selling secret battle plans to the enemy is violating impersonal role expectations, but those of his colleagues who knew him would very likely consider it a personal betrayal. Similarly, did the rate-buster in the Bank Wiring Room violate his personal relationship with each of his coworkers, or did he betray a normative expectation pertaining to his work group? Organizations are mixes of role and personal obligations, and transgressions of role obligations that threaten individuals' understanding of their workplace, threaten their security or their own identities are as likely to be seen as betrayals as are violations of informal personal understandings.

Finally, members of organizations certainly may experience an enraging sense of betrayal from another's betrayal of the organization. Examples might include a colleague you do not know personally agreeing to testify for the government in its lawsuit against the company, or when a fellow employee (who is a stranger to you) gets caught accepting a bribe and brings embarrassment to everyone working for the organization. Transgressions of impersonal role obligations can be the most stinging of betrayals—those which endanger the safety of the group.

After all, the term betrayal was first applied to selling secrets which harmed the clan; the word betrayal comes from the Latin word *tradere*, 'to hand over', as in secrets to an enemy. The application of this concept to personal relationships, such as friendships or marriage, is a comparatively recent attempt to indicate that threatening transgressions can occur at the personal as well as the collective level. (And perhaps reflects the fact that in modern societies our personal security is dependent on smaller groupings—couples rather than clans.) Individuals who work enter into obligations to organizations, occupations, and work groups; obligations to these entities, if violated, may be very threatening and so may be seen by their fellows as betrayals. Therefore, we suggest that acts which transgress expectations regarding both personal and impersonal relationships can be perceived as betrayals.

## The Necessity of Intent

It is generally agreed that betrayal harms the victim in some way (hence the term victim). However, less clear is whether the perpetrator must intend to harm the victim. Harm, in the sense used here, can refer to any negative outcome of the betrayal episode from physical forms of betrayal (e.g. abuse) to psychological outcomes (e.g. loss of self-identity). Does it matter whether the employees who sell secret product innovations to the company's competitor do so in a deliberate attempt to harm the organization, or are they just indifferent to the harm their greed may cause? To be seen as a betrayal must the act be calculated to harm the victim? It turns out that one's answer to this question rests on the theoretical perspective one takes and, empirically, who is studied.

The most ardent claims for the necessity of intentional harm-doing in determining whether an action is a betrayal comes from research on the victim's interpretive or sense-making process (Bies, 1987; Morris & Moberg, 1994; Robinson, 1996). Each of these theorists agreed that betrayal must be perceived by the victim as an act whereby the perpetrator intentionally causes harm. Thus Morris and Moberg argued that 'the victim must convince himself or herself not only that it was the violator who caused the harm but also that he or she did so freely and deliberately' (1994, p. 179).

However, theorists from other disciplines suggest that it isn't necessary to require perpetrators' intention to harm, simply that they intend to behave opportunistically. As Elangovan and Shapiro stated, 'although violations of trust need to be voluntary to be considered betrayal, some of them may be unintentional' (1998, p. 551). These authors used both the presence of intent and the timing of intent (whether prior to or after the initiation of a relationship) to develop a typology of betrayal which distinguishes between acts of 'accidental' betrayal—the absence of intent—from 'intentional', 'premeditated,' and 'opportunistic' types. For example, numerous accounts of studies of espionage highlight the idealistic motives of the perpetrator—selling intelligence for the common good—and not their intent to harm the unfortunate victims (Åkerström, 1991).

Finally, there is considerable ambiguity about intent when perpetrators and victims are directly queried. Jones and Burdette (1994) provided evidence gleaned from retrospective narratives that both perpetrators and victims perceive opportunistic motives yet differ in their attributions of cause. That is, while both agreed that the act of betrayal was intentionally performed, perpetrators overwhelmingly attribute their own motives to unstable causes (e.g. fit of rage). Victims, on the other hand, were much more likely to perceive the motives of the perpetrator as intentional, stable, and internal (e.g. dispositional character flaw). In addition, Baumeister, Stillwell and Wotman (1990) discovered that victims and perpetrators have substantially different subjective interpretations of the consequences of betrayals. Perpetrators are more likely to see the incident as isolated and without lasting implications, while the victims believed it caused lasting harm and continuing grievance. Such differing subjective perceptions of betrayal are not surprising—a betrayal is such an extreme violation that we would expect perpetrators to minimize and mitigate it if at all possible. As Jones and Burdette reasoned, 'Perhaps such explanations reduce one's sense of moral responsibility for undesirable behaviors' (1994, p. 258).

Thus, requiring intent to harm victims probably is too strict a requirement. Particularly when we consider impersonal betrayals, it seems clear that many betrayals are undertaken for gain and the harm to the victim is a byproduct rather than the primary purpose of the act. Anyway, perpetrators can always claim they meant no harm or hadn't realized the implications (and we really cannot read their thoughts). As Elangovan and Shapiro (1998) suggested, it is not the intent to harm which leads an act to be seen as a betrayal but an indifference to the harm caused to those who placed their trust in the perpetrator. We recognize that many actions which victimize individuals in organizational settings are compelled by circumstances or are accidental and participants do seek to differentiate those from betrayals. However, future work would benefit from a more precise focus on indifference to or devaluing of harm, rather than intent to harm, as the requirement for eliciting feelings of betrayal.

### Victim, Perpetrator, and Third Parties

In industrial/organizational psychology the focus has been on the victim–perpetrator dyad. Typically, third parties are incidental to the betrayal episode, relegated instead to the status of a comparison standard (Morrison & Robinson, 1997) or a source of influence (Morris & Moberg, 1994). Yet theorists in other disciplines focus on the role of third parties, some insisting that acts of betrayal inherently require third parties (Baxter, Mazanec, Nicholson et al., 1997).

Shackelford and Buss (1996) suggested that betrayal involves the potential threat of diverting valued resources to persons outside the primary relationship. Likewise, Argyle and Henderson (1984) hypothesized that relationship rules are created to deal with potentially negative consequences related to third parties (e.g. ensuring that self-disclosures are kept in confidence). Their research suggests that the violation of rules concerning third parties is one of the most crucial in terms of the consequences to the relationship, with over one-third of the respondents rating them as either 'moderately' or 'very important' in the relationship's subsequent dissolution.

Some theorists require that any act of betrayal involve a third party. Baxter et al. examined betrayal from a dialectic perspective—that loyalty is meaningful only in unity with its opposite, disloyalty (or, the act of betraying)—and argued that third parties are required in any account of betrayal: 'There are always three parties, A, B, C, in a matrix of loyalty. A can be loyal to B only if there is a third party C who stands as a potential competitor . . . thus the concept of loyalty becomes meaningful to us only when united conceptually with the possibility of betrayal' (1997, p. 656). Thus, third parties are central to many scholarly theories of what it means to betray.

Industrial/organizational psychologists probably also should recognize the implicit and sometimes explicit third party in acts of betrayal. For example, as members of social groups, third parties are implicated to the extent that shared norms, agreements, and expectations concerning appropriate conduct are developed. In this way third parties constitute a powerful source of influence (Morris & Moberg, 1994), or 'clan control' (Ouchi, 1980). Yet typically I/O psychologists place the role of third parties outside the primary betrayal episode. For example, Robinson (1996) limited the role of third parties to a source of comparative information in the victim's sense-making process of a potential violation. For others, third parties are implicit at best. Bies, for example, focused on outrage over underpayment of expected compensation. Third parties would be implicit in this betrayal, in the form of alternative employers forgone, based on the false promise of high compensation. An explicit recognition of the role of third parties would help enrich our understanding of the kind of reactions individuals may have to violated expectations. Who those third parties are and how they are involved in workplace betrayals would be a fruitful area for future research.

## The Necessity of Shared Knowledge

To what extent must the victim and perpetrator share knowledge concerning expectations and their importance to the relationship? Here again there appears to be little consensus in the literature. Robinson (1996) argued that the lack of mutality concerning the content of expectations is a common condition. Alternatively, Elangovan and Shapiro (1998) stated that both must agree on the contents of expectations but may disagree on the extent to which these are important to the relationship. Still others, such as Bies (1987) and Metts (1994), suggested that knowledge of the facts is negotiated between the victim and perpetrator through social accounts or other remedial efforts.

Robinson did not require that the victim and perpetrator agree on expectations for the relationship. Commensurate with the current definition of the psychological contract as individual employees' perception of their own and their organization's reciprocal obligations (Rousseau, 1989, 1995), Robinson focused exclusively on the individual employee's perception that they are a victim of a psychological contract breach. Since psychological contracts are inherently perceptual and idiosyncratic to each individual, it follows that 'an employee's beliefs about the obligations underlying his or her employment relationship are not necessarily shared by agents of the organization' (Robinson, 1996, p. 228). She based her model in part on the possibility of 'incongruence' because each may have divergent schemata by which to interpret expectations, many expectations are complex and ambiguous, and the level of communication will vary. What matters is that the employee perceives a breach and, through an interpretative process, comes to feel that it constitutes a violation of an important promissory agreement. Thus, the victim and perpetrator need not agree on the contents, importance, or even the behaviors involved for a breach to be classified as a betrayal.

Elangovan and Shapiro (1998) disagree. Arguing from the perpetrator's perspective, they stated that mutuality is a precondition for betrayal. They require that both victim and perpetrator be 'mutually aware' of the expectations, otherwise there could be no intent on the part of the perpetrator, hence no actual betrayal. This definitional condition allows for the distinction between an act of opportunistic betrayal and an oversight or accident. If both agree on the expectations the transgression cannot be attributed away as an accident, misunderstanding, or other mere disappointment. However, the two parties do not have to agree on the extent to which the expectations are pivotal or important to the relationship. Thus, they may still disagree on whether an act of betrayal occurred. In fact, the victim need not even be aware of the betrayal, since Elangovan and Shapiro focused exclusively on the perpetrator's decision to betray.

Further, Metts (1994) and Bies (1987) proposed that expectations are negotiated, sometimes even after the transgression has occurred. Both Metts and Bies focused on how the knowledge of a betrayal episode may be altered through social accounts or other remedial efforts. In both cases, the perpetrators use any inherent ambiguity concerning the contents of expectations to ameliorate the harm or intention attributed to them and their act. In Metts' (1994) discussion of relational transgressions, the consequences of a particular transgression are largely the outcome of a negotiation process consisting of several factors: severity of offence, explicitness, motivations, attributions, understanding, and insight. Similarly, Bies (1987) discussed the social accounts provided by perpetrators that served to mitigate the negative implications for the harm-doer.

Like intent to harm, the requirement for mutuality seems too strict for workplace settings. There is simply too much that is ambiguous, so many ways in which behavior can be compelled by changing circumstances. Acts which are serious threats to an employee's security or identity can occur because the market for the company's product has collapsed. Employees may have worked for many years for a public utility that has now been privatized and finds that it must operate in a more efficient manner than the employees had expected. Or an unexpected opportunity for a better job may induce an engineer to leave the project at a critical time. While there will always be mutual agreement that a general's selling secrets to the enemy is a betrayal, many of the changes organizations and individuals working in them undertake cannot be so unambiguously understood by all to be betrayals. There seems to be no way to escape the fact that what are betrayals in work settings will often be matters of dispute.

## Dispositional vs. Situationally Driven Betrayal

There has been a long-standing tension between dispositional theories, on the one hand, and situational theories, on the other, in social science. Despite widespread agreement that, in the famous equation of Lewin (1951), behavior is a function of both the person and the environment there remains only a limited number of truly interactionist models (see Eoyang, 1994, for a notable exception). The same pattern exists among those studying betrayal.

The clearest example of the dispositional approach to betrayal is provided by Jones and Burdette (1994) who conceptualized betrayal as driven by a personality trait; in addressing betrayal from this perspective they have developed a measure of an individual's propensity to betray, called the Interpersonal Betrayal Scale. In contrast, several other scholars have embraced the notion of situational relativity and argue for differences in interpretations of acts as betrayals as dependent on the nature of the relationship (Baxter et al., 1997; Clark & Waddell, 1985; O'Connell, 1984; Shackelford & Buss, 1996). For example, Baxter and colleagues argued that perceptions of an act as a betrayal will vary from one context to the next depending on the loyalty demands present. Similarly, Clark & Waddell (1985) examined differences in betrayal as a function of the type of relationship. According to their previous research (Clark & Mills, 1979) they argued that the rules concerning the benefits one expects to give and receive will vary depending on the type of relationship. Using the distinction between communal—whereby 'members feel a special obligation for the other's welfare' (Clark & Waddell, 1985, p. 404)—and exchange-based relationships (defined by the lack of this special obligation) these authors argued that 'behaviors considered unjust in one relationship may be considered perfectly acceptable in another' (p. 403). Echoing this sentiment, Shackelford and Buss (1996, p. 1152), argued from an evolutionary perspective to suggest, 'one way to predict and explain which behaviors will be interpreted as a betrayal of a relationship is to identify the adaptive benefits that might have accrued to ancestral humans forming that relationship'. From Baxter et al., Clark and Waddell, and Shackelford and Buss's perspectives different relationships are developed to reap different benefits and to the extent that the expected benefits differ across relationships there should be different perceptions of what constitutes a betrayal in the various contexts.

In order to better understand workplace betrayal we can draw on both perspectives. For example, research might seek to establish the validity of Jones and Burdette's (1994) Interpersonal Betrayal Scale for selection decisions. Similarly, we might be able to begin to identify those situations where perception of betrayal is a possibility by learning more about the loyalty demands in different situations, or the importance of different relationships and memberships to participants' self-identity. To assist the latter work, Baxter et al. (1997) reported a measure that can be used to determine the importance of relationships to one's sense of self, the Inclusion-of-Other-in-the-Self Scale (Aron, Aron & Smollan, 1992) and Luhtanen and Crocker (1992) have developed a measure of the importance of various social-group identities to the individual.

## IMPLICATIONS

As complex, global organizational forms and contractual relationships increase in importance questions of trust, injustice and psychological contracts become more salient to the organizational enterprise. We identified betrayal as a concept central to these fields of study and to a better understanding of interpersonal relationships that was ill-understood. This review sought to introduce industrial/organizational psychologists to the wider literature on betrayal and to clarify its applications to the workplace. These arguments have several implications for current issues in research and practice in industrial/organizational psychology, which are elaborated below.

## Clarifying Workplace Betrayal

First, we discovered that there are several different and conflicting understandings of workplace betrayal. We drew on the more extensive literatures on betrayal in social psychology, sociology, and political science to develop a more comprehensive understanding of workplace betrayal. First, we saw that simply stating that a transgressed expectation must be important or pivotal to elicit feelings of betrayal provides insufficient guidance. Specifying what is important and why, as social psychologists such as Shackelford and Buss have done, is necessary to theory development. Here we provided those features other scholars have said characterize important expectations and applied them to organizational settings, proposing that transgressions which violate constitutive expectations, violate a We-boundary, threaten a victim's sense of security, or threaten self-identity are more likely to be seen as betrayals. We hope these can provide a basis for theory development and testing of what leads to feelings of betrayal in the workplace.

Second, we suggested that defining impersonal betrayal as outside the scope of workplace betrayal was both misguided and unnecessary. Impersonal betrayals can be every bit as threatening as personal ones. Further, concerns about having one party to the transgression be a collective fade once we relax the requirement that a perpetrator must intend to harm the victims. If the perpetrator is aware of and indifferent to the potential harm he or she may cause, impersonal betrayal can be accommodated. Role obligations are simply too important to industrial/organizational psychology, to define them out of consideration.

Third, in industrial/organizational psychology normative advice on averting moral outrage has centred on admonitions to provide explanations and information to prevent an interpretation of the act as a betrayal. Yet this work suggests that transgressions of constitutive, relationship-forming rules that threatens one's security or identity are not likely to be mitigated with soothing words. Most people aren't going to be talked out of their perception that an action threatens the very basis of the relationship or is not a threat to their security or identity. Once such suspicions are engaged it would be difficult to present any sort of argumentation that would not be viewed as cravenly self-serving. Rather we would suggest that ambiguous acts which may or may not be interpreted as betrayals are comparatively rare in organizational settings. In functioning organizations many participants have extensive experience with one another and the setting and the areas of ambiguity are concomitantly small. This is not to say that explanation would not help to support employees' perceptions that they are respected and have standing (Tyler, 1998) or perhaps shift blame elsewhere, just that it would probably not lead individuals to be less likely to interpret an act as a betrayal, or to mitigate their rage once they have done so. Thus, at best, forestalling perceptions of betrayal would depend more on an advance understanding of employees' perceptions of their We-groups, their constitutive rules governing their relationships and memberships, and which relationships are important to their senses of security and self-identity. Only such foreknowledge would provide the information necessary to either shift expectations before the act or gird for the consequences if that is not possible.

Finally, we know too little about cross-cultural differences in perceptions of acts of betrayal or in reactions to felt betrayal. The extent to which culture influences the rules of relationships and perceptions of betrayal remains an as yet unexplored area of inquiry (Argyle & Henderson, 1984; Clark & Waddell, 1985). If transgressions are subject to ambiguity in a single organization in one society, the potential for differences in what constitutes a betrayal in cross-cultural settings is immense. For example, the first author has conducted research in formerly communist countries in transition to market economies, and she has found that newly installed American and British managers were engaging in what their subordinates believed to be acts of betrayal: violations of their employees' expectations that bosses should act as caring parents (e.g., Pearce, 1995). Even when these expatriate executives understood their subordinates' expectation they tended to dismiss them as wrong, expecting the employees to adopt their own constitutive rules once they had been shown their 'errors'. Clearly, constitutive rules are not so easily changed, and these subordinates' feelings of betrayal certainly were not mitigated by such instruction. Helping to identify differences in constitutive rules, We-boundaries, sources of security and the importance of memberships to self-identity could prove useful in averting serious breakdowns of trust in cross-cultural collaborations.

## Extreme Emotions as Motivators of Workplace Behavior

One of the defining aspects of betrayal is that it evokes strong negative emotions. These strong emotions, in turn, hold great motivating power. As Ellsworth (1994, p. 25) has stated, 'many scholars believe that the primary function of emotion is to move the organism to appropriate action in circumstances consequential for its well-being.' We have argued that betrayal often involves a fundamental threat to one's security (i.e. well-being). As such, it provides a unique opportunity to examine the motivating potential of emotions. Given industrial/organizational psychology's long-standing interest in motivation, it is surprising that the emotions and the behaviors thereby motivated are only now coming under scrutiny.

Betrayal forms the basis for two suggestions for future research with respect to betrayal and the emotions evoked. First, research on betrayal has been relatively silent about the actual emotion elicited by an act interpreted as a betrayal. While almost everyone would agree that betrayal evokes strong negative emotions (Bateson, 1977) the actual form taken may vary considerably from feelings of sorrow to extreme rage. Åkerström (1991) uses a host of terms to express the negative emotions aroused, including indignation, contempt, revenge, and rage. Morrison and Robinson suggest that 'central to the experience of violation are the feelings of anger, resentment, bitterness, indignation, and even outrage' (1997, p. 231). It would be useful to illuminate the various scope conditions concerning the manifestation of the negative emotions involved in betrayal. For example, when will a terminated employee who had expected lifetime employment feel outrage versus bitterness? Perhaps the research on betrayal in I/O psychology has gotten ahead of itself by focusing on how to mitigate the consequences of the resultant negative emotions (e.g. Bies, 1987), while neglecting the various forms and consequences of negative emotion that may occur in the first place.

Attribution theories of emotion (e.g. Smith & Ellsworth, 1985; Ortony, Clore & Collins, 1988; Scherer, 1984; Weiner, 1985) could provide a useful starting point for understanding the workplace consequences of strong negative emotion. According to these attribution theorists, emotions result from an individual's appraisal of their environment along a number of dimensions. It is noteworthy that our review of the defining features of acts that elicit betrayal reflects some of the more general dimensions proffered by attribution theorists of emotion. That is, attribution theorists discuss the dimensions of novelty, agency, and norm/self-concept compatibility (see Ellsworth, 1994) which correspond to our discussions of security, intent, and identity centrality, respectively. For example, Ellsworth discussed evidence that the attribution of agency plays a crucial role in differentiating the resultant negative emotion. Thus, the employee who attributes the cause of her or his termination to fate or market conditions may feel bitterness, whereas an attribution of cause to a manager's betrayal may engender extreme feelings of outrage (cf. Frijda, 1986; Scherer, 1984).

This also illustrates the influential role of culture. For example, Matsumoto, Kudoh, Scherer & Wallbott (1988) reported that Japanese were less likely to assign blame to individuals than were American participants. When asked to assign responsibility, these participants were more likely to respond 'non-applicable' than were their American counterparts. This is particularly important with respect to betrayal, since research generally supports the notion that without blame there is generally little anger (Mesquita & Frijda, 1992). Indeed, there is some evidence provided by cultural psychologists suggesting that a situation that would evoke anger in more individualist cultures may actually evoke feelings of shame in more collectivist or interdependent cultures (e.g. Markus & Kitayama, 1991). Thus, the interdependence of emotion and culture suggests a variant of our situational argument concerning betrayal. To what extent does knowledge of betrayal developed in the more individualist cultures of North America and Northern Europe apply to cultures with different value systems? The role of culture suggests a host of scope conditions that need to be explored with increasing urgency in the globally integrated workplace.

Our second suggestion for future research has to do with the behaviors which result from an experienced emotion. That is, there is surprisingly little empirical research or theory in I/O psychology that predicts the actions of those who experience different emotions. Instead, most research and theory concerning the role of emotions at work has focused predominantly on their expression as distinct from their experience (e.g. Hochschild, 1983; Rafaeli & Sutton, 1989). Unfortunately, to our knowledge no one has yet conducted systematic empirical research about reactions to the experience of different workplace emotions (Jones and George, 1998, presented persuasive theory but, as yet, no empirical tests). How does the victim respond to the rage engendered by betrayal? How does the perpetrator respond to the guilt they feel upon their act of betrayal? When will the doctoral student who feels betrayed murder the offending professor (or himself)? These are just some of the questions that a review of betrayal suggests. The time is ripe to begin to develop a more nuanced understanding of the behavioral reactions to emotions at work.

## CONCLUSIONS

Betrayal is vital to an understanding of the more interpersonally based networked organizational forms, and also is a surprisingly versatile reflection of many of the current interests of industrial/organizational psychologists. The concept is central to theories of trust, justice, and psychological contracts, and suggests productive areas of research in cross-cultural normative expectations, the efficacy of mitigating accounts in workplace settings, and the effects of strong emotion on workplace action. This review suggests that if it is something we are talking about more, such a conversation can be illuminating.

## ACKNOWLEDGEMENTS

The authors wish to thank Greg Bigley, Marta Elvira, Gil Geis, Paul Olk, Amy Randel, and Chris Zatzick for their penetrating comments on an earlier draft.

## REFERENCES

Afifi, W. A. & Metts, S. (1998). Characteristics and consequences of expectation violations in close relationships. *Journal of Social and Personal Relationships*, 15, 365–392.
Åkerström, M. (1991). *Betrayal and Betrayers: The Sociology of Treachery*. London: Transaction.
Argyle, M. & Henderson, M. (1984). The rules of friendship. *Journal of Social and Personal Relationships*, 1, 211–237.
Aron, A., Aron, E. N. & Smollan, D. (1992). Inclusion of other in the self scale and the structure of interpersonal closeness. *Journal of Personality and Social Psychology*, 63, 596–612.
Bateson, G. (1997). *About Bateson: Essays on Gregory Bateson*. New York: Dutton.
Baumeister, R. F., Stillwell, A. & Wotman, S. R. (1990). Victim and perpetrator accounts of interpersonal conflict: Autobiographical narratives about anger. *Journal of Personality and Social Psychology*, 59, 994–1005.
Baxter, L. A., Mazanec, M., Nicholson, J., Pittman, G., Smith, K. & West, L. (1997). Everyday loyalties and betrayals in personal relationships. *Journal of Social and Personal Relationships*, 14, 655–678.
Bies, R. J. (1987). The predicament of injustice: The management of moral outrage. *Research in Organizational Behavior*, 9, 289–319.
Bies, R. J. & Tripp, T. M. (1998). Revenge in organizations: The good, the bad, and the ugly. In R. W. Griffin, A. O'Leary-Kelly & J. M. Collins (Eds), *Dysfunctional Behavior in Organizations: Non-violent Dysfunctional Behavior* (pp. 49–67). Greenwick, CT: JAI Press.
Bies, R. J., Tripp, T. M. & Kramer, R. M. (1997). At the breaking point: Cognitive and social dynamics of revenge in organizations. In R. A. Giacalone & J. Greenberg (Eds), *Antisocial Behavior in Organizations* (pp. 18–36). Thousand Oaks, CA: Sage.
Bigley, G. A. & Pearce, J. L. (1998). Straining for shared meaning in organization science: Problems of trust and distrust. *Academy of Management Review*, 23, 405–421.
Clark, M. S. & Mills, J. (1979). Interpersonal attraction in exchange and communal relationships. *Journal of Personality & Social Psychology*, 37, 12–24.
Clark, M. S. & Waddell, B. (1985). Perceptions of exploitation in communal and exchange relationships. *Journal of Social and Personal Relationships*, 2, 403–418.
Elangovan, A. R. & Shapiro, D. L. (1998). Betrayal of trust in organizations. *Academy of Management Review*, 23, 547–566.
Ellsworth, P. C. (1994). Sense, culture, and sensibility. In S. Kitayama and H.R. Markus (Eds), *Emotion and Culture: Empirical Studies of Mutual Influence* (pp. 23–50). Washington DC: American Psychological Association.
Eoyang, C. (1994). Models of espionage. In T. R. Sarbin, R. M. Carney & C. Eoyang (Eds), *Citizen Espionage* (pp. 69–92). London: Praeger.
Frijda, N. H. (1986). *The Emotions*. Cambridge: Cambridge University Press.
Greenberg, J. & Scott, K. S. (1996). Why do workers bite the hands that feed them? Employee theft as a social exchange process. *Research in Organizational Behvavior*, 18, 111–156.
Hansson, R. O., Jones, W. H. & Fletcher, W. L. (1990). Troubled relationships in later life: Implications for support. *Journal of Social & Personal Relationships*, 7, 451–463.
Hochschild, A. (1983). *The Managed Heart*. Berkeley, CA: University of California Press.
Jones, G. R. & George, J. M. (1998). The experience and evolution of trust: Implications for cooperation and teamwork. *Academy of Management Review*, 23, 531–546.

Jones, W. H. & Burdgette, M. P. (1994). Betrayal in relationships. In A. L. Weber & J. H. Harvey (Eds), *Perspectives on Close Relationships* (pp. 243–262). Boston: Allyn & Bacon.

Lewin, K. (1951). *Field Theory in Social Sciences.* New York: Harper & Row.

Luhtanen, R. & Crocker, J. (1992). A collective self-esteem scale: Self-evaluation of one's social identity. *Personality and Social Psychology Bulletin*, **18**, 302–318.

Markus, H. R. & Kitayama, S. (1991). Culture and the self: Implications for cognition, emotion and motivation. *Psychological Review*, **98**, 224–253.

Masumoto, D., Kudoh, T., Scherer, K. & Wallbott, H. (1988). Antecedents of and reactions to emotions in the United States and Japan. *Journal of Cross Cultural Psychology*, **19**, 267–286.

Mesquita, B. & Frijda, N. H. (1992). Cultural variations in emotions: A review. *Psychological Bulletin*, **412**, 179–204.

Metts, S. (1989). An exploratory investigation of deception in close relationships. *Journal of Social and Personal Relationships*, **6**, 159–179.

Metts, S. (1994). Relational transgressions. In W.R. Cupach and B.H. Spitzberg (Eds), *The Dark Side of Interpersonal Communication* (pp. 217–239). Hillsdale, NJ: Erlbaum.

Morris, J. H. & Moberg, D. J. (1994). Work organizations as contexts for trust and betrayal. In T. R. Sarbin, R. M. Carney & C. Eoyang (Eds), *Citizen Espionage* (pp. 163–201). London: Praeger.

Morrison, E. W. & Robinson, S. L. (1997). When employees feel betrayed: A model of how psychological contract violation develops. *Academy of Management Review*, **22**, 226–256.

North, D. (1990). *Institutions, Institutional Change and Economic Performance.* London: Cambridge University Press.

O'Connell, L. (1984). An exploration of exchange in three social relationships: Kinship, friendship, and the marketplace. *Journal of Social and Personal Relationships*, **1**, 333–345.

Ortony, A., Clore, G. & Collins, A. (1988). *The Cognitive Structure of Emotions.* New York: Cambridge University Press.

Ouchi, W. G. (1980). Markets, bureaucracies and clans. *Administrative Science Quarterly*, **25**, 129–141.

Pearce, J. L. (1995). A reviewer's introduction to staging the new romantic hero in the old cynical theatre: On managers, roles and change in Poland. *Journal of Organizational Behavior*, **16**, 628–630.

Rafaeli, A. & Sutton, R. I. (1989). The expression of emotion in organizational life. In L. L. Cummings & B. M. Staw (Eds), *Research in Organizational Behavior*, Vol. 11 (pp. 1–42). Greenwich, CT: JAI Press.

Robinson, S. L. (1996). Trust and breach of the psychological contract. *Administrative Science Quarterly*, **41**, 574–599.

Robinson, S. L., Kraatz, M. S. & Rousseau, D. M. (1994). Changing obligations and the psychological contract: A longitudinal study. *Academy of Management Journal*, **37**, 137–152.

Roethlisberger, F. J. & Dickson, W. J. (1939). *Management and the Worker.* Cambridge, MA: Harvard University Press.

Rousseau, D. M. (1989). Psychological and implied contracts in organizations. *Employee Responsibilities and Rights Journal*, **2**, 121–139.

Rousseau, D. M. (1995). *Psychological Contracts in Organizations.* Thousand Oaks, CA: Sage.

Scherer, K. R. (1984). On the nature and function of emotions: A component process approach. In P. Ekman & K. Scherer (Eds), *Approaches to Emotion* (pp. 293–317). Hillsdale, NJ: Erlbaum.

Shackelford, T. K. (1997). Perceptions of betrayal and the design of the mind. In J. A. Simpson and D. T. Kenrick (Eds), *Evolutionary Social Psychology* (pp. 73–107), Hillsdale, NJ: Erlbaum.

Shackelford, T. K. & Buss, D. M. (1996). Betrayal in mateships, friendships, and coalitions. *Personality and Social Psychology Bulletin*, **22**, 1151–1164.

Shale, T. (1993). What went wrong? *AsiaMoney*, 4(6), 14–16.

Simmel, G. (1964). *The Sociology of Georg Simmel.* Trans., ed. K. Wolff. Part 4, *The Secret and the Secret Society* (pp. 307–355). New York: Free Press.

Smith, C. A. & Ellsworth, P. C. (1985). Patterns of cognitive appraisal in emotion. *Journal of Personality and Social Psychology*, **48**(4), 813–838.

Tyler, T. R. (1998). The psychology of authority relations. In R. M. Kramer & M. A. Neale (Eds), *Power and Influence in Organizations*. Thousand Oaks, CA: Sage.

Weinber, B. (1985). An attributional theory of achievement motivation and emotion. *Psychological Review*, **92**, 548–573.

Zucker, L. G. (1986). The production of trust: Institutional sources of economic structure 1840–1920. *Research in Organizational Behavior*, **8**, 53–111.

# Chapter 6

# WORKING TIME, HEALTH AND PERFORMANCE

Anne Spurgeon
*University of Birmingham*

Cary L. Cooper
*University of Manchester*

## INTRODUCTION

During the 1990s substantial changes took place in international legislation on working time. The new European Directive on Working Hours (1993) introduced specific measures relating to the scheduling of shifts and rest breaks and to the maximum number of hours permissible within set periods, whilst more globally, the International Labour Organisation (ILO) introduced radical new standards for working patterns, focusing particularly on night work (1990). These measures reflect an increasing awareness of the potential implications for health and safety of the number and pattern of hours which people are required to work. Moreover there have been marked and rapid changes in these patterns in recent years, most obviously in the area of shiftworking, which in many countries involves up to 25% of the workforce. Shiftwork may be broadly defined as work which takes place either permanently or frequently outside normal daytime working hours. It may, for example, consist of permanent night work, permanent evening work or a rotational pattern where a certain number of days is spent on each shift. Today these patterns are becoming increasingly complex, comprising complicated combinations of different shift times and lengths, which change or rotate according to a variety of schedules. These may be either continuous, running for 24 hours per day and 7 days per week, or semi-continuous, running for two or three shifts per day with or without weekends. An increasingly popular format is the long shift, usually 12 hours, which compresses the working week into fewer days. Added to this are numerous flexible working arrangements which have developed in

*International Review of Industrial and Organizational Psychology, 2000 Volume 15*
Edited by C.L. Cooper and I.T. Robertson. © 2000 John Wiley & Sons, Ltd

recent years such as flexitime, annualised hours contracts, job sharing and school-term working. Alongside these changes, which are essentially about the way working time is organised, there is a further trend towards extended working hours (Wedderburn, 1996a), either as formally constituted overtime, or as an informal, often unpaid, response to high work demands. In contrast to shiftworking as defined, overtime work consists of extensions to the normal working day which are not part of a predetermined schedule and which may also, for example, include holiday and weekend working. These emerging patterns have developed largely in response to the rapid economic and social change which is taking place in both industrialised and developing countries. New technologies, increased competitiveness and new customer demands for round the clock services have all combined to produce much more irregularity in peoples' working hours. Indeed in some cases the advent of sophisticated communications systems has meant that the distinction between work time and home time is becoming increasingly blurred.

Given these trends, it has become a matter of some importance to understand the potential effects of working time arrangements on the health and well-being of employees, and on their associated work performance. The role of occupational psychology in this process has in the past been somewhat variable. It has always been clear, for example, that psychological methods and tools were central to the assessment of performance decrements resulting from the fatigue and circadian disruption common in shiftworkers. Perhaps less obvious has been the psychologist's role in assessing the risk in terms of the physical health outcomes of particular work patterns and in devising interventions to help reduce those risks. In recent years however, the somewhat artificial distinction between physical and psychological health has been largely replaced by a biopsychological approach which recognises the essential interaction between the two. For example, psychosocial stressors in the working environment may have a significant part to play in the development of health problems such as coronary heart disease and gastrointestinal disorders. Current evidence suggests that the stress derived from the pattern and duration of working time may be particularly important in this respect. Further, the physiological response to potential stressors in the workplace is likely to be mediated by a number of psychological variables, ranging from personality factors, through attitudes and belief systems to the presence of other environmental stressors. From the psychologist's point of view therefore, the subject of working time presents a number of interesting challenges.

The development of human performance testing both in relation to work efficiency and to occupational safety is a continuing requirement, with the need for more sophisticated approaches which closely mimic the real working environment and which also take account of the role of psychosocial mediators. In addition, however, the study of working time may be seen as a particular branch of organisational stress research, where the role of the psychologist is central to the process of assessment and subsequent intervention. This chapter therefore aims to provide an overview of what is currently known about the effects of different patterns of working time on health, well-being and performance, with a view to defining the future role of psychology in this field. A comprehensive picture of current thinking in this area necessarily involves a multidiscilinary perspective which in particular draws extensively on evidence from occupational medicine and epidemiology, where much of the information is derived from data sets on large populations. However, in recent years more attention has focused on individual differences and vulnerable groups in the workplace and these will also be highlighted. It should also be noted that much of what we know at the moment relates to shiftworking in its various forms, since this has been much more extensively studied than, for example, overtime work. However, as far as possible non-shiftwork issues will also be considered.

It is clear that complex patterns of working time will be an integral part of working life in the future for many people. Yet in the course of this chapter it will also become evident that many of these patterns pose potential problems for peoples' health, well-being and performance. A final section therefore, will deal with the important area of intervention and the various approaches which have been designed to address these problems.

## METHODOLOGICAL ISSUES

Research into the potential health effects of working time has been concerned both with short-term complaints about fatigue and general well-being and with longer term risks of more serious disease. Where shiftwork is concerned, most of these problems are thought to relate directly or indirectly to the regular disruption of the body's normal circadian rhythms which involve a range of physiological processes such as changes in heart rate and blood pressure, respiration, temperature, production of certain hormones and digestive and excretory functions. Under normal circumstances these processes function in such a way that individuals are programmed for daytime work and leisure, and for night-time sleep, a pattern which is determined both by endogenous factors, the internal body clock, and by exogenous environmental influences such as daylight, noise and the general social habits of the individual. Regular disturbance of these body rhythms can result in a cumulative sleep deficit, resultant fatigue and symptoms of general malaise. The association between shiftworking and this type of complaint is therefore a fairly direct one. However, in the case of some other aspects of health, notably cardiovascular disease, gastrointestinal disturbance, reproductive effects and mental ill-health, the relationship with shiftworking appears to be mediated by psychological stress, although the precise mechanisms involved remain unclear. The primary means of studying these effects and those relating to other patterns of working time is via large-scale epidemiological studies either on a cross-sectional or a longitudinal basis. Studies of this type can identify an association between working time and certain health outcomes, but not necessarily a causal relationship or an explanatory mechanism.

A reasonably consistent and convincing body of evidence has now accumulated in this area, but there are some well-established methodological problems which need to be borne in mind. The most obvious of these relates to population self-selection, generally termed 'the healthy worker' or 'survivor' effect. Workers who are better able to cope with the problems of shiftwork or overtime are more likely to select themselves into this work initially and are less likely to select themselves out later on as a result of health problems. Consequently both cross-sectional and longitudinal data may be drawn from a population where 'healthy workers' are over-represented and such data may therefore represent an underestimate of the real prevalence of health effects.

Other problems common in epidemiological studies related to the difficulty of establishing appropriate control groups matched for important variables such as age, gender, social class and smoking habits and which differ only in respect of the single variable of work pattern. The influence of a variety of potential confounders is often difficult to control. For example, higher rates of gastrointestinal problems in night workers as compared with day workers may simply reflect a reduction in the quality of catering services available at night. It is well known that in many organisations working conditions at night differ markedly from those during the day, for example in respect of the type of work, the numbers of workers present, the amount of supervision, the application of health and safety procedures and the facilities of all types which are generally available.

Finally, problems have been identified in relation to the definition of outcome measures. A number of categories of disease which have been associated with shiftworking and overtime are not discrete conditions but contain a range of disorders which it may be inappropriate to group together. The most obvious example of this is the case of 'karoshi', a phenomenon identified in Japan, which literally translated means 'death from overwork'. Here a causal link has been postulated between prolonged excessive working hours and sudden death in relatively young and apparently healthy workers. Postmortem results however, have revealed a range of causes of death in this group, including stroke of various types, acute heart failure, myocardial infarction and aortic rupture (Uehata, 1991), although all would fall under the general heading of 'vascular event'. Similar problems exist in relation to effects on reproductive health and gastrointestinal disturbance, each of which can take many forms.

In the case of shorter term health complaints such as self-reported symptoms of fatigue and depressed mood, investigations in the past have suffered from a lack of standardisation and attention to psychometrics in the questionnaire measures employed. This has recently been addressed, in particular by the development of the Standard Shiftwork Index (Barton, Spelten, Totterdell et al., 1995) which provides a psychometrically sound instrument for assessing the most often reported symptoms in shiftwork research.

Notwithstanding these difficulties there has been a large amount of research effort directed towards the problem of shiftworking, and to a lesser extent overtime working, during the last 30 years. Early research in this field was carried out by Taylor and colleagues who published a series of excellent studies documenting morbidity and mortality in shiftworkers (Taylor, 1967; Taylor, Pocock & Sergean, 1972; Pocock, Sergean & Taylor, 1972). Building on these data, subsequent researchers have carried out studies which have served both to define the potential risks to health from shiftwork and overtime and to inform the development of approaches most likely to reduce those risks.

## SHIFTWORK AND HEALTH

### Stress and Mental Health

It is fairly clear that shiftworking constitutes a potential psychosocial stressor. A number of self-report studies confirm this, using a variety of measures of perceived stress and well-being (Hurrell & Colligan, 1987; Estryn-Behar, Kaminski, Peigne et al., 1990; Barton & Folkard, 1991; Imbernon, Warret, Roitg et al., 1993; Cervinka, 1993; Prunier-Poulmaire, Gadbois & Volkoff, 1998). While shiftworking has been linked to a range of physical health problems, therefore, its relationship to mental health disturbance is probably the most direct one. Several studies have used measures of specific mental health outcomes in addition to self-reported strain, and have demonstrated increased risks of both anxiety and depression in shiftworkers. For example Imbernon et al. (1993) studied electricity and gas supply workers in France and found significant levels of disturbance on a measure of 'psychological equilibrium'. Similarly Estryn-Behar et al. (1990), studying female hospital workers, found a significant association between job strain due to shiftwork and poor mental health as measured by a well-established mental health screening tool, the General Health Questionnaire (GHQ) (Goldberg & Williams, 1988). The GHQ is a measure of general mental health covering both anxiety and depression. A much earlier study demonstrated in particular an increased incidence of clinical depression in shiftworkers (Michel-Briand, Chopard & Guiot, 1981). Some recent research has concentrated on the relationship between shiftwork and personality disturbance. A range of studies in different countries (reviewed by Cole, Loving & Kripke, 1990) indicate a strong association between shiftwork and neuroticism. There are some difficulties in interpreting the direction of causality in this relationship (see later section on Individual Differences). However, the balance of opinion suggests that neurotics adapt more poorly to shiftwork than do non-neurotics. In general therefore, current evidence suggests that, as a significant source of occupational stress, shift-working is likely to increase the risk of mental health problems in all workers, and that this risk may be magnified in certain vulnerable groups.

## Cardiovascular Disorders

The result of early studies on the incidence of cardiovascular disease (CVD) in shiftworkers (reviewed by Harrington, 1978) provided few grounds for concern. Since the early 1980s however, the position has reversed, with the majority of studies indicating a significant association between various types of shiftwork, particularly nightwork, and cardiovascular disorders. The methodology in these more recent studies was considerably better, particularly in respect of the problem of selection. A large-scale longitudinal study carried out on Swedish paper-mill workers (Alfredsson, Karasek & Theorell, 1982; Knutsson, Akerstedt, Jonsson & Orth-Gomer, 1986) followed up workers for 15 years and compared the risk of ischaemic heart disease (IHD) in shift-workers with that of day workers. Shiftworkers had a significantly elevated risk which rose with increasing duration of shiftworking and which was independent of age and smoking history. Further, it was noted that there were few drop-outs in the study population. Interestingly, however, in those who had been shiftworkers for more than 20 years there was a fall in the relative risk of IHD. The authors attribute this to selection factors since within the group who had begun shiftworking more than 20 years earlier, a large percentage (63%) had selected themselves out of shiftwork within three years, in that they had changed over to day work. This observation underlines the importance of the healthy worker effect which may well account for the negative results of earlier studies. In one of the very few negative studies in recent years (McNamee, Binks, Jones et al., 1996) the authors also cite this factor as a potential explanation for their results. Two further studies in Denmark (Tüchsen, 1993) and in Finland (Tenkanen, Sjoblom, Kalimo et al., 1997) confirmed evidence of an association between shiftworking and cardiovascular disorders, although the Danish data suggested that night work specifically, rather than shiftwork in general, was responsible for a raised risk of IHD. An interesting approach adopted by Olsen and Kristensen in Denmark (1991) involved reviewing existing quantitative epidemiological data concerned with a range of possible causes of coronary heart disease and estimating the aetiological fraction for shiftworking. This fraction is defined as 'the proportion of the disease which would not have occurred if the risk factor had not occurred in the population'. For shiftwork this fraction was calculated to be 7%.

In summary, therefore, the evidence of an association between shiftworking and an increase in CVD is difficult to dismiss. The precise causal mechanism involved in this association is perhaps less clear. However, most hypotheses invoke factors conventionally viewed as resulting directly or indirectly from psychosocial stress. Hence shiftwork and particularly night work is seen as a source of occupational strain which may act to increase physiological risk factors for CVD, notably high arterial blood pressure, increased heart rate, and increased blood lipid concentrations. It may also encourage behaviour patterns associated with increased risk such as poor diet, limited physical activity and smoking. Studies which have investigated blood pressure and heart rate have usually failed to find evidence of increases in shiftworkers as a group compared with the general population (Bursey, 1990; Stoynev & Minkova, 1998). However, individual differences in cardiovascular reactivity to stress are well-established (Carroll, Harris & Ross, 1991) and it is noteworthy that a study in Japan (Kobayashi, Watanabe, Tanaka & Nakagawa, 1992) found significant differences between normotensive and hypertensive workers in the effects of shiftwork on blood pressure and heart rate at different times of the day. A further study in Japan (Nakamura, Shimai, Kikuchi et al., 1997) found that workers on a rotating three-shift system, as compared with day workers, had a higher risk of CVD, higher levels of serum total cholesterol and a greater tendency towards obesity. The authors suggest that these findings may be explained in terms of stress-induced hypercholestrolemia which has been demonstrated in animal experiments (Servatius, Ottenweller & Natelson, 1994). Current data are limited in this area but generally support the view that the demands of shiftwork act both as a direct physiological stressor and as a psychological stressor by encouraging the development of health-threatening coping behaviours.

## Digestive Disorders

The most frequently reported health complaints of shiftworkers relate to digestive problems. A number of early studies found an increase of gastroduodenitis and peptic ulcers among those working rotational shifts (reviewed by Vener, Szabo & Moore, 1989). Although many of these studies have been heavily criticised on methodological grounds a more recent review (Costa, 1996) confirms early findings and concludes that there is sufficient evidence to consider shiftwork as an important risk factor for digestive disorders, particularly peptic ulcers. Again night work seems to cause the most problems. In a study of textile workers who developed gastrointestinal problems Costa, Apostoli, d'Andrea and Gaffuri (1981) calculated the time interval between workers beginning a particular type of work and the diagnosis of a digestive disorder. The shortest time interval for both gastroduodenitis and peptic ulcer was repsectively 4.7 and 5.6 years for night workers as compared with 12.6 and 12.2 years for day workers. An important factor in the development of appetite disturbance and gastrointestinal disorders in shiftworkers is likely to be their long-term irregular and inappropriately timed eating habits. For example, physiologically speaking, the body is not geared to cope with the quantity and composition of a normal daytime meal during the night, implying some scope for behavioural modification as an approach to reducing the risk of these problems. In addition, however, gastrointestinal problems have, like CVD, frequently been viewed as resulting at least in part from long-term exposure to occupational stress.

### Reproductive Disorders

A number of problems included under the general heading of reproductive disorders have been associated with shiftworking. These include subfecundity (Bisanti, Olsen, Basso et al., 1996, Ahlborg, Axelsson & Bodin, 1996), spontaneous abortion (Axelsson, Ahlborg & Bodin, 1996), pre-term birth and low birthweight (Nuriminen, 1989; Xu, Ding, Li & Christiani, 1994). Although the literature in this area is not large it is fairly consistent and suggests special risks for women of child-bearing age. The suggestion is that negative effects may in part be due to hormonal disturbance (Daleva, 1987), but also to the psychosocial stress which accompanies shiftworking. As with other health outcomes effects appear to derive from an interaction between direct physiological and indirect psychological mechanisms.

### Shiftwork and Social Disruption

Running alongside the normal physiological rythms of the body is a societal rhythm which has developed in parallel with the body clock. Hence, most people's activities (sleeping, eating, working, leisure, and family duties) are programmed into blocks of time which appear to be remarkably similar within and even across different cultures (Gadbois, 1984). An important factor is that not all blocks of time are interchangeable and some are much more suited to certain activities than others. For example, time appropriate for spending with children, for certain organised leisure activities or for viewing the most popular TV programmes, is subject to external constraints. Shiftworkers may therefore lose the opportunity for these activities. The importance of this has been demonstrated in studies which have attempted to quantify the value to individuals of having time off at different times of the day (Wedderburn, 1981; Hornberger & Knauth, 1993). Shiftworkers, in common with day workers, tend to place a high value on time off during evenings and weekends and much less value on time off in the daytime. It is unsurprising, therefore, that a number of studies have demonstrated that disturbances of social and family life are at least as important to the overall well-being of shiftworkers as are the physiological effects of circadian disruption.

A large survey of shiftworkers in the UK found that levels of concern about home and family life, and about social life, showed highly significant correlations with feelings of chronic tiredness and general malaise (Smith & Bennett, 1983). Other effects on leisure and social life have been measured either via semi-objective criteria such as participation in specific activities or by self-reports of satisfaction. An early study by Mott, Mann, McLoughlin et al (1965), for example, showed that membership of voluntary organisations averaged 1.4 for day workers as compared with 1.3 for those on nights and rotating shifts and 1.2 for those on fixed afternoon shifts. Similarly Frost and Jamal (1979) found significantly fewer hours were spent on organisational activities by rotating shiftworkers as compared with non-shiftworkers. However, many studies in this area point to the importance of a variety of mediating factors such as the prevalence of shiftwork generally in the geographical area which may promote a culture conducive to adjustment, the compensatory effects of high wages and the availability of choice in shift allocation.

Clearly disruption of family and social life is likely to vary between sub-groups defined by certain demographic characteristics. Several studies have explored the particular problems of women shiftworkers with children. These studies tend to document self-reported problems of reduced time with children (Lushington, Lushington & Dawson, 1997), diminished ability to fulfil the role of parenthood and to maintain family relationships (Greenwood, 1983). However, the findings are not consistent across all shift patterns. Comparisons between women who work night shifts only, with those who work rotating shifts, suggest that the former may experience fewer problems since regular permanent night work enables them to develop a satisfactory pattern of childcare and fulfilment of domestic responsibilities (Alward & Monk, 1990, Barton & Folkard, 1991). Again, an additional important determinant of well-being appears to be the opportunity to choose the preferred shift pattern.

There is some evidence that the self-reported concerns of women shiftworkers may translate into adverse effects on children's development. Studies by Leonard and Claisse in Belgium and by Knauth and by Gadbois in Germany (reported in Wedderburn, 1993) all indicated poorer long-term educational success in the children of shiftworkers as compared with day workers even after taking account of factors such as the qualifications and social class of the parents. A recent investigation by Barton, Aldridge and Smith (1998) also indicated adverse emotional effects on children. However, these studies were concerned with shiftworking parents rather than predominantly shiftworking mothers. While they raise concerns about potential effects on children therefore, the picture is not a straightforward one.

Other family disturbance may relate to effects on the quality of the relationship between partners. A variety of problems have been documented, for example reduced social contacts and joint special activities, different mealtimes and requirements for daytime silence in the house (Nachreiner, Baer, Diekmann & Ernst, 1984) and detrimental effects on sexual life (Wedderburn, 1978; Thierry, 1980). Evidence about actual separation and divorce however, is sparse and somewhat contradictory (Bunnage, 1984).

## SHIFTWORK AND PERFORMANCE

### Sleep Disturbance

One of the most obvious effects of shiftwork is the disturbance it causes to the length and quality of sleep. Numerous self-report surveys have documented these problems in rotating shiftworkers (Khaleque, 1991; Escriba, Perez-hoyos & Bolumar, 1992; Poole, Evans, Spurgeon & Bridges, 1992; Barak, Achiron, Lampl et al., 1995), in night workers (Chan, Gan, Ngui & Phoon, 1987, Alfredsson, Akerstedt, Mattsson & Wilborg, 1991; Smith & Folkard, 1993; Neidhammer, Lert & Marne, 1994) and in people working other irregular hours (Fletcher, Colquhoun, Knauth et al., 1988; Rutenfranz, Plett, Knauth et al., 1988; Sparks, 1992; Koh, Chia & Lee, 1994). Evidence from the wider literature on sleep research suggests that these effects have two components, firstly a reduction in the actual number of hours of sleep, and secondly fragmentation of sleep, both effects resulting from the requirement to sleep at inappropriate times in the circadian rhythm. Normal sleep appears to consist of two distinct types, predominantly slow wave sleep which is required for brain restitution, and apparently less crucial 'facultative' sleep (Horne, 1985, 1988). The former 'obligatory' sleep tends to occupy the first five hours of the night. Provided individuals are not deprived of 'obligatory' sleep, effects on performance appear to be minimal even where sleep loss extends over several months (Webb & Agnew, 1974). However, displacement of sleep appears to have much more significant effect than does sleep curtailment. Where sleep is displaced to an inappropriate point in the circadian cycle, when hormonal activity in the body is geared to promote wakefulness, sleep is much more difficult to maintain and therefore becomes fragmented. Thus shiftworkers may suffer both from a reduction in hours of sleep, which may extend into the 'obligatory' sleep requirement, and from a lack of sleep continuity. Added to this they are then required to work at a time which is suboptimal from the point of view of their circadian cycle. Taken together, these factors predict that shiftworking is likely to be associated both with a reduction in the quality of performance at work and with an increase in errors and accidents.

### Errors and Productivity

Despite a substantial body of laboratory-based research on circadian rhythms, sleep loss and performance (reviewed by Alluisi & Morgan, 1982) workplace-based investigations are relatively rare. This is due in part to the considerable methodological difficulties which arise when attempting to demonstrate intershift differences in performance. These centre on the well-known differences between daytime and night time working environments, which make it very difficult to separate out the effects of time of day per se. Despite this, however, the results are fairly consistent in demonstrating that errors are more frequent on rotating shifts and particularly the night shift when compared with daytime working. This has been shown in studies assessing real errors in a range of occupations such as meter readers (Bjerner, Holm & Swensson, 1955), pilots in flight simulators (Klein, Bruner & Holtman, 1970), train drivers (Hildebrandt, Rohmert & Rutenfranz, 1974) and truck drivers (Harris, 1977). Some more recent studies have used laboratory-type tests such as reaction time and mental arithmetic to demonstrate slower and less accurate performance on the night shift (Tepas, Walsh, Moss & Armstrong, 1981; Tilley, Wilkinson & Warren, 1982).

Studies which investigate the relationhip between shiftwork schedules and productivity are particularly scarce. However, again the data which do exist all appear to point to higher productivity on day shifts. For example, an early study of shift changes in the UK showed that when the same workers worked day and night shifts alternately most achieved higher productivity during the day (Wyatt & Marriott, 1953). A study by Murrel (1965) also noted decreased productivity in night workers employed in various jobs and a more recent study in Taiwan showed that optimum performance was achieved on the day shift and worst performance on the night shift. Within night shifts however, those that were part of a fixed shift system produced higher productivity than those that were part of a rotating system (Liou & Wang, 1991).

## Accidents

Errors may affect work quality and speed of performance but perhaps more seriously, they may also cause accidents. Accident investigation data show that fatigue, defined as 'sleepiness' has contributed to a large number of industrial and transportation accidents (Mitler, Carskadon, Czeisler et al., 1988). A substantial body of epidemiological evidence exists which links the night shift in particular to an increased risk of industrial accidents. (Wojtczak-Jaroszowa & Jarosz, 1987; Ong et al., 1987; Lauridsen & Tonnessen, 1990; Novak, Smolensky, Fairschild & Reeves, 1990; Laundry & Lees, 1991; Gold, Rogacz, Bock et al., 1992). A recent study in a UK engineering company with three rotating shifts showed that the relative risk of sustaining an injury at work was 1.23 times higher on the night shift than on the morning shift (Smith, Folkard & Poole, 1994). These results are despite the fact that in many organisations accidents and injuries are less likely to be reported at night thus producing a potential underestimate of the true figure. The evidence that shiftworking results in an increased risk of accidents at work is therefore a matter of some concern.

## COMPRESSED WORKING TIME

Most of the literature on shiftwork is concerned with rotating 8 hour shifts. In recent years however, work schedules which compress the working week into a smaller number of longer shifts have become increasingly popular with both employers and employees. By concentrating work into fewer days workers have longer and more frequent rest breaks. For example, a continuously operating 12-hour shift system generates four days off for every four days worked. The advantages for employees include an extended period for leisure or domestic activities, fewer work days with no loss of pay, a reduction in commuting problems and costs and a regular work week. From the employers' point of view these systems provide greater flexibility for covering all jobs at required times and a decrease in start-up times, hence a more efficient continuous stock or service provision flow and a generally better service for customers. In addition more time is available for extra activities such as meetings and training sessions. These are, however, some potential disadvantages which centre on the problem of fatigue which may translate into errors, accidents or health problems. Research on the potential effects of these work schedules has proliferated in recent years. Most has been concerned with evaluating the 12-hour shift system which is by far the most common form of compressed working time.

Initial attention has focused on the workers' general level of satisfaction with 12-hour as opposed to conventional 8-hour shifts. Generally these results have been positive, with workers reporting greater preference for compressed working time, largely on the grounds of the increased leisure time it provides (Ivancevich & Lyon, 1977; Peacock, Glube, Miller & Clune, 1983; Cunningham, 1989; Daniel, 1990; Rosa, 1991; Tucker, Barton & Folkard, 1996). Additional data from Lees and Laundry (1989) indicated a reduction in minor morbidity, especially stress-related complaints associated with a change to 12-hour shifts. However, there are some dissenters to this generally positive view. A survey of nurses in the UK who changed to 12-hour shifts felt that these actually disrupted their social and fmaily life (Thompson, 1989). Similarly a study of nurses in Australia also found more favourable ratings for 8-hour shifts (Kundi, Koller, Stefan et al., 1995). The results of one study of manufacturing workers indicated that while the workers themselves were satisfied with the change to 12-hour shifts, this opinion was not shared by their partners (Wallace, Owens & Levens, 1990). It would seem that attitudes to different shift systems are unlikely to be generalisable across organizations and that numerous demographic and social mediators, including employee choice, need to be taken into account.

Other studies have been concerned with aspects of performance in terms both of productivity and of the potemtial for errors and accidents. The concern here, even when shifts do not rotate is that cumulative fatigue may be engendered by long hours. It should be noted, however, that 12-hour shifts differ markedly from overtime work (discussed below) and that the data are not transferable between the two situations. Unlike overtime, compressed time schedules are predictable in terms of timing and length and do not involve extra remuneration. Further, they continue in the same form for months, or years, rather than involving short periods of extended activity. The attitudes and motivations of employees are therefore likely to differ accordingly.

Studies of potential performance decrements in 12-hour shiftworkers have largely involved self-reports of fatigue or occasionally completion of cognitive tests at different points in the shift schedule. The majority of studies which have used questionnaires indicate that employees do report considerable fatigue towards the end of a 12-hour shift. Daniel (1990) found that workers at a chemical plant reported more fatigue and subsequently slept significantly longer than comparable workers on 8-hour shifts, including night workers. Another study of chemical workers in the UK (Tucker, Barton & Folkard, 1996) which used the Standard Shiftwork Index, found that one of the few differences between those on 8-hour and 12-hour shifts was their self-rated level of alertness, less in the 12-hour shiftworkers, at certain times of the day. By contrast Lowden, Kecklund, Axelsson and Akerstedt (1998), also studying workers at a chemical plant, found that alertness actually increased following a change from an 8-hour to a 12-hour shift system. However, not surprisingly, the particular time of day when reports are recorded appears to be of major importance here. A further study by Tucker, Smith, Macdonald and Folkard (1998) involving manufacturing and engineering companies found that 8-hour workers reported higher levels of alertness in the afternoons, while 12-hour workers were more alert in the mornings. Further, beginning a shift at 6.00 a.m. (a common occurrence in industry) appeared to have particularly deleterious effects on alertness. A study in Sweden also underlines the complexity of the situation. Axelsson, Kecklund, Akerstedt & Lowden (1998) compared sleepiness and physical effort in power plant workers who worked 12-hour shifts during weekends and 8-hour shifts during the week. When 12-hour and 8-hour night shifts were compared sleepiness was greater, and physical effort less, on the 12-hour shift. When morning shifts were compared however, sleepiness was greater on the 8-hour shifts. The authors suggest that reported sleepiness on morning shifts might relate to differences in sleep length prior to the shift, while on the night shift it might relate to differences in physical effort. One cannot conclude therefore, that 12-hour shifts necessarily produce increased sleepiness. In summary, the data on how people actually feel when working on 12-hour shifts are contradictory. Different points in the cycle induce differing levels of fatigue. Further, it has been suggested that the nature of the work, particularly in terms of its physical demands, is an important factor in determining whether or not workers wish to retain a 12-hour system (Wedderburn, 1996b).

Data from actual performance tests are relatively rare. The studies quoted above by Lowden et al. (1998) and Axelsson et al. (1998) also included reaction time, and in the case of the Axelsson study, a vigilance test. In neither study were significant differences in test performance observed between 8-hour and 12-hour shifts. However, an earlier study by Rosa (1991), using a battery of cognitive tests, found performance decrements attributable to 12-hour shiftworking in control room operators who had been working on this schedule for 7 months. These decrements persisted at follow-up 3.5 years later. Unfortunately, time of testing was somewhat variable in these studies and once more the likelihood is that different shift systems produce problems at different points in the cycle.

Whether fatigue problems on 12-hour shifts are translated into increased accident rates is currently unknown. The result of a study by Laundry and Lees (1991) in a yarn manufacturing company supported this view. Further, a recent analysis of 1.2 million accidents in Germany for the year 1994 indicated that there are clear time-related effects on occupational accident risks with the risk increasing exponentially after the ninth hour of work (Hanecke, Tiedemann, Nachreiner & Grzech-Sukalo, 1998). There was also a significant interaction betwen number of hours at work and time of day, data which appear to raise considerable concerns about shiftworking in general, and longer shifts in particular.

Information on productivity relating to 12-hour shifts is largely anecdotal, although some data from Holland did show that operating time in 28 companies studied increased by an average of 15% following the introduction of compressed working weeks (Hoekstra, Jansen & VanGoudoever, 1994). Operating time is not necessarily synonymous with productivity however, a factor of relevance to the next section on extended working hours.

## OVERTIME WORK

The tendency to work beyond the length of a regular shift or of a standard (usually 8-hour), working day appears to be increasing in many countries, including developed ones. This is a reversal of previous twentieth century trends, (Wedderburn, 1996a). Much of this overtime, particularly in managerial and professional groups, may be unpaid and in response to increasing workloads and decreasing staff resources. The potential health and safety implications of long working hours were brought into sharp focus by the introduction of the European Directive on Working Time (1993) which among other things introduced a limit of 48 hours per week on working time, unless an alternative agreement had been reached between employer and employees. Certain groups of workers are currently exempt from the directive, notably junior doctors and various types of transport workers, mainly because of practical difficulties in its application. An initial but ultimately unsuccessful challenge to the legislation by the UK government on the grounds that it was not a health and safety issue, prompted a number of reviews of what is actually known about the effects on health and performance of certain patterns of working time, particularly long hours (Harrington, 1994; Spurgeon, Harrington & Cooper, 1997; Sparks & Cooper, 1997). The general consensus view, derived from an admittedly small database, is that the risk to health is sufficient to raise significant concern. As in the case of shiftworking many of the effects of overtime work appear to be mediated by stress. While circadian disruption is not a factor, increasing fatigue and increased duration of exposure to other workplace stressors are important. The current literature on this subject is limited in the main to potential effect on mental health and CVD, with some additional consideration of effects on performance and safety.

## Mental Health

The majority of modern studies which explore the association between long working hours and the development of mental health problems have been carried out in the context of occupational stress research, where length of working hours constitutes one potential stressor. Most studies use well-established measures of psychological well-being or mental health. For example, Duffy and McGoldrick (1990) investigated the mental health of urban bus drivers as compared with that of a matched group of general practice patients. Mental health as measured by the Crown–Crisp Experiential Index (Crown & Crisp, 1979) was significantly poorer in the bus drivers, with family problems related to long hours identified as a major source of stress. In a study of UK accountants (Daniels & Guppy, 1995), quantitative work overload of which long hours was a major component, was significantly related to scores on a measure of psychological well-being (Warr, 1990) and on the General Health Questionnaire (GHQ). In Japan a study of factory workers demonstrated that working hours of more than 9 hours a day was significantly related to psychological distress also measured by the GHQ (Ezoe & Morimoto, 1994). Similarly in a UK study, the GHQ scores of junior doctors increased significantly between commencing their first post and eight weeks later during which time they were working on average 73 hours per week (Houston & Allt, 1997). Clearly in all these cases it is not possible to attribute psychological distress solely to the factor of long hours, since overtime work by its very nature tends to occur concomitantly with high levels of other work stressors. Further, some studies have highlighted the importance of individual difference such as gender (Galambois & Walter, 1992), personality type (Watanabe, Torii, Shinkai & Watanabe, 1993) and motivation (Bliese & Halverson, 1996) in moderating the response to long hours. For many workers, however, the demands of excessive overtime may significantly reduce their ability to cope with other occupational stressors.

## Cardiovascular Disorders

Unsurprisingly, extended working hours sustained over long periods have also been linked to an increased risk of CVD. Two early studies identified an association between CVD and 'severe occupational strain' which at that time was measured solely in terms of long working hours. Russek and Zohman (1958) found that 71 of 100 coronary patients under the age of 40 had worked more than 60 hours per week over a prolonged period, more than four times the number in the control group. Two years later Buell and Breslow (1960) published the results of a three-year mortality study and concluded that the risk of mortality from CVD in men under the age of 44 was significantly greater in those who worked more than 48 hours a week. Interestingly, heavy physical work seemed to offer some protection from the working hours risk factor. Further support for an association between long hours and CVD has come from another UK study of telephone company employees who were also regular night school attenders (Hinkle, Whitney & Lehman et al., 1968). More recently a study in Japan of men admitted to hospital with acute myocardial infarction demonstrated an increasing trend in the risk of infarction with an increase in working hours (Sokejima & Kagamimori, 1998). Concerns about 'karoshi', which so far seems to be a peculiarly Japanese phenomenon, have already been mentioned.

Other studies, however, have produced contradictory data. For example morbidity and mortality data collected in Sweden over a 20-year period up to 1983 (Starrin, Larsson, Brenner et al., 1990), failed to find any association between CVD-related morbidity in males and long hours, although interestingly, an association was identified in females which may be explained by gender differences in additional domestic workloads. In America no relationship was identified between long hours and risk factors for CVD such as high blood pressure and serum cholesterol concentrations (Sorenson, Pirie, Folsom et al., 1985). Current thinking favours the view that individual differences are important moderators of the relationship between overtime work and CVD. These include factors such as gender (women having dual roles), personality (for example Type A), physiological susceptibility and the presence of other sources of stress. Other, as yet unexplored, factors include differences in attitudes and motivation which are likely to be crucial in determining whether exposure to a potential stressor is translated into a health problem.

## Performance Effects

As noted earlier, performance may be assessed in a number of ways, in terms of productivity, errors, accidents or surrogate measures in the form of cognitive tests. In most areas of research there is an understandable preference for data produced from more recent studies, employing as they do the latest methodological approaches. Surprisingly, where long hours and performance are concerned some of the most useful data were collected by an engineering works in the UK at the end of the last century (Mather, 1884). In a series of elegantly designed experiments the management at Mather & Platt in Manchester were able to demonstrate that when weekly hours were reduced from 53 to 48 production levels remained the same. Moreover, absenteeism was reduced. A short time later a German factory producing optical goods reduced daily hours from 9 to 8, resulting in a 3% rise in production (Abbe, 1901). These studies were the first to demonstrate that increased operating time does not necessarily translate into increased production. Since these pioneering experiments a series of others, in different parts of the world, have produced similar findings (reviewed by Alliusi & Morgan, 1982).

In recent years, more attention has focused on the use of performance testing to assess the effects of the fatigue presumed to result from long working hours. In a controlled laboratory experiment student volunteers performed cognitive tests for different time periods (Okogbaa & Shell, 1986). Performance deteriorated with time spent on task and was 6% better with scheduled rest breaks than without such breaks. Performance tests have been applied particularly in the area of driver fatigue (reviewed by Brown, 1994) and to the problems experienced by junior doctors (reviewed by Spurgeon & Harrington, 1989). Data from these studies and from laboratory investigations indicate that, as in the case of CVD, the effects of long working hours are moderated by a range of task-based and individual factors. These include the type of task, for example routine and monotonous versus complex and stimulating (Monk & Folkard, 1985), the motivation of the person, including the perceived cost of errors (Craig, 1984), and the presence or absence of other stressors (Craig, 1984). In common with compressed work schedules therefore, the evidence for performance effects is sufficient to raise concern but proper understanding will require attention to a complex interaction of mediating factors.

## INDIVIDUAL AND GROUP DIFFERENCES

Some people seem well able to tolerate the demands of shiftworking and overtime while others seem particularly vulnerable to their effects. Both patterns of work merit study in this respect. However, the information in this section is currently limited to shiftworking since to date no one has studied the particular characteristics of those who respond well to overtime work. Shiftwork tolerance has been defined as 'an absence of complaints with regard to sleep, digestive and nervous disorders or psychological well-being' (Harma, 1993a). Being able to identify the individual and social determinants of increased tolerance or vulnerability is important for two reasons. First, it could be helpful in terms of selecting more suitable people into this kind of work, or at least being in a position to counsel applicants more clearly about the potential risks to their health. Second, it can inform the development of appropriately focused programmes to manage shiftwork problems and thus reduce the risk. A range of factors have been investigated in recent years including age, gender, aspects of lifestyle, health status, personality traits and behaviour patterns.

## Age

It is well established that the ability to tolerate shiftwork decreases with age (Oginski, Pokorski & Oginski, 1993; Harma, Hakola, Akerstedt & Laitinen, 1994; Reilly, Waterhouse & Atkinson, 1997; Brugere, Barrit, Butat et al., 1997). Symptoms of intolerance frequently begin to develop around the late forties and early fifties in workers who have often worked on shifts for many years without significant problems. A number of contributory factors have been suggested. First, since age is usually associated with long experience of shiftworking, adverse effects may be cumulative. A study of 750 shiftworkers in an oil refinery was able to show that even in particular age groups, including younger groups, length and quality of sleep decreased with longer experience of shiftwork (Foret, Bensimon, Benoit & Vieux, 1981). Second, there is also a well-documented change or flattening of circadian rhythms as people get older (Czeisler, Dumont, Duffy et al., 1992; Reilly, Waterhouse & Atkinson, 1997). This leads to an increased tendency towards 'morningness', coupled with general phase shifting. Added to this is an increased tendency to shorter sleep and frequent waking with age (Bliwise, 1993). All of these factors make adjustment to any disruption of the normal body clock and compensation for lost sleep more difficult. Harma et al. (1994), in a laboratory-based experiment, showed that older postal workers (mean age 57) were less able to recover from several night shifts than younger subjects (mean age 24) in terms of performance on a letter-sorting task which mimicked their real jobs. Finally, it has been suggested that general deterioration in physical health and the ability to cope with other life stressors may also play a part in the difficulties experienced by older workers.

## Health Status

It has often been suggested in the past that those with particular health problems, notably diabetes, thyrotoxicosis, epilepsy, and renal disease should be counselled against shiftworking. Much of this thinking was based on concerns about exacerbating these workers' existing conditions and about disruption of their medication regimes. There is some evidence however, that problems in this area may be much less than was originally thought. For example Poole, Wright and Nattrass (1992) showed that in insulin-dependent diabetes, control of diabetes was no worse in those working shifts than in those who worked days only. In many countries attitudes to physically vulnerable groups are more flexible than hitherto and tend to be based on individual circumstances rather than on blanket policy. This is particularly the case in the UK where the Disability Discrimination Act (HMSO, 1995) now makes it illegal to discriminate against employees on the grounds of physical disability unless it can be demonstrated that employment will significantly increase the risk to their health. This is an issue which tends to be of concern to the occupational physician, specifically in relation to pre-employment screening, rather than to the occupational psychologist, however.

## Gender

Traditionally, night work and hence rotating shifts have been discouraged for women. This dates back to an International Labour Organisation convention in 1948 outlawing such work, a convention which is still adhered to in many countries. However, with the emergence of legislation on equality and of a generally anti-discriminatory culture in many developed countries, the number of women involved in shiftwork has gradually increased. In fact for some jobs where shiftwork is unavoidable, notably nursing, women have always been over-represented. There are, however, well-documented differences in the ability of men and women to cope with shiftwork with significantly more problems being experienced by women (Oginski, Pokorski & Oginski, 1993; Beermann & Nachreiner, 1995; Nachreiner, Lubeck-Ploger & Grzech-Sukalo, 1995). Laboratory-based investigations indicate that these findings are not explained by physiological differences (Hakola, Harma & Laitinen, 1995) and it is generally accepted that the problem of women shiftworkers tend to be related to factors such as differences in social and domestic pressures, family and childcare responsibilities and the difficulties of transport and safety during unsocial hours (Hakola, Harma & Laitinen, 1995; Beerman & Nachreiner, 1995). Further, there is evidence that the existence of a partner (Beerman & Nachreiner, 1995), and social support within the family (Louden & Bohle, 1997) are both important moderators of any effect. Interestingly, women over the age of 50 appear to suffer less from shiftwork intolerance than their male counterparts. In one study (Oginski, Pokorski & Oginski, 1993) it was observed that in women, self-reported health complaints decreased significantly in this age group, presumably as a result of a reduction in domestic responsibilities.

## Personality Factors

A number of aspects of personality have been investigated in an attempt to predict which types of people are likely to be best suited to shiftwork. The majority of these studies are cross-sectional and product interesting correlational data. However, they raise inevitable questions about causation. Do certain features of personality predict shiftwork tolerance or are they actually an effect of long-term adjustment? The most consistent associations have been obtained in relation to neuroticism which is highly correlated with shiftwork tolerance (Iskra-Golec, Marek & Noworol, 1995; Taylor, Folkard & Shapiro, 1997). However, a rare longitudinal study by Kaliterna, Vidacek, Prizmic and Radosevic-Vidacek (1995) was unable to demonstrate that neuroticism actually predicted shiftwork tolerance and suggested it might be better viewed as a potential confounder in future studies.

Similar problems exist in relation to a number of other factors. Shiftworkers are more likely to have an internal locus of control (Smith, Spelten & Norman, 1995), to be 'flexible' rather than 'rigid' (Gallway & McEntee, 1997) an to be 'evening' rather than 'morning' circadian types (Breithaupt, Hildebrandt & Dohre et al., 1978). Most recently, the concept of 'hardiness' has been investigated (Wedderburn, 1994). In a sample of male and female shiftworkers in a textile and an electronics factory 'hardiness' was positively correlated with increased liking for shiftwork and reduced reporting of physical complaints. Again however, one cannot deduce from these results whether this factor is a predictor or an outcome measure.

The focus in all the above investigations has been on coping styles rather than on actual coping behaviour. Since correlational data provide rather shaky ground on which to base pre-employment selection, recent thinking in this area suggests that the identification of effective patterns of coping behaviour in shiftworkers would be a more useful approach (Nachreiner, 1998). Here the emphasis would be on intervention and training of existing employees to reduce problems and risks rather than attempting to screen out unsuitable individuals. A variety of coping behaviours, particularly the organisation of social, domestic and transport arrangements, appear to be associated with improved attitudes to shiftwork (Greenwood, 1995; Harma, Rosa & Pulli et al, 1995; Blood, Sack, Lewy & Monk, 1995; Pisarski, Bohle & Callan, 1998). There is also evidence that regular exercising and physical fitness are related to shiftwork tolerance in terms of decreased reports of fatigue and of health complaints (Harma, Ilmarinen, Knauth et al., 1988a, b; Harma, 1993b). Predictive data are limited but, as Nachreiner (1998) points out, coping behaviours are amenable to modification and it should therefore be possible to carry out well-controlled intervention studies to inform new approaches to shiftwork management. Current thinking in the area of management and intervention is the subject of the final section of this chapter.

## INTERVENTION AND MANAGEMENT

### Shiftwork

It is clear from the preceding sections that better adjustment to shiftwork will both enhance the health and well-being of employees and promote safer and more productive work performance. To this end a variety of different approaches to shiftwork management have been introduced with varying degrees of success. Broadly these fall into three categories: (a) interventions which focus on the design of the work/rest schedule itself; (b) interventions which focus on aspects of the work environment in which shiftworking takes place; (c) interventions which focus on the individual, either pharmacologically or in terms of attitudes and behaviour.

## Work Schedule Design

Although a large number of shift patterns exist one of the most common is the three 8-hour shift rotation. Consequently most effort in the area of system design has been directed towards this pattern. Essentially two questions have been addressed. First, in what direction should shifts rotate and second, how fast should the rotation occur? Shift systems may rotate in a forward direction (mornings, afternoons, nights), usually called a 'delaying' system or in a backward direction (nights, afternoons, mornings), usually called an 'advancing' system. While there is no ideal shift system, the bulk of evidence suggests that in terms of the health and well-being of the workers a forward rotation which occurs slowly (for example over 3–4 weeks) is preferable (Rosa, Bonnet, Bootzin et al., 1990; Knauth, 1993). This allows the body to adjust fully to each new pattern, a process which normally takes from two to three weeks (Akerstedt, 1985) and ensures that workers are not in a continual state of circadian disruption. In addition, forward rotation is in harmony with the fact that, without external cues which force the body clock into a 24-hour cycle, the normal endogenous period is 25 hours. This has been observed in laboratory situations where external cues are removed (Wever, 1979). Under these circumstances there is a forward moving tendency, with sleep times occurring later and later.

Current data also suggest that night work is best kept to a minimum where possible. Although negative effects on productivity are unproven the evidence for adverse health and social consequences is compelling. In fact only a small minority of employees actually appear to prefer permanent night shifts and an early doctoral thesis on this subject (McDonald, 1958) suggested that night work 'veterans' were a somewhat unusual group both socially and psychologically.

The timing of shifts has also received attention since it has been observed that an early start to the morning shift increases fatigue and errors on this shift (Moors, 1990; Hildebrandt, Rohmert & Rutenfranz, 1974). This is apparently because workers beginning a shift at 6 a.m. tend to go to bed at the usual time the night before. Despite this observation however, optimal timing of shifts depends on a range of local factors from specific elements of the job (for example whether it is the night or the morning shift which is responsible for waking up patients in a hospital ward) to the geography and culture of the area, which may influence optimal times for leisure. These factors point above all to the need for flexibility in shift timing which takes into account local conditions.

In addition to scheduling of the work pattern there have also been suggestions that scheduling of short naps during working hours may offset fatigue effects during night shifts. These have generally been referred to as 'maintenance' naps and have become common practice in Japan where rooms are provided for the purpose. Few evaluations of their effectiveness in terms of increasing alertness have been carried out although one laboratory study (Gillberg, 1984) was able to demonstrate that one hour of sleep, as compared with one hour of rest while awake, improved alertness in an experiment which required subjects to stay awake all night. Currently there is an absence of data on the usefulness of formally sanctioned napping in the workplace and concerns have been raised as to whether napping on successive nights might actually reduce circadian adaptation. As a potentially useful intervention, however, it does merit further investigation.

## The Work Environment

In terms of adapting the work environment only two factors have received substantial attention. The first of these is the introduction of bright light during night shifts in an attempt to replicate one of the exogenous factors which encourage wakefulness. The capacity for controlled light exposure to shift the phase of circadian rhythms is well established in animals (Pittendrigh, 1981), but data on humans are contradictory. For example, Costa, Ghirlanda, Minors and Waterhouse (1993) assessed the effects on nurses of short periods of bright light on two consecutive night shifts as compared with two nights with normal lighting. The nurses reported less tiredness and sleepiness and a more balanced sleeping pattern following bright light exposure. In addition, performance on a letter cancelling test was enhanced. No change in physiological correlates of phase shifting (hormonal excretion and body temperature) were observed, however. By contrast Budnick, Lerman and Nicolich (1995) were able to demonstrate significant changes in morning urinary melatonin levels in nightshift workers during a three-month trial of exposure to bright light during the shift. Despite this no significant changes in self-reported alertness were recorded. Current opinion is that more information is needed on the precise timing, intensity and duration of light exposure needed to produce phase shifting but that this intervention holds considerable promise.

The second aspect of the work environment which has been considered is the actual workload both in terms of its physical intensity and its duration. The thinking here is that, for night workers in particular, the activation of body systems conducive to performance via changes in the relationships between cardiac, respiratory and metabolic variables, is much reduced (Rosa et al., 1990). Some studies of energy expenditure in male shiftworkers tend to support this in showing that more energy is expended to achieve a similar level of work on some shifts than on others. For example, a study by Wojtczak-Jaroszowa in Poland (quoted in Rosa et al., 1990) of workers in a glass factory showed that when workers were examined before work and at four points during the work shift, pulmonary ventilation, oxygen uptake and energy expenditure were significantly higher on the night shift than on other shifts. Energy expenditure was 10% higher on this shift despite work speed being slightly slower. It is known that, in any case, under normal daytime conditions, work capacity decreases over the period of an 8-hour shift (Mital, 1986). Therefore for night workers this normal decrease appears to interact with the effects of nocturnal working. These and other data have led to suggestions that in order both to maximise efficiency and to protect the long-term health of the workers different work schedules might be appropriate to different phases in shift cycles. To date, however, there have been no systematic investigations of this approach.

## The Individual

Interventions which focus on the individual may be either pharmacologically or behaviourally based. Pharmacological approaches include sedative-hypnotics designed to increase sleep during non-work hours, stimulants to improve alertness during work hours and drugs designed to manipulate the normal circadian sleep/wake cycle. Of these the first two are generally regarded as unhelpful, particularly over the long term since their effectiveness tends to decline with use and the potential for abuse is a significant concern (Kales, Soldatos, Bixler & Kales, 1983; Weiss & Laties, 1962). The effective use of drugs to control the normal sleep/wake cycle, particularly the use of melatonin, which is known to be effective in regulating the sleep patterns of insomniacs (Zhdanova, Wurtman, Lynch et al., 1995), is currently speculative but is regarded as promising. However, the use of this type of drug over a long period, as opposed to its current short-term application for jet-lag sufferers, seems likely to meet with some resistance. For this reason perhaps the most effective long-term interventions are likely to lie in the area of human attitudes and behaviour. Some of these relate simply to improvements in physical fitness and changes in lifestyle patterns and it is these which have so far received the most attention in terms of intervention studies.

The findings relating to energy expenditure discussed earlier have led a number of researchers to investigate the effects of increased regular exercise and physical fitness on adaptation to shiftwork. The results have been generally encouraging. For example Harma et al. (1988a, b) evaluated the effects of a four-month physical training programme on the mood, sleep and symptom reporting of a group of shiftworking nurses. Those participating in the programme showed on average a 5-beat decrease in heart rate and a 5% increase in maximal volume of oxygen as compared with the control group. Importantly, they also reported decreased fatigue, improved sleep and fewer musculoskeletal problems. Disappointingly, manipulation of meal timing and diet content appears to be less successful in terms of promoting circadian adjustment. Much of the early enthusiasm for this approach was based on a study of jet-lag sufferers (Graeber, 1989) which assessed the effects of a particular 'feasting and fasting' regime with positive results. However, it has never been replicated in shiftworkers and the authors of the study have themselves raised doubts about its applicability to patterns of working time. It is perhaps rather too early to dismiss this type of approach completely however, since there have been few well-controlled trials of different regimes.

Manipulation of sleeping patterns in shiftworkers has been similarly limited and current advice seems to centre on avoidance of caffeine near sleep time, advice which is hardly specific to this particular group. However one study by Sharratt and Davis (1991) investigated what was termed a 'chronohygiene programme' for employees on a 12-hour shift system. This incorporated both diet and exercise together with advice about sleep patterns. Workers kept to a specific programme of physical activity and relaxation, together with specific types of food at certain times of the day. After a four-week trial there were several positive results in terms of self-reported increased alertness and de-creased fatigue, improved reaction time and reduced errors on a simulated work task. Other evaluative data in this field are limited. However a number of organisations are beginning to introduce such approaches as part of an overall shiftwork policy. The role of the behavioural scientist in introducing and maintaining such programmes is likely to increase.

From the psychologist's point of view perhaps the most interesting pos-sibility lies in the area of individually-based stress management which to date has received very little attention. Rosa et al. (1990) point to several potential applications of different approaches drawn from the psychological literature. They note, for example, that many of the adverse effects of shiftwork are derived from sleep deprivation and that establishing and maintaining good sleep habits would seem to be central to satisfactory adjustment. A number of successful behavioural modification programmes have been developed for the treatment of insomniacs, such as stimulus control instructions (Bootzin & Nicassio, 1978), which simply consist of a set of procedures for optimising the home surroundings for sleep. These might readily be adapted for shiftworkers. In addition, assuming that patterns of working time constitute a potential stressor, a range of well-established stress reduction techniques would also merit exploration in this context. These include for example, relaxation train-ing (Benson, 1975), visualisation training shown to be successful in improving sporting and academic performance (Mahoney, 1984), and biofeedback, also shown to be effective in enhancing alertness and performance (Druckman & Swets, 1988). Finally, and perhaps most importantly, forms of cognitive-behavioural therapy aimed at promoting self-efficacy and positive coping be-haviour might be a powerful tool in effecting better adjustment via attitude change. As Rosa and colleagues note, counselling, both for shiftworkers and for their families, is a much neglected area. To date there has been little application of these methods within the workplace to cope with the specific problems of working time. Yet their success in other areas suggests that alongside other organisational interventions they could have an important role to play, not least because of the importance of placing the control of successful adjustment in the hands of the workers themselves.

## FUTURE DIRECTIONS

From the evidence presented in this review it is clear that the pattern and length of hours that people work frequently constitute a risk to their health and well-being. Conventional health and safety practice usually prescribes a policy of removal of workplace hazards rather than requiring that the individual employee adjust to those hazards. However, where shiftwork and to a lesser extent overtime work are concerned, it is clear that the hazards in question cannot be removed and are in fact likely to become more pervasive in the future. As a result attention is increasingly turning to the development of policies designed to reduce risks and minimise effects on performance. To date these policies have tended to focus on manipulation of the work enviornment either in terms of optimum shift scheduling or physical interventions such as bright light introduction or workload reduction. While these approaches are of considerable importance and many are derived from a sound evidence base, they have rarely been complemented by attention to the behavioural patterns of the employees themselves. Increasingly, however, the results of studies which investigate the effects of working time are pointing to the importance of attitudes and motivation in promoting satisfactory adjustment to irregular hours. Exploring individual differences in terms of these variables is important to our understanding of some current contradictions in the data on working time in that they supply us with important explanatory mediating factors. Further, they point the way to effective interventions which can enhance those already in place. Epidemiological research can go some way towards defining these factors by careful analysis of the data in terms of age, gender, health status and lifestyle variables. However, an in-depth understanding of how such factors operate requires exploration of the field within a framework which includes the attitude and belief systems of the individuals concerned, their coping strategies and how their working patterns interact with aspects of their domestic and social lives. To date there has been little systematic study in this area either in terms of defining these important psychosocial mediators or in implementing controlled intervention studies. Both aspects will require input from psychological theory and methodology. Further, in the study of lifestyle change, for example, the modification of sleeping and eating patterns, approaches developed within the related fields of health psychology and health promotion, will be of central importance.

Management of working time in its broader sense is currently at an early stage, with some limited attention to better organisation of shiftwork scheduling and virtually none to reducing the risks associated with long, irregular or unsocial hours. Future progress in this area will require a substantial extension of current organisational initiatives but in particular will need a new emphasis on psychosocial issues and on assisting individual employees to develop appropriate adjustment strategies. In this field therefore, as in many others, the biopsychosocial model provides the only meaningful perspective.

# REFERENCES

Abbe, E. (1901). Cited in J. Goldmark (Ed.), *Fatigue, Efficiency: a Study in Industry*, 1912, New York: Russell Sage Foundation.

Ahlborg, G., Axelsson, G. & Bodin, L. (1996). Shift work, nitrous oxide exposure and subfertility among Swedish midwives. *International Journal of Epidemiology*, **25**(4), 783–790.

Akerstedt, T. (1985). Adjustment of physiological circadian rhythms and the sleep-wake cycle to shiftwork. In S. Folkard & T. H. Monk (Eds.), (pp. 185–198). New York: Wiley.

Alfredsson, L., Akerstedt, T., Mattsson, M. & Wilborg, B. (1991). Self-reported health and well-being amongst night security guards: A comparison with the working population. *Ergonomics*, **34**(5), 525–530.

Alfredsson, L., Karasek, R. & Theorell, T. (1982). Myocardinal infarction risk and psychosocial work environment: An analysis of the male Swedish working force. *Social Science and Medicine*, **16**, 463–467.

Alluisi, E. A. & Morgan, B. B. (1982). Temporal factors in human performance and productivity. In E. A. Alluisi & A. Fleishman (Eds), *Human Performance and Productivity: Stress and Performance Effectiveness* (pp. 165–247), Vol. 3. A. Erlbaum, Hillsdale, NJ.

Alward, R. R. & Monk, T. H. (1990). A comparison of rotating-shift and permanent night nurses. *International Journal of Nursing Studies*, **27**(3), 297–302.

Axelsson, G., Ahlborg, G. & Bodin, L. (1996). Shift work, nitrous oxide exposure, and spontaneous abortion among Swedish midwives. *Occupational and Environmental Medicine*, **53**, 374–378.

Axelsson, J., Kecklund, G., Akerstedt, T. & Lowden, A. (1998). Effects of alternating 8- and 12-hour shifts on sleep, sleepiness, physical effort and performance. *Scandinavian Journal of Work Environment and Health*, **24**(3), 62–68.

Barak, Y., Achiron, A., Lampl, Y., Gilad, R., Ring, A., Elizur, A. & Sarova-Pinhas, I. (1995). Sleep disturbances among female nurses: Comparing shift to day work. *Chronobiology International*, **12**(5), 345–350.

Barton, J., Aldridge, J. & Smith, P. (1998). The emotional impact of shift work on the children of shift workers. *Scandinavian Journal of Work and Environmental Health*, **24**(3), 146–150.

Barton, J. & Folkard, S. (1991). The response of day and night nurses to their work schedules. *Journal of Occupational Psychology*, **64**, 207–218.

Barton, J., Spelten, E., Totterdell, P., Smith, L., Folkard, S. & Costa, G. (1995). The standard shiftwork index: A battery of questionnaires for assessing shiftwork-related problems. *Work and Stress*, **9**(1), 4–30.

Beermann, B. & Nachreiner, F. (1995). Working shifts—different effects for women and men? *Work and Stress*, **9**(2/3), 289–297.

Benson, H. (1975). *The Relaxation Response*. New York: Morrow.

Bisanti, L., Olsen, J., Basso, O., Thonneau, P. & Karmaus, W. (1996). Shift work and subfecundity: A European multicenter study. *Journal of Environmental Medicine*, **38**(4), 352–358.

Bjerner, B., Holm, A. & Swensson, A. (1955). Diurnal variation in mental performance: A study of three shift workers. *British Journal of Industrial Medicine*, **12**, 103–110.

Bliese, P. D. & Halverson, R. R. (1996). Individual, nomothetic models of job stress: An examination of work hours, cohesion and well-being. *Journal of Applied Social Psychology*, **26**, 1171–1181.

Bliwise, D. L. (1993). Sleep in normal aging and dementia. A review. *Sleep*, **15**, 40–81.

Blood, M. L., Sack, R. L., Lewy, A. J. & Monk, T. H. (1995). Regular social rhythms are associated with circadian phase shifts in night workers. *Shiftwork International Newsletter*, **12**(1), 112.

Bootzin, R. R. & Nicassio, P. M. (1978). Behavioural treatment for insomnia. *Programmes for Behavioural Modification*, **6**, 1–45.

Breithaupt, H., Hildebrandt, G., Dohre, D., Josch, R., Sieber, U. & Werner, M. (1978). Tolerance to shift of sleep as related to the individual's circadian phase position. *Ergonomics*, **21**, 767–774.

Brown, I. D. (1994). Driver fatigue. *Human Factors*, **36**(2), 298–314.

Brugere, D., Barrit, J., Butat, C., Cosset, M. & Volkoff, S. (1997). Shiftwork, age, and health: An epidemiologic investigation. *International Journal of Occupational and Environmental Health*, **3**(2), 15–19.

Budnick, L. D., Lerman, S. E. & Nicolich, M. J. (1995). An evaluation of scheduled bright light and darkness on rotating shiftworkers: Trial and limitations. *American Journal of Industrial Medicine*, **27**, 771–782.

Buell, P. & Breslow, L. (1960). Mortality from CHD in Californian men who work long hours. *Journal of Chronic Disease*, **II**(b), 615–626.

Bunnage, D. (1984). The consequences of shift work on social and family life. In A. Wedderburn & P. Smith (Eds), *Psychological Approaches to Night and Shiftwork*. Edinburgh: Herriot-Watt University.

Bursey, R. G. (1990). A cardiovascular study of shift workers with respect to coronary artery disease risk factor prevalence. *Journal of the Society of Occupational Medicine*, **40**, 65–67.

Carroll, C., Harris, M. G. & Ross, G. (1991). Haemodynamic adjustments to mental stress in normotensives and subjects with mildly elevated blood pressure. *Psychophysiology*, **28**, 438–446.

Cervinka, R. (1993). Night shift dose and stress at work. *Ergonomics*, **36**(1–3), 155–160.

Chan, O. Y., Gan, S. L., Ngui, S. J. & Phoon, W. H. (1987). Health of night workers in the electronics industry. *Singapore Medical Journal*, **28**(5), 390–399.

Chan, O. Y., Gan, S. L. & Yeo, M. H. (1993). Study on the health of female electronics workers on 12 hours shifts. *Occupational Medicine*, **43**, 143–148.

Cole, R. J., Loving, R. T. & Kripke, D. F. (1990). Psychiatric aspects of shiftwork. *Occupational Medicine*, **5**(2), 301–314.

Costa, G. (1991). *Social and Family Life as Important Criteria for the Construction of Shift Systems*. Dublin: European Foundation for the Improvement of Living and Working Conditions.

Costa, G. (1996). The impact of shift and nightwork on health. *Applied Ergonomics*, **27**(1), 9–16.

Costa, G., Apostoli, P., d'Andrea, G. & Gaffuri, E. (1981). Gastrointestinal and neurotic disorders in textile shift workers. In A. Reinberg, N. Vieux & P. Andlauer (Eds) *Night and Shift Work: Biological and Social Aspects* (pp. 215–221). Oxford: Pergamon Press.

Costa, G., Ghirlanda, G., Minors, D. S. & Waterhouse, J. M. (1993). Effect of bright light on tolerance to night work. *Scandinavian Journal of Work and Environmental Health*, **19**, 414–420.

Council of the European Communities (1993). Concerning certain aspects of the organisation of working time. Council Directive 93/104/EC. Luxembourg. *Official Journal of the European Communities*, **L307** (13-12-93), 18–24.

Craig, A. (1984). Human engineering. In J. S. Warr (Ed.), *The Control of Vigilance in Sustained Attention and Human Performance*. Chichester: Wiley.

Crown, S. & Crisp, A. H. (1979). *Manual of the Crown–Crisp Experiential Index*. London: Hodder & Stoughton.

Cunningham, J. Barton (1989). A compressed shift schedule: Dealing with some of the problems of shift-work. *Journal of Organizational Behaviour*, **10**, 231–245.

Czeisler, C., Dumont, M., Duffy, J., Steinberg, J., Richardson, G., Brown, E. et al. (1992). Association of sleep-wake habits in older people with changes in output of circadian pacemaker. *The Lancet*, **340**, 933–936.

Daleva, M. (1987). Metabolic and neurohormonal reactions to occupational stress. In R. M. Kalimo, A. El-Batawi & C. L. Cooper (Eds), *Psychosocial Factors at Work and Their Relation to Health* (pp. 48–63). Geneva: WHO.

Daniel, J. (1990). Sociopyschological studies of operators of 8 and 12 hour shifts in continuous production. *Travail Humain*, **53**(3), 277–282.

Daniels, K. & Guppy, A. (1995). Stress, social support, and psychological well-being in British accountants. *Work and Stress*, **19**(4), 432–447.

Druckman, D. & Swets, J. A. (1988). *Enhancing Human Performance*. Washington, DC: National Academy.

Duffy, C. A. & McGoldrick, A. E. (1990). Stress and the bus driver in the UK transport industry. *Work and Stress*, **4**(1), 17–27.

Escriba, V., Perez-hoyos, S. & Bolumar, F. (1992). Shiftwork: Its impact on the length and quality of sleep among nurses of the Valencian region in Spain. *International Archive of Occupational and Environmental Health*, **64**, 125–129.

Estryn-Behar, M., Kaminski, M., Peigne, E., Bonnet, N., Vaichere, E., Gozlan, C., Azoulay, S. & Giorgi, M. (1990). Stress at work and mental health status among female hospital workers. *British Journal of Industrial Medicine*, **47**, 20–28.

Ezoe, S. & Morimoto, K. (1994). Behavioural lifestyle and mental health status of Japanese factory workers. *Preventive Medicine*, **23**, 98–105.

Fletcher, N., Colquhoun, W. P., Knauth, P., DeVol, D. & Plett, R. (1988). Work at sea: A study of sleep, and of circadian rhythms in physiological and psychological functions, in watchkeepers on merchant vessels. *International Archives of Occupational and Environmental Health*, **61**, 51–57.

Foret, J., Bensimon, G., Benoit, O. & Vieux, N. (1981). Quality of sleep as a function of age and shiftwork. In A. Reinberg, N. Vieux & P. Andlauer (Eds), *Aspects of Human Efficiency* (pp. 273–282). London: English Universities Press.

Frost, P. J. & Jamal, M. (1979). Shiftwork attitudes and reported behavioural individual characteristics and hours of work and leisure. *Journal of Applied Psychology*, **64**, 77–81.

Gadbois, C. (1984). Time budget and strategies regulating off the job activities of night nurses. In A. Wedderburn (Ed.), *Psychological Approaches to Night and Shiftwork*. Edinburgh: Heriot-Watt University.

Galambois, N. L. & Walters, B. J. (1992). Work hours, schedule inflexibility, and stress in dual-earner spouses. *Canadian Journal of Behavioural Science*, **24**(3), 290–302.

Gallway, T. J. & McEntee, J. J. (1997). Effects of individual differences and shift systems on workers' health. *Shiftwork International Newsletter*, **14**(1), 83.

Gillberg, M. (1984). The effects of two alternative timings of a one-hour nap on early morning performance. *Biological Psychology*, **19**, 45–54.

Giovanni, C. (1991). Shiftwork and circadian variations of vigilance and performance. In J. Wise, V. D. Hopkin & M. L. Smith (eds), *Automation and Systems Issues: Air Traffic Control*, Vol. F73, NATO ASI Series edn. Heidelberg, Berlin: Springer-Verlag.

Gold, D. R., Rogacz, S., Bock, N., Tosteson, T. D., Baum, T. M., Speizer, F. E. & Czeisler, C. A. (1992). Rotating shift work, sleep, and accidents related to sleepiness in hospital nurses. *American Journal of Public Health*, **82**(7), 1011–1014.

Goldberg, D. & Williams, P. A. (1988). *Users' Guide to the General Health Questionnaire (GHQ)*. Windsor: Nelson.

Graeber, R. C. (1989). Jet lag and sleep disruption. In M. Kryger, H. T. Roth & W. C. Dement (Eds), *Principles and Practice of Sleep Medicine* (pp. 324–33). Philadelphia: W.B. Saunders.

Greenwood, K. (1983). Report on the SECV quality of life shiftworkers survey. In M. Wallace (Ed.), *Shiftworkers in Australia* (pp. 10–14). Melbourne, Victoria: Brain-Behaviour Research Institute, La Trobe University.

Greenwood, K. M. (1995). Strategies used by shiftworkers to improve sleep following the night shift. *Shiftwork International Newsletter*, **12**(1), 23.

Hakola, T., Harma, M. I. & Laitinen, J. T. (1995). Sex and circadian adjustment to night shifts. *Shiftwork International Newsletter*, **12**(1), 74.

Hanecke, K., Tiedemann, S., Nachreiner, F. & Grzech-Sukalo, H. (1998). Accident risk as a function of hour at work and time of day as determined from accident data and exposure models for the German working population. *Scandinavian Journal of Work Environment and Health*, **24**(3), 43–48.

Harma, M. (1993a). Individual differences in tolerance to shiftwork: A review. *Ergonomics*, **36** (1–3), 101–110.

Harma, M. (1993b). Ageing, physical fitness and shiftwork tolerance. *Applied Ergonomics*, **27**(1), 25–29.

Harma, M. I., Ilmarinen, J., Knauth, P., Rutenfranz, J. & Hanninen, O. (1988a). Physical training intervention in female shift workers: I. The effects of intervention on fitness, fatigue, sleep, and psychosomatic symptoms. *Ergonomics*, **31**(1), 39–50.

Harma, M. I., Ilmarinen, J., Knauth, P., Rutenfranz, J. & Hanninen, O. (1988b). Physical training intervention in female shift workers. II. The effects of intervention on the circadian rhythms of alertness, short-term memory, and body temperature. *Ergonomics*, **31**(1), 51–63.

Harma, M. I., Hakola, T., Akerstedt, T. & Laitinen, J. T. (1994). Age and adjustment to night work. *Occupational and Environmental Medicine*, **51**, 568–573.

Harma, M., Rosa, R. R., Pulli, K., Mulder, M. & Nasman, O. (1995). Individual factors associated with positive attitudes toward later shift start-end times in rotating shift work. *Shiftwork International Newsletter*, **12**(1), 76.

Harrington, J. M. (1978). *Shiftwork and Health: A Critical Review of the Literature*. London: HMSO.

Harrington, J. M. (1994). Shift work and health—a critical review of the literature on working hours. *Annals of the Academy of Medicine*, **23**(5), 699–705.

Harris, W. (1977). Fatigue, circadian rhythms, and truck accidents. In R. Mackie (Ed.), *Vigilance: Theory, Operational Performance and Physiological Correlates* (pp. 133–146). New York and London: Plenum Press.

Hildebrandt, G., Rohmert, W. & Rutenfranz, J. (1974). 12- and 24-hour rhythms in error frequency of locomotive drivers and the influence of tiredness. *International Journal of Chronobiology*, **2**, 175–180.

Hinkle, L. E., Whitney, L. H., Lehman, E. W., Dunn, J., Benjamin, B. & King, R. (1968). Occupation, education, and coronary heart disease. *Science*, **161**, 238–248.

HMSO (1995). Disability Discrimination Act 1995. London: HMSO.

Hoekstra, F., Jansen, B. & VanGoudoever, B. (1994). *The Compressed Working Week*. Dublin: European Foundation for the Improvement of Living and Working Conditions.

Hornberger, S. & Knauth, P. (1993). Interindividual differences in the subjective valuation of leisure time utility. *Ergonomics*, **36**(1–3), 255–264.

Horne, J. (1985). Sleep loss: Underlying mechanisms and tiredness. In S. Folkard & T. Monk (Eds), *Hours of Work: Temporal Factors in Work Scheduling*. New York: Wiley.

Horne, J. (1988). *Why We Sleep: The Functions of Sleep in Humans and Other Mammals*. New York: Oxford University Press.

Houston, D. M. & Allt, S. K. (1997). Psychological distress and error making among junior house officers. *British Journal of Health Psychology*, **2**, 141–151.

Hurrell, J. J. & Colligan, M. J. (1987). Machine pacing and shiftwork: Evidence for job stress. *Journal of Organizational Behaviour*, **8**(2), 159–175.

Imbernon, E., Warret, G., Roitg, C., Chastang, J. & Goldberg, M. (1993). Effects on health and social well-being of on-call shifts: An epidemiologic study in the French national electricity and gas supply company. *Journal of Occupational Medicine*, **35**(11), 1131–1137.

International Labour Organisation (ILO) (1990). *The Hours We Work: New Work Schedules in Policy and Practice*. Geneva: ILO.

Iskra-Golec, I., Marek, T. & Noworol, C. (1995). Interactive effect of individual factors on nurses' health and sleep. *Work and Stress*, **9**(2/3), 256–261.

Ivancevich, J. M. & Lyon, H. L. (1977). The shortened workweek: A field experiment. *Journal of Applied Psychology*, **62**(1), 34–37.

Kales, A., Soldatos, C. R., Bixler, E. O. & Kales, J. D. (1983). Early morning insomnia with rapidly eliminated benzodiazepines. *Science*, **229**, 95–97.

Kaliterna, L., Vidacek, S., Prizmic, Z. & Radosevic-Vidacek, B. (1995). Is tolerance to shiftwork predictable from individual difference measures? *Work and Stress*, **9**(2/3), 140–147.

Khaleque, A. (1991). Effects of diurnal and seasonal sleep deficiency on work effort and fatigue of shiftworkers. *International Archives of Occupational and Environmental Health*, **62**, 591–593.

Klein, D. E., Bruner, H. & Holtman, H. (1970). Circadian rhythm of pilot's efficiency, and effects of multiple time zone travel. *Aerospace Medicine*, **41**, 125–132.

Knauth, P. (1993). The design of shift systems. *Ergonomics*, **36**(1–3), 15–28.

Knauth, P. & Rutenfranz, J. (1987). Shiftwork. In J. M. Harrington (Ed.) *Recent Advances in Occupational Health*, Vol. 3 (pp. 263–281). Edinburgh, London, Melbourne and New York: Churchill Livingstone.

Knutsson, A., Akerstedt, T., Jonsson, B. B. & Orth-Gomer, K. (1986). Increased risk of ischaemic heart disease in shift workers. *The Lancet*, **336**, 89–92.

Knutsson, A., Akerstedt, T. & Jonsson, B. G. (1988). Prevalence of risk factors for coronary artery disease among day and shift workers. *Scandinavian Journal of Work Environment and Health*, **14**, 317–321.

Kobayashi, F., Watanabe, T., Tanaka, T. & Nakagawa, T. (1992). Effect of shift work and time of day on blood pressure and heart rate in normotensive and hypertensive workers. *Journal of Occupational Medicine, Singapore*, **4**(2), 58–63.

Koh, D., Chia, H. P. & Lee, S. M. (1994). Effects of a double day shift system on sleep patterns of hotel workers. *Journal of Occupational Medicine, Singapore*, **6**(1), 27–31.

Kundi, M., Koller, M., Stefan, H., Lehner, L., Kaindlsdorfer, S. & Rottenbucher, S. (1995). Attitudes of nurses towards 8 hour and 12 hour shift systems. *Work and Stress*, **9**(2/3), 134–139.

Laundry, B. R. & Lees, R. (1991). Industrial accident experience of one company on 8- and 12-hour shift systems. *Journal of Occupational Medicine, Singapore*, **33**(8), 903–906.

Lauridsen, O. & Tonnessen, T. (1990). Injuries related to the aspects of shift working: A comparison of different offshore shift arrangements. *Journal of Occupational Accidents*, **12**, 167–176.

Lees, R. & Laundry, B. R. (1989). Comparison of reported workplace morbidity in 8-hour and 12-hour shifts in one plant. *Journal of the Society of Occupational Medicine*, **39**, 81–84.

Liou, T. S. & Wang, M. J. (1991). Rotating-shift system vs. fixed-shift system. *International Journal of Industrial Ergonomics*, **7**, 63–70.

Loudon, R. & Bohle, P. (1997). Work/non-work conflict and health in shiftwork: Relationships with family status and social support. *International Journal of Occupational and Environmental Health*, **3**(2), 71–77.

Lowden, A., Kecklund, G., Axelsson, J. & Akerstedt, T. (1998). Change from an 8-hour shift to a 12-hour shift, attitudes, sleep, sleepiness and performance. *Scandinavian Journal of Work Environment and Health*, **24**(3), 69–75.

Lushington, W., Lushington, K. & Dawson, D. (1997). The perceived social and domestic consequences of shiftwork for female shiftworkers (nurses) and their partners. *Journal of Occupational Health and Safety, Australia and New Zealand*, **13**(5), 461–469.

Mahoney, M. J. (1984). Cognitive skills and athletic performance. In W.F. Straub & J.M. Williams (Eds), *Cognitive Sport Psychology*, Lansing, MI: Sport Science Associates.

Mather, W. (1884). The forty-eight hour week: A year's experiment and its results. Guardian Printing Works.

McDonald, J. C. (1958). Social and psychological aspects of night shiftwork. PhD. Thesis, University of Birmingham.

McNamee, R., Binks, K., Jones, S., Faulkner, D., Slovak, A. & Cherry, N. M. (1996). Shiftwork and mortality from ischaemic heart disease. *Occupational and Environmental Medicine*, **53**, 367–373.

Michel-Briand, C., Chopard, J. L. & Guiot, A. (1981). The pathological consequences of shift work in retired workers. In A. Reinberg, N. Vieux & P. Andlauer (Eds), *Night and Shiftwork: Biological and Social Aspects*, (pp. 399–407). Oxford: Pergamon Press.

Mital, A. (1986). Prediction models for psychophysical lifting capabilities and the resulting physiological responses for work shifts of varied durations. *Journal of Safety Research*, **17**, 155–163.

Mitler, M., Carskadon, M., Czeisler, C., Dement, W., Dinges, D. & Graeber, R. (1988). Catastrophes, sleep and public policy: Consensus report. *Sleep*, **11**(1), 100–109.

Monk, T. H. (1990). Shiftworker performance. *Occupational Medicine: State of the Art Reviews*, **5**(2), 183–198.

Monk, T. H. & Folkard, S. (1985). Individual differences in shiftwork adjustment. In S. Folkard & T. H. Monk (Eds), *Hours of Work: Temporal Factors in Work Scheduling*. Chichester: Wiley.

Moors, S. H. (1990). Learning from a system of seasonally-determined flexibility: Beginning work earlier increases tiredness as much as working longer days. In G. Costa, G. Cesana, K. Kogi & A. Wedderburn (Eds), *Shiftwork Health, Sleep and Performance*. Frankfurt: Peter Lang.

Mott, P. E., Mann, F. C., McLoughlin, Q. & Warwick, D. P. (1965). *Shiftwork: The Social Psychological, and Physical Consequences*, Ann Arbor, MI: University of Michigan Press.

Murrel, K. F. (1965). *Ergonomics: Man in his Working Environment*, Vol. 18. London: Chapman & Hall.

Nachreiner, F. (1998). Individual and social determinants of shiftwork tolerance. *Scandinavian Journal of Work Environment and Health*, **3**, 35–42.

Nachreiner, F., Baer, K., Diekmann, A. & Ernst, G. (1984). Some approaches in the analysis of the interference of shiftwork with social life. In A. Wedderburn & P. Smith (Eds), *Psychological Approaches to Night and Shiftwork*. Edinburgh: Heriot-Watt University.

Nachreiner, F., Lubeck-Ploger, H. & Grzech-Sukalo, H. (1995). Changes in the structure of health complaints as related to shiftwork exposure. *Work and Stress*, **9**(2/3), 227–234.

Nakamura, K., Shimai, S., Kikuchi, S., Tominaga, K., Takahashi, H. & Tanaka, M. (1997). Shift work and risk factors for coronary heart disease in Japanese blue-collar workers: Serum lipids and anthropometric characteristics. *Occupational Medicine*, **47**(3), 142–146.

Niedhammer, I., Lert, F. & Marne, M. J. (1994). Effects of shift work on sleep among French nurses. *Journal of Occupataional Medicine*, **36**(6), 667–674.

Novak, R. D., Smolensky, M. H, Fairchild, E. J. & Reeves, R. R. (1990). Shiftwork and industrial injuries at a chemical plant in Southeast Texas. *Chronobiology International*, **7**(2), 155–164.

Nuriminen, T. (1989). Shift work, fetal development and course of pregnancy. *Scandinavian Journal of Work Environment and Health*, **15**, 395–403.

Oginski, H., Pokorski, J. & Oginski, A. (1993). Gender, ageing and shiftwork intolerance. *Ergonomics*, **36**(1–3), 161–168.

Okogbaa, G. O. & Shell, R. L. (1986). The measurement of knowledge of worker fatigue. *IIE Transactions*, **18**(4), 335–342.

Olsen, O. & Kristensen, T.S. (1991). Impact of work environment on cardiovascular diseases in Denmark. *Journal of Epidemiology and Community Health*, **45**, 4–10.

Ong, C. N., Phoon, W. O., Iskandar, N. & Chia, K. S. (1987). Shiftwork and work injuries in an iron and steel mill. *Applied Ergonomics*, **18**(1), 51–56.

Peacock, B., Glube, R., Miller, M. & Clune, P. (1983). Police officers' response to 8 and 12 hour shift schedules. *Ergonomics*, **26**(5), 479–493.

Pisarski, A., Bohle, P. & Callan, V. J. (1998). Effects of coping strategies, social support and work-nonwork conflict on shift worker's health. *Scandinavian Journal of Work and Environmental Health*, **24**(3), 141–145.

Pittendrigh, C. S. (1981). Circadian systems: Entrainment. In J. Aschoff (Ed.), *Handbook of Behavioural Neurobiology*, Vol. 4, *Biological Rhythms* (pp. 95–124). New York: Plenum.

Pocock, S. J., Sergean, R. & Taylor, P. J. (1972). Absence of continuous three-shift workers: A comparison of traditional and rapidly rotating systems. *Occupational Psychology*, **46**, 7–13.

Poole, C. J., Evans, G. R., Spurgeon, A. & Bridges, K. W. (1992). Effects of a change in shift work on health. *Occupational Medicine*, **42**, 193–199.

Poole, C. J., Wright, A. D. & Nattrass, M. (1992). Control of diabetes mellitus in shift workers. *British Journal of Industrial Medicine*, **49**, 513–515.

Prunier-Poulmaire, S., Gadbois, C. & Volkoff, S. (1998). Combined effects of shift systems and work requirements on customs officers. *Scandinavian Journal of Work Environment and Health*, **24**(3), 134–140.

Reilly, T., Waterhouse, J. & Atkinson, G. (1997). Ageing, rhythms of physical performance, and adjustment to changes in the sleep-activity cycle. *Occupational and Environmental Medicine*, **54**, 812–816.

Rosa, R. R. (1991). Performance, alertness, and sleep after 3.5 years of 12 hour shifts: A follow-up study. *Work and Stress*, **5**(2), 107–116.

Rosa, R. R., Bonnet, M. H., Bootzin, R. R., Eastman, C. I., Monk, T., Penn, P. E., Tepas, D. I. & Walsh, J. K. (1990). Intervention factors for promoting adjustment to nightwork and shiftwork. *Occupational Medicine: State of the Art Reviews*, **5**(2), 391–415.

Russek, H. I. & Zohman, B. L. (1958). Relative significance of heredity, diet and occupational stress in coronary heart disease of young adults. *American Journal of Medicine*, **325**, 266–275.

Rutenfranz, J., Plett, R., Knauth, P., Condon, R., DeVol, D., Fletcher, N., Eickhoff, S., Schmidt, K. H., Donis, R. & Colquhoun, W. P. (1988). Work at sea: A study of sleep, and of circadian rhythms in physiological and psychological functions, in watchkeepers on merchant vessels. *International Archives of Occupational and Environmental Health*, **60**, 331–339.

Servatius, R. J., Ottenweller, J. E. & Natelson, B. H. (1994). A comparison of the effects of repeated stressor exposures and corticosterone injections on plasma cholesterol, thyroid hormones and corticosterone levels in rats. *Life Science*, **55**, 1611–1617.

Sharratt, M. T. & Davis, S. (1991). The effects of a chronohygiene program on fatigue, alertness and performance levels of 12-hour shift operators. In W. Karwowski & J. W. Yates (Eds) *Advances in Industrial Ergonomics and Safety III* (pp. 669–674). London: Taylor & Francis.

Smith, L. & Folkard, S. (1993). The impact of shiftwork on personnel at a nuclear power plant: An exploratory survey study. *Work and Stress*, **7**(4), 341–350.

Smith, L., Folkard, S. & Poole, C. J. (1994). Increased injuries on night shift. *The Lancet*, **344**, 1137–1139.

Smith, L., Spelten, E. & Norman, P. (1995). Shiftwork locus of control: Scale development. *Work and Stress*, **9**(2/3), 219–226.

Smith, P. & Bennett, S. (1983). Report of the joint University of Bradford and Civil Service Union studies of shiftwork. In A. Wedderburn (Ed.), *Social and Family Factors in Shift Design*, 1993 edn, Vol. 5. Dublin: European Foundation for the Improvement of Living and Working Conditions.

Sokejima, S. & Kagamimori, S. (1998). Working hours as a risk factor for acute myocardial infarction in Japan: Case-control study. *British Medical Journal*, **317**, 775–780.

Sorensen, G., Pirie, P., Folsom, A., Luepker, R., Jacobs, D. & Gillum, R. (1985). Sex differences in the relationship between work and health: The Minnesota heart survey. *Journal of Health and Social Behaviour*, **26**, 379–394.

Sparks, K. & Cooper, C. (1997). The effects of hours of work on health: A meta-analytic review. *Journal of Occupational and Organizational Psychology*, **70**, 391–408.

Sparks, P. J. (1992). Questionnaire survey of masters, mates and pilots of a state ferries system on health, social and performance indices relevant to shift work. *American Journal of Industrial Medicine*, **21**, 507–516.

Spurgeon, A. & Harrington, J. M. (1989). Work performance and health of junior hospital doctors: A review of the literature. *Work and Stress*, 9(2/3), 368–376.

Spurgeon, A., Harrington, J. M. & Cooper, C. L. (1997). Health and safety problems associated with long working hours: A review of the current position. *Occupational and Environmental Medicine*, **54**(6), 367–376.

Starrin, B., Larsson, G., Brenner, S. O., Levi, L. & Pettersen, I. L. (1990). Structural changes, ill health and mortality in Sweden. *International Journal of Health Services*, **20**, 27–42.

Stoynev, A. G. & Minkova, N. K. (1997). Circadian rhythms of arterial pressure, heart rate and oral temperature in truck drivers. *Occupational Medicine*, 47(3), 151–154.

Stoynev, A. G. & Minkova, N. K. (1998). Effect of forward rapidly rotating shift work on circadian rhythms of arterial pressure, heart rate and oral temperature in air traffic controllers. *Occupational Medicine*, **48**(2), 75–79.

Taylor, P. J. (1967). Shift and day work: A comparison of sickness absence, lateness and other absence behaviour at an oil refinery from 1962–65. *British Journal of Industrial Medicine*, **24**, 93–102.

Taylor, E., Folkard, S. & Shapiro, D. (1997). Shiftwork advantages as predictors of health. *International Journal of Occupational and Environmental Health*, 3(2), 20–29.

Taylor, P. J., Pocock, S. J. & Sergean, R. (1972). Absenteeism of shift and day workers: A study of six types of shift system in 29 organisations. *British Journal of Industrial Medicine*, **29**, 208–213.

Tenkanen, L., Sjoblom, T., Kalimo, R., Alikoski, T. & Harma, M. (1997). Shift work occupation and coronary heart disease over 6 years of follow-up in the Helsinki heart study. *Scandinavian Journal of Work Environment and Health*, **23**, 257–265.

Tepas, D. I. & Carvalhais, A. B. (1990). Sleep patterns of shiftworkers. *Occupational Medicine: State of the Art Reviews*, 5(2), 199–208.

Tepas, D. I., Walsh, J. K., Moss, P. D. & Armstrong, D. (1981). Polysomnographic correlates of shift worker performance in the laboratory. In A. Reinberg, N. Vieux & P. Andlauer (Eds), *Night and Shift Work: Biological and Social Aspects* (pp. 179–186). New York: Pergamon.

Thierry, H. (1980). Compensation for shiftwork: A model and some results. In W. P. Colquhoun & J. Rutenfranz (Eds), *Studies of Shiftwork* (pp. 449–462). London: Taylor & Francis.

Thompson, J. (1989). Rigour round the clock. *Nursing Times*, **85**, 21.

Tilley, A. J., Wilkinson, R. T. & Warren, P. (1982). The sleep and performance of shift workers. *Human Factors*, **24**, 629–641.

Tüchsen, (1993). Working hours and ischaemic heart disease in Danish men. A 4-year cohort study of hospitalisation. *International Journal of Epidemiology*, **22**(2), 215–221.

Tucker, P., Barton, J. & Folkard, S. (1996). Comparison of 8 and 12 hour shifts: Impacts on health, well-being and alertness during the shift. *Occupational and Environmental Medicine*, **53**, 767–772.

Tucker, P., Smith, L., Macdonald, I. & Folkard, S. (1998). Shift length as a determinant of retrospective on-shift alertness. *Scandinavian Journal of Work and Environmental Health*, **24**(3), 49–54.

Uehata, T. (1991). Karoshi due to occupational stress-related cardiovascular injuries among middle-aged workers in Japan. *Journal of Science of Labour*, **67**, 20–28.

Vener, K. J., Szabo, S. & Moore, J. G. (1989). The effect of shiftwork on gastrointestinal function: A review. *Chronobiology*, **12**, 421–439.

Wallace, M., Owens, W. & Levens, M. (1990). Adaptation to twelve hour shifts. In G. Costa, G. Cesana, K. Kogi & A. Wedderburn (Eds), *Shiftwork: Health, Sleep and Performance*. Frankfurt am Main: Peter Lang.

Warr, P. B. (1990). The measurement of well-being and other aspects of mental health. *Journal of Occupational Psychology*, **63**, 193–210.

Watanabe, S., Torii, J., Shinkai, S. & Watanabe, T. (1993). Relationships between health status and working conditions and personalities among VDT workers. *Environmental Research*, **61**, 258–265.

Webb, W. & Agnew, H. (1974). The effects of a chronic limitation of sleep length. *Psychophysiology*, **11**(3), 265–274.

Wedderburn, A. (1978). Some suggestions for increasing the usefulness of psychological and sociological studies of shiftwork. *Ergonomics*, **21**, 827–833.

Wedderburn, A. (1981). Is there a pattern in the value of time off work? In A. Reinberg, N. Vieux & P. Andlauer (Eds), *Night and Shift Work: Biological and Social Aspects*. Oxford: Pergamon Press.

Wedderburn, A. (Ed.) (1993). *Social and Family Factors in Shift Design*, 1st edn, Vol. 5. Dublin: European Foundation for the Improvement of Living and Working Conditions.

Wedderburn, Z. (1994). Shiftwork, health and personality hardiness: An apparent double link. Paper presented at the 1994 Occupational Psychology Conference, London.

Wedderburn, A. (Ed.) (1996a). 'Statistics and News', *Bulletin of European Studies on Time*, Vol. 9. Dublin: European Foundation for the Improvement of Living and Working Conditions.

Wedderburn, A. (ed.) (1996b). 'Compressed Working Time', *Bulletin of European Studies on Time*, Vol. 10. Dublin: European Foundation for the Improvement of Living and Working Conditions.

Weiss, B. & Laties, V. G. (1962). Enhancement of human performance by caffeine and the amphetamines. *Pharmacological Review*, **14**, 1–36.

Wever, R. A. (1979). *The Circadian System of Man*. New York: Springer Verlag.

Wojtczak-Jaroszowa, J. & Jarosz, D. (1987). Chronohygienic and chronosocial aspects of industrial accidents. *Programmes in Clinical and Biological Research*, **227B**, 415–426.

Wyatt, S. & Marriott, R. (1953). Night work and shift changes. *British Journal of Industrial Medicine*, **10**, 164–172.

Xu, X., Ding, M., Li, B. & Christiani, D. C. (1994). Association of rotating shiftwork with preterm births and low birth weight among never smoking women textile workers in China. *Occupational and Environmental Medicine*, **51**, 470–474.

Zhdanova, I. V., Wurtman, R. J., Lynch, H. J., Ives, J. R., Dollins, A. B., Morabito, C. et al. (1995). Sleep inducing effects of low doses of melatonin ingested in the evening. *Clinical Pharmacological Theories*, **57**, 552–558.

# Chapter 7

# EXPERTISE AT WORK: EXPERIENCE AND EXCELLENT PERFORMANCE

Sabine Sonnentag
*University of Amsterdam*

The question of what makes someone an expert in a field is a topic which fascinates many people. International bestsellers such as *In Search of Excellence* (Peters & Waterman, 1982) or *How to be a Star at Work* (Kelley, 1998) reflect the interest of a broader audience in this area. Many individuals and organizations want to learn more about the 'secrets' of expert performance in order to improve their own way of task accomplishment or to draw conclusions for human resource management within the organization.

Within the academic literature, research on expertise has a long tradition. However, it is not until the past 10 to 15 years that a greater number of researchers have become interested in expertise *at work*. This chapter reviews research on expertise. It covers studies within the field of industrial and organizational psychology as well as studies which examined activities closely related to specific activities performed in work settings (e.g., computer programming and medical diagnosis). The chapter mainly concentrates on research conducted within the past 15 years—but will also include major findings from earlier studies.

The first section provides a definition of expertise and distinguishes between two conceptualizations of expertise. The second section gives an overview over main approaches to expertise research. Section three is the core of this chapter and reviews study findings on the differences between experts and non-experts. It will cover the following areas: knowledge, problem comprehension, goal setting and planning, feedback processing and communication and cooperation. Section four addresses the question of how expertise develops. Finally the fifth section specifies directions for future research.

*International Review of Industrial and Organizational Psychology, 2000 Volume 15*
Edited by C.L. Cooper and I.T. Robertson. © 2000 John Wiley & Sons, Ltd

## Definition and Concept of Expertise

Psychological research on expertise is built on de Groot's studies of world-class chess players, mainly conducted during the thirties and forties (Groot, 1978). De Groot himself, however, referred more to the term 'mastership' rather than to 'expertise'. He described a master as 'someone who has attained a high, generally recognized, degree of competence in a special trade or field (p. 316). Within the psychological literature, the term 'expertise' began to gain broader acceptance during the seventies (Chase & Simon, 1973) and eighties (Chi, Glaser & Farr, 1988; Chi, Glaser & Rees, 1982). Increased research effort resulted in various definitions of 'expert' and 'expertise':

- 'we refer to expertise as the ability, acquired by practice, to perform qualitatively well in a particular task domain' (Frensch & Sternberg, 1989, p. 158).
- 'On the most general level, the study of expertise seeks to understand and account for what distinguishes outstanding individuals in a domain from less outstanding individuals in that domain, as well as from people in general' (Ericsson & Smith, 1991, p. 2).
- 'An "expert" is typically defined as an individual who possesses a large body of knowledge and procedural skill. This ability to bring to bear a large amount of relevant information quickly and efficiently is tied to a particular area of expertise' (Green & Gilhooly, 1992, p. 46).
- 'In my research, experts are operationally defined as those who have been recognized within their profession as having the necessary skills and abilities to perform at the highest level' (Shanteau, 1992, p. 255).
- 'Expertise is defined as the achievement of consistent, superior performance through the development of specialized mental processes acquired through experience and training .... Successful performance is a necessary but not sufficient condition for defining expertise. Expertise involves the possession of a well-organized domain-specific knowledge base' (Ford & Kraiger, 1995, p. 7).
- 'In research on expertise, an expert is usually defined in a very pragmatic way as someone who performs at the level of an experienced professional: an MD in medicine, a Master or Grandmaster in chess, an experienced systems programmer, a practicing attorney, an engineer employed in design, and so on' (Richman, Gobet, Staszewski & Simon, 1996, p. 168).

Taken together, researchers define expertise as high, outstanding, and exceptional performance which is domain-specific, stable over time, and related to experience and practice. Additionally, some authors regard the possession of knowledge as an essential aspect of expertise (Ford & Kraiger, 1995; Green & Gilhooly, 1992). Despite this overall agreement, the expertise concept becomes much more fuzzy when addressing the question of who is a non-expert.

In the expertise literature, two different conceptualizations can be found (for a similar distinction cf. Tynjälä, Nuutinen, Eteläpelto, Kirjonen & Remes, 1997). One group of authors focuses on the notion of experience in the expertise concept and therefore regards persons with long experience as experts and persons with short experience as non-experts. It is assumed that because of their limited experience, non-experts have not—or: not yet—attained an expert performance level but can reach it in the future. This approach is reflected in the operationalization of expertise adopted in a huge amount of studies in which individuals with long years of experience, for example professionals or graduate students, were assumed to be experts and individuals with a few years or even only some months of experience, for example undergraduate students, were regarded as non-experts or novices (Batra & Davis, 1992; Jeffries, Turner, Polson & Atwood, 1981; Voss, Wolfe, Lawrence & Engle, 1991).

Another group of authors explicitly focuses on the performance aspect of expertise and therefore regards high and excellent performers as experts. Persons who do not exceed a moderate performance level are seen as non-experts. This line of research describes characteristics of high performers—as opposed to moderate or average performers.

Both conceptualizations are relevant for work and organizational psychology. The first conceptualization, which concentrates on the experience aspect of expertise, can provide useful information about skill acquisition processes (Ackerman & Humphreys, 1990). Studies which show how experienced and inexperienced individuals differ in their approaches to task accomplishment point to the skills and strategies inexperienced individuals have to learn. It is assumed that the performance of inexperienced individuals will improve when they learn experienced individuals' skills and strategies. The second conceptualization explicitly aims at the description and explanation of performance differences. Several researchers are particularly interested in performance differences which are not attributable to differences in length of experience (e.g., Hacker, 1992; Sonnentag, 1988a). Studies based on this conceptualization focus on performance differences among individuals with a comparable length of experience.

This chapter reviews literature conducted within both conceptualizations of expertise. The first approach will be referred to as the 'experience conceptualization', the second approach will be referred to as the 'excellence conceptualization'.

## Approaches of Expertise Research

*Research focus*

Expertise research focuses on *process* aspects of individual performance. Within this line of research it is studied how experts approach their tasks and what strategies they use in order to accomplish these tasks. It is assumed that experts' ways of approaching and accomplishing tasks are particularly smart and more efficient than those of non-experts. By concentrating on what experts do and how they do it, expertise research differs from other research approaches within industrial and organizational psychology which study factors such as intelligence or achievement motivation as predictors of performance without looking at the processes of task accomplishment (O'Reilly & Chatman, 1994).

Expertise research has its origin in the field of cognitive psychology (Groot, 1978). Researchers have paid much attention to differences between experts and non-experts with respect to cognitive processes. In a great number of studies it has been shown that experts and non-experts differ with respect to domain-specific problem-solving processes and domain-specific knowledge (for overviews cf., Ericsson & Lehmann, 1996; Green & Gilhooly, 1992). When examining differences between experts and non-experts with respect to work processes, work and organizational psychologists can build on these findings from cognitive psychology. However, work does not comprise cognitive processes only and work performance cannot be completely explained just by referring to cognitive processes (Campbell, McCloy, Oppler & Sager, 1993; O'Reilly & Chatman, 1994). For example, Hoffman, Feltovich and Ford (1997) criticized the fact that past expertise research has largely ignored factors such as social, motivational, and emotional processes which might also play a great role in expert performance.

Therefore, expertise research within the field of work and organizational psychology should not only study differences between experts and non-experts with respect to cognitive processes, but should also address other potential differences. This chapter will include a review of already existing studies on communication and cooperation.

*Study designs*

For examining differences between experts and non-experts, many researchers adopt a contrastive approach (Voss, Fincher-Kiefer, Greene & Post, 1986). Within this approach, two groups of individuals, that is experts and non-experts, are compared with respect to differences and similarities in performing a specific task. Very often, experienced study participants have been compared with less experienced individuals (e.g., Eteläpelto, 1993; Jeffries et al., 1981; Voss, Greene, Post & Penner, 1983; Wiggins & O'Hare, 1995), but this approach can be easily applied to the study of high versus moderate performers (e.g. Elstein, Shulman & Sprafka, 1978; Koubek & Salvendy, 1991; Leithwood & Steinbach, 1995). Some researchers extended this two-group comparison to a multiple-group design without giving up the basic idea of the contrastive approach. For example, Patel and her coworkers compared medical experts who were specialized in various subdisciplines (Patel & Groen, 1991; for a similar approach cf. Voss et al., 1983).

Other researchers assume a continuum from being an expert to not being an expert—rather than a clear distinction between the two groups. When following such an approach, expertise is conceptualized as a continuous variable and subsequently related to process aspects of task accomplishment by correlational analyses (Sujan, Weitz & Kumar, 1994; Tripoli, 1998). This approach is more often implemented when studying the excellence aspect of expertise than the experience aspect.

Another part of expertise research is based on case studies. In such studies, researchers locate a group of experts and analyse in detail these persons' knowledge and approaches to task accomplishment (e.g., Adelson & Soloway, 1988; Berlin, 1993; Crandall & Getchell-Reiter, 1993; Guindon, 1990; Reed & Johnson, 1993). Such case studies provide detailed descriptions and illustrations of experts' action processes and can therefore contribute to a deeper understanding of expert performance. However, most of these case studies are associated with two major methodological problems. First, it often remains unclear how the experts were identified and whether the experts were regarded as highly experienced or whether they were excellent performers. Second, without a comparison with a group of less experienced or less well performing persons, it remains unclear whether process characteristics of task accomplishment found in the studied experts are specific for these experts or whether non-experts also show the same characteristics.

*Identification of experts and non-experts*

If one concentrates on the experience aspect of expertise, experts and non-experts can be identified relatively easily. Based on a person's years of experience in a domain, this person is either regarded as an expert (i.e., experienced) or a non-expert. However, when conceptualizing expertise as excellent performance, the answer to the question of how to identify experts and non-experts is less straightforward. Three major approaches can be distinguished: a first approach which focuses on task performance, a second approach which focuses on social recognition and evaluation, and a third approach which focuses on career-related measures.

The task-performance approach suggests identifying expert performers by consistently superior performance on a set of tasks (Ericsson & Smith, 1991). This set of tasks should be representative for the domain and should be administerable to any person under laboratory conditions. When following this approach and identifying experts by their task performance, one has to define cut-off scores for 'superior performance'. Ericsson and Charness (1994) suggested regarding as experts those individuals who perform at least two standard deviations above a population's mean performance level.

If researchers succeed in identifying a set of representative tasks and in developing valid performance measures, this task-performance approach offers the advantage of comparing experts' and non-experts' processes of task accomplishment under standardized task conditions. However, in many domains, particularly in complex work settings, it might be difficult to design a set of standardized tasks which capture all relevant aspects of expertise. For example, tasks which are accomplished over a long period of time cannot be easily administered in a laboratory setting. Moreover, the mastery of novel and emerging tasks as one aspect of expertise (Hesketh, 1997) might not be covered by such standardized tasks.

A second approach takes a completely different look at the question of how to identify expert performers and bases the identification of experts on social recognition and evaluation. For example, Shanteau (1992) suggested 'let those in a domain define the experts' (p. 255). The use of peer or supervisory assessments is one way to implement this approach. There is a number of studies in which high performers were identified on the basis of assessments provided by peers, supervisors, or others familiar with individuals' performance (e.g., Elstein, Shulman & Sprafka, 1978; Ericsson, Krampe & Tesch-Römer, 1993; Klemp & McClelland, 1986; Sonnentag, 1998a; Stein, 1995).

Such an approach to identifying expert performers seems to be justified in the light of validity studies on peer assessments (Harris & Schaubroeck, 1988; Norton, 1992). However, it has been argued that social evaluations such as peer assessments might suffer from a likeability or friendship bias (Salthouse, 1991). The existence of such a bias would imply that persons who are liked more by their peers or by their broader social network would have a greater chance of being regarded as high performers. Recent research has shown that there is some relationship between likeability and perceived performance; but peer assessment outcomes cannot be accounted for by such a likeability bias (Schmitt, Pulakos, Nason & Whitney, 1996; Sonnentag, 1998b). These results suggest that friendship or likeability biases do not substantially effect the validity of peer assessments.

Nevertheless, social evaluations of high performance do not overlap completely with task-performance measures (Sonnentag, 1998a; Vessey, 1986). This finding implies that these two measures cover different aspects of expertise. As a consequence for future expertise research it might be most appropriate to use a combination of task-performance and social-evaluation measures.

The third approach uses measures of career advancement and the position held within the organization as indicators for high performance. Individuals who were promoted very quickly or who work at a higher hierarchical level are regarded as excellent performers (Luthans, Rosenkrantz & Hennessey, 1985). This approach seems appealing in those domains where objective task performance is difficult to assess. Additionally, there are studies which suggest that high performers do work at higher organizational levels (Sonnentag, 1995; Stein, 1995). However, there are some problems with operationalizating excellent performance by these measures. First, career advancement and promotion to high organizational levels might depend on other factors than excellent task performance alone. Second, jobs at different organizational levels might be associated with different tasks and ways of accomplishing these tasks. Therefore, differences between assumed high performers working in higher positions and assumed lower performers working in lower positions cannot be unequivocally attributed to the persons' performance levels.

## Data collection methods

Expertise research is primarily interested in process aspects of task accomplishment and its underlying knowledge. There is a great number of methods which aim at the assessment of experienced versus less experienced and excellent versus moderate performers' working processes and knowledge (for overviews cf., Cooke, 1994; Hacker, 1992; Hoffman, Shadbolt, Burtin & Klein, 1995; Olson & Biolsi, 1991).

Among the most widely used approaches are process-tracing methods based on verbal data. Typically, study participants are asked to work on a specific task and to think aloud while working on this task, that is to verbalize their thoughts concurrently. These thinking aloud reports are later analyzed by protocol-analysis methods. In the past, the validity of verbal reports has been seriously questioned (Nisbett & Wilson, 1977). However, more specific studies on the thinking aloud method suggest that this method provides valid measures of thinking processes (Ericsson & Simon, 1993). Nevertheless, it could not yet be ruled out completely that thinking aloud might be differentially valid (Speelman, 1998).

An alternative to verbal data is observations of the task-accomplishment process. Observations are particularly useful when assessing processes which are not consciously accessible, be it that they are largely based on sensorimotor processes—or be it that they are highly routinized because of extended practice. Some researchers studied the problem-solving processes of experts and non-experts within complex, computer-based simulations (e.g., Dörner & Schölkopf, 1991; Schaub & Strohschneider, 1992). Within such a framework, study participants' behaviour can be directly observed and analyzed on the basis of the recordings made by the computer system.

Several researchers used retrospective methods based on stimulated recall (e.g., Elstein, Shulman & Sprafka, 1978) as a supplement to concurrent verbalizations and observations. When applying such a retrospective method, in a first step the working process and concurrent verbalizations of study participants while working on a task are video-taped. In the second step, this tape is shown to the participants, who are asked to comment on their task accomplishment process.

Additionally, researchers often used interview methods for eliciting experts' and non-experts' knowledge. These interviews can be unstructured or can follow a structured format. During the past decade, several researchers provided overviews over such interview methods (Cook, 1994; Hoffman, Crandall, & Shadbolt, 1998; Hoffman et al., 1995).

Although the assessment of thinking aloud protocols, observations and interviews form the core of data collection methods within expertise research, there are various other methods which are used to a somewhat lesser degree, such as self-report questionnaire scales. Questionnaire measures have been used to measure motivational orientations (Sujan, Weitz & Kumar, 1994) or specific planning behaviors (Tripoli, 1998). Particularly when examining knowledge differences between experts and non-experts, researchers asked study participants to work on specific tasks such as recall tasks or fill-in-the-blank tasks (Soloway, Adelson & Ehrlich, 1988). Subsequently, experts' and non-experts' responses to these tasks were analyzed.

A completely different way of gathering data about experts' task-accomplishment processes is to approach individuals who are familiar with the expert and to elicit characterizations of this expert's behavior. This can be done by relatively unstructured interview methods (Sonnentag, 1995) or more sophisticated card-sorting procedures (Turley & Bieman, 1995).

Most of the data collection methods are very time-consuming, both during the period of data gathering and during data analysis. Therefore, researchers often decide to study only a small number of experts and non-experts. As a consequence, in many studies the power to detect differences between experts and non-experts is low. This implies that often significant differences found between the two groups correspond to relatively large effect sizes.

## Differences Between Experts and Non-experts

Experts' work processes are characterized by a great number of various process characteristics which centre around five major topics: (a) possessing and using knowledge; (b) problem comprehension; (c) goal setting and planning; (d) feedback processing; and (e) communication and cooperation. This section reviews research on these topics and presents findings for both conceptualizations of expertise, the experience conceptualization and the excellence conceptualization.

Research within the experience conceptualization mainly compared professionals (or other groups of individuals with real world working experience) with students. There are only a few studies in which individuals with a long working experience were compared with those with a shorter real world working experience (e.g., Kirschenbaum, 1992; Schenk, Vitalari & Davis, 1998; Wiggins & O'Hare, 1995). This implies that research within the two expertise conceptualizations not only conceptualized expertise differently but referred to partially different samples and comparisons. More specifically, studies within the excellence conceptualization are not redundant to the experience studies but examine performance differences within the groups of experienced individuals.

### Knowledge

Since the early years of expertise research, knowledge differences between experts and non-experts have been regarded as one of the crucial distinguishing factors between experts and non-experts (Groot, 1978). For example, in their classical paper, Chase and Simon (1973) have argued that chess experts have stored a large amount of chessboard patterns in long-term memory and that these representations belong to the basic features of skilled chess performance.

*Knowledge in experienced versus inexperienced individuals.* Many studies which adopted the experience-based conceptualization of expertise revealed differences in domain-specific knowledge between experienced and less experienced individuals with experts possessing more domain-specific knowledge. Often, such knowledge differences were not examined directly, but inferred from experienced individuals' superior performance on comprehension or recall tasks (e.g. Adelson, 1981; McKeithen, Reitman, Rueter & Hirtle, 1981). These studies provide evidence that experts outperform inexperienced individuals when working on—or recalling—meaningful material and that experts' performance is reduced when they are confronted with meaningless, such as randomly configurated, material.

Some studies applied knowledge elicitation methods in order to address knowledge differences more directly. For example, Wiedemann (1995) examined maintenance specialists who were experienced in diagnosing faults in a flexible production system and trainees lacking such a specific experience. More specifically, Wiedemann studied differences with respect to knowledge about potential causes associated with specific fault symptoms and knowledge about symptoms associated with specific fault causes. Maintenance specialists, that is the more experienced workers, had a more comprehensive knowledge about symptoms associated with specific fault causes. Furthermore, maintenance specialists' knowledge about possible causes tended to be more comprehensive and more correct than trainees' knowledge.

In addition, research has shown that not only do experienced persons possess more domain-specific knowledge, their mental representations are more abstract (Wiedenbeck, Fix & Scholz, 1993) and mirror the deep structure of a problem domain (Schoenfeld & Herrmann, 1982). Moreover, experienced individuals' knowledge is characterized by a higher degree of detail (Lurigio & Carroll, 1985).

Possessing the relevant domain-specific knowledge allows experienced persons to adopt specific efficient strategies when working on a task or solving a problem. For example, because of their domain-specific knowledge experienced persons can apply a forward reasoning strategy (Patel & Groen, 1991). Forward reasoning implies working from the problem and the available information towards the goal, for example a specific diagnosis. Inexperienced individuals who lack domain-specific knowledge often have to adopt a backward reasoning strategy and work from a hypothesis (e.g. about a diagnosis) back to the available information. Backward reasoning puts high demands on working memory. Additionally, experienced individuals' comprehensive domain-specific knowledge allows them to retrieve already existing solutions from memory (Jeffries et al., 1981). However, the experts' domain-specific knowledge which is very helpful when applied to routine tasks might be detrimental when transfer to an unfamiliar task is needed (Frensch & Sternberg, 1989; Marchant, Robinson, Anderson & Schadewald, 1991).

More experienced persons not only possess more domain-specific knowledge, but also more meta-cognitive knowledge, that is knowledge of their own cognitions and behavior. Eteläpelto (1993) conducted a study of meta-cognitive knowledge in computer program comprehension and compared professional programmers with computer science students. It turned out that the more experienced professional programmers had more meta-cognitive knowledge about the task. They knew more about a good strategy and more often reported that their own comprehension strategy corresponded to that good strategy. Furthermore, the experienced programmers were more aware of their specific problems in comprehension while the students only knew about their difficulties at a general level.

In the medical domain, researchers examined the use of knowledge in more detail and paid specific attention to the use of biomedical, that is basic science, knowledge (Patel, Kaufman & Magder, 1996). A number of studies on diagnostic reasoning tasks showed that more experienced individuals demonstrated less overt application of biomedical knowledge than did less experienced individuals (for a review cf., Boshuizen & Schmidt, 1992; for contradicting findings cf., Lesgold, Rubinson, Feltovich et al., 1988). Further analyses by Boshuizen and Schmidt (Boshuizen & Schmidt, 1992; Schmidt & Boshuizen, 1993) showed that biomedical knowledge does not become 'inert' or even irrelevant in experienced physicians' diagnostic reasoning processes. Rather, experienced physicians used their biomedical knowledge in an encapsulated form. Through practice, experienced physicians have subsumed detailed, lower level propositions under higher level propositions, which might not even appear as biomedical, but as clinical knowledge. This implies that experienced individuals do possess more domain-specific knowledge, but do not explicitly verbalize it when using it. Simpson and Gilhooly (1997) reported similar findings for an electrocardiogram analysis task.

However, *possessing* relevant knowledge is not sufficient for successfully accomplishing a task. For example, Voss et al. (1983) who analyzed problem-solving processes in social sciences, observed that inexperienced persons possessed knowledge about the problem domain but were not effective in applying their knowledge to the problem to be solved. Wiedemann (1995) correlated trainees' and maintenance specialists' knowledge with their performance in six diagnostic tasks. For the maintenance specialists, Wiedemann found a correlation of $r = 0.63$ between completeness of knowledge and performance and a correlation of $r = 0.66$ between amount of incorrect knowledge and performance. Thus, in experienced individuals, knowledge was highly correlated with performance. For the trainee group, however, there was no significant relationship between knowledge and performance. These findings suggest that particularly inexperienced individuals are not necessarily able to 'translate' their knowledge into performance-relevant actions. A study on aeronautical decision making offers a similar conclusion (Stokes, Kemper & Kite, 1997). Experienced and inexperienced pilots did not differ in a declarative knowledge test comprised of standard questions. However, in a flight simulation, which depended highly on declarative knowledge, experienced pilots outperformed inexperienced pilots. This implies that inexperienced persons might possess the basic declarative knowledge but fail in applying it in complex actions.

Taken together, experienced persons possess a more comprehensive and better organized knowledge which is a prerequisite for more efficient problem-solving strategies, such as forward reasoning. However, particularly in inexperienced persons, knowledge was found to be not directly linked to performance. This finding suggests that with increasing experience not only the amount and organization of knowledge develops but also its application in the task-accomplishment process. More specifically, experienced persons make better use of their knowledge.

*Knowledge in excellent versus moderate performers.* Studies which addressed knowledge as a potential distinguishing factor between high and moderate performers found superior knowledge in the highly performing group. For example, Hacker, Rühle and Schneider (1976) studied performance differences in the textile industry and compared high and lower performers. All study participants had a job experience of at least 5 years. Main tasks of the textile workers included machine monitoring, error detection, and error rectification. The performance difference between the high and low performance group was 20%. Analyses showed that high performers had a more adequate knowledge of the most frequent causes of machine stoppages and of indicators of such causes.

In his study on fault diagnosis in a flexible production system, Wiedemann (1995) concentrated on knowledge differences between experienced maintenance specialists and less experienced workers. However, he additionally analyzed knowledge differences between high and moderate performers. High performers' knowledge turned out to be more complete and to include less incorrect knowledge (for a similar finding cf., Schaper & Sonntag, 1998).

Research suggests that high and lower performers do not only differ in their amount of knowledge. In addition, high performers seem to possess a more integrative knowledge structure. For example, Sujan, Sujan and Bettman (1988) studied the knowledge of salespeople in a telephone marketing operation. The authors found that more effective sellers—as rated by their supervisors—differed from less effective sellers in their knowledge structures. The more effective sellers had more interrelated knowledge structures about their customers and associated sales strategies. Smith and Good

(1984) studied problem-solving processes in genetics and observed that low performers often got confused because of their poorly integrated and partly irrelevant knowledge. Moreover, poorly integrated and partly irrelevant knowledge overloads low performers' working memory. Based on the findings of their field study in software design projects, Curtis, Krasner and Iscoe (1988) also stressed the importance of knowledge for expertise. More specifically, Curtis, Krasner and Iscoe described that mapping of knowledge from various domains as a crucial characteristic of exceptional software designers. These software designers succeeded in linking their computational knowledge with extensive knowledge about the software's application domain.

There are a few studies which tried to assess the more procedural aspects of knowledge. For example, highly performing software professionals studied by Sonnentag (1998a) expressed more knowledge about useful strategies, that is strategies about how one should proceed when solving a software design problem. In addition, studies on tacit knowledge showed that high performers know better how to proceed. Tacit knowledge can be defined as 'practical know-how that usually is not openly expressed or stated and which must be acquired in the absence of direct instruction' (Wagner, 1987, p. 1236). Wagner and Sternberg (1985) found that bank managers' tacit knowledge was positively related to performance, as measured by routine annual performance evaluations. In a study with faculty members of psychology departments, Wagner and Sternberg (1985) found that a total tacit knowledge score was positively related to a number of performance measures. Tacit knowledge about managing oneself and managing one's career turned out to be most important. From this study one may conclude that it is not only domain-specific knowledge which differentiates high from moderate performers but a more procedural aspect of knowledge referring to meta-cognition and self-regulation.

Taken together, research identified knowledge differences between high and moderate performers. In particular, differences in integrated knowledge structures and procedural aspects of knowledge were found to be associated with performance differences.

### Problem comprehension

Problem comprehension is an important phase within the task-accomplishment process. During problem comprehension one builds a representation of the problem, that is develops an understanding of the task or the problem to be solved. Typical problem-comprehension activities include a search for information and exploration of the problem domain. Researchers paid much attention to the problem-comprehension activities of experts and non-experts, both within an experience conceptualization and an excellence conceptualization of expertise.

*Problem comprehension in experienced versus inexperienced individuals.* There are many studies which examined the amount of problem-comprehension activities of experienced and less experienced individuals. A number of studies showed that experienced individuals searched for information to a greater extent and spent more time on problem comprehension than did less experienced individuals. In their classical study on software design, Jeffries et al. (1981) compared the design processes of experienced designers with those of undergraduate computer science students. Experienced designers spent more effort on understanding the design problem before developing a design solution. Inexperienced individuals proposed a design solution without having explored the problem domain sufficiently. Also Sutcliffe and Maiden (1991) compared students and more experienced professional software engineers. While working on a software task, experienced software engineers showed substantially more information-gathering activities than did students. Batra and Davis (1992) examined the role of experience in database design and compared the design activities of experienced designers with those of students. Although the overall amount of time devoted to task accomplishment did not differ substantially between the two groups, the authors observed differences in the type of activities. Compared to students, experienced designers spent more time in gathering information about the task and in developing a good understanding of the problem domain.

Similarly, in a study on problem solving in international relations, Voss et al. (1991) found that professors with long years of experience paid more attention to problem representation issues than did undergraduate students. The authors assumed that lack of knowledge hindered the inexperienced students from developing an adequate problem representation. Schaub and Strohschneider (1992) asked managers and students to work on a complex simulation task. There was no difference with respect to the total number of questions asked during the whole working process. However, compared to students, managers devoted more time on information gathering during the early phases of task accomplishment. During this time, managers did not act but concentrated on information search.

When summarizing these study findings, there is some evidence that experienced individuals pay more attention to problem comprehension than do less experienced individuals. This seems to be particularly true when working on design and complex problem-solving tasks. In most of these studies, experienced individuals' extensive information-gathering and problem-comprehension activities were most prominent in the early phases of the working process. This finding suggests that experienced individuals aim at building a comprehensive representation of the problem before they continue working on the task (Hershey, Walsh, Read & Chulef, 1990; Jeffries et al., 1981; Schaub & Stohschneider, 1992).

However, there are studies which resulted in opposite findings. Most of these studies examined decision-making processes. In their study on a financial decision-making task, Hershey et al. (1990) found that experienced participants asked for less information while working on the task than did naïve participants. However, the experienced participants had requested most of the relevant information *before* working on the task.

Kirschenbaum (1992) studied naval officers while accomplishing a decision task. She compared experienced officers with less experienced instructors and students lacking experience within the domain. The experienced officers tended to gather less information than the two other groups. However, due to the small sample size, the difference did not reach significance. Bédard and Mock (1992) compared the information-search strategies of experienced and less experienced auditors. Analyses showed that experienced auditors acquired less information. Wiggins and O'Hare (1995) reported a similar finding. When working on an aeronautical decision task, experienced pilots searched for less information and spent less time on information acquisition than did less experienced pilots.

Experienced individuals' less intensive information-search behavior does not imply that this group regards information search as irrelevant. In contrast, Bédard and Mock's study (1992) revealed that the experienced auditors searched for less information but attached more importance to the information they did acquire. A number of studies suggests that experienced persons spend less time on information-gathering activities because they search for information more efficiently while inexperienced individuals' information-gathering activities include recursions, redundancies, and inefficiencies (Bédard & Mock, 1992; Hershey et al., 1990; Schaub & Strohschneider, 1992; Wiggins & O'Hare, 1995).

Taken together, results on the amount of problem-comprehension activities of experienced and less experienced individuals seem to be mixed. However, the pattern of findings is quite clear. When working on design and other complex problem-solving tasks, experienced individuals show a greater amount of problem-comprehension activities (Batra & Davis, 1992; Jeffries et al., 1981; Sutcliffe & Maiden, 1991; Voss et al., 1991) while when working on decision-making tasks, experienced individuals show fewer problem-comprehension activities (Bédard & Mock, 1992; Kirschenbaum, 1992; Wiggins & O'Hare, 1995). One explanation might be that in the context of decision-making tasks, experienced individuals have already built problem representations on rather general and abstract levels. Because of their experience, they have scripts of prototypical problem situations and their relevant cues (Hershey et al., 1990). Thus, when confronted with a decision-making task, they can search for these cues very quickly. In contrast, inexperienced individuals do not possess an abstract representation of prototypical situations and therefore it takes them longer to gather the potentially relevant information.

However, the case might be different in the context of design and other complex problem-solving tasks. Here also experienced individuals do not yet have an abstract representation of the specific problem to be solved but must build it during the course of problem solving. Thus, in this context experienced individuals invest in problem-comprehension activities. Inexperienced individuals stop their problem comprehension prematurely. Lack of knowledge might be a reason for it (Voss et al., 1991).

There are some studies which addressed the question as to what kind of information experienced and less experienced individuals pay attention to. In their study on problem solving in the social sciences, Voss et al. (1983) observed that experienced social scientists concentrated on abstract or general problems as the underlying causes of the specific problem to be solved. Lower level problems thereby became subordinate to the more abstract problem. Studies in other domains confirmed that experienced participants focus on higher level and more general information while inexperienced participants request more specific information (Hershey et al., 1990; Wiedemann, 1995), particularly early in the task-accomplishment process (Bédard & Mock, 1992).

Kirschenbaum (1992) found that experienced naval officers more often searched for history and raw data information, that is information which is difficult to understand, but can be very useful in decision making because it helps in predicting future developments.

Crandall and Getchell-Reiter (1993) studied expertise in neonatal intensive care and interviewed experienced nurses about the information they gathered in critical and challenging cases. The authors found that nurses paid attention to very subtle and early symptoms often not described in the medical literature, such as an infant's skin colour or muscle tone. The experienced nurses paid much attention to changes in infants' status over a period of time (e.g., a shift) and interpreted discrepancies between a previous and a current status as a cause for concern. Unfortunately, no comparisons with inexperienced nurses are reported, but the findings are consistent with the results from Kirschenbaum's study (1992), which described the use of history information as a distinguishing factor between experienced and inexperienced naval officers.

The observation that experienced individuals pay attention to very subtle cues and integrate these into a comprehensive picture over the course of time seems to show that they mainly use their 'intuition' (Benner, 1984). Often, the experienced persons themselves are unable to verbalize how they arrived at an adequate understanding of a situation and attribute it to their 'feeling' and 'intuition'. However, as the study by Crandall and Getchell-Reiter (1993) suggests it is rather the perception and integration of very subtle information which enables rapid and adequate problem comprehension.

*Problem comprehension in excellent versus moderate performers.* High performers regard intensive problem comprehension and information collection as a highly important strategy for successfully accomplishing a task (Leithwood &

Steinbach, 1995; Sonnentag, 1998a). However, there is rarely any evidence that high performers spend more time on problem-comprehension activities. Studies from various domains show that high and moderate performers do not differ in the amount of problem-comprehension activities or that high performers even spend less time on these activities.

For example, Vessey (1986) studied the process of debugging computer programs and analyzed various information-gathering activities of high and low performers. For most of the information-gathering activities she did not find a difference between high and low performers. In another study, Koubek and Salvendy (1991) compared highly performing computer programmers with programmers at a moderate performance level while accomplishing a program-modification task. Supervisors had rated the programmers' performance. Programmers who were among the 95% best performing programmers in their field were regarded as 'very best', programmers performing between the 70th and 80th percentile were regarded as 'above average'. Koubek and Salvendy did not find any difference in the amount of time devoted to information search.

Also Sonnentag (1998a) studied software professionals and compared the ways high and moderate performers proceeded when working on a software design task. High and moderate performers had been identified by peer nominations and by performance on this software design task. Two types of problem-comprehension activities were measured: analyzing requirements given in the task description and building scenarios of the problem domain. Analyses showed that over the whole working process, high performers spent *less* time in analyzing requirements. There were no differences between the two performance groups in early phases of task accomplishment, but moderate performers spent substantially more time analyzing requirements in later phases. With respect to the second problem-comprehension activity (i.e., building scenarios) no differences between high and moderate performers were found.

In a classical study on medical problem solving, Elstein, Shulman and Sprafka (1978) compared the information-search strategies of physicians who were identified as 'best diagnosticians' by their peers with the strategies of physicians who were not or were less often nominated. No differences in the activities between nominated and non-nominated physicians were found. The authors additionally compared those physicians who arrived at accurate diagnoses in the experimental tasks with physicians who did not. Analysis showed that the more accurate physicians acquired *more* cues during the diagnostic period, without necessarily spending more time on this activity. This finding suggests that accurate physicians work more efficiently.

Schaper and Sonntag (1998) examined diagnostic fault-finding processes in a manufacturing plant and compared high and moderate performers' information-gathering strategies while trying to find specific faults. For most of the information-gathering activities no differences between high and lower performers emerged. With respect to two activities, the authors did find differences, with lower performers showing these activities to a greater extent. Moreover, lower performers repeated their diagnostic actions more often. Again, this indicates that they were less efficient in problem comprehension.

Similarly, studies on activities of managers point in the same direction. Luthans, Rosenkrantz and Hennessey (1985) compared the work activities of successful and less successful managers with an observational method. Managers' success was operationalized by a promotion index. Successful and less successful managers did not differ with respect to exchange of information. Jansen and Stoop (1997) conducted a similar study and asked managers from a large Dutch company on which activities they spent their working time. Jansen and Stoop even found that successful managers, that is managers who had advanced in their career very quickly, spent less time on exchange of information than did less successful managers.

Taken together, research in various domains shows that high performers do not spend more time on problem-comprehension activities. One reason for this finding might be that high performers search for the most useful information. During problem comprehension, high performers focus on general, abstract, and evaluative information (Koubek & Salvendy, 1991; Vessey, 1986).

Studies in the domain of management additionally showed that highly performing managers concentrated their problem-comprehension activities on specific types of information. Isenberg (1986) conducted a study in which general managers from six cooperatives developed an action plan for a short business case. Independent, knowledgeable raters assessed the effectiveness of these action plans. Analyses showed that a specific information-processing strategy which went from general to more specific and concrete information was related to more effective action plans. However, an exclusive focus on specific facts was negatively related to the effectiveness of action plans.

Klemp and McClelland (1986) studied excellence among senior managers from six different organizations. The authors identified outstanding senior managers—as opposed to average performers—by a peer and supervisory assessment procedure. Managers participated in interviews which were based on a critical incident technique (Flanagan, 1954). Klemp and McClelland found that diagnostic information seeking was one of the most prominent intellectual competencies typical for outstanding senior managers. Diagnostic information seeking includes activities such as 'pushing' (p. 40) for concrete information in situations which are ambiguous, asking for information from a variety of sources, and making use of questions to gain a better understanding of the situation or problem. Thus, high performers' search for specific and highly relevant information can explain why they spent comparably little time on problem comprehension.

In addition, research suggests that high performers pursue a more efficient way of problem comprehension (Elstein, Shulman & Sprafka, 1978; Schaper & Sonntag, 1998). Studies which analyzed the *process* of problem comprehension in more detail demonstrated that high performers use very specific strategies in order to arrive quickly at an adequate problem representation. Pennington (1987) examined program comprehension strategies in the domain of computer programming. By contrasting comprehension activities of the top-performing quartile of her participants with the activities of the lowest-performing quartile, Pennington identified a 'cross-referencing strategy' as typical for the high performers. Such a cross-referencing strategy can be characterized as an alternation between 'systematic study of the program, translation into domain terms, and verification in program terms' (p. 111). In contrast to high performers, lower performers concentrated on one of the aspects (e.g., program *or* domain) without building connections. With respect to problem comprehension, this study indicates that high performers cover the whole task domain and integrate its various parts and aspects.

Findings from another study on computer program comprehension pointed in a similar direction. Computer programmers who showed a flexible program comprehension strategy and combined a top-down with a bottom-up approach tended to arrive at a better understanding of computer programs than did programmers who relied only on one approach (Shaft & Vessey, 1998).

Also Sonnentag (1998a) identified a specific problem-comprehension strategy of highly performing software designers. High performers tended to link the analysis of requirements directly to problem domain scenarios, that is they related the task description immediately to their knowledge about real-world processes. Taken together, these three studies showed that high performers succeed in combining and integrating various aspects of the task and the solution process. Their approach can be characterized as a 'relational strategy' in that they relate and closely link several parts of the solution process.

One might argue that such a relational strategy puts great demands on working memory and is therefore not a beneficial working strategy. However, due to their well-developed integrated knowledge and efficient problem-solving strategies such as forward reasoning (Smith & Good, 1984) high performers probably have working memory capacity available for applying such a relational strategy.

## Goal setting and planning

Goal setting and planning are crucial components of an action process (Frese & Zapf, 1994; Hacker, 1998). Goal setting and planning imply decisions about what to accomplish and how to proceed. Empirical expertise research has paid some attention to potential differences in goal setting and planning between experts and non-experts, within both the experience conceptualization and the excellence conceptualization.

*Goal setting and planning in experienced versus inexperienced individuals.* One can assume that goal setting and planning require some domain specific experience. Thus, one can expect that experienced and less experienced individuals differ in their goal-setting and planning activities. Particularly with respect to goal setting, empirical research supports this assumption. For example, Benner (1984) who studied expertise in clinical nursing practice, described that more experienced nurses saw their own actions in the context of long-range goals. Hershey et al. (1990) compared experienced financial planners with naïve participants while working on a financial decision-making task. The authors found that the experienced participants' behavior was more goal-directed than that of the inexperienced participants. In a recent study, Schenk, Vitalari and Davis (1998) compared inexperienced with experienced systems analysts. Experienced systems analysts verbalized more goals than did the inexperienced analysts.

Furthermore, experienced individuals do not only focus more on the goals of their own working processes. They additionally pay more attention to the goals associated with their working products and objects. For example, in Sutcliffe and Maiden's study (1991), experienced software engineers reasoned more about the goals of the computer system they had to develop (for a related finding within the domain of international relations cf. Voss et al., 1991).

To sum up, research suggests that experienced individuals are more goal-oriented in their working process. These results can be explained within a resource allocation framework as proposed by Kanfer and Ackerman (1989). Since experienced individuals are more advanced in the skill acquisition process they have more cognitive resources available for self-regulatory activities such as goal setting.

However, there is only limited empirical evidence that experienced individuals implement their goal-orientation by specific planning activities. Research which compared planning between experienced and inexperienced individuals resulted in inconsistent findings. On the one hand, there is some evidence that experienced individuals engage more in planning. For example Bryson, Bereiter, Scardamalia and Joram (1991), reported that experienced writers plan to a larger extent than do inexperienced writers. On the other hand, there are studies which did not find any differences in planning between experienced and less experienced individuals (Sonnentag, 1988a). Voss et al. (1983) observed that experienced social scientists did not articulate higher level plans when working on a problem within their domain of expertise. Benner's (1984) study on clinical nursing offers a similar conclusion. Benner observed that nurses with a moderate experience consciously planned their activities on an abstract and analytical level. Highly experienced nurses however, were found to be less involved in analytical problem-solving and planning processes.

It might be that there is a curvilinear relationship between experience and planning. Some amount of experience is needed for being able to plan one's task-accomplishment process and to make predictions about the effect of one's actions. With increasing experience, however, explicit and conscious planning becomes less necessary. This might be due to two mechanisms: first, the planning process itself becomes highly routinized and is therefore less conscious and less easily verbalizable. Second, an individual will have ready-made action plans available which he or she can apply without extensive reflection.

*Goal setting and planning in excellent versus moderate performers.*   Research based on the excellence conceptualization of expertise paid much attention to goal-setting and planning activities. In general, there is broad evidence that high and moderate performers differ with respect to goal setting and planning.

Hacker and Vaic (1973) analyzed the goal-setting activities of high and low performers in shopfloor-level jobs. Among the low performers, only 57% formulated a performance goal for the current working day, while all high performers formulated such a goal. Also, Vitalari and Dickson (1983), who examined problem solving in software systems analysis, found that high performers showed more goal-setting behavior. In a case study, Dylla (1990) examined the design processes of professional engineers who worked on a construction task under laboratory conditions. Analyses showed that high performers put greater focus on the goal development than did the weaker performers.

These findings, which were largely based on participants' concurrent verbalizations, are in line with results from questionnaire studies. Survey data from a service organization and a moving company showed that an individual's amount of specific goal setting was positively related to supervisory performance ratings (Earley, Wojnaroski & Prest, 1987). Tripoli (1998) examined working strategies in technical and administrative professionals. She found that priority focus—which can be regarded as a specific type of goal-orientation—was positively related to work performance as rated by supervisors or peers. Thus, individuals who experienced a clear and broad concentration on their work priorities showed higher performance.

There are also exceptions from these fairly consistent findings. Vessey (1986) examined professional programmers who had to debug computer programs and compared programmers with a high versus a low debugging performance. She found that the lower performing group verbalized *more* goal-setting behaviour. However, this finding does not necessarily contradict results from the other studies. It might be that high performers have automated their goal-setting behavior. This would imply that they set goals without verbalizing them.

High and moderate performers differ not only in the amount of goal setting but also in the type of goals they pursue. Hacker (1992, 1998) summarized studies on high performance in shopfloor jobs, particularly in the textile industry (cf. also Frese & Zapf, 1994). One major difference between high and lower performers was that high performers pursued long-range goals while lower performers were more oriented towards short-term goals.

In this context, workers with long-term goals anticipated events that might happen during the whole shift. They therefore engaged in a proactive planning strategy. Short-term goals, however, allowed only for a momentary, more reactive strategy. Hacker argues that the main prerequisite for pursuing long-range goals is a good mental representation of the task and the working process.

In a sample of salespeople, Sujan, Weitz and Kumar (1994) found that both learning and performance goal orientation (Dweek & Leggett, 1988) were positively related to sales performance. Interestingly, performance orientation was positively related to working hard, that is to working long hours, while learning orientation was positively related both to working hard and working smart. Working smart included behaviors such as engaging in planning, engaging flexibly in a wide range of selling behaviors and activities, and altering sales behaviors and activities for meeting situational requirements. Working hard as well as working smart in turn showed positive relationships with performance. Thus, high performance was closely related to the pursuit of learning goals—goals which can be regarded as a specific type of long-range goals.

Taken together, these studies suggest that high performers set more specific and more long-range goals. This more extensive goal-setting activity might be due to high performers' more comprehensive knowledge base. Furthermore, one can assume that goals in turn direct high performers' further activities such as gathering relevant information, planning and feedback processing.

Studies in several domains showed that high performers engaged more in planning than did moderate performers. Hacker and Vaic (1973), who studied performance differences in shopfloor-level jobs, found that highly performing operators spent significantly more time on preparatory tasks than did lower performers. For example, high performers spent 4.9% of their working time on planning while low performers spent 2.5% on this activity. Similarly, high performers spent 13.8% of their time on setting-up their machines while lower performers spent 9.0% on this activity. Moreover, Hacker and Vaic observed that high and lower performers not only differed with respect to the several activities but that high performers proactively structured their work in such a way that they could engage in planning and setting-up machines.

With respect to managerial jobs, empirical research showed positive relationships between planning and high performance. In this study with general managers who had to solve a business case, Isenberg (1986) found that planning for contingencies was positively correlated with the effectiveness of the developed action plans. Also Klemp and McClelland (1986) identified planning/causal thinking as a crucial competence of outstanding senior managers. In this study and task domain, planning implied the ability to see implications and to make predictions about the future, to analyze causal relationships, and to develop strategies and plans for goal attainment. Similarly, in their study about work activities of managers, Jansen and Stoop (1997) found a positive relationship between planning/coordination and managers' success (however, cf. Luthans et al., 1985).

Tripoli (1998), who examined professionals in complex jobs, found contingency planning to be positively related to peer ratings of performance. When working on a project, highly performing professionals anticipated obstacles and considered more than one approach in case the first approach did not work well.

Frese and his coworkers studied planning behavior in different samples of small-scale entrepreneurs (Frese, van Gelderen & Ombach, 1988; Rauch & Frese, in press; van Gelderen & Frese, 1988). Based on the analysis of interview and questionnaire data, the authors found that the lack of any planning behavior was negatively related to entrepreneurs' performance (Frese et al., 1988; van Gelderen & Frese, 1998). Thus, entrepreneurs who largely pursued a reactive strategy were least successful. Interestingly, in a longitudinal analysis the authors found support for an effect of performance on planning behavior. These findings suggest that high performance enhances a specific approach to task accomplishment which in turn has a positive impact on subsequent performance.

A study by Leithwood and Steinbach (1995) on problem solving by school principals showed that high and moderate performers did not differ in their planning activities when confronted with highly structured problems. In such situations, there was generally not much planning. However, when approaching an ill-structured problem, highly performing school principals engaged more much in detailed planning than did moderate performers.

In her study on high performance in software design, Sonnentag (1988a) differentiated between two types of planning: planning ahead and local planning. Planning ahead comprised reflections and decisions on the future course of action; local planning referred to explicit intentions about the next action step without extensively reflecting on it. Analyses showed that high and moderate performers differed with respect to local planning activities. Particularly while developing the design solution, high performers engaged more in local planning. However, there were no differences with respect to planning ahead.

The findings reported by Leithwood and Steinbach (1995) and Sonnentag (1998a) suggest that high performers' more extensive activity in planning ahead found in shopfloor and managerial jobs does not hold for all tasks and task domains. There are tasks—such as software design tasks accomplished in individual settings—which do not need to be accomplished in a relatively fixed sequence and which do not require much coordination (Guindon, 1990). These tasks therefore do not ask for much planning and the most appropriate way to accomplish them is to not plan too far ahead. Other tasks however—such as managerial or complex problem-solving tasks—require planning to a large extent. It seems that high performers do engage in extensive planning when it is needed but refrain from this activity when it does not help in accomplishing the task.

*Feedback processing*

Feedback processing is an important phase within an action process in which the present situation is compared with the cognitive representation of the goal. By processing feedback one evaluates whether, and to what extent, the pursued goal has been achieved. Feedback processing is helpful in detecting errors, inconsistencies and other suboptimalities in one's working process or product. Adequate feedback provides important information for initiating new action steps (Carver & Scheier, 1982). In work contexts, feedback is often provided by other persons or by the work process itself. Additionally, individuals can actively search for feedback (Ashford & Cummings, 1983). This section will focus on such feedback-seeking activities.

*Feedback processing in experienced versus inexperienced individuals.* Until now, expertise research has not paid much attention to feedback seeking. However, there are some studies which indicate that more experienced individuals tend to search more for feedback than do inexperienced persons. For example, Voss et al. (1983) studied problem-solving processes in social sciences and found that experienced social scientists showed greater skill in evaluating the implications of the solutions they had proposed. Inexperienced persons did not evaluate the consequences of their solutions and did not check for constraints in the problem domain which might hinder the implementation of their ideas. Similarly, in a more recent study in the domain of international relations, experienced study participants engaged more in a critical evaluation of their problem-solving process and their interpretation of the information (Voss et al., 1991).

In their study of software engineering students and professionals, Sutcliffe and Maiden (1991) found that professionals, that is the more experienced participants, evaluated and tested their solutions more often. Furthermore, experienced software engineers tended to test each of their solutions just after they had developed them while students postponed testing until the end of the task accomplishment. Schenk et al. (1998) reported a similar finding. Experienced system analysts tested their hypotheses more often than did inexperienced analysts. If necessary, these experienced analysts discarded their hypotheses more often.

Taken together, these empirical studies provide a consistent picture. More experienced individuals search for feedback to a greater degree than do inexperienced individuals.

*Feedback processing in excellent versus moderate performers.* Similarly, there is evidence from studies which followed the excellence conceptualization of expertise that high performers are more involved in feedback seeking than are moderate performers. In their study on software systems analysis, Vitalari and Dickson (1983) observed that high performers modified their strategies more often than did low performers. The authors interpret the modification of strategies as a response to a change in information gained from the environment. Feedback seeking can be seen as a necessary prerequisite in order to gather more information and a basis for modifying strategies.

Leithwood and Steinbach (1995) observed that when making assumptions during problem solving, highly performing school principals were very explicit about their assumptions while moderate performers were much less explicit. Being explicit about one's assumptions seems to be an important prerequisite for feedback seeking. When assumptions remain implicit there are not many possibilities for evaluating their correctness. Thus, high performers' way of approaching their tasks implies that they are more inclined to search for feedback.

Studies which examined feedback seeking more directly, support this interpretation. Highly performing software professionals spent significantly more time on feedback processing while working in a design task than did moderate performers (Sonnentag, 1998a). Similarly, information technology professionals who were nominated by two managers as excellent performers more often reported that they asked their coworkers for feedback (Sonnentag, de Gilder & Winkelman, 1999).

In this case study on construction processes, Dylla (1990) found that one of the weak performers spent only a very small amount of time on analyzing and evaluating his solution, that is on feedback processing. The other weak performer spent about the same relative amount of time on analyzing and evaluating his solution as the high performers did, but his analysis and evaluation were on a less detailed level and less accurate.

In summary, these studies showed that high performers seek more feedback. Thus, the findings within both conceptualizations of expertise are rather parallel: experienced individuals and high performers look more for feedback than do inexperienced and lower performing individuals. These differences in feedback seeking can be explained by differences in knowledge and problem-comprehension processes. Compared to less experienced individuals and lower performers, experienced and highly performing individuals were found to possess a more comprehensive knowledge about the domain and to proceed more efficiently during problem comprehension. Therefore they know better which aspects of the problem to look at and which information indicates a good versus a suboptimal solution. Furthermore, they might have higher performance expectations, which were found to be positively related to feedback seeking (Morrison & Cummings, 1992; Northcraft & Ashford, 1990).

*Communication and cooperation*

Most studies on expertise have examined thinking and action processes performed within individual task accomplishment. Nevertheless, several authors have turned to potential differences between experts and non-experts in cooperative work settings. Traditionally, researchers have been sceptical about whether experts possess good communication and cooperation skills (Shanteau, 1988; Stein, 1995). However, recent empirical research suggests that experts show positive characteristics in the domain of communication and cooperation. Most of these studies adopted the excellence conceptualization of expertise and compared high with lower performers.

However, there seems to be additional evidence that experienced individuals' communication processes are superior to those of less experienced persons. In a sea-combat simulation study, Lipshitz and Ben Shaul (1997) found that experienced commanders communicated more extensively with others, and asked for and provided more detailed information while inexperienced participants with no combat experience tended simply to instruct others.

With respect to the excellence conceptualization of expertise, a relatively large number of studies on communication and cooperation processes have been conducted in technical domains, such as software design or engineering. In their field study on software design in large projects, Curtis, Krasner and Iscoe (1988) identified exceptional communication skills as one of the essential characteristics of exceptional performers. These exceptional performers spent much time educating their coworkers and accomplished a great portion of their design work while interacting with others. Similar findings are reported by Riedl, Weitzenfeld, Freeman, Klein and Musa (1991) who observed highly developed interpersonal skills in expert software engineers.

Sonnentag (1995) asked members of software development teams to describe a highly performing coworker. More than 50% of the participants described a high performer as a person who is socially skilled. In this study, social skills included cooperation skills, communication skills, and team-leading competencies as well as being a 'good colleague' with whom it is easy to go along. In the same study, Sonnentag (1995) compared the work activities of high and average performing software professionals. Analyses showed that high performers spent more time in consultations with coworkers and participated more in review meetings. For example, they were more involved in exchanging information and supporting others in case of problems. Highly performing software professionals without supervisory tasks tended to spend more time in both formal and informal meetings than did moderate performers without any supervisory tasks; however, this difference did not reach the conventional significance level.

Some other studies, however, did not find superior cooperation skills in high performers. By using a network analysis, Stein (1995) identified experts and non-experts in a bio-technology start-up firm and an educational institution. Stein had expected that experts would be perceived as being less cooperative than non-experts. However, there were no differences in cooperativeness between experts and non-experts, as perceived by their peers. Experts were more trusted by the other network members and were perceived to have higher leadership qualities. Similarly, Turley and Bieman (1995) did not find differences in team-orientation between exceptional and non-exceptional software engineers. There are several explanations for these partially inconsistent findings. It might be that the differences are relatively small in size so that they do not become obvious in all studies. Furthermore, it might be that the differences in cooperation skills between high and moderate performers are dependent on cultural or task contexts.

There are two studies which support this assumption. Lange (1996) studied social competencies in highly and average performing engineers. She found that high performers showed high assertiveness and team competence, irrespective of the quality of team functioning. However, moderate performers' assertiveness and team competence declined in poorly functioning teams. An observational study in software development teams points in the same direction (Sonnentag, 1999). Analyses of video-taped team meetings showed that in general, high performers participated more in the meeting and contributed more to the meeting process. Additionally, when the meetings were poorly structured or characterized by conflicts and ambiguous situations, high performers engaged more in process-controlling activities, such as meeting management, goal setting, problem analysis, and feedback seeking. Taken together, these two studies suggest that differences between high and moderate performers become most evident in unfavourable situations, that is situations characterized by a poor quality of team functioning or by a low level of meeting structure. However, in more favourable situations the differences between high and moderate performers are less obvious.

Sonnentag and Lange (1999) examined *how* software professionals and engineers addressed cooperation situations. In two studies using scenario tasks, the authors found that high performers came up with more solution ideas for difficult cooperation situations. Compared to lower performers, high performers more often suggested addressing cooperation partners at an interpersonal level.

Furthermore, high performers' excellent technical skills seem to have an effect on cooperation patterns within teams. Turley and Bieman (1995) compared exceptional and non-exceptional software engineers who had been identified by their managers. In a Q-sort procedure, software engineers had to indicate which behavior was related to their 'personal best' performance. On average, exceptional software engineers reported having helped others to a greater degree while non-exceptional performers reported having sought help from others. Similarly, Sonnentag et al. (1999) found that information technology professionals described by their managers as excellent reported that they were more often asked by their coworkers for help and feedback.

Of course, differences in communication and cooperation-related skills and activities between high and lower performers are not unique to technical domains. They play an important role in other domains, particularly in managerial jobs. In their observational study on managerial activities, Luthans et al. (1985) found three important differences between successful and less successful managers. First, successful managers, that is managers who had advanced in their career more quickly, spent more time managing conflict than did less successful managers. Second, they were more involved in socializing/politicking activities. Third, they spent more time on interactions with persons from outside their organizations.

In their study on outstanding senior managers, Klemp and McClelland (1986) did not focus on communication or cooperation activities per se. However, they identified 'influence competencies' as crucial characteristics of high performers. Such influence competencies are often instantiated in cooperation situations. More specifically, the influence competencies included 'directive influence/personalized power' (e.g., confronting others directly in the event of problems), 'collaborative influence/socialized power' (e.g., dealing with groups and aiming at outcomes and cooperation), and symbolic influence (e.g., setting a personal example).

Leighwood and Steinbach (1995) examined elementary school principals' behavior during staff meetings with a stimulated recall method. The authors reported substantial differences between the activities of highly performing and more typical school principals. During problem interpretation high performers more often checked their own interpretations by eliciting staff members' views on the problem. Moreover, high performers interpreted the problems to be discussed within a larger context while moderate performers tended to view the problems in isolation. With respect to goals, high performers were more concerned with pursuing goals most staff members could agree on and were additionally less committed to a preconceived solution. Furthermore, high performers developed detailed plans for collaborative task accomplishment and were more explicit about their own views without intimidating or restraining others. High performers planned follow-ups of the meetings. Taken together, high performers' meeting behavior reflected to a large degree their activities in individual task settings, such as great emphasis on problem comprehension and planning. It seems that for doing this in an optimal way, they were less concerned with their own views but were open to the interpretations and suggestions of their staff.

To sum up, the majority of studies provided evidence for differences in cooperation activities and competencies between high and lower performers. Especially in difficult situations, high performers possess better communication skills and are more involved in cooperation processes.

However, up to now it is still unclear whether cooperation activities and competencies are an integral component of work-related expertise, that is whether cooperation is part of the 'essence of expertise' (Ericsson & Lehmann, 1996). On the basis of existing research it cannot be ruled out that high performers are superior in cooperation but that this superiority is a by-product of their excellence and their superiority in problem-solving processes and knowledge. This would imply that differences in cooperation processes between high and moderate performers are nothing more than a reflection of the respective differences in problem-solving processes and that work-related expert performance is possible without cooperation. Studies which found that high performers' activities in cooperative settings largely resemble their behavior in individual task settings (Leithwood & Steinbach, 1995; Sonnentag, 1999) are in line with this interpretation, although they do not rule out alternative interpretations.

Additionally, cooperation competencies and participation in cooperation settings could have a positive effect on expertise. Research has shown that explaining ideas and facts to oneself improves future performance (Chi, de Leeuw, Chiu & LaVancher, 1994). It is plausible to assume that the same is true for explanations provided to others within cooperation settings. This implies that high performers who participate more in cooperation situations and who are more often approached for help and feedback—and as a consequence will explain more to their coworkers—will themselves also gain from these explanation activities. Future studies are needed which test the—potentially reciprocal—relationships between expertise and cooperation in more detail.

*Summary*

Table 7.1 summarizes the main research findings on differences between experts and non-experts separately for both conceptualizations of expertise. The conceptualizations do not only differ in the way expertise was operationalized. Additionally, the types of samples studies overlap only partially. While study samples within the excellence conceptualization comprised only professionals (and other individuals working as employees in a specific job), studies within the experience conceptualizations were substantially based on comparisons between students and professionals (and other employees). Moreover, as will be described in more detail in the next section, excellence and experience are related only to a moderate degree.

A direct comparison between the findings originating from the two operationalizations is difficult, because not all aspects of experts' knowledge and task-accomplishment processes were covered to a similar degree within both conceptualizations. For example, research on knowledge encapsulation was done only within the experience conceptualization. Specific problem-comprehension strategies, that is, the application of a relational strategy, were studied only within the excellence conceptualization. Finally, studies on differences in communication and cooperation were predominantly done within the excellence conceptualization. Thus, it would be premature to conclude that it is mainly the high-performance aspect of expertise—and not the experience aspect—which is associated with a relational strategy during problem comprehension or high involvement in communication and cooperation.

**Table 7.1** Summary of research findings

| | Comparisons within the experience conceptualization | Comparisons within the excellence conceptualization |
|---|---|---|
| Knowledge | • Experienced individuals possess more complete and more correct knowledge<br>• Experienced individuals' knowledge is more abstract and more detailed<br>• Experienced individuals possess more meta-cognitive knowledge<br>• Experienced individuals use their knowledge in an encapsulated form and are generally better in using their knowledge | • Excellent performers possess more complete and more correct knowledge<br>• Excellent performers possess a better integrated knowledge structure<br>• Excellent performers possess more procedural and tacit knowledge |
| Problem comprehension | • Experienced individuals show more problem-comprehension activities in design and complex problem-solving tasks<br>• Experienced individuals show fewer problem-comprehension activities in decision-making tasks<br>• Experienced individuals focus on abstract and general information, less on specific information<br>• Experienced individuals search for 'history information', raw data and subtle cues<br>• Experienced individuals' problem-comprehension process is less recursive | • Excellent performers spend less or equal time on problem comprehension, also in design and complex problem-solving tasks<br>• Excellent performers focus on abstract and general information<br>• Excellent performers' problem-comprehension process goes from general to specific and concrete information<br>• Excellent performers apply a relational strategy |
| Goal setting and planning | • Experienced individuals are more goal-oriented<br><br>—Planning: inconsistent findings; maybe curvilinear relationship | • Excellent performers show more goal setting<br>• Excellent performers focus more on long-range goals<br>• Excellent performers show more planning in complex and ill-structured tasks, but not in well-structured tasks |
| Feedback processing | • Experienced individuals seek more for feedback | • Excellent performers seek more for feedback |
| Communication and cooperation | —Very rarely studied | • Excellent performers spend more time in cooperation-related activities<br>• Excellent performers show higher social skills and are more involved in specific team-oriented behaviors, particularly in difficult situations<br>• Excellent performers are more involved in helping processes and provide more feedback to others |

Nevertheless, similarities between experienced individuals and high performers become obvious. Both expert groups possess more correct and more complete knowledge than non-experts. Experienced individuals and high performers focus on general and abstract information during problem comprehension. They are more goal-oriented and engage more in goal setting. Furthermore, they show more feedback seeking.

However, some specific characteristics of high performers—contrasted with experienced individuals—also emerged. Compared to lower performers, high performers do not spend more time on problem comprehension, irrespective the type of task. Experienced individuals however, engage more in problem comprehension when working on design and other complex problem-solving tasks. It might be that with increasing experience, individuals know about the high importance of problem comprehension and therefore invest a lot of effort when the task requires complex problem solving. However, although experienced individuals proceed more efficiently than inexperienced individuals they do not necessarily possess high performers' extremely useful and successful approaches to problem comprehension.

With respect to planning, results were somewhat inconsistent within both comparisons. The pattern of study findings within the experience conceptualizations suggests a curvilinear relationship between experience and planning. However, within the excellence conceptualization the degree of planning seems to be more dependent on the task requirements. High performers showed more planning in complex, ill-structured tasks but not in tasks where no explicit planning is needed, such as well-structured tasks for which individuals already possess action plans or other tasks which do not require a fixed and pre-planned course of action. Thus, the findings indicate that high performers adjust their behavior to the task requirements while this seems to be less specific for experienced individuals. Research findings with respect to communication and cooperation point in the same direction. High performers showed specific process-controlling activities only in poorly structured meeting situations. Taken together, high performers display a high adaptation to task requirements (cf., Ericsson & Lehmann, 1996).

To sum up, experienced individuals and high performers share some knowledge features and ways to task accomplishment. But there are also some specific approaches which seem to be more strongly related to high performance than to experience. Thus, it seems warranted to keep up the distinction between the two conceptualizations of expertise.

## Development of Expertise

Experience is a core aspect in many expertise concepts (Ford & Kraiger, 1995; Frensch & Sternberg, 1989; Richman et al., 1996). This is explicitly reflected in the experience conceptualization of expertise. Within this conceptualization it is implicitly assumed that with increasing experience an individuals's level of performance increases. Studies which compared relatively inexperienced students with professionals and other more experienced individuals support this assumption. In many of the studies, experienced individuals showed a better performance than less experienced individuals, particularly students (e.g., Jeffries et al., 1981; Schaub & Strohschneider, 1992).

However, the finding that more experienced individuals show a better performance may not only be due to the performance-enhancing effects of experience. Additionally, selection and self-selection might prevent low-performing students and newcomers from starting or continuing a career in the respective domain. This implies that it is less likely that low performers will become experienced professionals. As a consequence, in empirical studies, the experienced subgroup might be pre-selected and might overrepresent higher performers.

Furthermore, studies which compared students with professionals do not provide an answer to the question of how excellence develops within individuals already working in a domain and why some of those who started a career in a domain become high performers while others' performance remains at a moderate level. Empirical studies showed that substantial performance differences do exist among individuals with a comparable length of experience (Batra & Davis, 1992; Jeffries et al., 1981; Reif & Allen, 1990; Simmons & Lunetta, 1993).

*Years of experience*

Within the expertise literature, it is often stressed that long years of experience are necessary for arriving at a high performance level. Based on biographical evidence, researchers argued that most individuals performing at an expert level have been active in the respective domain for at least ten years (Ericsson, Krampe & Tesch-Römer, 1993; Richman et al., 1996). However, this observation does not necessarily imply that individuals with at least ten years of experience in a domain perform at a high level.

Studies within the excellence conceptualization of expertise examined the relationship between years of experience and performance. Some of these studies reported positive relationships between years of experience and performance level. For example, Sujan, Sujan and Bettman (1988) found a strong positive correlation between experience in telephone marketing and supervisory ratings of effectiveness. However, the mean job experience for the overall sample was relatively low. Also Koubek and Salvendy (1991), who compared high-level performers in the software domain with somewhat lower performers found that the high-level performers had a significantly longer professional experience. Exceptionally performing software engineers studied by Turley and Bieman (1995) had more years of professional experience than non-exceptional performers. However, differences between the two groups could not be explained by differences in years of professional experience.

Other studies, however, did not find differences in years of experience between high and lower performers (Leithwood & Steinbach, 1995; Schenk et al., 1998; Sonnentag, 1995; Stein, 1995).

Taken together, these expertise studies are consistent with meta-analyses on the relationship between length of experience and performance conducted within the broader field of work and organizational psychology (McDaniel, Schmidt & Hunter, 1988; Quiñones, Ford & Teachout, 1995). For example, Quiñones et al. (1995) found a correlation (corrected for sampling error and criterion unreliability) of $r = 0.27$ between a time-based measure of experience and performance. Overall, years of experience are positively related to performance. Nevertheless, common variance is relatively low, suggesting that years of experience play only a minor role in the development of excellence.

*Variety of experience*

Other aspects of experience than its length might be more important (cf., Quiñones et al., 1995; Tesluk & Jacobs, 1998). Studies in the domain of software development and programming provide some support for this assumption. Highly performing software professionals had worked in more different projects and with more different programming languages than had moderate performers (Sonnentag, 1995). Thus, high performers have a broader and a more varied professional experience. In another study, Stanislaw, Hesketh, Kanavaros, Hesketh and Robinson (1994) found that computer programmers who reported that they would like to learn another programming language tended to score higher on self-rated performance than programmers who did not want to learn another programming language. Although these findings do not exclude the opposite causal explanation they might indicate that high performers wish to learn more while lower performers seem to be more satisfied with their current level of skill and knowledge.

It might be that the development of excellence is a self-enhancing process. Having worked in various subdomains and having accomplished a great variety of different tasks helps in developing more general principles and models (Hesketh, 1997), which in turn have a positive effect on performance. In addition, performing at a high level and having already gained much experience in learning might facilitate further learning activities.

*Deliberate practice*

Ericsson, Krampe and Tesch-Römer (1993) presented a theoretical framework in which they explained expert performance as the result of deliberate practice, that is goal-oriented, regular and individualized learning activities. The concept of deliberate practice refers to 'activities that have been specially designed to improve the current level of performance' (p. 368). Ericsson et al. (1993) described deliberate practice by three main features: (a) deliberate practice requires a huge amount of time and energy invested over a long period of time as well as teachers, training material and training facilities; (b) deliberate practice is not inherently enjoyable and motivating; (c) deliberate practice requires a lot of effort, therefore the daily amount of time which can be devoted to deliberate practice is limited. Until now, researchers have studied deliberate practice and its effects mainly in the domains of music, chess, and other sports.

In their studies, Ericsson and coworkers (1993) compared violin students identified by their teachers as 'best violinists' with violin students described as 'good violinists' and lower performing students who were trained to be music teachers. All students kept a diary over the period of seven days and participated in an interview in which they provided detailed biographical information. Analysis showed that 'best violinists' and 'good violinists' currently spent more time practising alone, that is on an activity which captures the essential features of deliberate practice, than did the lower performing group of students. Additionally, the authors calculated the students' accumulated amount of practice since the age of 4 and found it to be highly related with students' performance level. In another study, Ericsson et al. (1993) examined deliberate practice in pianists. Compared with piano amateurs, piano students who prepared for a solo career had spent more time on deliberate practice since their childhood (for a study on the role of deliberate practice on maintaining a high performance level cf., Krampe & Ericsson, 1996). Charness, Krampe and Mayr (1996) and Starkes, Deakin, Allard, Hodges and Hayes (1996) studied deliberate practice in the domains of chess and wrestling and obtained encouraging findings: cumulative amount of deliberate practice was positively related to performance level.

Studies which apply the deliberate practice concept to work settings are still rare. In a first cross-sectional study, Sonnentag and Kleine (in press) examined goal-oriented learning activities in insurance agents and found that deliberate practice also occurred in this work context. Typical activities in this domain which were performed as deliberate practice included extensive preparations for difficult tasks, mental simulation and searching for feedback. Furthermore, the amount of time currently spent on deliberate practice was significantly related to insurance agents' work performance. However, the amount of deliberate practice accumulated during insurance agents' careers showed no significant relationship with work performance.

Taken together, these studies on deliberate practice showed that high performers spent more time on deliberate practice activities. Additionally, there are good theoretical reasons to assume that deliberate practice has a causal effect on performance (Ericcson et al., 1993). However, due to the cross-sectional nature of the deliberate practice studies, which relied heavily on retrospective data, the conclusion that deliberate practice *leads* to high performance might be premature (for a critical evaluation of the deliberate practice approach cf. Sternberg, 1996).

## Directions for Future Research

Most expertise studies adopted the contrastive research approach (Voss et al., 1986) or correlational study designs. These studies provide descriptions of what experts do and what they know in comparison to non-experts. Thus, existing expertise research offers a relatively comprehensive picture of the differences between experts and non-experts. However, because of the limitations of these design approaches, many studies do not allow unequivocal conclusions about whether these differences are responsible for the performance differences or whether they are an epiphenomenon of superior performance. Strictly speaking, we do not know whether the application of a relational strategy leads to high performance in specific tasks or whether high performers possess the cognitive prerequisites for following such a strategy.

Future expertise research should adopt study designs which allow more definitive conclusions. In particular, more experimental studies are needed. Within experimental studies one might think of two different manipulations which can offer an answer to the question as to whether a specific aspect of knowledge or a specific way of approaching a task is responsible for superior performance. First, within training experiments one could provide non-experts with the knowledge experts possess or train non-experts to accomplish a task in the same way experts do. One would hypothesize that non-experts' performance improves. Second, one could prevent experts from using a specific strategy they typically use. One would hypothesize that experts' performance declines.

Additionally, longitudinal studies would allow more conclusive answers than do existing contrastive and correlational studies. Longitudinal studies are still very rare (for an exception cf., Eteläpelto, 1998), but would be particularly useful when examining the development of expertise. They are necessary for examining how the development of expertise unfolds over time and for testing whether specific learning processes such as deliberate practice have a *causal* effect on excellence. With respect to the development of expertise a number of further research questions needs to be addressed. It is still unanswered whether specific work situations or task assignments help in developing expertise. Additionally, attributions and expectations held by supervisors or peers might also have an effect on expertise development (Eden, 1984).

Recently, several researchers have suggested including motivational and self-regulatory concepts within research on expertise (Ericsson et al., 1993; Richman et al., 1996; Hoffman et al., 1995). However, extensive research is still lacking. One might think of specific motivational orientations as a prerequisite for engaging in extensive learning and practice activities necessary for attaining an excellent performance level (Ericsson et al., 1993). Additionally, within a resource allocation concept (Kanfer & Ackerman, 1989) one can argue that because of their better mastery of cognitive processes, high performers have more resources available for motivational and self-regulatory processes which in turn enhance performance. Furthermore, accomplishing tasks at a high performance level may have positive effects on beneficial self-regulatory mechanisms. For example, high performers' mastery experiences may foster their self-efficacy (Bandura, 1997).

Past expertise research has identified similarities and some differences in knowledge and aspects of work processes between experienced individuals and high performers. Furthermore, length of experience and degree of excellence were found to be—although weakly—correlated. Up to now, the experience and excellence conceptualizations have not been explicitly combined within *one* study. Thus, the relative contribution of experience versus excellence to specific knowledge and task accomplishment variables is still unclear. Future research should examine experience and excellence simultaneously within one study.

In recent years, researchers have increasingly stressed the distinction between routine and adaptive expertise (Gott, Parker Hall, Pokorny, Dibble & Glaser, 1993; Hesketh, 1997; Smith, Ford & Kozlowski, 1997). Routine expertise refers to a high level of fast, accurate, and automatic performance in the face of well-known tasks while adaptive expertise is characterized by flexibility and adaptability to new problems, including the invention of new procedures (Hatano & Inagaki, 1986). Thus, adaptive expertise can be conceptualized as high performance in novel and not completely predictable situations (Sloboda, 1991). It is assumed that a deep and principle-based understanding of the domain and the task is the essential prerequisite for adaptive expertise (Gott et al., 1993). Empirical research on work-related expertise is just beginning to adopt the notion of adaptive expertise (Kozlowski, Toney, Weissbein, Mullins & Brown, 1998).

One can expect that the distinction between routine and adaptive expertise will become increasingly relevant. Since work requirements are permanently changing and new tasks continuously emerge (Frese, 1997; Lawler, 1994), in today's and future work settings adaptive expertise will become more and more important.

## References

Ackerman, P. L. & Humphreys, L. G. (1990). Individual differences theory in industrial and organizational psychology. In M. D. Dunnett & L. M. Hough (Eds), *Handbook of Industrial and Organizational Psychology*, Vol. 1 (pp. 223–282). Palo Alto, CA: Consulting Psychologists Press.

Adelson, B. (1981). Problem solving and the development of abstract categories in programming languages. *Memory & Cognition*, **9**, 422–433.

Adelson, B. & Soloway, E. (1988). A model of software design. In M. T. H. Chi, R. Glaser & M. J. Farr (Eds), *The Nature of Expertise* (pp. 185–208). Hillsdale, NJ: Erlbaum.

Ashford, S. J. & Cummings, L. L. (1983). Feedback as an individual resource: Personal strategies of creating information. *Organizational Behavior and Human Performance*, **32**, 370–398.

Bandura, A. (1997). *Self-efficacy: The Exercise of Control*. San Francisco: Freeman.

Batra, D. & Davis, J. G. (1992). Conceptual data modelling in database design: Similarities and differences between expert and novice designers. *International Journal of Man–Machine Studies*, **37**, 83–101.

Bédard, J. & Mock, T. J. (1992). Expert and novice problem-solving behavior in audit planning. *Auditing: A Journal of Practice and Theory*, **11** (Suppl.), 1–20.

Benner, P. (1984). *From Novice to Expert: Excellence and Power in Clinical Nursing Practice*. London: Addison-Wesley.

Berlin, L. M. (1993). Beyond program understanding: A look at programming expertise in industry. In C. R. Cook, J. C. Scholz & J. C. Spohrer (Eds), *Empirical Studies of Programmers: Fifth Workshop* (pp. 6–25). Norwood, NJ: Ablex.

Boshuizen, H. P. A. & Schmidt, H. G. (1992). On the role of biomedical knowledge in clinical reasoning by experts, intermediates and novices. *Cognitive Science*, **16**, 153–184.

Bryson, M., Bereiter, C., Scardamalia, M. & Joram, E. (1991). Going beyond the problem as given: Problem solving in expert and novice writers. In R. J. Sternberg & P. A. Frensch (Eds), *Complex Problem Solving: Principles and Mechanisms* (pp. 61–84). Hillsdale, NJ: Erlbaum.

Campbell, J. P., McCloy, R. A., Oppler, S. H. & Sager, C. E. (1993). A theory of performance. In E. Schmitt, W. C. Borman & Associates (Eds), *Personnel Selection in Organizations* (pp. 35–70). San Francisco: Jossey-Bass.

Carver, C. S. & Scheier, M. F. (1982). Control theory: A useful conceptual framework for personality—social, clinical, and health psychology. *Psychological Bulletin*, **92**, 111–135.

Charness, N., Krampe, R. & Mayr, U. (1996). The role of practice and coaching in entrepreneurial skill domains: An international comparison of life-span chess skill acquisition. In K. A. Ericsson (Ed.), *The Road to Excellence: The Acquisition of Expert Performance in the Arts and Sciences, Sports and Games* (pp. 51–80), Mahwah, NJ: Erlbaum.

Chase, W. G. & Simon, H. A. (1973). The mind's eye in chess. In W. G. Chase (Ed.), *Visual Information Processing* (pp. 215–281). New York: Academic Press.

Chi, M. T. H., de Leeuw, N., Chiu, M.-H. & LaVancher, C. (1994). Eliciting self-explanations improves understanding. *Cognitive Science*, **18**, 439–477.

Chi, M. T. H., Glaser, R. & Farr, M. J. (Eds) (1988). *The Nature of Expertise*. Hillsdale, NJ: Erlbaum.

Chi, M. T. H., Glaser, R. & Rees, E. (1982). Expertise in problem solving. In R. J. Sternberg (Ed.), *Advances in the Psychology of Human Intelligence* (pp. 7–75). Hillsdale, NJ: Erlbaum.

Cooke, N. J. (1994). Varieties of knowledge elicitation techniques. *International Journal of Human–Computer Studies*, **41**, 801–849.

Crandall, B. & Getchell-Reiter, K. (1993). Critical decision method: A technique for eliciting concrete assessment indicators from the intuition of NICY nurses. *Advances in Nursing Science*, **16**, 42–51.

Curtis, B., Krasner, H. & Iscoe, N. (1988). A field study of the software design process for large systems. *Communications of the ACM*, **31**, 1268–1287.

Dörner, D. & Schölkopf, J. (1991). Controlling complex systems; or expertise as 'grandmother's know-how'. In K. A. Ericsson & J. Smith (Eds), *Toward a General Theory of Expertise: Prospects and Limits* (pp. 218–239). Cambridge: Cambridge University Press.

Dweck, C. S. & Leggett, E. L. (1988). A social-cognitive approach to motivation and personality. *Psychological Review*, **95**, 256–273.

Dylla, N. (1990). Denk- und Handlungsabläufe beim Konstruieren. Unpublished Dissertation, Technische Univeristät München. Fakultät für Maschinenwesen.

Earley, P. C., Wojnaroski, P. & Prest, W. (1987). Task planning and energy expended: Exploration of how goals influence performance. *Journal of Applied Psychology*, 72, 107–114.

Eden, D. (1984). Self-fulfilling prophecy as a management tool: Harnessing Pygmalion. *Academy of Management Review*, 9, 64–73.

Elstein, A. S., Shulman, L. S. & Sprafka, S. A. (1978). *Medical Problem Solving: An Analysis of Clinical Reasoning.* Cambridge, MA: Harvard University Press.

Ericsson, K. A. & Charness, N. (1994). Expert performance: Its structure and acquisition. *American Psychologist*, 49, 725–747.

Ericsson, K. A., Krampe, R. T. & Tesch-Römer, C. (1993). The role of deliberate practice in the acquisition of expert performance. *Psychological Review*, 100, 363–406.

Ericsson, K. A. & Lehmann, A. C. (1996). Expert and exceptional performance: Evidence of maximal adaptation to task constraints. *Annual Review of Psychology*, 47, 273–305.

Ericsson, K. A. & Simon, H. A. (1993). *Protocol Analysis. Verbal Reports as Data*, Revd edn. Cambridge, MA: Massachusetts Institute of Technology.

Ericsson, K. A. & Smith, J. (1991). Prospects and limits of the empirical study of expertise: An introduction. In K. A. Ericsson & J. Smith (Eds), *Toward a General Theory of Expertise: Prospects and Limits* (pp. 1–38). Cambridge: Cambridge University Press.

Eteläpelto, A. (1993). Metacognition and the expertise of computer program comprehension. *Scandinavian Journal of Educational Research*, 37, 243–254.

Eteläpelto, A. (1998). The development of expertise in information systems design. Unpublished Dissertation, University of Jyväskylä, Jyväskylä.

Flanagan, J. C. (1954). The critical incident technique. *Psychological Bulletin*, 85, 327–358.

Ford, J. K. & Kraiger, K. (1995). The application of cognitive constructs and principles to the instructional systems model of training: Implications for needs assessment, design, and transfer. In C. L. Cooper & I. T. Robertson (Eds), *International Review of Industrial and Organizational Psychology*, Vol. 10 (pp. 1–48). Chichester: Wiley.

Frensch, P. A. & Sternberg, R. J. (1989). Expertise and intelligent thinking: When is it worse to know better? In R. J. Sternberg (Ed.), *Advances in the Psychology of Human Intelligence*, Vol. 5 (pp. 157–188). Hillsdale, NJ: Erlbaum.

Frese, M. (1997). Dynamic self-reliance: An important concept for work in the twenty-first century. In C. L. Cooper & S. E. Jackson (Eds), *Creating Tomorrow's Organizations: A Handbook for Future Research in Organizational Behavior* (pp. 399–416). Chichester: Wiley.

Frese, M., van Gelderen, M. & Ombach, M. (1998). How to plan as a small scale business owner: Psychological process characteristics of action strategies and success. Amsterdam: University of Amsterdam.

Frese, M. & Zapf, D. (1994). Action as the core of work psychology: A German approach. In H. C. Triandis, M. D. Dunnette & L. M. Hough (Eds), *Handbook of Industrial and Organizational Psychology*, Vol. 4 (pp. 271–340). Palo Alto, CA: Consulting Psychologists Press.

Gott, S. P., Parker Hall, E., Pokorny, R. A., Dibble, E. & Glaser, R. (1993). A naturalistic study of transfer: Adaptive expertise in technical domains. In D. K. Detterman & R. J. Sternberg (Eds), *Transfer on Trial: Intelligence, Cognition, and Instruction* (pp. 258–288). Norwood, NJ: Ablex.

Green, A. J. K. & Gilhooly, K. J. (1992). Empirical advances in expertise research. In M. T. Keane & K. J. Gilhooly (Eds), *Advances in the Psychology of Thinking*, Vol. 1 (pp. 45–70). New York: Harvester Wheatsheaf.

Groot, A. D. d. (1978). *Thought and Choice in Chess*, 2nd edn. The Hague: Mouton.
Guindon, R. (1990). Designing the design process: Exploiting opportunistic thoughts. *Human–Computer Interaction*, **5**, 305–344.
Hacker, W. (1992). *Expertenkönnen: Erkennen und Vermitteln.* Göttingen: Verlag für Angewandte Psychologie.
Hacker, W. (1998). *Allgemeine Arbeitspsychologie: Psychische Regulation von Arbeitstätigkeiten.* Bern: Huber.
Hacker, W., Rühle, R. & Schneider, N. (1976). Psychologische Grundlagen von Arbeitsverfahren. *Sozialistische Arbeitswissenschaft*, **20**, 428–437.
Hacker, W. & Vaic, H. (1973). Psychologische Analyse interindividueller Leistungsdifferenzen als eine Grundlage von Rationalisierungsbeiträgen. In W. Hacker, W. Quaas, H. Raum & H.-J. Schulz (Eds), *Psychologische Arbeitsuntersuchung* (pp. 109–131). Berlin: Deutscher Verlag der Wissenschaften.
Harris, M. M. & Schaubroeck, J. (1988). A meta-analysis of self-supervisor, self-peer, and peer-supervisor ratings. *Personnel Psychology*, **41**, 43–62.
Hatano, G. & Inagaki, K. (1986). Two courses of expertise. In H. Stevenson, H. Azuma & K. Hakuta (Eds), *Child Development and Education in Japan* (pp. 262–272). San Francisco: Freeman.
Hershey, D. A., Walsh, D. A., Read, S. J. & Chulef, A. S. (1990). The effects of expertise on financial problem solving: Evidence for goal-directed, problem-solving scripts. *Organizational Behavior and Human Decision Processes*, **46**, 77–101.
Hesketh, B. (1997). Dilemmas in training for transfer and retention. *Applied Psychology: An International Review*, **46**, 317–386.
Hoffman, R. R., Crandall, B., & Shadbolt, N. (1998). Use of the critical decision method to elicit expert knowledge: A case study in the methodology of cognitive task analysis. *Human Factors*, **40**, 254–276.
Hoffman, R. R., Feltovich, P. J. & Ford, K. M. (1997). A general framework for conceiving of expertise and expert systems in context. In P. J. Feltovich, K. M. Ford & R. R. Hoffman (Eds), *Expertise in Context: Human and Machine* (pp. 543–580). Menlo Park, CA: AAAI Press.
Hoffman, R. R., Shadbolt, N. R., Burtin, A. M. & Klein, G. (1995). Eliciting knowledge from experts: A methodological analysis. *Organizational Behavior and Human Decision Processes*, **62**, 129–158.
Isenberg, D. J. (1986). Thinking and managing: A verbal protocol analysis of managerial problem solving. *Academy of Management Journal*, **29**, 775–788.
Jansen, P. & Stoop, B. (1997). Wat effectieve managers werkelijk doen. Uitkomsten von zelfbeschrijvingen en observatie-onderzoek [What effective managers really do. Results from self-reports and observations]. *Gedrag en Organisatie*, **10**, 78–94.
Jeffries, R., Turner, A. A., Polson, P. G. & Atwood, M. E. (1981). The processes involved in designing software. In J. R. Anderson (Ed.), *Cognitive Skills and their Acquisition* (pp. 255–283). Hillsdale, NJ: Erlbaum.
Kanfer, R. & Ackerman, P. L. (1989). Motivation and cognitive abilities: An integrative/aptitude–treatment interaction approach to skill acquisition. *Journal of Applied Psychology*, **74**, 657–690.
Kelley, R. E. (1998). *How to be a Star at Work: Nine Breakthrough Strategies You Need to Succeed.* New York: Times Books.
Kirschenbaum, S. S. (1992). Influence of experience on information-gathering strategies. *Journal of Applied Psychology*, **77**, 343–352.
Klemp, G. O. & McClelland, D. C. (1986). What characterizes intelligent functioning among senior managers? In R. J. Sternberg & R. K. Wagner (Eds), *Practical Intelligence: Nature and Origin of Competence in the Everyday World* (pp. 31–50). Cambridge: Cambridge University Press.
Koubek, R. J. & Salvendy, G. (1991). Cognitive performance of super-experts on computer program modification tasks. *Ergonomics*, **34**, 1095–1112.

Kozlowski, S. W. J., Toney, R. J., Weissbein, D. A., Mullins, M. E. & Brown, K. G. (1998). Developing adaptive expertise. Paper presented at the Fourth Conference on Naturalistic Decision Making, Warrenton, VA.

Krampe, R. T. & Ericsson, K. A. (1996). Maintaining excellence: Deliberate practice and elite performance in young and older pianists. *Journal of Experimental Psychology: General*, **125**, 331–359.

Lange, I. (1996). Die Rolle von sozialen Kompetenzen bei herausragender Leistung in Ingenieurberufen. Unpublished Diploma Thesis, University of Giessen, Giessen, Germany.

Lawler, E. E. (1994). From job-based to competency-based organizations. *Journal of Organizational Behavior*, **15**, 3–15.

Leithwood, K. & Steinbach, R. (1995). *Expert Problem Solving: Evidence from School and District Leaders*. Albany, NY: State University of New York Press.

Lesgold, A., Rubinson, H., Feltovich, P., Glasser, R., Klopfer, D. & Wang, Y. (1988). Expertise in a complex skill: Diagnosing X-ray pictures. In M. T. H. Chi, R. Glaser & M. J. Farr (Eds), *The Nature of Expertise* (pp. 311–342). Hillsdale, NJ: Erlbaum.

Lipshitz, R. & Ben Shaul, O. (1997). Schemata and mental models in recognitions—primed decision making. In C. E. Zsambok & G. Klein (Eds), *Naturalistic Decision Making* (pp. 293–303). Mahwah, NJ: Erlbaum.

Lurigio, A. J. & Carroll, J. S. (1985). Probation officers' schemata of offenders: Content, development, and impact on treatment decisions. *Journal of Personality and Social Psychology*, **48**, 1112–1126.

Luthans, F., Rosenkrantz, S. A. & Hennessey, H. W. (1985). What do successful managers really do? An observation study of managerial activities. *Journal of Applied Behavioral Science*, **21**, 255–270.

Marchant, G., Robinson, J., Anderson, U. & Schadewald, M. (1991). Analogical transfer and expertise in legal reasoning. *Organizational Behavior and Human Decision Processes*, **48**, 272–290.

McDaniel, M. A., Schmidt, F. L. & Hunter, J. E. (1988). Job experience correlates of job performance. *Journal of Applied Psychology*, **73**, 327–330.

McKeithen, K. B., Reitman, J. S., Rueter, H. H. Hirtle, S. C. (1981). Knowledge organization and skill differences in computer programmers. *Cognitive Psychology*, **13**, 307–325.

Morrison, E. W. & Cummings, L. L. (1992). The impact of feedback diagnosticity and performance expectations on feedback seeking behavior. *Human Performance*, **5**, 251–264.

Nisbett, R. E. & Wilson, T. D. (1977). Telling more than we can know: Verbal reports on mental processes. *Psychological Review*, **84**, 231–259.

Northcraft, G. B. & Ashford, S. J. (1990). The preservation of self in everyday life: The effects of performance expectations and feedback context in feedback inquiry. *Organizational Behavior and Human Decision Processes*, **47**, 42–64.

Norton, S. M. (1992). Peer assessments of performance and ability: An exploratory meta-analysis of statistical artefacts and contextual moderators. *Journal of Businesses and Psychology*, **6**, 387–399.

O'Reilly, C. A. & Chatman, J. A. (1994). Working smarter and harder: A longitudinal study of managerial success. *Administrative Science Quarterly*, **39**, 603–627.

Olson, J. R. & Biolsi, K. J. (1991). Techniques for representing expert knowledge. In K. A. Ericsson & J. Smith (Eds), *Toward a General Theory of Expertise: Prospects and Limits* (pp. 240–285). Cambridge: Cambridge University Press.

Patel, V. L. & Groen, G. J. (1991). The general and specific nature of medical expertise: A critical look. In K. A. Ericsson & J. Smith (Eds), *Toward a General Theory of Expertise* (pp. 93–125). Cambridge: Cambridge University Press.

Patel, V. L., Kaufman, D. R. & Magder, S. A. (1996). The acquisition of medical expertise in complex dynamic environments. In K. A. Ericsson (Ed.), *The Road to*

*Excellence. The Acquisition of Expert Performance in the Arts and Sciences, Sports and Games* (pp. 127–165). Mahwah, NJ: Erlbaum.

Pennington, N. (1987). Comprehension strategies in programming. In G. M. Olson, S. Sheppard & E. Soloway (Eds), *Empirical Studies of Programmers: Second Workshop* (pp. 100–113). Norwood, NJ: Ablex.

Peters, T. & Waterman, R. (1982). *In Search of Excellence: Lessons from America's Best-Run Companies.* New York: Warner.

Quiñones, M. A., Ford, J. K. & Teachout, M. S. (1995). The relationship between work experience and job performance: A conceptual and meta-analytic review. *Personnel Psychology*, **48**, 887–910.

Rauch, A. & Frese, M. (in press). A contingency approach to small scale business success: A longitudinal study on the effects of environmental hostility and uncertainty on the relationship of planning and success. *Frontiers of Entrepreneurship Research.*

Reed, N. E. & Johnson, P. E. (1993). Analysis of expert reasoning in hardware diagnosis. *Journal of Man–Machine Studies*, **38**, 251–280.

Reif, F. & Allen, S. (1990). Cognition for interpreting scientific concepts: A study of acceleration. *Cognition and Instruction*, **9**, 1–44.

Richman, H. B., Gobet, F., Staszewski, J. J. & Simon, H. A. (1996). Perceptual and memory processes in the acquisition of expert performance: The EPAM model. In K. A. Ericsson (Ed.), *The Road to Excellence: The Acquisition of Expert Performance in the Arts and Sciences, Sports and Games* (pp. 167–187). Mahway, NJ: Erlbaum.

Riedl, T. R., Weitzenfeld, J. S., Freeman, J. T., Klein, G. A. & Musa, J. (1991). What we have learned about software engineering expertise. *Proceedings of the Fifth Software Engineering Institute Conference on Software Engineering Education* (pp. 261–270). New York: Springer.

Salthouse, T. A. (1991). Expertise as the circumvention of human processing limitations. In K. A. Ericsson & J. Smith (Eds), *Prospects and Limits of the Empirical Study of Expertise: An Introduction* (pp. 286–300). Cambridge: Cambridge University Press.

Schaper, N. & Sonntag, K. (1998). Analysis and training of diagnostic expertise in complex technical domains. *European Journal of Work and Organizational Psychology*, **7**, 479–499.

Schaub, H. & Strohschneider, S. (1992). Die Auswirkungen unterschiedlicher Problemlöseerfahrung mit einem unbekannten komplexen Problem. *Zeitschrift für Arbeits- und Organisationspsychologie*, **36**, 117–126.

Schenk, K. D., Vitalari, N. P. & Davis, K. S. (1998). Differences between novice and expert system analysts: What do we know and what do we do? *Journal of Management Information Systems*, **15**, 9–50.

Schmidt, H. G. & Boshuizen, H. P. A. (1993). On the origin of intermediate effects in clinical case recall. *Memory & Cognition*, **21**, 388–351.

Schmitt, N., Pulakos, E. D., Nason, E. & Whitney, D. J. (1996). Likability and similarity as potential sources of predictor-related criterion bias in validation research. *Organizational Behavior and Human Decision Processes*, **68**, 272–286.

Schoenfeld, A. H. & Herrmann, D. J. (1982). Problem perception and knowledge structure in expert and novice mathematical problem solvers. *Journal of Experimental Psychology: Learning, Memory and Cognition*, **8**, 484–494.

Shaft, T. M. & Vessey, I. (1998). The relevance of application domain knowledge: Characterizing the computer program comprehension process. *Journal of Management Information Systems*, **15**, 51–78.

Shanteau, J. (1988). Psychological characteristics and strategies of expert decision makers. *Acta Psychologica*, **68**, 203–215.

Shanteau, J. (1992). Competence in experts: The role of task characteristics. *Organizational Behavior and Human Decision Processes*, **53**, 252–266.

Simmons, P. E. & Lunetta, V. N. (1993). Problem-solving behaviors during a genetics computer simulation: Beyond the expert/novice dichotomy. *Journal of Research in Science Teaching*, **30**, 153–173.

Simpson, S. A. & Gilhooly, K. J. (1997). Diagnostic thinking processes: Evidence from a constructive interaction study of electrocardiogram (ECG) interpretation. *Applied Cognitive Psychology*, **11**, 543–554.

Sloboda, J. (1991). Musical expertise. In K. A. Ericsson & J. Smith (Eds), *Towards a General Theory of Expertise* (pp. 153–171). Cambridge: Cambridge University Press.

Smith, E. M., Ford, J. K. & Kozlowski, S. W. J. (1997). Building adaptive expertise: Implications for training design strategies. In M. A. Quiñones & A. Ehrenstein (Eds), *Training for a Rapidly Changing Workplace: Applications of Psychological Research* (pp. 89–118). Washington, DC: American Psychological Association.

Smith, M. U. & Good, R. (1984). Problem solving and classical genetics: Successful versus unsuccessful performance. *Journal of Research in Science Teaching*, **21**, 895–912.

Soloway, E., Adelson, B. & Ehrlich, K. (1988). Knowledge and processes in the comprehension of computer programs. In M. T. H. Chi, R. Glaser & M. J. Farr (Eds), *The Nature of Expertise* (pp. 129–152). Hillsdale, NJ: Erlbaum.

Sonnentag, S. (1995). Excellent software professionals: Experience, work activities, and perceptions by peers. *Behaviour & Information Technology*, **14**, 289–299.

Sonnentag, S. (1998a). Expertise in professional software design: A process study. *Journal of Applied Psychology*, **83**, 703–715.

Sonnentag, S. (1998b). Identifying high performers: Do peer nominations suffer from a likability bias? *European Journal of Work and Organizational Psychology*, **7**, 501–515.

Sonnentag, S. (1999). High performance and meeting participation. Results from case studies in software design teams. Amsterdam: University of Amsterdam.

Sonnentag, S., de Gilder, D. & Winkelman, E. (1999). Excellent performers' involvement in helping and feedback behavior. Amsterdam: University of Amsterdam.

Sonnentag, S. & Kleine, B. M. (in press). Deliberate practice at work: A study with insurance agents. *Journal of Occupational and Organizational Psychology*.

Sonnentag, S. & Lange, I. (1999). No lonely heroes: High performers' approaches to cooperation situations. Paper presented at the Academy of Management Annual Conference, August 6–11, 1999, Chicago, IL.

Speelman, C. (1998). Implicit expertise: Do we expect too much from our experts? In K. Kirsner, C. Speelman, M. Maybery, A. O'Brien-Malone, M. Anderson & C. MacLeod (Eds), *Implicit and Explicit Mental Processes* (pp. 135–147). Mahwah, NJ: Erlbaum.

Stanislaw, H., Hesketh, B., Kanavaros, S., Hesketh, T. & Robinson, K. (1994). A note on the quantification of computer programming skill. *International Journal of Human–Computer Studies*, **41**, 351–362.

Starkes, J. L., Deakin, J. M., Allard, F., Hodges, N. & Hayes, A. (1996). Deliberate practice in sports: What is it anyway? In K. A. Ericsson (Ed.), *The Road to Excellence: The Acquisition of Expert Performance in the Arts and Sciences, Sports and Games* (pp. 81–106). Mahwah, NJ: Erlbaum.

Stein, E. W. (1995). Social and individual characteristics of organizational experts. *International Journal of Expert Systems*, **8**, 121–143.

Sternberg, R. J. (1996). Costs of expertise. In K. A. Ericsson (Ed.), *The Road to Excellence: The Acquisition of Expert Performance in the Arts and Sciences, Sports and Games* (pp. 347–354). Mahwah, NJ: Erlbaum.

Stokes, A., F., Kemper, K. & Kite, K. (1997). Aeronautical decision making, cue recognition, and expertise under time pressure. In C. E. Zsambok & G. Klein (Eds), *Naturalistic Decision Making* (pp. 183–196). Mahwah, NJ: Erlbaum.

Sujan, H., Sujan, M. & Bettman, J. R. (1988). Knowledge structure differences between more effective and less effective salespeople. *Journal of Marketing Research*, **25**, 81–86.

Sujan, H., Weitz, B. A. & Kumar, N. (1994). Learning orientation, working smart, and effective selling. *Journal of Marketing*, **58**, 39–52.

Sutcliffe, A. & Maiden, N. (1991). Analogical software reuse. *Acta Psychologica*, **78**, 173–197.

Tesluk, P. E. & Jacobs, R. R. (1998). Towards an integrated model of work experience. *Personnel Psychology*, **51**, 321–355.

Tripoli, A. M. (1998). Planning and allocating: Strategies for managing priorities in complex jobs. *European Journal of Work and Organizational Psychology*, **7**, 455–476.

Turley, R. T. & Bieman, J. M. (1995). Competencies of exceptional and nonexceptional software engineers. *Journal of Systems and Software*, **28**, 19–38.

Tynjälä, P., Nuutinen, A., Eteläpelto, A., Kirjonen, J. & Remes, P. (1997). The acquisition of professional expertise—a challenge for educational research. *Scandinavian Journal of Educational Research*, **41**, 475–494.

van Gelderen, M. & Frese, M. (1998). Strategy process as a characteristic of small scale business owners: Relationships with success in a longitudinal study. Amsterdam: University of Amsterdam.

Vessey, I. (1986). Expertise in debugging computer programs: An analysis of the content of verbal protocols. *IEEE Transactions on Systems, Man, and Cybernetics*, **16**, 621–637.

Vitalari, N. P. & Dickson, G. W (1983). Problem solving for effective systems analysis: An experimental exploration. *Communications of the ACM*, **26**, 948–956.

Voss, J. F., Fincher-Kiefer, R. H., Greene, T. R. & Post, T. A. (1986). Individual differences in performance: The contrastive approach to knowledge. In R. J. Sternberg (Ed.), *Advances in the Psychology of Human Intelligence*, Vol. 3 (pp. 297–334). Hillsdale, NJ: Erlbaum.

Voss, J. F., Greene, T. R., Post, T. A. & Penner, B. C. (1983). Problem-solving skill in the social sciences. In G. J. Bower (Ed.), *The Psychology of Learning and Motivation. Advances in Research and Theory*, Vol. 17 (pp. 165–213). New York: Academic Press.

Voss, J. F., Wolfe, C. R., Lawrence, J. A. & Engle, R. A. (1991). From representation to decision: An analysis of problem solving in international relations. In R. J. Sternberg & P. A. Frensch (Eds), *Complex Problem Solving: Principles and Mechanisms* (pp. 119–158). Hillsdale, NJ: Erlbaum.

Wagner, R. K. (1987). Tacit knowledge in everyday intelligent behavior. *Journal of Personality and Social Psychology*, **52**, 1236–1247.

Wagner, R. K. & Sternberg, R. J. (1985). Practical intelligence in real-world pursuits: The role of tacit knowledge. *Journal of Personality and Social Psychology*, **49**, 436–458.

Wiedemann, J. (1995). *Ermittlung von Qualifizierungsbedarf—am Beispiel der Störungsdiagnose in der flexiblen Fertigung*. Münster: Waxmann,.

Wiedenbeck, S., Fix, V. & Scholz, J. (1993). Characteristics of the mental representations of novice and expert programmers: An empirical study. *International Journal of Human–Computer Studies*, **39**, 793–812.

Wiggins, M. & O'Hare, D. (1995). Expertise in aeronautical weather-related decision making: A cross-sectional analysis of general aviation pilots. *Journal of Experimental Psychology: Applied*, **1**, 305–320.

# Chapter 8

# A RICH AND RIGOROUS EXAMINATION OF APPLIED BEHAVIOR ANALYSIS RESEARCH IN THE WORLD OF WORK

Judith L. Komaki, Timothy Coombs, Thomas P. Redding, Jr, and Stephen Schepman
*Baruch College, NY*

Three decades ago, at what many consider the height of American liberalism (Geoghegan, 1999), a motivational theory with a distinctly pro-social emphasis emerged in the field of psychology. Termed operant conditioning (Skinner, 1974), this theory is based upon the idea that when consequences—such as feedback and recognition—are judiciously rearranged so that they follow what is desired, dramatic improvements can and do occur in people's lives. A stream of studies geared toward examining the application of operant conditioning, or what is referred to as applied behavior analysis (ABA), appeared in the mid-1960s: Children previously viewed as 'autistic' and destined to spend the remainder of their lives institutionalized began to communicate and to help themselves when they were reinforced for successive approximations to desired behaviors (Lovaas, 1966), and first-graders in a ghetto neighborhood learned skills critical to further achievement following a combination reinforcement and extinction program of 'rules, praise, and ignore' (Becker, Madsen, Arnold & Thomas, 1967).

Shortly thereafter, operant researchers began to expand their reach. From the clients of organizations—students and patients, they began working with the members of organizations—mental health staff (Ayllon & Azrin, 1968; Panyon, Boozer & Morris, 1970) and teachers (Cooper, Thomson & Baer, 1970). Even army recruits in boot camp at Fort Ord served as subjects; a token economy program not only maintained the morale of the recruits, but it also met the rigorous standards of their superiors (Datel & Legters, 1971). The same positive reinforcement principle was applied in the private sector: when dock workers at Emery Air Freight were recognized for their efforts and received feedback, they worked more efficiently ('Where Skinner's theories work,' 1972).

*International Review of Industrial and Organizational Psychology, 2000 Volume 15*
Edited by C.L. Cooper and I.T. Robertson. © 2000 John Wiley & Sons, Ltd

Given these positive indications that the ABA approach works, industrial/organizational (I/O) psychologists began discussing its use as an innovative approach to motivation (Hamner, 1974; Nord, 1969; Porter, 1973; Whyte, 1972). Since then, hundreds of studies have been conducted in work settings and published in I/O (*Journal of Applied Psychology, Organizational Behavior and Human Decision Processes*) and ABA journals (*Journal of Applied Behavior Analysis*), as well as in a journal devoted to behavioral applications in business and industry (*Journal of Organizational Behavior Management*). Numerous reviews of the literature attest to the proliferation of studies conducted using the ABA approach (Balcazar, Shupert, Daniels, Mawhinney & Hopkins, 1989; Frederiksen, 1982; Hopkins & Sears, 1982; Merwin, Thomason & Sanford, 1989; O'Brien, Dickinson & Rosow, 1982; O'Hara, Johnson & Beehr, 1985; Stajkovic & Luthans, 1997).

Thirty years later, however, legitimate questions continue to be raised. Particularly with regard to adults in complex organizations, there is still debate as to whether the ABA approach has lived up to the best of its proponents' visions or the worst of its critics' fears.

In the first section of this chapter, we discuss the ABA approach in terms of its aims, its features, and its applications in work settings. Next, we describe some of the criticisms, which range from the effectiveness to the generality of the ABA approach. Following the criticisms is the review itself, where we report on three decades of studies (all of which are meticulously controlled) that range from the earliest studies done in the late 1960s to the latest appearing in 1998. We end with recommendations for the next millennium.

## APPLIED BEHAVIOR ANALYSIS APPROACH

### Its Aims

Reflecting the 'vigor of John and Robert Kennedy, the righteousness of Martin Luther King Jr. and the freedom riders, the ardor and agony of the Vietnam War protesters and the fervor of the women's rights movement' (Reich, 1999, p. 8) in the late 1960s, ABA researchers hoped to make the world a better place. In fact, the founders of the field—Don Baer, Mont Wolf, and Todd Risley (1968)—heralded 'socially important behaviors, such as mental retardation, crime, mental illness, or education' in the first issue of the *Journal of Applied Behavior Analysis*. They actually went on record and forecast that research in these areas 'may well lead to the widespread examination of these applications, their refinement, and eventually their replacement by better applications. Better applications, it is hoped, will lead to a better state of society' (p. 91).

### Its Features

The ABA approach has three features which distinguish it from other motivation theories: (a) its emphasis on the consequences of performance; (b) its pinpointing and direct sampling of relevant behaviors or outcomes; and (c) its insistence on the evaluation of effectiveness.

### Focus on performance consequences

The consequences of our performance—the feedback we receive, the comments we hear—are thought to have a powerful impact on what we do from day to day. When frequent, positive consequences are made contingent on performance, substantial and meaningful improvements have occurred in literally thousands of experiments conducted at all levels of the phylogenetic scale (Honig, 1966; Ulrich, Stachnik & Mabry, 1966; 1970; 1974). In fact, one of the major tenets of operant conditioning theory is that behavior is a function of its consequences.

The ABA approach is unique in that two of its major concepts are based on the time at which they occur: (a) antecedents such as the providing of training, the setting of goals, and the communication of company policy which typically precede performance and occur *before* the behavior of interest, and (b) consequences such as the providing of feedback, recognition, and incentives which usually follow performance and take place *after* the behavior.

In motivating others, antecedents are secondary to consequences. Although antecedents serve valuable educational or cuing functions in that they clarify expectations for performance, specify the relationship between behavior and its consequences, and/or signal occasions in which consequences are likely to be provided, consequences are considered superior to antecedents in their motivational role. Hence, the mainstay of virtually all ABA interventions is the delivery of one or more different types of consequences.

### Pinpointing and directly measuring germane dependent variables

The second feature concerns the dependent variable, particularly the substance and assessment of the target behaviors or outcomes. Influenced by the field's pro-social bent, ABA researchers do not choose dependent variables that are 'convenient for study,' but instead focus on those that are 'socially important' (Baer, Wolf & Risley, 1968, p. 92) in spite of the fact that these targets may be considerably more difficult to assess (Komaki, 1998a). Hence, rather than assessing nonsense syllables or reaction times or even the amount of time spent interacting, ABA researchers identify what employees actually say and do when interacting with patients or customers.

At the same time, it is critical to directly sample when measuring performance. Rather than relying on reports of safety awareness or workers' scores during safety training, for instance, the practices of workers on the job are assessed directly. Similarly, Baer, Wolf and Risley (1968) attach 'little applied value in the demonstration that an impotent man can be made to say that he no longer is impotent,' preferring that the emphasis should be on 'what subjects can be brought to do rather than what they can be brought to say' (p. 93). In short, when specifying and measuring the dependent variable, the relevancy and the directness of measurement is critical.

### Emphasis on rigorous evaluation

Another noteworthy characteristic of the ABA approach is its emphasis on evidence in the form of empirical data. No number of expert opinions or testimonials can substitute for the collection and presentation of data that a given result actually occurred. In fact, the *Journal of Organizational Behavior Management* was started not by academics, but by members of a behaviorally-based consulting firm called Tarkenton and Associates that was headed up by clinical psychologist Aubrey Daniels and former quarterback Fran Tarkenton.

Besides wanting to know that X actually changed, ABA researchers also want to know if the relationship between X and Y is a result of happenstance, or if Y was truly responsible for X, that is, if a cause and effect relationship actually exists. To make causal conclusions with confidence requires the rigorous evaluation of the effectiveness of programs and the use of an internally valid design. Two families of designs are considered internally valid: (a) the traditional between-group control group designs such as the pretest-posttest control group design (Campbell & Stanley, 1963); and (b) the within-group designs such as the reversal and the multiple-baseline designs (Kazdin, 1998; Komaki & Jensen, 1986).

Within-group designs have the advantage of allowing one to draw cause–effect conclusions with assurance. At the same time, they do not require the random assignment of subjects to either a treatment or a control group. Rarely is it possible in the wrapping and make-up departments of a bakery, for example, to randomly assign workers so that two new groups are formed, one of which is treated and one of which is not treated. With within-group designs, each group serves as its own control. Perhaps not surprisingly, these within-group designs are the designs of choice in most ABA studies.

Hence, the ABA approach differs from other motivational theories in (a) its emphasis on consequences rather than the antecedents of performance as the motivational force; (b) its choice and sampling of socially important targets rather than those that are more convenient for study; and (c) its insistence on determining whether the program or happenstance is responsible for the changes.

## Its Three-step Process

Consistent with the characteristics of the approach, ABA researchers typically implement three steps when trying to improve performance: (a) specifying and measuring desired behaviors; (b) rearranging consequences to ensure that positive, frequent ones are contingent on desired behaviors; and (c) evaluating the effectiveness of the program. To get an idea of how this process usually works, let us take as an example a program that was introduced to two departments of a wholesale bakery (Komaki, Barwick & Scott, 1978). The management at the bakery had become alarmed when the injury rate jumped sharply. In order to encourage employees to maintain safe practices, a positive reinforcement program was introduced that was very different from the usual approach of posting signs and admonishing workers to be careful.

*Step 1: Specify and measure desired behavior*

First, desired work practices were defined. To establish what workers should do to avoid having similar accidents in the future, verbs such as 'turn off' and 'release' (rather than adjectives such as 'careful' and 'conscientious') were encouraged. A list of definitions was generated (e.g. walk around conveyer belt). To ensure that the definitions were objective, each definition had to meet the test of interrater reliability. Furthermore, independent raters had to consistently agree on their recordings and obtain interrater reliability scores of 90% or better before they were considered trained. Trained raters then went to the work site and recorded the percentage of incidents performed in a safe or unsafe manner. They collected data frequently—on the average of four times a week. Furthermore, during the formal data collection period, the raters continued to check their interrater reliability.

*Step 2: Provide frequent, contingent, positive consequences*

The consequence for safe practices was primarily informational. The department's safety scores were presented on a graph, so workers could see at a glance how their group had done and how this compared to their previous record. The graph was posted publicly in the work area, thus fostering a healthy competition between the departments. When workers asked, they were also told what they had done correctly and incorrectly.

*Step 3: Evaluate effectiveness on the job*

To assess whether or not the program was effective, a within-group research design—the multiple-baseline design across groups—was used. The two groups were the wrapping and make-up departments in the bakery. Data were collected in both groups. The program was introduced in a staggered manner: after 5½ weeks in the wrapping department and after 13½ weeks in the make-up department.

As shown in Figure 8.1, employees in the two departments substantially improved their safety performance from 70 and 78% of the time to 96 and 99%, respectively. Within a year, the number of lost-time injuries dropped from 53 to 10. Although this is only one example, it shows the three steps involved in sustaining the motivation of workers.

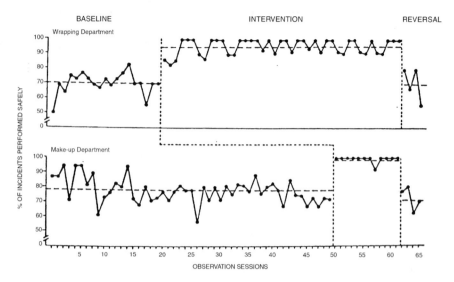

**Figure 8.1**    Graph illustrating the results of a positive reinforcement program
From J.L. Komaki, K.D. Barwick and R. Scott (1978). A behavioral approach to occupational safety: Pinpointing and reinforcing safety performance in a food manufacturing plant. *Journal of Applied Psychology*, **63**, 434–445. © American Psychological Association. Reproduced by permission of the American Psychological Association

## Its Criticism when Used with Working Adults

Despite the impassioned beliefs of ABA researchers that the approach could make a meaningful difference and the generally positive reviews of positive reinforcement in the public and private sectors (Aamodt, 1996; Balcazar et al., 1989; Frederiksen, 1982; Hopkins & Sears, 1982; Komaki, Coombs & Schepman, 1996; Lee & Earley, 1992; Merwin, Thomason & Sanford, 1989; O'Brien, Dickinson & Rosow, 1982; O'Hara, Johnson & Beehr, 1985; Stajkovic & Luthans, 1997), skepticism still lingers particularly when the focus is on working adults.

*Doubts about the effectiveness of the approach*

Even critics acknowledge that the theory of operant conditioning can and does have an impact. They question, however, whether it can be meaningfully applied to working adults. Some of the criticisms go back 20 years: Landy and Trumbo (1980), in their book on the psychology of work behavior, concluded the section on the reinforcement approach by noting: 'While we accept the basic proposition that contingent rewards affect behavior, we are not convinced that the behaviorist model can be usefully applied in any meaningful sense to a wide range of work behavior' (p. 355). Miner (1980), too, in his book on organizational theory, summarized its impact as follows: 'There is good reason to question whether behavior modification theory makes a useful independent contribution' (p. 223).

Seventeen years later, the same complaints are being made. Muchinsky (1997), in comparing reinforcement theory with five other motivational approaches, rated goal-setting and expectancy theories 'strong' in industrial applicability and 'moderate–strong' in empirical support. Reinforcement theory, on the other hand, was rated only 'moderate' in industrial applicability and empirical support (p. 375). (Note: Among the reasons for Muchinsky's lackluster ratings might be his sources of evidence. In his section on 'Empirical Tests of the Theory,' Muchinsky stated that the 'empirical tests of reinforcement theory have involved determining which schedule of reinforcement has the greatest effect on increasing the occurrence of the desired behavioral response' (p. 344); he goes on to identify four studies, none of which were published after 1976 [Pedalino & Gamboa, 1974; Pritchard, Leonard, Von Bergen & Kirk, 1976; Yukl & Latham, 1975; Yukl, Latham & Pursell, 1976].)

## Lack of generality

Another common complaint is the ABA approach's lack of generality or external validity. For example, the ABA approach has been described as being 'extremely controversial when applied to humans—as compared to, say pigeons or other similar lab animals on which the principles were originally developed' (Steers & Porter, 1987, p. 60).

*Confined to workers at lowest levels in highly structured settings.*  A related criticism concerns the applicability of the approach with high level job incumbents and in less structured situations. Miner (1980), for example, reports that 'the most favorable findings for the theory appear to occur in highly controllable contexts such as very small business(es)' (p. 224) and that 'almost all of the research has focused on relatively low level employees rather than on managers or professionals' (p. 224).

*Restricted to narrow range of dependent variables.*  Another concern involves the nature of the tasks. Muchinsky (1997) acknowledged that 'research clearly indicates that the principles of reinforcement theory do "work"' (p. 345). However, he pointed out that the research 'has primarily been limited to studies of quantity of production. We don't know very much about how quality of performance is affected' (p. 345). Miner (1980) went further to state that: 'As research moves to more complex situations involving quantity–quality interactions, interdependent work, and the like, the theory predicts less well, if at all' (p. 224).

I/O psychologists have also raised questions about employees' reactions to reinforcement programs. Muchinsky (1997) reported that few studies have assessed 'people's attitudes toward such incentive methods' (p. 345). The implication is that when workers increase their productivity but suffer a decline in their satisfaction with the work, the ABA approach may be only partially successful. Aamodt (1996) cited two 'incentive' studies which show that 'when designed poorly, they can result in such negative outcomes as increased stress, decreased health, and decreased safety' (p. 460) (Schleifer & Amick, 1989; Schleifer & Okogbaa, 1990). Two other typical incentive plans fared no better: Aamodt (1996) cited further evidence that employees may not be entirely satisfied with pay-for-performance plans (Brown & Huber, 1992) and that research is mixed for merit pay (Gilchrist & White, 1990; Hills, Scott, Markham & Vest, 1987; Wisdom & Patzig, 1987).

*Limited to short duration.*   Lastly, concerns are expressed about the generality of the approach over extended periods of time. Miner (1980) states: 'Yet even when favorable findings do occur and can realistically be attributed to behavior modification procedures, there is reason to believe that the improvements may dissipate over time if the procedures were instituted on a continuing basis' (p. 224).

As we can see, besides questions about effectiveness, concerns have been expressed about the extent to which the approach can be generalized to situations other than the lowest level work populations, the most simple dependent variables, and relatively short time periods.

## Lack of scholarly advancement

Another set of concerns regards its scientific aspects. This time, however, it is consummate insiders who are raising issue about the lack of conceptual progress in advancing the knowledge of theoretical principles and the lack of decision criteria with which to make sound judgments about the success or failure of studies.

*Glacial conceptual progress.*   Founders Baer, Wolf and Risley (1968) expressed hope that the approach would go beyond a bag of tricks and 'strive for relevance to principle' (p. 96). In discussing conceptual systems, they made the point that: 'To describe the exact sequence of color changes whereby a child is moved from a color discrimination to a form discrimination is good; to refer also to 'fading' and "errorless discrimination"' is better' (p. 96). The same can be said for the independent variables used in work settings. To describe feedback in the form of publicly posted graphs as the consequence in an intervention is good; to refer also to the principle of 'positive reinforcement' and its essential characteristics of being response-contingent and involving the presentation, rather than the removal, of a positive reinforcer, is better. Reference to a higher order lifts the discussion of the intervention from idiosyncratic details in a particular experiment to the essential characteristics of the scientific principles.

Apprehensions about the glacial movement of scholarly progress have been expressed by ABA researchers, Hayes, Rincover, and Solnick (1980). They are particularly concerned that the field is 'becoming a more purely technical effort with less interest in conceptual questions.' They point to the following evidence. The empirical studies published in the first 10 years of the *Journal of Applied Behavior Analysis* were divided into three types: (a) technical: studies oriented toward 'how to' questions of applied interest (e.g., how to use police patrols to reduce theft), but with no reference to principles of behavior such as reinforcement or stimulus control; (b) direct application: studies test the generality of known principles with new behaviors, in new settings, or with new populations; and (c) systematic application: studies advancing our basic knowledge of the principles. They found that the majority of studies 'have always been, and continue to be, simple applications, testing the applicability of known behavioral principles' (Hayes et al., 1980, p. 280) with as many of 74% fitting into the classification of direct application. At the same time, the percentage of articles categorized as technical rose dramatically—to a high of 22%—over the 10-year period, whereas studies 'devoted to the development and extension of behavioral principles in applied settings . . . is fast disappearing' (p. 281). Hayes, Rincover and Solnick (1980) muse that 'these trends may indicate a developing polarization in applied behavior analysis between its purely technical and more conceptual aspects' (p. 284).

*Problems interpreting research results when using within-group designs.* Another issue concerns the making of inferences when using within-group designs. Although ABA researchers pride themselves on the internal validity of their preferred within-group designs, they sometimes have difficulty drawing consistent conclusions about the results of studies. Among the problems is that time-series analyses are rarely done and the criteria for a visual inspection, which is commonly done, have not been specified. For example, after reviewing 10 years of studies, three ABA researchers with 30 plus years of experience among them admitted that they 'were not able to measure reliably whether the behavior changes reported in JABA studies were large enough' (Hayes, Rincover, & Solnick, 1980, p. 276).

Not surprisingly, reviews of ABA research follow the same disturbing pattern. That is, they are not able to separate successful from unsuccessful studies. They do not even discuss behavior changes. Instead, the reviewers simply repeat the generally glowing conclusions of the authors, or they leave as vague whether the studies were effective or not. For instance, Merwin, Thomason and Sanford (1989), following the lead of Andrasik (1979), update his review by doing another 'methodological and content' (p. 39) review of 35 experiments published between 1978 and 1986. While they identify for each study the subjects, design, the dependent and independent variables and their reliability, the benefit/cost ratio, and the reactions of on-site personnel, there is little if any mention of any 'data' in the form of improvements in production or safety. Instead, they summarize the so-called reactions or resistance shown by workers and management; in the safety experiment by Komaki, Barwick and Scott (1978) (detailed in Figure 8.1), Merwin, Thomason and Sanford (1989) indicate that 'workers accepted [the] program . . . [but that] managers [were] not accepting of support' (p. 49). Andrasik (1979) went further than listing the designs by identifying whether they met the Systematic Intervention criterion which assessed whether the studies 'were sufficiently well-controlled to support cause and effect interpretations' (p. 59). He even identified whether any follow-up assessments were made, described the intervention, but again there was no mention of the effects. Unless one can definitively determine whether a study does or does not support the principle in question, it is difficult to draw conclusions about either the principle or the approach. Perhaps even more critical, one cannot profit from one's mistakes. Lacking this accumulated knowledge has deleterious implications for the future of the field.

In short, despite the promise of the ABA approach in the heady, idealistic days of the late 1960s, concerns continue to be expressed about (a) its effectiveness as a viable motivational approach with working adults, (b) the generality of the approach; (c) its conceptual advancement; and (d) the bases used in making judgments about effectiveness with within-group designs.

## REVIEW OF THE LITERATURE

In the review, we report on studies that range from the earliest studies done in the late 1960s to the latest appearing in 1998. All were done in the field—with employees in work settings; all were experiments—in which some program was introduced with the aim of enhancing performance; and all were rigorously controlled. In an effort to rule out Terpstra's (1981) 'positive bias' findings in which an inverse relationship exists between the degree of methodological rigor and reported outcome success, only studies considered internally valid were included.

Instead of assuming that all studies addressed the same research question, we examined each study to determine the question that could be answered. The first set of questions asked whether the approach works, what we referred to as program evaluation questions. These studies were subdivided by principles which ranged from the use of positive reinforcement to punishment. An example of a program evaluation question was: Does positive reinforcement work? The second set of questions involved multiple treatments and asked whether one treatment adds to or facilitates another treatment, where contingent pay can be one treatment and full pay the other treatment. Hence, one of the facilitative questions was: Does contingent pay improve performance over and above that of full pay?

Using a specially developed set of decision criteria for the results of within-group designs, we scrutinized each study, examining the data in the graphs to determine whether and at what level support was found for the question.

Quantitative information is provided in one of eight tables for each study. The means (where given) are listed by phase or group so that it is possible to see the magnitude of the changes taking place. Information is also provided about the duration of the intervention phases. Furthermore, the graphs of 11 studies are presented so that it is possible to see whether trends emerge in the data over time as well as the overlap in data points from phase to phase.

Adding to the richness of the information obtained, the review describes each study qualitatively. The subjects and setting, as well as the target behaviors or outcomes, are detailed in the tables. Furthermore, tallies show the relative proportions of studies conducted in the public and private sectors and also indicate whether the targets focus on the negotiation or the execution of tasks.

The present review differs from previous reviews: (a) in breadth—30 years of studies are reviewed; (b) in rigor—only studies meeting strict content and methodological standards are included and an explicit set of decision criteria is used to determine the magnitude of support; and (c) in richness—the studies are presented question-by-question, and for each study, information is presented about the subjects and setting and the dependent variable.

The following sections detail the methods we used in identifying and pruning the studies we used in the review.

## Search Strategy

Pertinent studies were identified in three ways:

1. A computer-based information search was conducted of the PsycLit Psychological Abstracts. The key terms used in the search were behavior modification, behavior analysis, contingency management, self-management, and operant. Because of the widespread use of behavior modification techniques in clinical and educational settings, the computer search was restricted to studies listed: (a) in the Applied Psychology category under the following subcategories—Occupational Attitudes & Interests & Guidance (3610), Personnel Selection & Training (3620), Personnel Evaluation & Performance (3630), Management & Management Training (3640), Organizational Behavior and Job Satisfaction (3650), and Human Factors Engineering (3660); and (b) in the Social Processes and Social Issues under the Social Structure & Social Roles (2910) subcategory. The end point for the search was 1998.

2. The reference lists of pertinent studies and literature reviews were examined.

3. Letters were sent to approximately 50 contributors to the literature. Their assistance was requested in tracking down studies that might be in press or in out-of-the-way venues.

## Standards for Being Included as a Study in the Review

To be included in the review, the study had to meet two standards, one concerning content and the other methodology.

### Appropriate content

For a study to be considered as having the appropriate content; (a) the study had to include an independent variable; (b) the independent variable had to include at least one consequence; (c) the dependent variable had to assess performance at work; and (d) the subjects had to be functioning normally in a setting enabling continuity over time.

*Independent variable.*   Because one of the aims of the review is to determine if the interventions result in improvements, each study had to include at least one intervention or independent variable. Descriptive or correlational studies in which observations were made 'only of what is there without disturbing it' (Runkel & McGrath, 1972, p. 90) were excluded from the review. These studies can be 'a matchless way of learning the variables, their ranges and combinations, but the investigator does not know with high confidence just what he has learned' (Runkel & McGrath, 1972, p. 94). Excluded were studies that: (a) included a dependent variable about performance at work but assessed only individual differences such as personality (McCredie, 1991); (b) those that discussed potentially viable independent variables such as self-provided consequences (Diamante & Giglio, 1991) or interventions in the total quality movement (Mawhinney, 1992; Redmon, 1992), but did not introduce them; and (c) those that measured ongoing rather than manipulated management practices (e.g., Komaki, Desselles & Bowman, 1989; Podsakoff, Todor, Grover & Huber, 1984).

*At least one consequence.*   The major tenet of operant conditioning theory is that behavior is a function of its consequences, hence each study had to include an independent variable with at least one consequence. The consequences could be (but were not limited to those that were): (a) informational, such as feedback; (b) social, such as praise and recognition; (c) activity, such as the opportunity to sell renewal contracts following the selling of a new contract; or (d) they could be a combination of one or more types. The consequence(s) could be delivered: (a) by the persons themselves, such as when self-praise was used; or (b) by someone else, such as the boss.

Although the independent variable had to include at least one consequence, it could include components other than consequences. A common intervention was one which combines a consequence such as feedback and an antecedent such as rules and reminders. Excluded were programs consisting of only antecedents (e.g., introducing only an antecedent such as training, Briscoe, Hoffman & Bailey, 1975; or using only antecedents such as modeling, cognitive restructuring, reframing, thought stopping, and relaxation, Webb, 1991).

*A dependent variable about performance at work.* Given the fact that one of the aims of the review is to see whether the approach can be applied to tasks conducted in work settings, the dependent variable had to possess two critical attributes: (a) employees in the studies had to be accountable for performing the tasks; and (b) superiors of these employees had to be likely to take corrective actions should problems persist. The following dependent variables were generally considered work-related: attendance, punctuality, productivity, service as it related to customers or clients or patients, sales, occupational safety, and supervision.

Dependent variables involving smoking, drugs, stress, burnout, job searches, and aerobic exercise were not included. The reasons were twofold: workers in these studies were not considered directly responsible, and they would probably not be reprimanded by their superiors when they maintained their baseline rate of performance. Management personnel, for example, might encourage workers to curb their smoking and to increase their exercising, but they would generally not require them to do so. Along the same lines, seat-belt usage (Rudd & Geller, 1985) was not included when it referred to workers driving to and from work, as opposed to when it related to their usage on the job. Attitudes toward the job, while acknowledged as critical to a full definition of productive, satisfied workers, were also excluded if the attitudinal measure was the only dependent variable, or if it was not accompanied by a measure of performance (e.g., Schay, 1988). In short, at least one dependent variable had to assess performance at work.

*Normally functioning subjects in an ongoing setting.* Because the review focuses on working adults, studies were limited to those with subjects considered to be functioning normally. Excluded were studies of adults who worked, but who were confined as patients to mental health wards (e.g., Ayllon & Azrin, 1968).

The studies in the review were also limited to those settings in which perrsons had some continuity over time, so that the 'relationships have, or quickly acquire, some history and some anticipated future' (McGrath, 1984, p. 8). Excluded were short-term studies conducted in laboratory settings (e.g., Cherrington, Reitz & Scott, 1971; Erez, 1977; Jorgenson, Dunnette & Pritchard, 1973) or simulations (e.g., Garson & Stanwyck, 1997), with their 'ad hoc groups which are convened for such a short time that the group does not have a chance to develop its own history or its own unique normative structure' (Hackman & Morris, 1975, p. 59).

*Methodologically rigorous*

Methodologically, the research design used in the study had to be internally valid. Either of two major design types qualified as being internally valid: (a) the between-group design; and (b) the within-group design, specifically the reversal or multiple-baseline design across individuals, groups, behaviors, or settings.

*Internally valid designs making comparisons between groups.*   Studies with a pretest-posttest control group design, a posttest only design, or a Solomon four-group design were acceptable (Campbell & Stanley, 1963). Excluded were one-shot case studies that simply reported increases following the program (e.g., Datel & Legters, 1971). Also excluded were nonequivalent control group designs in which comparisons were made between intact groups (such as Siero, Boon, Kok and Siero's 1989 study using groups of employees who were in two postal districts) but were not randomly assigned to one of the groups).

*Internally valid designs making comparisons within groups.*   Both the reversal and the multiple-baseline designs were acceptable; however, they differ in important ways from one another. Because they are less commonly known than the traditional control group design, their characteristics and rationale are briefly detailed.

   *Reversal design.* A study with a reversal design has at least three phases: (1) the baseline phase in which data are collected before the intervention; (2) the intervention phase during which the treatment is introduced; and (3) the reversal phase, which is the essential phase during which the treatment is discontinued.

   A study with an ABA (where A = baseline, B = intervention, and A = return to baseline) reversal design is illustrated in Figure 8.2 (Kortick & O'Brien, 1996). As can be seen, the performance of the workers dramatically improved when the treatment was introduced, *and* declined back to baseline during the reversal phase. As a result, the authors concluded that the treatment was responsible for the improvements. The rationale is as follows: it is not likely that another significant event, referred to as history (Campbell & Stanley, 1963), would occur and fade at precisely the same time as the intervention was introduced and removed. Furthermore, if maturation, another plausible alternative hypothesis, was the primary reason for the changes, then one would expect that performance would gradually change as time passed; it is also unlikely that performance would change directions during the reversal phase. Another source of internal invalidity, statistical regression, was also ruled out. Regression artifacts would be likely to appear in any series of repeated measurements and not just after the introduction and reintroduction of the intervention. Because these plausible alternative hypotheses could be ruled out, it is possible to say with confidence that the intervention was responsible for the improvements.

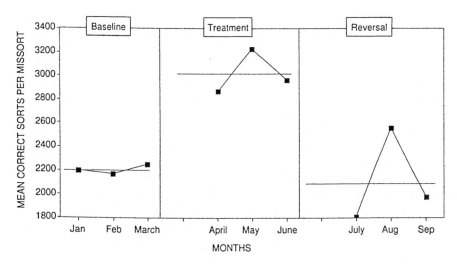

**Figure 8.2**   Graph illustrating the use of a reversal design
Reproduced with permission from S.A. Kortick and R.M. O'Brien (1996). The world
series of quality control: A case study in the package delivery industry. *Journal of
Organizational Behavior Management*, **16**(2), 77–93. © The Haworth Press

The reversal phase is critical. Hence, studies with a baseline and a treatment
phase but no reversal phase were excluded. For example, ABC or ABCD
designs in which two or more different interventions are introduced suc-
cessively after an initial baseline period do not include a reversal phase. Pritchard and his colleagues used an ABCD design in which they introduced
feedback (B) after a nine-month baseline period (A) (Pritchard, Jones, Roth,
Stuebing & Ekberg, 1988). Next, goal setting was added to the feedback (C).
Finally, incentives (D) were added to the goal setting and feedback. Although
they were mainly interested in knowing if 'giving group-based feedback with
the productivity measurement system increase(s) productivity' (p. 341), they
could not answer this question with confidence because of the design they
used. The problem with this design is that there was no reversal phase which
makes it difficult to rule out plausible alternative hypotheses such as history
involving extraneous changes made organization-wide. Even Pritchard et al.
(1988) acknowledged that 'there could have been changes occurring in the
larger organizations of which the five experimental units were a part that were
causing general increases in productivity for all units' (p. 347).

*Multiple-baseline design.* The multiple-baseline design is also an internally
valid design. Fox, Hopkins and Anger (1987) used a multiple-baseline design
to determine if a token economy program was successful in improving safety.
As can be seen in Figure 8.3, the two essential characteristics for the multiple-
baseline design are included: (a) concurrent baselines in which there are two
or more baselines in which data are collected at the same time—data were

collected beginning in 1970 in two mines; and (b) staggered interventions in which the intervention is introduced at different times to the different baselines—a token economy intervention was introduced in 1971 to the Shirley Basin mine and in 1974 to the Navajo mine. Causal conclusions can be drawn when a multiple-baseline design is used, performance improves during and not before the intervention, and this result is repeated each time the intervention is introduced. Both results occurred, as shown in Figure 8.3. The same rationale holds: it is possible that an event other than the intervention (history) might occur at time X for baseline 1. However, the more baselines there are, the less likely it is that the same event would have a similar effect on baseline 2 at the same time in exactly the same order. It is also not likely that maturation would measurably influence the baselines at the same times and in the same order. Similarly, regression effects would be seen in any repeated measurements and not just after the interventions. Thus, Fox, Hopkins and Anger (1987) were justified in concluding that 'the tokens given to workers as a consequence of periods without lost-time injuries or equipment-damaging accidents apparently benefited all parties immediately involved' (p. 221).

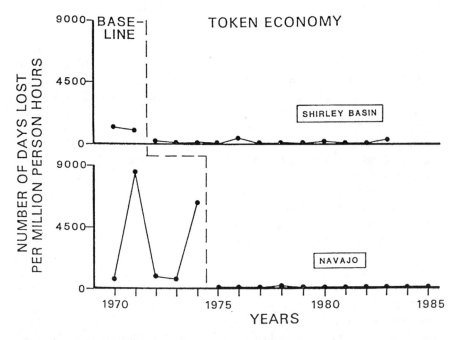

**Figure 8.3**  Graph illustrating the use of a multiple baseline design
Reproduced with permission from D.K. Fox, B.L. Hopkins and W.K. Anger (1987). The long-term effects of a token economy on safety performance in open-pit mining. *Journal of Applied Behavior Analysis*, **20**(3), 215–224. © The Society for the Experimental Analysis of Behavior

Excluded were studies that did not include both (a) concurrent baselines and (b) staggered interventions. For example, Austin, Kessler, Riccobono and Bailey (1996) collected data on two baselines at the same time, the percentage of safety behaviors on the ground and on the roof. But they did not stagger the timing of the intervention. Instead, they introduced it at the same time. Although the roofing 'crew improved from average baseline safety compliance levels of 51% on the ground and 55% on the roof to 90% on the ground and 95% on the roof', (pp. 49–50), it was difficult to rule out that plausible alternative hypotheses were responsible for the changes.

Hence, to meet the criteria of methodological rigor, either a between-group control design or a within-group reversal or multiple-baseline design had to be used. Only studies meeting both methodological rigor and content criteria were included in the review.

## Studies Meeting Methodological and Content Criteria

A search of the literature resulted in the identification of 126 studies that were appropriate in content and methodological rigor. These 126 studies were contained in 124 articles or book chapters. Each article and chapter contained one study, with the exception of two articles that contained two studies. A study was defined as an independent set of subjects and an independently reported set of results. The Shook, Johnson and Uhlman (1978) article, for example, included two studies because two independently reported sets of results for two sets of subjects and settings were reported.

## Coding Procedures

Each study was coded by at least one and, for approximately 70% of the studies, two or three authors of the review. The coding was checked to see if agreement existed on the scoring of each and every item. Each disagreement was resolved by discussion.

### Properties of the studies recorded

For each study in the review, the following information was recorded:

1. The research question answered (e.g., does negative reinforcement work?).
2. The subjects, including the number and organizational level (e.g., non-supervisory, supervisory) and setting, including the types (e.g., public, private sector).
3. The dependent variable (e.g., functional service behaviors), the unit of analysis (e.g., #, %) as well as its coordination requirements and the processes involved (e.g., execution of psycho-motor tasks, negotiation and resolution of conflicts).

4.  The independent variable, including its type (e.g., informational, social), aggregation level (e.g., delivered to an individual or a group), and the frequency of its delivery (e.g., daily, monthly).
5.  The type of research design (e.g., the within-group reversal or multiple-baseline, or the between-group control group).
6.  Measures of central tendency and, where available, dispersion: for within-group designs, data are given by phase; for between-group designs, data are given by group; where means were not provided, another measure of central tendency was used, such as the median, mode, or another summary statistic (e.g., change from initial baseline, range).
7.  The 'test' used in drawing inferences (e.g., visual, ARIMA, $t$-test).
8.  The support provided for the question (e.g., including 'yes' and 'no' as well as 'inconclusive' and 'indeterminate'); for within-group designs where the level of support is 'yes,' the level of support could range from 1 to 3 with 1 indicating more support than 3.

*Research questions.*    To determine the question answered by each study, we first identified the research design—whether a between- or within-group design was used—and the type of question(s) posed by the investigator(s). Among the questions that could be raised are: (a) *program evaluation*: 'Does the program or treatment work?' (b) *facilitative*: 'Does treatment C add to or facilitate treatment B?' and (c) *comparison*: 'Is treatment C better than treatment B?'

*When the research design was appropriate to answer the question.* The program evaluation and facilitative questions could be addressed using both designs; the comparison question could be addressed using only a between-group design. When investigators' designs were suited to addressing their questions, we used the questions posed by the investigators. For example, when researchers used a between-group design with a treatment group and a control (or no-treatment) group to see if the program worked, then their study was classified, as the investigator had identified, as program evaluation. Likewise, when researchers used a within-group design, and they wished to address a program evaluation question, then their study was identified as answering that question. Similarly, if researchers wished to see if program C was better than program B and they used a between-group design comparing a treatment B group and a treatment C group, then this study would have been categorized as answering a comparison question.

*When there was a discrepancy between the research question posed and the design used.* On the other hand, when the investigators' design did not permit an answer to the question, then a discrepancy was said to occur. The most common mismatches were those in which investigators used an ABC or ABCD design with a single group, introduced multiple treatments one after another to the same group, and then wished to compare the treatments. It is difficult to answer these comparison questions with confidence because of a problem, referred to as 'multiple-treatment interference.'

As an illustration, let us look at a study by Anderson, Crowell, Doman and Howard (1988). Using an ABCD design, they wanted to compare the effects of individual feedback, goal setting, and praise on hockey team members. After baseline recording (A), they first publicly posted individual feedback (B), then introduced goal setting (C), and finally added praise (D). The fact that the group is exposed first to one treatment and then another opens up the possibility of *multiple-treatment interference*. When the same players performed first on system B, then switched to system C, and then to system D, it is difficult to rule out that one system might have had an impact on a subsequent one. Hence, because the same individuals are exposed to more than one treatment, 'interference' may occur and thus limit the generality of the results.

Two types of interference can be major threats to the generalizability of the findings. One type, termed the *contrast effect*, results from juxtaposing treatments in such a way that individuals can contrast treatment B with treatments C and D and perhaps behave differently. It is possible in the aforementioned study by Anderson et al. (1988) that goal setting increased performance further only because subjects already had the feedback introduced in phase B, and therefore had the benefit of being able to contrast their goals with their previous performance. 'Exposure to one manipulation or test may produce persistent consequences . . . that influence the subject's response to any subsequent manipulation' (Neale & Liebert, 1986, p. 175).

The second type of interference, called the *sequence effect*, results from introducing treatments in a particular order. In this case, B was introduced first, followed by C, and finally D. Practice and experience are two of the many factors that could contribute to sequence effects. For example, when players are given the same treatments in the same order, it is likely that they 'would improve as they became more familiar with the procedure, more comfortable with the . . . setting, and more practiced in the task' (Neale & Liebert, 1986, p. 176). In the above study, Anderson et al. (1988) found that feedback was associated with larger effects than were goal setting and praise, but they note the possibility of a sequence effect: 'this may have been due to the temporal precedence of this treatment' (p. 92). Hence, using this ABCD design may compromise the conclusions that can be made about comparing the different treatments because of limitations in generalizability.

In short, because of multiple-treatment interference, within-group designs in general and ABC or ABCD designs in particular could not be used to answer comparison questions with confidence.

*Using select designs with multiple treatments to address facilitative questions.* Although investigators using within-group designs could not satisfactorily compare treatments, we had established that they could use the information they had collected to determine whether one treatment *adds* to the effectiveness of another treatment. In answering this facilitative question, however, it is essential that the designs allow one to rule out sources of internal invalidity such as history and maturation. To do this, the designs had to include either a reversal phase (as in a reversal design) or the staggered introduction of treatments across two or more baselines (as in a multiple-baseline design).

A design with the series of phases—either BCB or BCBC—incorporates a reversal phase, and it can be used to address a facilitative question. Chhokar and Wallin (1984) used an ABCBC design which included the critical BCBC reversal phase: Baseline (A), Antecedents (training and goal setting) (B), and Antecedents with Consequences (feedback) (C), a reversal back to Antecedents alone (B), and a reintroduction of Antecedents with Consequences (C). With this design, they could determine if adding a second treatment (C) would facilitate an increase in addition to that of the first treatment (B) and hence answer the facilitative question: 'What is the additional effect of feedback (C) when goal setting and training (B) are already in place?'

Another way to address facilitative questions is to use an extension of the traditional multiple-baseline design. Treatments were introduced in a ABC sequence across four departments but at staggered intervals in a study by Komaki, Collins and Penn (1982). After Baseline (A), they introduced training only (B) followed by feedback (C) to the first department. A number of weeks later, they introduced the training only and then feedback to the second department. They continued to stagger the introduction of the treatments to the third and fourth departments, thus enabling them to answer the facilitative question: 'What is the additional effect of feedback when training is already in place?' When during the C phase, performance significantly improved in all the groups over and above that of B, the authors concluded that feedback *added* to the effectiveness of the training, despite the fact that in some groups significant changes had already occurred prior to the addition of the feedback.

In short, with the proper extensions of the reversal and multiple-baseline designs, one can examine the effects of multiple treatments by looking at whether one treatment adds to another.

*Types of questions answered.* Two sets of research questions were addressed. The first concerned *program evaluation*. Because different principles were used, the studies were subdivided by the primary principle involved and identified as answering one of the following questions: (a) Does *positive reinforcement* work?; (b) Does *negative reinforcement* work and (c) Does *punishment* work?

The other set were considered *facilitative*. They were grouped according to the different treatments: (d) Do consequences improve performance above and beyond that of antecedents alone? (e) Does contingent reinforcement improve performance above and beyond that of full pay? (f) Does praise improve performance above and beyond that of feedback alone? and (g) Does individual feedback improve performance above and beyond that of group feedback?

Unfortunately, no comparison questions were addressed in this review because no studies were identified with multiple treatments using control group designs.

*Support provided for the question.* Once we determined which research question could be answered with confidence, the results were categorized in terms of the support they did or did not provide for the question as: (a) 'yes,' providing support, (b) 'no,' providing no support, and (c) 'mixed,' providing support in some cases but not in all. Studies in which it was not possible to make judgments about support were classified as: (d) 'inconclusive,' in which it could not be determined whether the changes were or were not the result of the program or (e) 'indeterminate' in which insufficient data were given to make the judgment; the most common problems occurred when no graph was provided or when individual data points were not plotted on the graphs.

The criteria used to determine support differed depending on the research design used.

*For between-group designs, traditional criteria were used.* For studies with between-group designs, the traditional indices were used: (a) the results of standard statistical tests comparing groups such as the analysis of variance ($F$) or the $t$-test; and (b) the probability levels ($p$) of these results occurring by chance if there were no differences between the groups.

*For within-group designs, there was a lack of agreed-upon indices.* No such traditional criteria exist for judging data when using within-group designs. Among the reasons is that data are collected repeatedly over time, an essential characteristic of within-group designs, as shown in Figures 8.1 to 8.11. When drawing conclusions, ABA researchers do not pore over $t$-test scores and probability levels. Instead, they scrutinize the graph and do what is referred to as a visual inspection, or an 'eyeball' test.

The problem with visual inspection, however, is that there are no agreed-upon criteria. According to DeProspero and Cohen (1979), seasoned ABA researchers use a 'wide range' of indices. They can visually assess the 'trends' or 'slopes' of the scores within and between baseline and intervention phases, the 'means' or levels of phases and the amount of 'overlap' between scores of adjacent phases, the 'stability' and 'variability' of the scores within and across conditions, and the 'number of data points in each phase', and the 'number of times the effect is replicated' within each study. In fact, when seasoned researchers independently examined the graphs of the same studies and interpreted the results, the correlation was 0.61, indicating only 'modest' agreement (p. 578). DeProspero and Cohen concluded that 'a behavioral researcher seeking corroboration on the interpretation of results would not be likely to get the same answer twice' (p. 578). With different researchers using different indices, it is difficult to replicate the inference process.

To date, few attempts have been made to address the lack of agreed-upon criteria. Instead, the usual recommendation is to supplement the visual analysis with a time-series analysis or an auto-regressive moving averages analysis (ARIMA) (Jones, Weinrott & Vaught, 1978; McCain & McCleary, 1979). With a time-series analysis, one assesses the significance of level changes— changes in means from baseline to intervention and slope changes—as well as changes in trend within and across phases (e.g., Chokkar & Wallin, 1984). The advantage is that time-series analysis provides standard criteria that researchers can agree upon to interpret the results of studies. (Note: The recommendation is not a blanket one, however. For 'large-effect' studies where no reasonable critic would disagree with the inference(s) drawn by the author(s), Jones, Weinrott and Vaught (1978) do not recommend time-series analysis. For non-obvious cases, they do.) Jones, Weinrott and Vaught (1978) also hold out the enticing possibility that researchers may be overlooking meaningful effects. 'If time-series analysis were used . . ., researchers probably would infer meaningful changes in their data more often than if visual inferences alone were used' (p. 280).

Despite the recommendations to conduct time-series analysis, they are rarely done. Studies in this review relied mainly on visual inspection, with only 7 of the 120 studies using within-group designs (less than 6%), conducting time-series analyses. Among the reasons is the lack of familiarity with the analysis. In introducing time-series analysis, McCain and McCleary (1979) note that 'readers may be disconcerted . . . because the analysis seems so different from the statistical work they are used to' (p. 233). There are differences in the assumptions that can be made about the data. There are differences in the data analysis procedures. The reason for the differences is in the nature of the data. Studies using within-group designs have an essential characteristic—the collection of data on the same group and in the same setting repeatedly over time. For example, in the previously discussed study (Fox, Hopkins & Anger, 1987), data were collected about workers in each mine and posted each year for 15 years. With time-series data, the problem is the scores may be serially dependent. This means that temporarily adjacent scores may be related to or predictive of one another. Shirley Basin mine's score for Year 1 may predict the mine's score on Year 2. The Year-2 score may predict the Year-3 score and so on. Serial dependency, however, violates the assumption of independence underlying traditional statistical methods. Hence, the first step in a time-series analysis is to assess and then if necessary transform the raw scores to uncorrelated or serially independent scores. To do this, auto-correlation functions are computed. The second step is to compare the transformed scores from adjacent phases in the design. To do this, one specifies a tentative transfer functional model and estimates the joint transfer function auto-regressive integrated moving averages model parameters. As Jones et al. (1977) readily admit, these computations are outside the realm of 'conventional graduate-school-learned statistical procedures' (p. 155).

Another reason why time-series analysis is rarely done relates to confusion surrounding its use. Initially, a bewildering array of recommendations were offered ranging from the traditional $t$- and $F$-test to the 'C' statistic (e.g., Gentile, Roden & Klein, 1972; Hartmann, 1974; Thoresen & Elashoff, 1974). It was not until the late 1970s that time-series analysis was established as the preferred analysis (Jones, Vaught & Weinrott, 1977; McCain & McCleary,

1979). Even in the late 1980s, debates continue over the application and interpretation of time-series models (Busk & Marascuilo, 1988; Huitema, 1988; Sharpley & Alavoisius, 1988; Suen, 1987; Suen & Ary, 1987).

Another reason why ABA researchers eschew time-series analysis is philosophical. In striving to make a difference, ABA researchers were not satisfied with the conventional criteria of a probability level at the 0.05 level that may be statistically, but not practically, significant (Sidman, 1960). Hence, they tended to eschew statistical analysis in general and time-series analysis in particular.

*Newly proposed decision criteria.* Because no traditional indices existed with which to evaluate the results of studies using within-group designs, we devised a new set of criteria. Termed OCT, the criteria identified key features of the data, with O standing for overlap in data point between phases, C for the measure of central tendency, and T for trends in the direction of the subsequent phase. When the results met support levels 1, 2, or 3, then we considered them to provide support for the question.

As shown in Table 8.1, the standards differed depending on the level of support:

1. Level 1: No overlap whatsoever between the data points of each phase and the subsequent phases and no trends in the direction of the subsequent phase.
2. Level 2: One third or fewer of the data points in each phase overlap with any data points in the subsequent phases and no trends in the direction of the subsequent phase.
3. Level 3: One third or fewer of the data points in one phase overlap with the mean in the subsequent phases and no trends in the direction of the subsequent phase. If the mean was not given, the median was used.

Level 2 changes differed from level 1 changes in that an overlap was allowed as long as one third or fewer of the data points in one phase overlapped with data points in the subsequent phase. Level 3 changes differed from Level 2 changes in that the overlap could occur with the mean of the subsequent phase rather than the stricter requirement of any one of the data points.

The OCT criteria were applied with all studies using within-group designs, assuming graphs with data points on were provided, and whether or not they had statistically significant and appropriate repeated measures test results (i.e., ARIMA [auto-regressive integrated moving averages analysis]). By articulating the essential features of the data, we can identify what is needed to conclude that the results provide support for the question, thus explicating our inference process and making it possible for others to replicate our decisions. The OCT criteria are similar to but not identical to the criteria recently suggested by Miller (1997) in that he too computes overlap and determines trends. Unique to the OCT criteria, however, are: (a) the use of the mean or

**Table 8.1** OCT decision criteria used to determine if results provided support for research questions of studies using a within-group design

| When results are from: | | | Results supported |
|---|---|---|---|
| Multiple baseline studies | Reversal studies | | |
| Changes in the predicted direction when and only when the same intervention is introduced, and these changes occur every time the intervention is introduced | Changes in the predicted direction during the intervention and the reversal phases | | Yes: Program is effective |
| | Levels of support | | |
| | 1. *No overlap whatsoever* between the data points of each phase and the subsequent phases and no trends in the direction of the subsequent phase | | |
| | 2. *One third or fewer* of the data points in each phase *overlap with any data points* in the subsequent phases and no trends in the direction of the subsequent phase | | |
| | 3. *One third or fewer* of the data points in one phase *overlap with the mean* in the subsequent phases and no trends in the direction of the subsequent phase. If the mean was not given, the median was used | | |
| No changes during the intervention | No changes during the intervention | | No: Program is *not* effective |
| With three or more baselines, changes occur during at least two interventions but *only one* change does *not* occur | With two or more reversal phases, changes occur during at least one reversal but changes do *not* occur during another | | Mixed: Program is effective in some cases, but not in all |
| Changes during at least one intervention, but *not* during the other intervention(s) | Changes during the intervention, but *not* during the reversal | | Inconclusive: The changes may or may not be the result of the program |

Note. OTC where O = overlap in data point between phases, C = the measure of central tendency, and T = trends in the direction of the subsequent phase median (measures of central tendency) of the entire set of observations in determining whether overlap occurs; (b) the differentiation made among different levels of support, with Level 1 changes being more robust than Levels 2 or 3; and (c) the identification of classifications such as mixed, inconclusive, and indeterminate. The latter was identified when no data points were plotted on the graph, thus making it difficult to use the OCT criteria to determine whether the results provided support for the question.

After recording properties ranging from the support provided for the question to the subjects and setting of each study, the results were aggregated by question. The next sections detail the results.

## Findings: Program Evaluation Questions

The results are first reported for program evaluation questions, and in particular those using the principle of positive reinforcement.

### Does positive reinforcement work?

To answer the question as to whether the principle of positive reinforcement resulted in changes on the job, an evaluation was made of 88 rigorously controlled studies in which employees were provided consequences that usually were frequent, positive, and contingent.

*Overall success rate.* Of the 88 studies, 58 were classified as 'yes,' 10 as 'mixed,' 4 as 'no,' 7 as 'inconclusive,' and 9 as 'indeterminate.' Of the studies for which we could make judgments about support, 58 studies were in support, 10 showed mixed support, and only 4 did not show any support, for a success rate of 93%. These results are consistent with previous reviews of the literature, which indicate the effectiveness of the ABA approach in work settings (Balcazar et al., 1989; Frederiksen, 1982; Hopkins & Sears, 1982; Merwin, Thomason & Sanford, 1989; O'Brien, Dickinson & Rosow, 1982; O'Hara, Johnson & Beehr, 1985; Stajkovic & Luthans, 1997).

To convey some of the richness of the results and to allow readers to see the bases on which we drew our conclusions, data from each of the studies are presented in Tables 8.2a, 8.2b, and 8.2c. The tables differ from one another in: (a) the research design used, with Table 8.2a displaying studies using multiple-baseline designs, Table 8.2b reversal, and Table 8.2c control-group; and (b) the reporting of measures of central tendency, with Tables 8.2a and 8.2b further divided into those that do and do not provide these measures.

Each table contains the following information: (a) The *author(s)* and in parenthesis the publication date; (b) the *dependent variable* (e.g., functional service behaviors) and in parenthesis the unit of analysis (e.g., #, %); (c) the *design* (e.g., reversal, multiple-baseline); (d) where available, the *means* and *standard deviations* either by phase or group depending on the design; (e) the

**Table 8.2a**   Multiple baseline studies pertinent to the question: Does positive reinforcement work?

| Article | Dependent variable | Means by condition | | Test | Results supported |
|---|---|---|---|---|---|
| | | Baseline | Positive reinforcement | | |
| Brown & Redmon (1989) | Unscheduled sick leave hours (#) | | | Visual | Yes[3] |
| | Group 1 | 27.2 | 11.1 | | |
| | Group 2 | 33.8 | 7.2 | | |
| | Group 3 | 46.0 | 7.6 | | |
| | Group 4 | 27.7 | 1.7 | | |
| | Group 5 | 23.2 | 16.0 | | |
| Carnine & Fink (1978) | Teacher giving appropriate signal (#) | | | Visual | Yes[2] |
| | Teacher 1 | 23.2 | 93.4 | | |
| | Teacher 2 | 26.1 | 97.5 | | |
| | Teacher 3 | 28.9 | 95.7 | | |
| | Rate of disruptive behavior by students (#/sec) | | | | |
| | Teacher 1's class | 15.6 | 8.5 | | |
| | Teacher 2's class | 15.8 | 6.6 | | |
| | Teacher 3's class | 17.4 | 6.3 | | |
| Carter, Holstrom, Simpanen & Melin (1988) | Missing value of items from area of store ($) | | | Visual | Mix. |
| | Department 1 | 4.7 | 1.2 | | |
| | Department 2 | 1.6 | 0.8 | | |
| | Department 3 | 2.0 | 0.1 | | |
| Cooper, Thomson & Baer (1970) | Teacher attention to appropriate behavior (%) | | | Visual | Yes[1] |
| | Teacher 1 | 9.0 | 30.0 | | |
| | Teacher 2 | 14.0 | 21.0 | | |
| Deluga & Andrews (1985–1986) | Workers departing early (%) | 1.9 | 1.7 | Visual | Yes[3] |
| | Workers tardy (%) | 4.9 | 1.4 | | |
| | Workers absent (%) | 5.3 | 1.9 | | |
| Fellner & Sulzer-Azaroff (1984) | Safe conditions (%) | 79.0 | 85.0 | Visual | Yes[3] |
| | Safe practices (% checklist items) | 78.0 | 86.0 | | |

| Study | Measure | | | ARIMA | |
|---|---|---|---|---|---|
| Fellows & Mawhinney (1997) | Sales calls (#) | | | ARIMA | Yes[3] |
| | Group 1 | 32.0 | 56.0 | | |
| | Group 2 | 35.8 | 66.8 | | |
| Fleming & Sulzer-Azaroff (1992) | Teacher interactions with students (%) | | | Visual | Inc. |
| | Subject 1 | 14.8 | 23.5 | | |
| | Subject 2 | 17.5 | 20.3 | | |
| | Subject 3 | 2.9 | 9.0 | | |
| | Subject 4 | 8.2 | 12.6 | | |
| | Subject 5 | 8.6 | 14.2 | | |
| | Subject 6 | 9.4 | 16.2 | | |
| Fox & Sulzer-Azaroff (1989) | Giving information about client behavior (%) | | | Visual | Inc. |
| | Team 1 | 50.0 | 100.0 | | |
| | Team 2 | 0.0 | 100.0 | | |
| | Team 3 | 25.0 | 60.0 | | |
| | Team 4 | 50.0 | 99.9 | | |
| | Team 5 | 0.0 | 50.0 | | |
| | Team 6 | 0.0 | 60.0 | | |
| Henry & Redmon (1990) | Statistical process control task (%) | | | Visual | Yes[3] |
| | Subject 1 | 77.8 | 100.0 | | |
| | Subject 2 | 75.7 | 100.0 | | |
| | Subject 3 | 84.2 | 100.0 | | |
| Iwata, Bailey, Brown et al. (1976) | Appropriate dental care as graded (%) | | | Visual | Yes[3] |
| | Unit C | 12.0 | 19.0 | | |
| | Unit D | 9.0 | 31.0 | | |
| | Time spent on scheduled task (%) | | | | |
| | Unit C | 5.0 | 17.0 | | |
| | Unit D | 5.0 | 20.0 | | |
| Johnson & Fawcett (1994) | Courteous service behaviors (%) | | | Visual | Yes[1] |
| | Person 1 | 25.0 | 73.0 | | |
| | Person 2 | 14.0 | 77.0 | | |
| | Person 3 | 12.0 | 72.0 | | |

**Table 8.2a**  (*Continued*)

| Article | Dependent variable | Means by condition | | Test | Results supported |
|---|---|---|---|---|---|
| | | Baseline | Positive reinforcement | | |
| Johnson & Frederiksen (1990) | Caregiver–patient interactions (#) | | | | |
| | Unit 1 | 116.59 | 174.30 | Visual | Ind. |
| | Unit 2 | 146.72 | 149.46 | | |
| Johnson & Masotti (1990) | Waitperson sales (%) | | | Visual | Yes[3] |
| | Cocktails | 36.0 | 39.0 | | |
| | Appetizers | 15.0 | 19.0 | | |
| | Deserts | 4.0 | 8.0 | | |
| Jones, Morris & Barnard (1985/1986) | Forms completed (%) | | | Visual | Yes[3] |
| | Rights | 54.0 | 96.0 | | |
| | Applications | 67.0 | 85.0 | | |
| | Witness list | 67.0 | 91.0 | | |
| Komaki (1994) | Ordnance group | | | ARIMA | Yes[3] |
| | Deficiencies detected (%) | 26.0 | 52.0 | | |
| | Action taken (%) | 17.0 | 75.0 | | |
| | Motor transport group | | | | |
| | Deficiencies detected (%) | 26.0 | 60.0 | | |
| | Action taken (%) | 23.0 | 54.0 | | |
| Komaki & Barnett (1977) | Stages completed during football game (%) | | | Visual | Yes[3] |
| | Play A | 61.7 | 81.5 | | |
| | Play B | 54.4 | 82.0 | | |
| | Play C | 65.5 | 79.8 | | |
| Komaki, Barwick & Scott (1978)[a] | Safe practices (% checklist items) | | | Visual | Yes[2] |
| | Wrapping department | 70.0 | 95.8 | | |
| | Make-up department | 77.6 | 99.3 | | |
| Komaki, Blood & Holder (1980) | Time spent smiling at customers (%) | 41.2 | 67.5 | Visual | Mix. |
| | Time spent talking to customers (%) | 88.1 | 90.9 | | |

| Study | Measure | | | | |
|---|---|---|---|---|---|
| Komaki, Collins & Penn (1982) | Motor transport group | | | Visual | No |
| | Individuals working (#) | 2.4 | 4.0 | | |
| | Time supervisor present (%) | 43.0 | 50.0 | | |
| | Action taken (%) | 49.0 | 50.0 | | |
| | Ordnance group | | | | |
| | Individuals working (#) | 1.9 | 1.7 | | |
| | Time supervisor present (%) | 46.0 | 46.0 | | |
| | Action taken | 65.0 | 43.0 | | |
| Komaki, Collins & Temlock (1987) | Quality service items rendered (#) | | | Visual | Yes[3] |
| | Group 1 | 3.9 | 6.2 | | |
| | Group 2 | 3.9 | 5.5 | | |
| Komaki, Waddell & Pearce (1977, study 2) | Being present 'in-store' (%) | 53.0 | 86.0 | Visual | Yes[3] |
| | Assisting customers (%) | 35.0 | 87.0 | | |
| | Filling shelf/counter (%) | 57.0 | 86.0 | | |
| Lamal & Benfield (1978)[a] | Arrival time (a.m.) | 10:45 | 8:15 | Visual | Yes[1] |
| | Time working (%) of total time | 50.6 | 84.6 | | |
| Lovett, Bosmajian & Frederiksen (1983)[a] | Charts completed (%) | | | Visual | Yes[1] |
| | Intake summaries | 71.0 | 94.0 | | |
| | Progress notes | 33.0 | 64.0 | | |
| | Treatment plans | 54.0 | 82.0 | | |
| Maher (1982) | Programs completed (%) | | | Visual | Yes[1] |
| | School A | 8.8 | 82.1 | | |
| | School B | 17.4 | 93.3 | | |
| | Information recorded (%) | | | | |
| | School A | 9.5 | 95.2 | | |
| | School B | 20.8 | 95.8 | | |
| McGinsey, Greene & Lutzker (1995) | Proper teaching technique (%) | | | Visual | Yes[1] |
| | Setting 1 | 22.0 | 100.0 | | |
| | Setting 2 | 0.0 | 100.0 | | |
| | Setting 3 | 10.0 | 95.0 | | |

**Table 8.2a**   (*Continued*)

| Article | Dependent variable | Means by condition | | Test | Results supported |
|---|---|---|---|---|---|
| | | Baseline | Positive reinforcement | | |
| Methot, Williams, Cummings & Bradshaw (1996) | Supervisors giving proper feedback (%) | | | Visual | Yes[3] |
| | Supervisor 1 | 20.0 | 85.0 | | |
| | Supervisor 2 | 0.0 | 63.0 | | |
| | Supervisor 3 | 25.0 | 99.0 | | |
| | Supervisor 4 | 50.0 | 68.0 | | |
| | Supervisor 5 | 36.0 | 83.0 | | |
| Nordstrom, Hall, Lorenzi & Delquadri (1987) | Pages typed correctly (%) | | | Visual | Yes[3] |
| | Individual 1 | 55.0 | 82.0 | | |
| | Individual 2 | 64.0 | 87.0 | | |
| Shoemaker & Reid (1980) | Workers absent (%) Both shifts but only those chronically absent | 11.7 | 8.5 | Visual | Mix. |
| | Day shift | 13.2 | 6.6 | | |
| | Night shift | 8.6 | 12.3 | | |
| Sulzer-Azaroff & de Santamaria (1980) | Hazardous conditions (#) | | | Visual | Mix. |
| | Department 1 | 30.1 | 13.2 | | |
| | Department 2 | 28.8 | 5.7 | | |
| | Department 3 | 38.6 | 12.9 | | |
| | Department 4 | 13.2 | 8.4 | | |
| | Department 5 | 14.8 | 1.8 | | |
| | Department 6 | 14.0 | 9.9 | | |
| Wilk & Redmon (1990) | Office tasks completed (#) | | | Visual | Yes[3] |
| | Person 1 | 23.0 | 180.0 | | |
| | Person 2 | 47.0 | 89.0 | | |
| | Person 3 | 30.0 | 90.0 | | |
| Wilk & Redmon (1998) | Clerical tasks completed (#) | | | Visual | Yes[3] |
| | Filing | 983.0 | 1703.0 | | |
| | Mailroom | 5077.0 | 8822.0 | | |
| | Credit evaluation | 685.0 | 861.0 | | |
| | Data entry | 582.0 | 994.0 | | |

| Article | Dependent variable | Changes from baseline or preceding phase, ranges, or other | | Test | Results supported |
|---|---|---|---|---|---|
| | | Baseline | Positive reinforcement | | |
| Zohar & Fussfeld (1981) | Earplug usage (%) | | | Visual | Yes[1] |
| | Group A | 70.0 | 87.0 | | |
| | Group B | 70.0 | 89.0 | | |
| | Group C | 72.0 | 88.0 | | |
| | Group D | 30.0 | 95.0 | | |
| Alavosius & Sulzer-Azaroff (1986)[b] | Care of clients (%) | | | Visual | Inc. |
| Arco (1997)[b] | Instructions, prompts & feedback (%) | | | Visual | Ind. |
| Fox, Hopkins & Anger (1987)[b] | Days lost due to injuries (#) | | | Visual | Yes[1] |
| | Shirley Basin mine | | 11.0[c] | | |
| | Navajo mine | | 2.0[c] | | |
| | Injuries resulting in lost time (#) | | | | |
| | Shirley Basin mine | | 15.0[c] | | |
| | Navajo mine | | 32.0[c] | | |
| Fulton & Malott (1981–1982) | Tasks completed (%) | 50.5[d] | 96.5[d] | Visual | Yes[3] |
| | Subject 1 | | | | |
| | Subject 2 | | | | |
| | Subject 3 | | | | |
| | Subject 4 | | | | |
| Harchik, Sherman, Sheldon & Strouse (1992)[b] | Direct careworkers' interaction with client | | | Visual | Yes[3] |
| | Using token reinforcement | | | | |
| | Participation by clients | | | | |
| | Content of interactions | | | | |

**Table 8.2a** *(Continued)*

| Article | Dependent variable | Changes from baseline or preceding phase, ranges, or other | | Test | Results supported |
|---|---|---|---|---|---|
| | | Baseline | Positive reinforcement | | |
| Hopkins, Conard & Smith (1986) | Work behaviors (% of intervals) | 49–76[e] | > 90 | Visual | Yes[1] |
| | Plant 1 | | | | |
| | Plant 2 | | | | |
| | Plant 3 | | | | |
| | Housekeeping practices (% of observations) | | | | |
| | Plant 1 | | > 85 | | |
| | Plant 2 | | > 90 | | |
| | Plant 3 | | > 90 | | |
| Hopkins et al. (1986)[b] | Working safely (%) | | 6 workers improved 3 workers unchanged | Visual | Inc. |
| Kreitner, Reif & Morris (1977)[b] | Completion of daily routine (#) | | | Visual | Yes[1] |
| | Completion of '1 on 1' sessions (#) | | | | |
| | Completion of group sessions (#) | | | | |
| LaMere et al. (1996)[b] | Waste disposal rating (#) | | | ANOVA | Yes |
| | Group A | | | | |
| | Group B | | | | |
| McKenzie & Rushall (1974)[b] | Swimmers absent (%) | | −45.0[f] | Visual | Yes[3] |
| | Swimmers arriving late (%) | | −63.0[f] | | |
| | Swimmers departing early (%) | | −100.0[f] | | |
| Panyan, Boozer & Morris (1970) | Patient sessions conducted by attendant (%) | 20.0– 63.0[e] 8.0– 79.0[e] | 99.0[g] 100.0[g] | Visual | Yes[3] |
| | Hall E | | | | |
| | Hall C | | | | |

| Study | Dependent variable | Results | | Support |
|---|---|---|---|---|
| Prue, Krapfl, Noah et al. (1980)[b] | Staff treatment (hours) | Group 1 +680.0[f]<br>Group 2 +37.0[f]<br>Group 3 +32.0[f]<br>Group 4 +100.0[f] | Visual | Yes[3] |
| Reid, Schuh-Wear & Brannon (1978)[b] | Workers absent (%)<br>Morning<br>Unit 1<br>Unit 2<br>Unit 3<br>Afternoon<br>Shift 1<br>Shift 2<br>Shift 3 | -3.4[f]<br>+1.3[f]<br>-0.9[f]<br>-5.0[f]<br>-0.8[f]<br>-1.7[f] | Visual | Mix. |
| Sulzer-Azaroff (1978)[b] | Safety behaviors (#) | 20 of 30 labs improved<br>2 labs worsened<br>8 labs unchanged | Visual | Mix. |
| Sulzer-Azaroff et al. (1990)[b] | Safety behaviors (%) | 3 of 3 departments improved | Visual | Yes[2] |
| Welch & Holborn (1988)[b] | Behavioral contract writing & negotiation (%) | 4 of 4 caregivers improved | Visual | Yes[1] |
| Welsh, Bernstein & Luthans (1992)[b] | Quality of food delivery<br>Quality of food preparation (#) | 1 of 8 employees improved<br>4 employees unchanged<br>3 employees unreported | Visual | Inc. |

Note. Numbers in parentheses = standard deviations. For support levels (1 = highest), refer to text. Inc. = inconclusive. Ind. = indeterminate. Mix. = mixed results.

[a]Refer to article for results from additional conditions or phases.
[b]No measures or only some measures of central tendency or other summary statistics given.
[c]% of average baseline level.
[d]Mean for all subjects.
[e]Range per phase.
[f]% change from initial baseline.
[g]Maximum per phase.

**Table 8.2b**  Reversal studies pertinent to the question: Does positive reinforcement work?

| Article | Dependent variable | Means by condition | | | | Test | Results supported |
|---|---|---|---|---|---|---|---|
| | | Baseline | Positive reinforcement | Baseline | Positive reinforcement | | |
| Dillon, Kent & Malott (1980) | Thesis tasks completed (%) | —[a] | 91.0 | 65.0 | 81.0 | Visual | Yes[1] |
| Fox & Sulzer-Azaroff (1987)[b] | Items on safety forms completed (#) | 11.1 | 13.7 | 12.6 | 13.0 | Visual | Yes[1] |
| Frederiksen, Richter, Johnson & Solomon (1981/1982) | Errors in recording (#): Completeness Status | 22.0 3.8 | 11.0 2.1 | 15.1 2.6 | | Visual | Inc. |
| Gillat & Sulzer-Azaroff (1994) | Principal's supervisory behavior (%): Goal setting Non-verbal feedback Praise | 17.0 13.0 5.0 | 71.3 57.0 53.5 | 40.0 49.0 52.5 | 83.8 82.0 88.0 | Visual | Inc. |
| Godbey & White (1992) | Accuracy of report (%) | 45.0 | 79.0 | 79.0 | | Visual | Ind. |
| Gupton & LeBow (1971) | Warranty calls resulting in sale (%): Person 1 Person 2 | 13.0 10.0 | 23.0 31.0 | 0.0 0.0 | | Visual | Yes[2] |
| Haynes, Pine & Fitch (1982)[b] | Accident rate per 100 operators (#) | 8.7 | 8.8 | 6.0 | | Visual | No |
| Hermann, DeMontes, Dominguez et al. (1973)[b] | Group members that are tardy (%) | 15.0 | 2.5 | 8.0 | 1.8 | Visual | Yes[2] |

| Study | Dependent variable | | | | | | |
|---|---|---|---|---|---|---|---|
| Heward (1978) | Baseball team efficiency (combination of statistics) | 0.7 | 0.8 | 0.8 | 0.7 | Visual | Ind. |
| Houmanfar & Hayes (1998) | Assignments completed (%) | 85.0 | 100.0 | 97.0 | 97.0 | Visual | Ind. |
| Johnson, Welsh, Miller & Altus (1991) | Jobs completed (%) | —[a] | 83.0 | 63.0 | 93.0 | Visual | No |
| Kreitner & Golab (1978) | Salespersons meeting criterion (#) | 2.6 | 5.9 | 4.3 | | Visual | Yes[2] |
| Luthans, Paul & Taylor (1985) | Functional service behaviors (#) | 49.6 | 54.9 | 50.6 | | Visual | Yes[2] |
| | | (5.1) | (5.2) | (4.8) | | | |
| | Dysfunctional service behaviors (#) | 45.9 | 40.6 | 45.1 | | | |
| | | (4.5) | (4.7) | (5.1) | | | |
| McCarthy (1978) | High bobbins (#) | 55.9 | 14.2 | 8.7 | 8.1 | Visual | Inc. |
| Nasanen & Saari (1987) | Correct housekeeping practices (%) | 62.0 | 85.0 | 84.0 | | Visual | Inc. |
| Nordstrom, Hall, Lorenzi & Delquadri (1987)[b] | Time working (%) Person 1 | 48.0 | 78.0 | 51.0 | 77.0 | Visual | Inc. |
| | Person 2 | 65.0 | 78.0 | 83.0 | —[c] | | |
| Pedalino & Gamboa (1974) | Workers absent (%) | 3.0 | 2.5 | 3.0 | | Visual | Yes[3] |
| Pommer & Streedback (1974)[b] | Tasks completed (%) Assigned jobs | 42.0 | 77.0 | 58.0 | 93.0 | Visual | Yes[2] |
| | Planned procedures | 40.0 | 77.0 | 56.0 | 93.0 | | |
| Quilitch (1978) | Suggestions submitted (#) | —[a] | 4.0 | 0.8 | 2.3 | Visual | Yes[2] |
| Shook, Johnson & Uhlman (1978) | Graphs completed (%) | 0.0 | 46.5 | 0.0 | | Visual | Yes[1] |

**Table 8.2b** (Continued)

| Article | Dependent variable | Means by condition | | Baseline | Positive reinforcement | Test | Results supported |
|---|---|---|---|---|---|---|---|
| | | Baseline | Positive reinforcement | | | | |
| Silva, Duncan & Doudna (1981)[b] | Workers absent (%) | 4.8 | 2.4 | 4.7 | 6.0 | Visual | Inc. |

Changes from baseline or preceding phase, ranges, or other

| Article | Dependent variable | Baseline | Positive reinforcement | Baseline | Positive reinforcement | Test | Results supported |
|---|---|---|---|---|---|---|---|
| Abernathy, Duffy & O'Brien (1982)[b] | Items processed per hour (#) | 1465.0 | 2250.0 | —[c] | | Visual | Ind. |
| Anderson, Crowell, Succec et al. (1982)[b] | Potential buyers contacted (#) | | | | | Visual | Yes[3] |
| Brand, Staelin, O'Brien & Dickinson (1982)[c] | Transactions complete (%) | | | | +295.0[a] | Visual | Ind. |
| | Claims researched (%) | | | | +150.0[a] | | |
| | Refinancing researched (%) | | | | +132.0[a] | | |
| | Rejects processed (%) | | | | +264.0[a] | | |
| Carlson & Hill (1982)[c] | Hours lost (#) | | | | | Visual | Ind. |
| | Factory workers | | | | | | |
| | Administrative workers | | | | | | |
| Elizur (1987)[b] | Words of greeting (#) | 0.52–0.53[e] | 1.24–2.32[e] | 2.89 | | Visual | Inc. |
| | Words of courtesy (#) | 0.87–1.13[e] | 2.35–3.36[e] | 3.75 | | | |
| | Eye contact (#) | 7.17 | 11.38 | 11.57 | 12.20 | | |
| | Smile (#) | 0.59 | 1.92 | 1.61 | 2.38 | | |

| Study | Measure | | | | | | |
|---|---|---|---|---|---|---|---|
| Frost, Hopkins & Conrad (1981) | Prep time (minutes) | —c | -5.3f | +0.4f | -2.8f | Visual | Ind. |
| | Fill time (minutes) | —c | | | -21.3 / 22.5e | Visual | No |
| Gaetani & Johnson (1983, group C) | Efficiency estimates (%) | | +40.0d | +8.0d | | Visual | Yes3 |
| Gaetani, Johnson & Austin (1983) | Minutes late (#) | 226.0 | 0–110.0g | 59.0 | | Visual | Yes1 |
| Kortick & O'Brien (1996)c | Properly sorted packages (%) Properly loaded onto trucks (rating) | | | | | Visual | |
| Makin & Hoyle (1993) | Engineering schemes produced (#) | —c | +270.0d | -8.5d | +127.0d | None | Ind. |
| McKenzie & Rushall (1974)c | Laps swum (# per minute) | | | | | Visual | Yes2 |
| Welsh, Luthans & Sommer (1993)c | Functional job behaviors (#) Dysfunctional job behaviors (#) | | | | | Visual | Inc. |

Note. Number in parentheses = standard deviations. For support levels (1 = highest), refer to text. Inc. = inconclusive. Ind. = indeterminate.

a Condition not implemented.
b Refer to article for results from additional conditions or phases.
c No measures or only some measures of central tendency or other summary statistics given.
d % change from initial baseline.
e Means of subphases per phase.
f Change from preceding phase.
g Range per phase.

**Table 8.2c**   Between-group studies pertinent to the question: Does positive reinforcement work?

| Article | Dependent variable | Means by condition | | Test | Results supported |
|---|---|---|---|---|---|
| | | Control group | Treatment group | | |
| Frayne & Latham (1987) | Hours group worked (#) | 403.2 (22.8) | 458.4 (32.7) | $t$-test | Yes |
| Hundall (1969) | Pieces finished (#) | | | | |
| | Pretest | 38.7 | 38.3 | $t$-test | Yes |
| | Posttest | 40.2 | 44.3 | | |
| Luthans, Paul & Baker (1981) | Customer service behaviors (#) | 362.2 | 433.2 | $t$-test | Yes |
| Orpen (1978) | Absenteeism (%) | | | | |
| | Baseline | 3.8 | 3.9 | $t$-test | Yes |
| | Intervention | 3.7 | 2.6 | | |
| | Baseline | 3.7 | 3.7 | | |
| | Intervention | 3.7 | 2.0 | | |

*statistical test* (e.g., *t*-test, ARIMA) or inference process such as visual analysis; and (f) whether the *results supported* the question (e.g., yes, no, mixed) with an indication, for studies using within-group designs, of the level of support.

*Magnitude of changes in on-the-job performance.*   In study after study, it was shown that using the principle of positive reinforcement resulted in substantial and meaningful changes. For example, in a multiple-baseline study by McGinsey, Greene and Lutkert (1995) as shown in Table 8.2a, baseline rates ranged from 0 to 22%, indicating that the teachers rarely used the proper techniques. Following the intervention, however, the teachers began using the proper techniques 95 and 100% of the time, on average. Similar mean increases can be seen in Table 8.2b in the reversal design study by Pommer and Streedbeck (1974). During baseline, workers were completing only 42% of their assigned jobs. After introducing the positive reinforcement program, workers were completing 77% of their jobs. Performance declined to 58%, however, when the positive reinforcer was removed. Only when the positive reinforcer was again reinstated did performance soar to 93%.

The graphs provide an even fuller picture. One can see the level and the trend of the changes over time, the overlap in the data points in one phase with the data points in the subsequent phase, and the dispersion of data points around the mean of each phase. In order to better illustrate the large amount of information portrayed in the graphs and to allow readers to see how we used the OCT criteria to make judgments about the levels of support, we present 8 more graphs to bring the total to 11.

In the next subsections, we present examples of results classified as providing support at Levels 1, 2, and 3, as well as those indicating no support, mixed support, and those considered inconclusive.

*Support Level 1 changes.* The changes from phase to phase are most dramatic in results classified as attaining Level 1 changes. Two indications of a level 1 change—the lack of overlap between the data points in one phase and the data points in the subsequent phase, and the lack of trend in the data points within each phase—can be seen in Figures 8.2, 8.3, 8.4, and 8.5.

To see how the graphs support and expand what we know, let us look at Figure 8.4, from an experiment by Johnson and Fawcett (1994). Interested in improving the service provided by staff members of a human services agency, they introduced a positive reinforcement program and evaluated it using a multiple-baseline design. If we were to rely only on the mean figures in Table 8.2a, we would know only that during baseline, the first, second, and third staff members performed 25, 14 and 13% of the behaviors, respectively, but that after the intervention, each staff member improved substantially and ended up with means of 73, 77 and 72%, respectively. Figure 8.4 substantially amplifies the picture, however, showing that the changes from baseline to the positive reinforcement phase—introduced at staggered intervals—occurred immediately *when and only when* the intervention was implemented. Figure 8.4 also indicates no trends in the direction of the subsequent phase; the baseline data were relatively stable, and if any trends existed during the intervention, they were not in the direction of the baseline phase. Furthermore, as one can see in Figure 8.4, there was not a single overlap in the data points in the baseline phase and the intervention phase; during baseline, the highest data point for the first staff member was 40%, whereas during the intervention, the lowest data point was 46%. Viewing the graph, one can literally 'see' why Johnson and Fawcett (1994) concluded that their intervention 'was effective in increasing (the) provision of courteous service to consumers' (p. 151).

Likewise, Figure 8.5 portrays the striking changes that took place during the presence and absence of an incentive system. Aware of the perennial procrastination associated with long-range, relatively unstructured projects, Dillon, Kent, and Malott (1980) set up an incentive system designed to aid students in the completion of their Master's theses. As Figure 8.5 confirms, graduate students 'produced a high and steady rate of completion of the weekly research tasks when it was present, while the rate of completion was considerably lower during the baseline phase, when the incentive system was absent' (p. 213). Not only were there no trends in the data from phase to phase, but there was no overlap in the data points from phase to phase.

Similarly, Kortick and O'Brien (1996) found that the quality of sorting needed in a package delivery company was far below standard during baseline. Figure 8.2 not only illustrates how far below standard the workers were, but

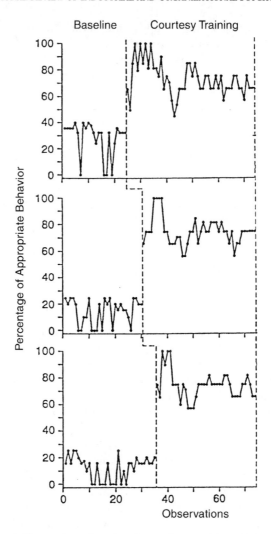

**Figure 8.4** Graph illustrating a Level 1 change in a positive reinforcement study
Reproduced with permission from M.D. Johnson and S.B. Fawcett (1994). Courteous
service: Its assessment and modification in a human service organization. *Journal of
Applied Behavior Analysis*, **27**, 145–152. © The Society for the Experimental Analysis of
Behavior

also the lack of trends indicating no shifts in the direction of the subsequent
phase. Only during the intervention did the organization reach the company
standard of 3000 packages sorted correctly for every missorted package.
When the intervention was reversed, performance declined. And, as shown
in Figure 8.2, there was not a single data point overlapping between the
phases.

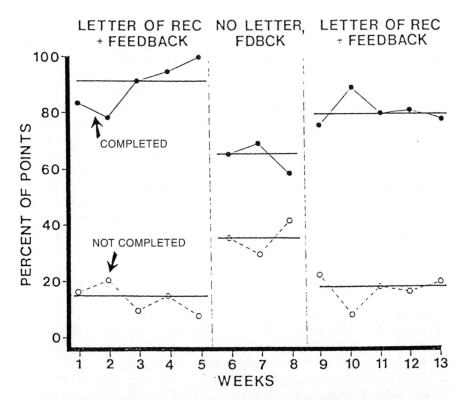

**Figure 8.5**   Graph illustrating a Level 1 change in a positive reinforcement study Reproduced with permission from M.J. Dillon, H.M. Kent and R.W. Malott (1980). A supervisory system for accomplishing long-range projects: An application to masters thesis research. *Journal of Organizational Behavior Management*, **2**(3), 213–228. © The Haworth Press

Similarly, the number of days lost per million person hours worked dramatically declined when a token economy program was introduced (Fox, Hopkins & Anger, 1987). In addition, as shown in Figure 8.3, none of the data points during baseline overlapped with any of the data points during the intervention, indicating a Level 1 change.

*Support Level 2 changes.* Level 2 changes in which one third or fewer of the data points in each phase can overlap with any data points in the adjacent phases can be seen in Figure 8.1. Although the safety level immediately increased when feedback was provided, several of the data points during baseline overlapped with those during the intervention phase (Komaki, Barwick & Scott, 1978). Hence, this experiment (described above) was classified as providing support for the principle of positive reinforcement, but at a level of 2.

*Support Level 3 changes.* Although Level 3 changes allowed for one third or fewer of the data points in one phase to overlap with the mean (or if not given, the median) of the subsequent phase, this requirement was still quite strict. To assess the effectiveness of their goal-setting and feedback program, Wilk and Redmon (1990) used a multiple-baseline design across persons; in this case, across the three processors in a university admissions department. As detailed in Table 8.2a, when the program was introduced, performance for each processor increased dramatically. The first processor increased the number of tasks completed from an average of 22 to 180. Furthermore, examination of Figure 8.6 shows no overlap whatsoever between baseline and intervention. The third processor also improved from an average of 30 to 99 tasks completed. Overlap did occur, however, as shown in Figure 8.6; 2 of 17 data points from baseline overlapped with the data points during the intervention. Even greater overlap occurred in the second processor's performance: Although the second processor made improvements from a mean of 47 to 89, she completed approximately 100 tasks one week during baseline. This single score of 100 overlapped the mean of 89 of the subsequent phase. Because only 1 of 10 (or 10%) of the data points during baseline overlapped, these results met the requirement that one third or fewer of the data can overlap with the mean of the subsequent phase. Based on the data of this lone processor, the results were categorized as a Level 3 change. An examination of Table 8.2a and Figure 8.6, however, shows that the changes, while not as dramatic as Level 1 or 2 changes, warranted Wilk and Redmon's (1990) conclusion that these results 'clearly support the effectiveness of a combined daily goal-setting and feedback program to increase employee productivity' (p. 69).

In short, whether the changes were classified as Level 1, 2, or 3, the improvements were still sizable.

*Mixed.* Studies classified as mixed were those in which some of the data indicated support, but other data did not. The study by Sulzer-Azaroff and de Santamaria (1980), using a multiple-baseline design, is an example. As shown in Figure 8.7, improvements occurred in five of the six departments. One department, Department 1, did not change from baseline to the feedback/suggestion phase because of the downward trend during the baseline phase in the direction of the intervention. Because changes occurred in five departments but not in one, this study was classified as mixed, indicating that the program was effective in some cases but not in all.

*No support.* The results of the studies discussed above were all considered to provide support. For some studies, that was not the case. As Figure 8.8 illustrates, no changes in preventive maintenance (PM) of heavy equipment in the Marine Corps were forthcoming (Komaki & Collins, 1982). Despite the fact that the researchers developed a new measure of PM and set up a program that included graduated goals *and* a potent consequence (time off with pay, which has been shown in a previous military setting to be among the top-rated [Datel & Legters, 1971]), the results were either short-lived or nonexistent. Hence, this experiment was classified as providing no support.

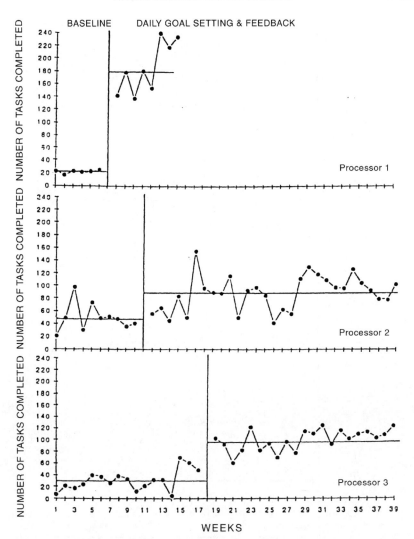

**Figure 8.6**    Graph illustrating a Level 3 change in a positive reinforcement study Reproduced with permission from L.A. Wilk and W.K. Redmon (1990). A daily adjusted goal-setting and feedback procedure for improving productivity in a university admissions department. *Journal of Organizational Behavior Management*, **11**(1), 55–75. © The Haworth Press

*Inconclusive.* In some studies, it could not be determined whether the changes were the result of the program or not. These studies were classified as inconclusive. Figure 8.9 illustrates the results of just such a study. Although an ABA design was appropriately used to examine the effectiveness of an intervention consisting of praise and corrective feedback in a Russian textile mill

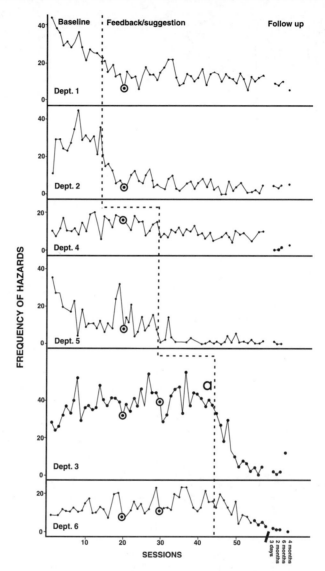

**Figure 8.7**   Graph illustrating mixed support in a positive reinforcement study
Reproduced with permission from B. Sulzer-Azaroff and M.C. de Santamaria (1980).
Industrial safety hazard reduction through performance feedback. *Journal of Applied
Behavior Analysis*, **13**(2), 287–295. © The Society for the Experimental Analysis of
Behavior

(Welsh, Luthans & Sommer, 1993), and improvements were obtained during
the intervention, performance remained the same during the reversal phase.
As a result, it was not possible to rule out alternative explanations to make a
causal inference. Furthermore, Welsh, Luthans and Sommer (1993) properly

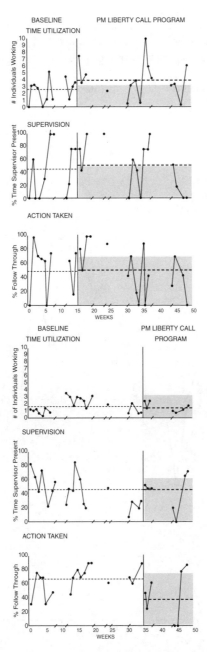

**Figure 8.8** Graph illustrating no support in a positive reinforcement study
Reproduced with permission from J.L. Komaki and R.L. Collins (1982). Motivation of
preventive maintenance performance. In R.M. O'Brien, A.M. Dickinson and M.
Rosow (Eds), *Industrial Behavior Modification: A Learning-based Approach to Business
Management* (pp. 243–265). New York: Pergamon. © Pergamon Press

note that 'the absence of a true reversal weakens the arguments that the intervention was the whole "cause" of increased (decreased) behavior frequencies' (p.30). Because it was not possible to rule out sources of internal

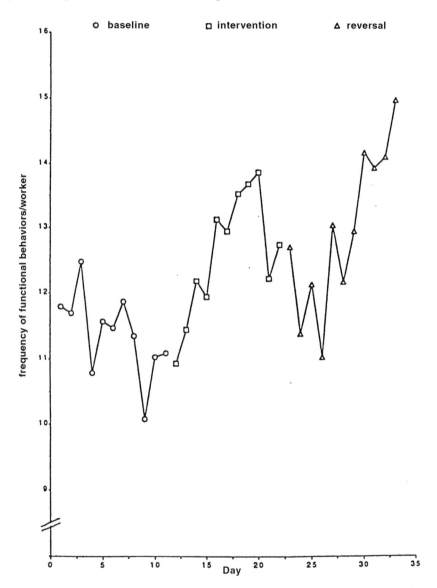

**Figure 8.9**   Graph illustrating inconclusive results in a positive reinforcement study Reproduced with permission from D.H.B. Welsh, F. Luthans and S.M. Sommer (1993). Organizational behavior modification goes to Russia: Replicating an experimental analysis across cultures and tasks. *Journal of Organizational Behavior Management*, **13**(2), 15–35. © The Haworth Press

invalidity and to draw conclusions about causality with confidence, this study was classified as inconclusive.

As can be seen, using the OCT criteria, studies ranged from those showing support ('yes,' 'mixed') to those studies that were inconclusive. A high percentage of studies—93%—had results showing support for the use of positive reinforcement.

*Duration of changes.* To see whether the changes might be substantial but short-lived, we tallied for each of the within-group studies concerning positive reinforcement the duration of the entire study as well as the longest intervention. As shown in Table 8.3, almost half of the studies lasted 26 weeks or longer, and in over 40% of the studies, the longest intervention was at least 12 weeks or longer. In fact, the experiments, conducted during the last 10 years,

**Table 8.3** Duration and delivery of methodologically rigorous positive reinforcement studies

| Duration[a] | % |
|---|---|
| Total | |
| Less than 12 weeks | 31 |
| 12–25 weeks | 25 |
| 26–38 weeks | 16 |
| 39–52 weeks | 10 |
| 1–4 years | 15 |
| 15 years | 1 |
| Longest intervention | |
| Less than 12 weeks | 59 |
| 12–25 weeks | 25 |
| 26–38 weeks | 7 |
| 39–52 weeks | 1 |
| 1–2 years | 4 |
| 12 years | 1 |
| **Delivery** | **%** |
| How often | |
| Daily | 34 |
| Weekly | 49 |
| Monthly | 7 |
| Unspecified | 10 |
| To whom[b] | |
| Individual | 80 |
| Group | 30 |

Note. $n = 88$

[a]Omitting the four between-groups studies that typically use a single pretest and posttest score

[b]Figures add up to more than 100% because some reports included two or more categories

were conducted on average 6.8 months and data were collected about the interventions on average 3.3 months. What this means is that the results were not ephemeral, lasting only a day, a week, or even a month. Rather, the changes, on average, continued over an extended period. Illustrating the potential longevity of any positive reinforcement program, Fox, Hopkins and Anger (1987) introduced a token economy program, shown in Figure 8.3, that was successful in reducing accidents in one mine for 11 years and in another for 12 years.

*Delivery of consequences.    How often.* Unlike the typical annual performance appraisal interview, consequences were delivered fairly often: from once a day to once a month. As can be seen in Table 8.3, 42% were delivered daily. Almost half, 48%, were delivered weekly. Only 5% were delivered monthly.

*To whom.* Consequences could be delivered to an individual or to a group, or both; because consequences could be distributed to both individuals and groups, the percentages tally to more than 100% in Table 8.3. The focus was on the individual, with 79% of the studies providing consequences on an individual basis, and only 30% to the group as a whole.

*Types of consequences.*    At least five different classes of consequences were provided in the positive reinforcement programs. Because all of the classes of consequences are not in everyday parlance, they are described below in more detail:

1.    *Organizational* : Organizational consequences include promotions, special training opportunities, and benefits indigenous to the particular organization. The latter were used by Haynes, Pine and Fitch (1982) in a regional transportation authority; they offered benefits such as free gasoline and free monthly passes on the bus system to workers as an incentive for reducing accidents.

Another powerful and potentially reinforcing event in academic settings, the sending out of letters of recommendations, was among the consequences successfully used by Dillon, Kent and Malott (1980). Rather than sending out the letters when students or potential employers requested them, Dillon, Kent and Malott (1980) arranged for the students' advisors to send them out when and only when students were making progress toward completing their Masters' theses.

2.    *Activity* : Another class of consequences, derived from the Premack (Premack, 1965) principle, is referred to as an activity consequence. The Premack principle states that any activity which workers engage in more regularly than another activity can be used as a consequence for the lower frequency activity. A novel application of the Premack principle took place in a sales organization. When Gupton and LeBow (1971) found new sales (where the customer purchases a new contract) to be much lower in frequency than renewal sales (where the customer merely renews a contract), they made the lower

frequency activity contingent on the higher frequency activity. In this case, the making of a new sale, the lower frequency activity, was the desired outcome; the opportunity to sell five renewal contracts, the higher frequency activity, was the activity consequence.

3. *Social* : Typically expressed by individuals, social consequences include commendations, compliments, criticism, reviews, and recognition for a job well done. For example, a manager in an agency in city government wrote down comments about the clerk typists' performance: 'Your typing percentage is up 15% over last week. Keep it up!' 'Your score was 100% this week. I knew you could do it. Fantastic!' (Nordstrom, Hall, Lorenzi & Delquadri, 1988, p. 100). In another example, hospital supervisors made comments to staff members, saying such things as 'I'm pleased to see you interacting with clients, but I'm sure Mary [the client] is even more pleased' (Brown, Willis & Reid, 1981).

4. *Informational* : Informational consequences, as the label suggests, are ones in which information is provided about a person's performance. The information can be conveyed in a variety of different ways. For example, feedback notes were passed on to supervisors to encourage the completion of accident reports; the number of total items that had been included, as well as any increases in completeness over prior submissions were mentioned (Fox & Sulzer-Azaroff, 1987). In other studies, graphs of baseline and intervention levels of workers' performance were used (Komaki & Collins, 1982; Komaki, Collins & Temlock, 1987; Nasanen & Saari, 1987; Sulzer-Azaroff & de Santamaria, 1980). The information itself can also vary. In the area of safety, the information provided included the percentage of incidents performed safely by the group (Komaki, Barwick & Scott, 1978; Komaki, Heinzmann & Lawson, 1980), the frequency of hazards (Sulzer-Azaroff & de Santamaria, 1980), the percentage of correct housekeeping practices (Nasanen & Saari, 1987), and audiograms at the beginning and at the end of workers' shifts, showing the temporary hearing losses that occurred when ear plugs were not worn (Zohar, Cohen & Azar, 1980).

5. *Generalized* : Generalized reinforcers derive their potency from the fact that they can be exchanged for back-up reinforcers. Examples of generalized reinforcers include cash, frequent flyer coupons, and trading stamps. Trading stamps were given to miners who had not suffered a lost-time injury during the month (Fox, Hopkins & Anger, 1987). With the trading stamps, they could exchange them for various household and recreational items which served as back-up reinforcers.

Another back-up reinforcer in a job training center for trainees who had earned coupons included the opportunity to select a clerical assignment including who, what, and where you worked (Deluga & Andrews, 1985–1986). Similarly, the chance to win a television set was used as a back-up reinforcer with a group of telemarketers who had participated in a lottery system (Fellows & Mawhinney, 1997).

In short, a wide variety of consequences were used as positive reinforcers, ranging from the sending out of letters of recommendation to the provision of information about one's performance.

*Using a single consequence or a combination of consequences* . In some cases, only one type of consequence was used. For instance, Gupton and LeBow (1971) used only one consequence to good effect, as shown in Table 8.2a. When the callers could make renewal calls—the consequence—after making a service sale, they substantially increased new service sales. In fact, the authors conclude by recommending that 'costly job analyses designed to increase productivity could perhaps be replaced by observing response rates, designating high and low probability behaviors, and instituting the appropriate contingencies' (p. 82).

Two or more types of consequences were combined in many interventions. A prevalent pairing was social and informational consequences. Besides praise, managers often provided feedback. A manager in the Nordstrom et al. (1988) study not only wrote down comments such as 'fantastic,' but he would also describe how 'the percent of pages typed correct was determined' when providing information to the typists about their performance (p. 102).

Three types of consequences were provided to winning transportation teams: (a) organizational—free gasoline and free monthly passes in the regional transportation authority, as well as (b) feedback about the teams' standings with respect to accidents, and (c) praise, with the winning teams being 'personally congratulated by the director of operations' (Haynes, Pine & Fitch, 1982).

To help graduate students complete long-range, relatively unstructured projects, Dillon, Kent and Malott (1980) used a host of consequences: (a) organizational, in that the advisor would send out letters of recommendation based only on students' satisfactory progress; (b) generalized, in that a point system was developed in which students could earn positive (and negative) points toward having letters of recommendation sent; and (c) informational, in that the students 'received a weekly feedback form, showing . . . the number of points (they) had earned for the previous week and cumulatively throughout the semester' (p. 219).

*How often.* The percentage of studies delivering the different types of consequences is shown in Table 8.4; because more than one type of consequence could be provided during the intervention, the percentages tally up to more than 100%.

Informational consequences predominated, with 72% of the studies providing feedback. Social and organizational consequences were next: 42% provided social consequences such as recognition, and 25% provided organizational consequences such as financial incentives or time off from work. Relatively few generalized consequences were delivered; only 10% of the studies provided chances to win in a lottery or tokens earned toward back-up reinforcers.

**Table 8.4** Different types of consequences in methodologically rigorous positive reinforcement studies

| Type of consequence | %[a] |
| --- | --- |
| Informational | 72 |
| Social | 42 |
| Organizational | 25 |
| Financial | 16 |
| Time off | 5 |
| Other | 4 |
| Generalized | 10 |
| Chances to win a lottery | 7 |
| Tokens earned toward back-ups | 3 |
| Activity | 1 |

Note. $n = 88$

[a]Figures add up to more than 100% because some reports included two or more categories

In short, what these findings indicate is when positive reinforcement programs were set up so that positive consequences, whether singly or in combination, were provided relatively frequently, substantial improvements occurred in performance. Furthermore, the percentage of studies showing support for the principle of positive reinforcement was reasonably high with 93% of the studies showing support.

### Does negative reinforcement work?

In contrast to the 88 positive reinforcement studies, only two studies addressed the use of negative reinforcement, and only two studies examined punishment. Furthermore, the findings were considerably more variable. For instance, one negative reinforcement study provided support, whereas the other was inconclusive. Given the sparsity of studies and the inconsistency of results, the subsequent discussions will not focus on the results, but on contextual issues.

Both negative and positive reinforcement are similar in that they aim to promote performance, but they differ in terms of whether the consequences are: (a) presented or removed, and considered (b) positive or aversive (Malott, Whaley & Malott, 1997). With positive reinforcement, something positive is presented: salutary comments are made; congratulations are offered; plaques, pizza and beer are provided; points are accrued; televisions are won. With negative reinforcement, nothing is presented. Instead, something—often considered distasteful or aversive—is removed or avoided: nagging ceases; complaints stop; frowns disappear; receiving penalties for tardiness is escaped; and having to punch out at time clocks is avoided. For example, workers in the study by Ford (1981) could avoid the aversive condition of having to report directly to their supervisor and to hear what impact their absence would have on the operation of the facility by taking vacation time instead of sick time.

An example of how and why negative reinforcement is used can be seen in the study by Kempen and Hall (1977). Because absenteeism was viewed as 'a chronic and worsening problem' (p. 1), management approached Kempen, an internal consultant within the Western Electric Company, to help develop procedures to reduce it. In reviewing the literature on absenteeism, the authors were disappointed that two previous field experiments conducted by Lawler and Hackman (1969) and Pedalino and Gamboa (1974) did not include 'a description of any historical or concurrent factors, such as disciplinary procedures, absence payment policies, or previous control efforts, which might have influenced the effects of the experimental interventions, . . . that the target employees in the studies were not typical of the bulk of industrial workers . . ., and lastly, that both interventions used monetary incentives' (p. 3), which were not practical or possible at Western Electric due to labor contracts stipulating that any monetary considerations be negotiated.

When Kempen and Hall looked at the previous efforts to reduce absenteeism, they found the primary method that had been used in the past consisted of strict controls in terms of clocking in and out and numerous penalties for noncompliance in terms of disciplinary procedures and ladders. In Plant A, for example, management had previously maintained 'a punitive absence control plan which consisted of four steps of progressive discipline, ranging from an informal discussion with the employee to consideration for termination of employment. The disciplinary process was begun when an employee accumulated four occasions of absence, regardless of length, during the most recent 26 week period' (Kempen & Hall, 1977, p. 9). Perhaps not surprisingly, these procedures did not result in significantly reducing absenteeism. During baseline, absenteeism averaged 6.2% at Plant A and 7.8% at Plant B, with absenteeism reaching as high as 10.2% in the seven months before the intervention.

Taking into consideration the punitive efforts that had been made to reduce absenteeism in the past and given the stark conditions that still existed, Kempen and Hall (1977) introduced a system, which allowed employees to avoid such aversive conditions as a high position on the disciplinary ladder and having to punch the time clock. In the intervention in Plant A: (a) The disciplinary procedures were redefined so as to focus on the employee's total time absent regardless of the number of occasions of absence; and (b) 'four types of reinforcement for good or improving attendance were provided: (1) freedom from the requirement to 'punch' the time clock, (2) earned time off without pay, (3) temporary immunity from discipline regardless of incurred absences, and (4) reduction in position on the disciplinary ladder' (p. 11). Because the only 'positive' consequence for attendance was the opportunity to earn time-off without pay and, in three instances, workers could avoid or escape aversive conditions such as a high position on the disciplinary ladder and having to punch the time clock, this system was designated as negative reinforcement. (Note: As shown in Table 8.5, it had the effect of reducing absenteeism to 4% in Plant A and 6.7% in Plant B.)

The differences in baseline conditions between negative and positive reinforcement studies are sometimes striking. In contrast to the harsh baseline conditions of Kempen and Hall's (1977) factory, baseline conditions in positive reinforcement studies tend to be less punitive, in fact, some may be described as ones of benign neglect. During baseline in the area of safety, for instance, in Komaki et al. (1978) nothing much happens when persons perform as desired; coworkers rarely comment and management recognition is rare. At the same time, nothing much happens when persons perform unsafely; no derogatory comments are made by coworkers or supervisors, no penalties are levied, and no disciplinary procedures are instituted. Even the aversive consequence of performing unsafely—having an accident—is typically, albeit fortunately, missing. Perhaps because there are few consequences for either desired or undesired performance, the interventions typically involve the introduction of primarily positive consequences. In contrast, with negative reinforcement programs, the aversive conditions already exist. Under these circumstances, investigators like Kempen and Hall (1977) could not ignore the stark baseline conditions. Necessitated by conditions which already existed and banned (no doubt) from making more use of positive consequences, Kempen and Hall (1977) wisely chose to allow workers to avoid or escape some of the most distasteful conditions. Although negative reinforcement is not the preferred principle to use in promoting performance, the study by Kempen and Hall (1977) illustrates why circumstances sometimes necessitate its use.

*Does punishment work?*

Despite perennial interest in punishment (e.g., Arvey & Jones, 1985; Baron, 1988), only two studies broached this question (Table 8.6). In one, a pay penalty in which cash shortages were subtracted from workers' daily salaries was successfully introduced by Marholin and Gray (1976); in the other, Ford (1981) combined negative reinforcement (described above) and punishment by requiring workers who wanted to take sick time to document their illness and to hear the supervisor tell them 'the number of staff remaining to meet work area responsibilities' (p. 73), but the results were inconclusive.

Given the nature of punishment which entails the use of aversive control procedures, we were chagrined to note that no compelling arguments were presented by either Marholin and Gray (1976) or Ford (1981) as to why it was necessary to use punishment. Furthermore, even if punishment were warranted, why was it not paired with positive reinforcement? Why were workers not positively reinforced for an incompatible behavior—for Marholin and Gray (1976) accuracy, for Ford (1981) the taking of sick leave and vacation time appropriately?

**Table 8.5**   Studies pertinent to the question: Does negative reinforcement work?

| Article | Dependent variable | Means by condition | | | | Design | Test | Results supported |
|---|---|---|---|---|---|---|---|---|
| | | Baseline | Negative reinforcement | Baseline | Negative reinforcement | | | |
| Ford (1981) | Vacation time taken (hours) | 103.5 | 145.6 | 161.0 | 199.1 | Rev. | Visual | Inc. |
| Kempen & Hall (1977) | Workers absent (%) Plant A Plant B | 6.2 7.8 | 4.0 6.7 | | | MB | Visual | Yes[3] |

Note. Rev. = reversal. MB = multiple baseline. Inc. = inconclusive. For support levels (1 = highest), refer to text

**Table 8.6** Studies pertinent to the question: Does punishment work?

| Article | Dependent variable | Means by condition | | | | Design | Test | Results supported |
| | | Baseline | Punishment | Baseline | Punishment | | | |
|---|---|---|---|---|---|---|---|---|
| Ford (1981) | Sick leave taken (#) of hours) | 102.8 | 57.1 | 56.5 | 49.7 | Rev. | Visual | Inc. |
| Marholin & Gray (1976) | Cash shortages based on register receipts (%) | 4.0 | 0.4 | 3.7 | 0.04 | Rev. | Visual | Yes[2] |

Note. Rev. = reversal. Inc. = inconclusive. For levels of support (1 = highest), refer to text

Given these pressing but unanswered questions, we would welcome (a) a set of guidelines discussing the conditions under which the different principles can and should be used in the field, and (b) then research specifically geared to documenting the conditions identified in the guidelines. For example, it would be beneficial to determine if the potentially deleterious side-effects that have been documented in other, primarily laboratory settings also occur and what, if anything, can be done to mitigate these potentially deleterious side-effects.

In summary, the principles of positive reinforcement, negative reinforcement, and punishment have all been used to try and change workers' performance. Although the use of positive reinforcement is considerably more prevalent and the results consistently better, we recommend further probing into the context and the conditions surrounding their use in applied settings.

### Findings: Facilitative Questions

This section presents the results of studies asking whether one treatment *adds* to the effectiveness of another treatment. We will begin by addressing the popular question involving the use of consequences as one treatment and antecedents as the other treatment.

*Do consequences improve performance above and beyond that of antecedents alone?*

After positive reinforcement, this antecedent-consequence question was the second most frequently raised. A total of 17 studies addressed this research question, as shown in Table 8.7. Thirteen of the studies found support for the question; three were inconclusive; only one did not find support. The ABC multiple-baseline studies (where B = antecedents and C = consequences) by Alavosius and Sulzer-Azaroff (1990), Anderson et al. (1988), Brown et al. (1980), Cossairt, Hall and Hopkins (1973), Komaki, Collins, and Penn (1982), Langeland, Johnson and Mawhinney (1998), Reber and Wallin (1984), Richman (1988), and Saari (1987), as well as the ABCB or ABCBC reversal studies by Chhokar and Wallin (1984), Geller et al. (1980), and Shook, Johnson and Uhlman (1978) found that consequences improved performance above and beyond that of antecedents alone. Some of the studies (e.g., Chhokar & Wallin, 1984; Komaki, Collins & Penn, 1982; Reber & Wallin, 1984) went beyond the visual inspection of the data with the addition of an ARIMA analysis. In each study, both the OCT assessment and the ARIMA analysis indicated that the improvement in worker performance between the antecedent and consequence phases was significant.

The antecedents typically used were training, instructions, rules, reminders or some combination of these educational and/or cuing events. The consequences, on the other hand, usually consisted of feedback and, in some cases, praise. For instance, Chhokar and Wallin (1984) implemented the following phases: Baseline (A), Training and Goal-setting (B), Feedback (C), Training and Goal-setting only (B), and Feedback (C).

As shown in Figure 8.10, after measuring safety performance in a manufacturing and repair plant over a 10-month period, they found that performance significantly improved from a training and goal-setting (B) mean of 80.9% to means of 94.6 and 96.8% when feedback (C) was provided once or twice a week, *and* that performance declined to 89.1% after reversing to only training and goal-setting (B), and then improved to 93.9% when the consequence (C) was again provided. Based on the results of the ABCBC design, Chhokar and Wallin (1984) rightfully conclude that 'the results that performance reached the set goal level only after feedback was provided, . . . declined when feedback was withdrawn, and improved again when feedback was reintroduced, highlight the importance of feedback for improving performance over and above the level achieved with only goal setting' (p. 529).

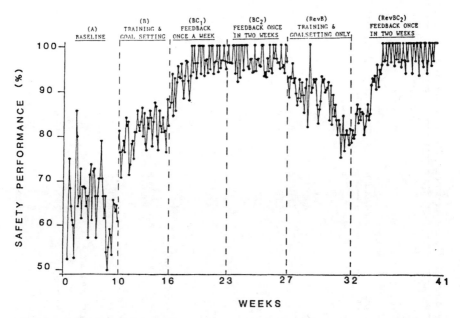

WEEKS

**Figure 8.10**   Graph illustrating Level 2 support for the effects of consequences over and above that of antecedents.
From J.S. Chhokar and J.A. Wallin (1984). A field study of the effect of feedback frequency on performance. *Journal of Applied Psychology*, **69**, 524–530. © American Psychological Association. Reproduced by permission of the American Psychological Association

The supportive results of 11 of 12 experiments indicate that, at least in some circumstances, antecedents alone may not be sufficient and that consequences are necessary to obtain substantial performance improvements. Given the prevalence of antecedents as a popular panacea, it is particularly salient to obtain evidence about the necessity of consequences.

**Table 8.7** Studies pertinent to the question: Do consequences improve performance above and beyond that of antecedents alone?

| Article[a] | Dependent variable | Means by condition | | | | Test | Results supported |
|---|---|---|---|---|---|---|---|
| | | Antecedent | Antecedent and consequence | Antecedent | Antecedent and consequence | | |
| *Multiple-baseline design :* | | | | | | | |
| Alavosius & Sulzer-Azaroff (1990) | Patient care (%) | | | | | Visual | Yes[3] |
| | Subject 1 | 60.0 | 94.0 | | | | |
| | Subject 2 | 60.0 | 95.0 | | | | |
| | Subject 3 | 75.0 | 94.0 | | | | |
| | Subject 4 | 50.0 | 93.0 | | | | |
| Anderson, Crowell, Hantula & Siroky (1988)[b] | Cleanliness of bar/restaurant (%) | | | | | Visual | Yes[2] |
| Brown, Malott, Dillon & Keeps (1980) | Customer service responses (%) | 59.3[c] | 84.7 | | | Visual | Yes[1] |
| Cossairt, Hall & Hopkins (1973) | Student praise (# of intervals) | | | | | Visual | Yes[3e] |
| | Teacher A | 1.4 | 0.7/ 5.0[d] | | | | |
| | Teacher B | 0.0 | 1.0/14.5[d] | | | | |
| Komaki, Heinzmann & Lawson (1980b) | Safety behaviors (%) | | | | | ARIMA[f] | Inc. |
| | Sweeper repair | 46.1 (21.0) | 68.4 (21.1) | | | | |
| | Preventive maintenance | 61.3 (17.1) | 76.2 (13.7) | | | | |
| | Light equipment repair | 73.8 (13.9) | 89.6 (13.0) | | | | |
| | Heavy equipment repair | 84.3 (16.6) | 92.3 (13.4) | | | | |

| Study | Measure | Baseline | Treatment | Analysis | Significant |
|---|---|---|---|---|---|
| Komaki, Collins & Penn (1982) | Safety incidents (%) | | | ARIMA | Yes[3] |
| | Chill & Pack | 83.0 (12.0) | 95.0 (8.0) | | |
| | Evisceration 1 | 66.0 (9.0) | 85.0 (7.0) | | |
| | Evisceration 2 | 84.0 (7.0) | 92.0 (4.0) | | |
| | Cut-up & bagging | 90.0 (11.0) | 96.0 (7.0) | | |
| Langeland, Johnson & Mawhinney (1998) | Office duties completed (%) | | | Visual | Yes[2] |
| | Admin. duties | 77.50 | 90.56 | | |
| | Record keeping | 71.50 | 82.55 | | |
| | Direct service | 87.50 | 89.20 | | |
| Parsons & Reid (1995) | Feedback from supervisors | | | Visual | Inc. |
| Ralis & O'Brien (1986) | Dinner orders with beverage (%) | | | Visual | No |
| | Red wine | 4.5 | 5.6 | | |
| | White wine | 16.5 | 17.9 | | |
| Reber & Wallin (1984) | Safety behaviors (%) | | | ARIMA | Yes |
| | Group 1 | 73.3g | 93.4 | | |
| | Group 2 | 75.2g | 96.0 | | |
| | Group 3 | 84.0g | 97.6 | | |
| Richman, Riordan, Reiss et al. (1988) | Workers on task (%) | | | Visual | Yes[3] |
| | House A | 80.0 | 94.0 | | |
| | House B | 75.0 | 81.0 | | |
| Saari (1987) | Correct safety practices (%) | | | Visual | Yes[2] |
| | Floor 2 | 68.0 | 81.0 | | |
| | Floor 1 | 76.0 | 83.0 | | |

**Table 8.7**  (*Continued*)

| Article[a] | Dependent variable | Means by condition | | | | Test | Results supported |
|---|---|---|---|---|---|---|---|
| | | Antecedent | Antecedent and consequence | Antecedent | Antecedent and consequence | | |
| Seaman, Greene & Watson-Perczel (1986) | CPR administration (% correct) | 46.0[h] | 95.0[h] | | | Visual | Yes[2] |
| Wittkopp, Rowan & Poling (1990)[b] | Machine set-up time (# of minues) | | | | | Visual | Inc. |

| Article[a] | Dependent variable | Means by condition | | | | Test | Results supported |
|---|---|---|---|---|---|---|---|
| | | Antecedent | Antecedent and consequence | Antecedent | Antecedent and consequence | | |
| *Reversal design:* | | | | | | | |
| Chhokar & Wallin (1984) | Safety behaviors (%) | 80.9 | 94.6/96.8[i] | 89.1 | 93.9 | ARIMA | Yes[2] |
| Geller, Eason, Phillips & Piesson (1980) | Hand washing following contamination (#) | 2.1[j] | 4.9 | 2.8 | | Visual | Yes[1] |
| Shook, Johnson & Uhlman Exp. 2 (1978) | Graphs completed (%) | 1.7 | 13.7/52.6[k] | 17.8 | 60.3 | Visual | Yes[21] |

Note. Numbers in parentheses = standard deviations. For support levels (1 = highest), refer to text. Inc. = inconclusive.

[a]Refer to article for results from additional conditions or phases.

[b]No measures or only some measures of central tendency or other summary statistics given.

[c]For two of three salespersons.

[d]The means of 0.7 and 1.0 refer to the antecedent and feedback condition; 5.0 and 14.5 refer to the antecedent, feedback, and praise condition.

[e]Yes, consequences improved performance above and beyond that of antecedents alone when feedback and then praise was provided.

[f]The data necessary to determine the level of support are not available.

[g]The means of 73.3, 75.2, and 84.0 refer to the second and most effective antecedent.

[h]The means are averaged across people.

[i]The mean of 94.6 refers to the antecedent and feedback once a week condition; 96.8 refers to the antecedent and feedback once every two weeks condition.

[j]The mean of 2.1 refers to the second and most effective antecedent.

[k]The mean of 13.7 refers to the antecedent and group feedback condition; the mean of 52.6 refers to the antecedent and individual feedback condition. Yes, consequences improved performance above and beyond that of antecedents alone when group feedback and then individual feedback were provided.

*Does contingent pay improve performance over and above that of noncontingent or full pay?*

The question about contingent and noncontingent reinforcement was the third most frequently raised question. Addressed by six studies as shown in Table 8.8, five of the six studies support the conclusion that contingent reinforcement improves performance over and above that of full pay when improved performance is the objective.

To see how timely the issue of contingent pay is, let us look at a study using a series of management strategies still in use today. Despite the fact that Pierce and Risley's (1974) study was done over 15 years ago, it still reflects the positions of many present-day managers. Confronted with what they considered inadequate performance, Pierce and Risley attempted to shore up workers' performance by implementing two classic management remedies: (a) using job descriptions that made it clear what workers were supposed to do—in fact, they even got new hires to sign an agreement that they knew what the job entailed and that they agreed to do it; and (b) threatening to fire the workers if they did not improve. As shown in Figure 8.11, the job descriptions had a minimal impact, with workers completing only 50 to 75% of their assigned tasks. The threats had an initial effect with improvements the first day, but after three days performance declined to their former levels. Only when a contingent pay system was instituted did performance improve so that workers were completing nearly 100% of their work. The director of the urban recreation program made it clear that 'instead of pay being based on the amount of time they spend in the community center, pay would instead be based on the proportion of their job they completed each day. They would now be paid for their work time instead of clock time' (p. 211). The impact of contingent pay can best be seen in its absence. When workers were told 'they were doing a fine job, . . . how much their work was helping the youths, . . . and that they would now receive full pay' (p. 211), the percentage of tasks completed plummeted to its lowest level, averaging 35%. When workers were again paid for the tasks they had completed, they immediately completed their assigned tasks.

The results of this study and the other four studies suggest that paying workers by clock time rather than work time will not necessarily translate into sustained improvements in performance, and that contingent pay can improve performance above and beyond that of full pay.

*Other facilitative questions*

Other questions have been raised, for example, about the impact of individual feedback over and above that of group feedback, and specific feedback over and above that of general feedback. For these facilitative questions, however, the numbers of the studies range from one to four. Moreover, the results are sometimes inconclusive. Hence, it is difficult to draw conclusions with

**Table 8.8** Studies pertinent to the question: Does contingent pay improve performance above and beyond that of noncontingent pay?

| Article | Dependent variable | Means by condition or group | | | | Design | Test | Results supported |
|---|---|---|---|---|---|---|---|---|
| | | Baseline | Contingent | Non-contingent | Contingent | | | |
| Allison, Silverstein & Galante (1992)[a] | Effective childcare (%) | | | | | MB | ANOVA | Ind. |
| George & Hopkins (1989)[b] | Sales per hour ($)<br>Restaurant 1<br>Restaurant 2<br>Restaurant 3 | 2.10<br>2.08<br>2.17 | 2.72<br>2.50<br>2.70 | | | MB | Visual | Yes[1] |
| Komaki, Waddell & Pearce (1977, study 1) | Time worked (%) | 63.0 | 93.0 | 62.0 | 97.0 | Rev. | Visual | Yes[1] |
| LaFleur & Hyten (1995) | Banquet staff quality of table setting (%) | 68.8 | 100.0 | 82.3 | 100.0 | Rev. | Visual | Yes[2] |
| Orpen (1974)[b] | Batches of error-free components (#) | | | 71.0<br>(8.6) | 82.0[c]<br>(16.2) | Con. grp | t-test | Yes |
| Pierce & Risley (1974) | Task completed (%) | | ≈100.0 | 35.0 | ≈100.0 | Rev. | Visual | Yes[2] |

Note. MB = multiple baseline. Rev. = reversal. Con. grp = control group. Ind. = indeterminate. For support levels (1 = highest), refer to text. Numbers in parentheses = standard deviation.

[a]No measures or only some measures of central tendency or other summary statistics given.
[b]Refer to article for results from additional conditions or phases.
[c]Gain scores.

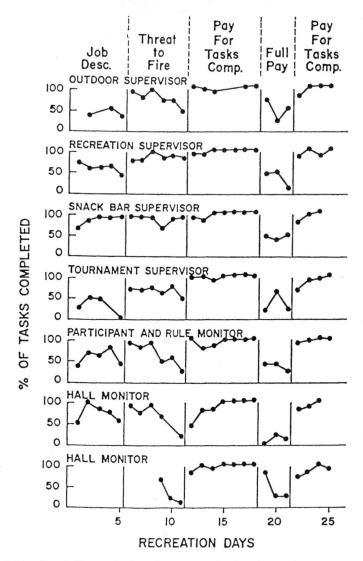

**Figure 8.11**  Graph illustrating Level 3 support for the effects of contingent pay over and above that of full pay

Reproduced with permission from C.H. Pierce and T.R. Risley (1974). Improving job performance of neighborhood youth corps aides in an urban recreation program. *Journal of Applied Behavior Analysis*, 7(2), 207–215. © The Society for the Experimental Analysis of Behavior

confidence. To foster further research about the questions raised, however, each of the studies are presented in Tables 8.9, 8.10 and 8.11. Rather than dwelling on how the results do or do not provide support, we will make recommendations for future research.

**Table 8.9** Studies answering other facilitative questions

| Facilitative question | Article | Dependent variable | Means by condition | | Design | Test | Results supported |
|---|---|---|---|---|---|---|---|
| | | | Baseline | Intervention | | | |
| Do antecedents improve performance over consequences alone? | Calpin, Edelstein & Redmon (1987) | Hours spent with clients (%) | | | MB | Visual | Inc. |
| | | Group 1 | 32.6 | 33.4 | | | |
| | | Group 2 | 26.6 | 27.0 | | | |
| | | Group 3 | 30.4 | 34.4 | | | |
| | Nemeroff & Cosentino (1979) | Days absent (#) | 0.9 (1.7) | 0.8 (1.1) | Con. grp | ANOVA | No |
| Does specific feedback improve performance over general feedback? | Ingham & Greer (1992) | Teacher performance (%) | | | MB | Visual | Yes[2] |
| | | Teacher C | −0.68 | 3.33 | | | |
| | | Teacher B | 0.01 | 5.35 | | | |

Note. Dashed line (e.g. – – –) divides different questions. Numbers in parentheses = standard deviations. MB = multiple baseline. Con. grp = control group. Inc. = inconclusive. For support levels (1 = highest), refer to text.

**Table 8.10** Studies pertinent to the question: Does praise improve performance above and beyond that of feedback alone?

| Article[a] | Dependent variable | Means by condition | | | | Design | Test | Results supported |
|---|---|---|---|---|---|---|---|---|
| | | Feedback | Feedback and praise | Feedback | Feedback and praise | | | |
| Brown, Willis & Reid (1981) | Hours spent with clients (%) | 20.0 | 37.0 | 13.0 | 35.0 | Rev. | Visual | Yes[3] |
| Crowell, Anderson, Abel & Sergio (1988) | Quality of bank transactions (%) | | | 85.0 | 83.0 | Rev. | Visual | Yes[2] |
| Wikoff, Anderson & Crowell (1982) | Standard output (%) | | | | | MB | Visual | Inc. |
| | Fiberglass | 99.0 (1.9) | 103.1 (2.5) | | | | | |
| | Upholstery | 85.7 (3.2) | 86.2 (3.9) | | | | | |
| | Punch press | 96.3 (1.8) | 97.7 (2.7) | | | | | |
| | Welding | 73.1 (2.1) | 79.1 (2.2) | | | | | |

Note. Rev. = reversal. MB = multiple baseline. For support levels (1 = highest), refer to text. Inc. = inconclusive. Numbers in parentheses = standard deviations.

[a]Refer to articles for results of additional conditions or phases.

**Table 8.11** Studies pertinent to the question: Does individual feedback improve performance above and beyond that of group feedback?

| Article[a] | Dependent variable | Group Feedback | Individual feedback | Individual and group feedback | Group feedback | Design | Test | Results supported |
|---|---|---|---|---|---|---|---|---|
| | | | Means by condition | | | | | |
| Burgio, Engel, Hawkins & McCormick (1990) | Nursing home duties (%) | | | | | MB | Visual | Yes[3] |
| | Group 1 | 59.8 | 81.6 | | | | | |
| | Group 2 | 44.4 | 85.4 | | | | | |
| Emmert (1978) | Tire splices (#) | | | | | MB | Visual | Inc. |
| | Crew A | 239.0 | 249.0 | | | | | |
| | Crew B | 258.0 | 258.0 | | | | | |
| | Crew C | 259.0 | 276.0 | | | | | |
| | Crew D | 268.0 | 274.0 | | | | | |
| Goltz, Citera, Jensen & Favero (1989) | Product handling (%) | 90.6 | | 96.4 | 95.2 | Rev. | ARIMA | Inc. |
| Newby & Robinson (1983)[b] | Cash shortages (%) | 2.3 | 0.5 | | | Rev. | Visual | Yes[3] |
| | Employee punctuality (%) | 62.5 | 86.0 | | | | | |
| | Checkout proficiency (%) | 71.4 | 92.0 | | | | | |

Note. MB = Multiple-baseline. Rev. = reversal. For levels (1 = highest), refer to text. Inc. = inconclusive.

[a]Refer to articles for results of additional conditions or phases.

[b]This study was not specifically designed to answer this question, but the data collected shed light on the issue.

*Does praise improve performance above and beyond that of feedback alone?*    The type of consequence—whether it be social or informational—continues to be of interest. Two of the three studies provide support for the question. Brown, Willis and Reid (1981), and Crowell et al. (1988) found that praise did improve performance above and beyond that of feedback alone. But the results of Wikoff, Anderson and Crowell (1982) were inconclusive. Hence, the results of the studies in Table 8.10 do not provide a definitive answer as to whether praise improves performance above and beyond that of feedback alone.

Rather than recommending that more empirical studies be done, however, we suggest that investigators should first define what they mean so that it is clear how the two differ from one another. In these three studies, as well as in the other studies in the review, we could not readily determine what were the essential and nonessential characteristics of feedback and praise. Brown, Willis and Reid (1981) have made a start. For instance, they operationalize feedback as 'the supervisor giving verbal feedback to the individual staff member immediately following the hourly time sample. The supervisor was instructed to provide no approving or disapproving remarks, only to present a description of what was being done' (p. 62). Praise, on the other hand, is identified as the evaluative (subjective) performance-related information given to employees, for instance, in the case of a supervisor giving 'approval statements for the target category chosen for that shift in addition to the feedback' (p. 62). But their definitions raised even more questions: Is feedback only descriptive? Can it not be evaluative as well? Furthermore, it was not clear how much the delivery made a difference, for instance, whether feedback was limited to verbal exchanges.

Once the essential and nonessential characteristics of praise and feedback are identified and operationalized, then investigators can go forward to address whether each should be used singly or in combination and whether praise adds to feedback. Doing this would shed light on the nature of praise and feedback in particular and consequences in general.

*Does individual feedback improve performance above and beyond that of group feedback?*    The question of to whom consequences should be delivered—to an individual or a group—has been of reoccurring interest. As shown in Table 8.11, four studies addressed this question. Two studies provided support but two studies were inconclusive.

Instead of conducting more studies along the same lines, we suggest reappraising the entire issue of what it means to set up an effective reinforcement system and identifying the host of factors that make an impact: (a) to whom the feedback is delivered; (b) the frequency of the feedback; (c) whether the feedback is contingent; (d) the sign of the feedback and its relative proportion given the rest of the feedback; (e) the substance (quantity, quality) of the feedback; and (f) the type of task (involving or not involving team coordination). In fact, we hypothesize that the individual–group issue is only one of many factors and that, all else being equal, it alone will not make a discernible impact on performance. Stated another way, the manner of delivery is neither necessary nor sufficient to cause performance improvements. Hence, we urge future researchers to shy away from testing single contributory factors and to test instead which mix of factors is optimal.

As can be seen, answers to the facilitative questions shed light on the importance of consequences and contingent pay, as well as raising intriguing research directions involving definitional and system-wide issues.

### Findings: Descriptive Information

After discussing the studies concerned with facilitative and program evaluation questions, let us now look at the subjects, settings, and dependent variables of all 126 studies in the review.

*Subjects*

*Levels of personnel.*   The subjects included both supervisory and nonsupervisory personnel. Among the nonsupervisory personnel were employees paid by the hour who were not exempt from being paid overtime, referred to as hourly/non-exempt personnel, such as bus drivers (Haynes, Pine & Fitch, 1982), nurses (Stephens & Burroughs, 1978) and factory workers (Welsh, Luthans & Sommer, 1993). Other nonsupervisory employees were baseball players (Heward, 1978), psychiatrists (Jones et al., 1985/1986) and real estate agents (Anderson et al., 1982) who were paid a salary and were exempt from being paid overtime, referred to as salaried/exempt personnel.

Non-supervisory personnel predominated, with 87% of the studies including hourly and/or salaried employees. But, as Table 8.12 shows, the studies were not confined to these lower-level workers; 5% percent of the studies included both supervisory and nonsupervisory personnel and another 6% included only supervisory personnel. Among the supervisory personnel were managers of an insurance company (Nemeroff & Consentino, 1979), an owner and operator of a small business (Gaetani, Johnson & Austin, 1983), and school principals (Gillat & Sulzer-Azaroff, 1994).

*Sample sizes.*   The sizes of the samples in the studies varied from as few as 1 subject to as many as 5000. As shown in Table 8.12, two-fifths of the studies had 10 or fewer subjects, whereas almost two-fifths had 20 or more subjects, with one-sixth of the studies having over 100 subjects.

*Settings*

Many of the earliest studies were conducted in the public sector in educational, social service, and institutional settings. Thirty years later, however, the

**Table 8.12** Subjects and settings in all of the methodologically rigorous studies

| Subjects | % |
|---|---|
| Organizational level[a] | |
| Only nonsupervisory personnel | 87 |
| Hourly/non-exempt | 72 |
| Salaried/exempt | 4 |
| Unspecified or mixed (nonexempt & exempt) | 11 |
| Both supervisory and nonsupervisory personnel | 5 |
| Only supervisory personnel | 6 |
| Number | |
| 1–5 | 21 |
| 6–10 | 21 |
| 11–20 | 18 |
| 21–50 | 14 |
| 51–100 | 8 |
| 101+ | 16 |
| Unspecified | 3 |
| Settings | % |
| Business | 54 |
| Service | 27 |
| Manufacturing | 24 |
| Other | 3 |
| Government | 46 |
| Institutional | 20 |
| Social service | 14 |
| Educational | 10 |
| Other | 2 |

Note. $N = 126$.

[a]Figures add up to more than 100% because some reports include two or more categories.

ratio was roughly half and half (Table 8.12). Slightly less than half of the studies—46%—took place in the public sector, with 20% taking place in institutions such as mental health facilities (Parsons & Reid, 1995), 14% connected to social service agencies such as group homes (Harchik, Sherman, Sheldon & Strouse, 1992), and 10% taking place in educational settings such as elementary schools or universities (Wilk & Redmon, 1998). Over half of the studies—54%—took place in the private sector, with 27% in service settings such as banks (Elizur, 1987) and department stores (Luthans, Paul & Taylor,

1985) and 24% in manufacturing settings such as shipyards (Nasanen & Saari, 1987) and factories (Kempen & Hall, 1977; Wittkopp, Rowan & Poling, 1990).

## Dependent variable

*Aspects of performance.* The target areas, as shown in Tables 8.2a, 8.2b, 8.2c, and in Tables 8.5 to 8.10, included soliciting suggestions for mental health employees for solving common problems (Quilitch, 1978), increasing the number of assignments completed by graduate students (Houmanfar & Hayes, 1998), increasing the amount of time resource room teachers actually spent instructing pupils (Maher, 1982), and promoting the set-up completion percentages for banquet employees (LaFleur & Hyten, 1995).

The most popular target area, accounting for almost one-fifth of the studies, was *production/production-related* (see Table 8.13). Improving the quality of

**Table 8.13** Dependent variables in all of the methodologically rigorous studies

| Dependent variable | % |
| --- | --- |
| Aspects of performance | |
| Production/production-related | 18 |
| Attendance/punctuality/early departures | 14 |
| Safety | 13 |
| Patient/client care | 11 |
| Customer service | 9 |
| Instructional/teaching technique | 9 |
| Record keeping/clerical | 7 |
| Supervision | 3 |
| Cash shortages | 2 |
| Sales | 2 |
| Other | 13 |
| Requiring coordination among group members[a] | |
| Yes | 7 |
| No | 94 |
| Processes involved[b] | |
| Executing psycho-motor tasks | 99 |
| Generating alternatives | 1 |
| Choosing among alternatives | 0 |
| Negotiating and resolving conflict | 1 |

Note. $N = 126$.

[a]Figures add up to more than 100% because some reports include two or more categories.
[b]McGrath (1984).

sorting and loading of packages in a package delivery company was considered a production-related task (Kortick & O'Brien, 1996).

The second highest dependent variable was *attendance and punctuality*, a critical factor in organizations which rely on having a certain number of qualified workers present before running equipment or assembly lines. Among the experiments trying to promote attendance were Hopkins, Conard and Smith (1986) at a unionized manufacturing/distribution center, Kempen and Hall (1977) in a factory, and Silva, Duncan, and Doudna (1982) at an insurance company.

Another area of concern to both management and workers—*safety and health*—has been the topic of 13% of the studies. Workers showed improvements in safety practices (Komaki, Barwick & Scott, 1978; Komaki, Blood & Holder, 1980), as well as other indices (housekeeping, Nasanen & Saari, 1987, hazards, Sulzer-Azaroff & de Santamaria, 1980, and ear plug usage, Zohar & Fussfeld, 1981), thus lessening the chance of incurring a disabling injury. Working together, employees in a fiberglass-reinforced plastics plant were also able to reduce their exposure to likely carcinogenic substances such as styrene and to enhance their chances of remaining healthy (Hopkins, Conard & Smith, 1986).

The *quality of service* has been a regular subject of interest in both the public and private sectors, accounting for 11 and 9%, respectively, of the studies. In the public sector, the focus is on *program implementation*, which ensures that programs developed for patients, clients, and students are delivered as planned. Langeland, Johnson, and Mawhinney (1998), for instance, set up a program to improve staff performance in a community mental health setting. Tellers in banks (Elizur, 1987), receptionists at a human service organization (Johnson & Fawcett, 1994), and salespersons in department stores (Komaki, Collins & Temlock, 1987; Luthans, Paul & Taylor, 1985) upgraded their interactions with customers in the private sector. Besides approaching customers more quickly, salespersons learned to assess customers' needs and then to provide relevant information.

*Coordination required.*    An overwhelming proportion of the dependent variables were considered independent—94%. Only 6% of the tasks were considered interdependent, requiring the cooperation of at least one group member to accomplish it. An example is that of preventive maintenance (PM) of equipment (Komaki, 1998). The first step in conducting PM is for group 1 to detect deficiencies on the equipment. To complete the PM cycle, further action must be taken by group 2 who must order the parts and make the repairs. If one group or the other fails to do its share, then this task will not be successfully completed.

In short, the descriptive information, gleaned from all 126 studies, provided a rich picture of the level and number of employees, the settings, and the different aspects of the dependent variables.

## DISCUSSION

To see if the ABA approach has lived up to the best of its proponents' visions or the worst of its critics' fears, let us now look at the pertinent findings.

### Living up to Proponents' Visions

*Using primarily positive reinforcement resulted in meaningful improvements in performance on-the-job*

As this review amply demonstrates, the use of the principle of positive reinforcement resulted in substantial and meaningful improvements in performance at work (Tables 8.2a, 8.2b, 8.2c; Figures 8.1–8.6). The reinforcers ranged from supervisors providing social consequences such as praise and informational ones such as feedback, to rearranging those that are indigenous to the job such as the opportunity for phone solicitors to sell renewal contracts. When these reinforcers were arranged singly or in combination to follow desired instances of performance, improvements typically occurred. The evidence of support was strong with a total of 72 meticulously controlled studies with which to make judgments about support and a 93% success rate. Furthermore, the strict criteria used in selecting the studies mandated that each study have an internally valid between- or within-group design, thus ruling out plausible alternative hypotheses such as the effect of practice, worsening economic conditions, or other improvement efforts. Hence, we can be reasonably confident that the changes in performance can be attributed to the programs themselves.

The positive reinforcement programs did not rely solely on rules, reminders, or training, which are the traditional forms of antecedents. Instead, ABA investigators went two steps further: (a) they measured employees' performance reliably as evidenced by obtaining consistently high agreement scores between observers and directly by sampling work behaviors and products; *and* (b) based on these measures of performance, they reinforced employees for jobs well done.

The importance of using consequences when motivating others was confirmed in experiments assessing what occurred when consequences were added after antecedents alone were provided (Table 8.7). When only antecedents were introduced, performance sometimes remained at baseline levels. Consequences, however, always added to the impact of antecedents. As shown in Figure 8.10 in the study by Chhokar and Wallin (1984), the antecedents of training and goal-setting were not sufficient to act as the sole motivating force; only when consequences in the form of feedback were provided did substantial improvements in safety performance occur.

Furthermore, an essential feature of consequences—ensuring the relationship or contingency between performance and the consequence—was highlighted. When pay was made contingent on performance, performance improved above and beyond that of full pay (Table 8.8). What these experiments show is that pay alone is not sufficient. In order to get quality performance, pay must be contingent on the caliber of the performance.

In short, these data effectively counter criticisms about the ABA approach's lack of usefulness in work settings and its weakness in empirical support. Soundly designed experiments demonstrated that positive reinforcement programs do work—not only were substantial improvements shown in individual experiments, but the overall success rate was 93%. Furthermore, the critical role of consequences and their contingent use was confirmed.

*Widespread generality.*    The 126 studies in the review, spanning three decades, bear testimony to the external validity of the approach.

*Across different levels and numbers of employees.* The subjects varied widely. White collar (e.g., supervisors), pink collar (e.g., real estate agents), and blue collar (e.g., factory workers) workers were represented. Both supervisory and nonsupervisory personnel were included.

Studies were conducted in small businesses, as well as large organizations. In fact, there were 50 or more subjects in almost one quarter of the studies, with 100 or more subjects in one-sixth of the studies, with some organizations including from 1000 to 5000 employees.

*Across dependent variables concerned with quantity as well as quality* . The dependent variables were also a diverse lot. Some such as attendance have been primarily concerned with quantity, but many focus on quality. For example, in safety, the aim is not the efficiency with which workers do their jobs, but rather with the manner in which they perform them. Likewise, the studies dealing with the provision of care to clients or patients and service to customers are primarily concerned with quality. Similarly, the improvement of teaching techniques is rarely operationalized as increasing the number of hours spent with students but rather the way in which instructors interact with the students. These four aspects of performance alone—safety (13%), patient/client care (11%), customer service (9%), and instructional techniques (9%)—comprise 42% of the dependent variables. Furthermore, not all production tasks which comprise 18% of the tasks are necessarily focused on quantity. For example, Kortick and O'Brien (1996) attempted in a package delivery company to improve the quality of sorting and loading of packages.

*Over extended periods of time.* The interventions were not necessarily short-lived. In fact, of the studies conducted in the past 10 years, data were collected during the interventions for an average of 3.3 months, indicating that the changes were not ephermeral.

As can be seen, based on the meticulously designed studies chosen for the review, it is possible to conclude with confidence that the positive reinforcement programs resulted in meaningful improvements in work settings. Furthermore, the studies taken collectively included a wide variety of subjects, settings, and dependent variables, and they show the viability of the approach over time.

## But Providing Little Evidence to Quell Some Other Complaints

While the review has provided evidence showing the effectiveness and generality of the ABA approach, two criticisms remain: the failure to gain input from workers in making program refinements, and the lack of a more conceptual discussion of the independent variables.

*Despite recent emphasis on social validity, workers' viewpoints were only sporadically sought out*

Employees' reactions to ABA programs have rarely been assessed (cf., Komaki, Collins & Penn, 1982; LaMere, Dickinson, Henry, Henry & Poling, 1996), in spite of lip service given to soliciting their opinions. Instead, ABA researchers are not unlike their colleagues using more traditional approaches; they implement programs as they more or less see fit. Although careful to measure worker performance, they do not necessarily measure their attitudes. I/O psychologists, on the other hand, typically do not measure performance reliably, directly, and repeatedly, but they solicit employees' viewpoints and assess their satisfaction with their jobs and their supervision.

Why is there such a difference? It is not for a lack of emphasis. ABA researchers have coined a new concept, termed social validity, which stresses the importance of determining whether the target behaviors—as well as the treatment and outcomes—have a positive and meaningful impact on the client (Bem & Funder, 1978; Cone, 1980; Schwartz & Baer, 1991; Winett, Moore & Anderson, 1991; Wolf, 1978). In fact, when researchers Wolf, Kirigin, Fixsen, Blase, and Braukmann (1995) were in charge of a massively funded effort to replicate a community-based program for youth, they described 'the pain, humiliation, and the cruel and unusual punishment' that occurred when they failed to 'develop a consumer feedback system' that was 'as sensitive as possible to every complaint by every important consumer' (p. 29). In their first attempt to replicate the group home program, they failed (as most program developers do) to systematically survey the consumers of the program, in this case, 'the youths, their parents and teachers, social workers, probation officers, board of directors' (p. 24) who were involved in the treatment of delinquent youths in group homes. Unfortunately, their first attempt to replicate ran into serious problems. Wolf began to get calls from friends and board members alike describing concerns of teachers, probation officers, 'and what seemed like dozens of others' (p. 29). Wolf reports that 'he was embarrassed and defensive and maybe a little hostile' to these early complaints, but relieved when the calls eventually stopped. After some number of months, the board president let him know that:

the board was going to terminate their relationship with us, and invited us to a final meeting. We had never seen such an angry group. The board members poured out complaints about our program. We asked them why they had not kept us informed about these problems all along so that we could have tried to remedy them. The board members claimed that they had tried to . . . We told the board that it was their fault that they had not told us soon enough or in sufficient detail to allow us to deal with their complaints. They dismissed us and told us that they would write us about their decision. Well, you know the outcome: they fired us! (p. 29)

Eventually, Wolf et al. (1995) decided on a defensive strategy of sending out questionnaires to all interested parties ranging from the probation officers from the juvenile court to the youths themselves. Based on the responses, wide-ranging changes were made. For example, when teachers reported a lack of help with the youths' school problems, guidance was provided so the house parents could deliver the help that was needed.

In light of the Wolf et al. (1995) experience, as well as the urgings of ABA researchers, we recommend systematically assessing workers' viewpoints *and* then fine-tuning the work environment to reflect both positive and negative opinions. Doing so will not only help prevent potentially negative side-effects, but it will also promote positively received practices and, as Wolf et al. (1995) found, the longevity of the interventions.

*Independent variables while effective rarely described in terms of abstract concepts*

The split in ABA research 'between its purely technical and more conceptual aspects,' as Hayes, Rincover and Solnick (1980, p. 284) pointed out two decades ago, still exists. The bulk of the studies fall into the category of (a) technical, making no reference to principles of behavior such as reinforcement or stimulus control, or (b) direct application, in which the generality of known principles is tested with new behaviors, in new settings, or with new populations. In the studies classified as positive reinforcement, the principle is sometimes not even mentioned; instead, the only reference made is to an example of a type of consequence (e.g., feedback, praise). Other investigators mention the principle, but they do a simple application that goes no further than assessing whether the principle of positive reinforcement works with a different behavior, in a different setting, or with a new population.

A third category, what Hayes et al. (1980) consider a systematic application, is addressed by some studies in the review. What is not clear, however, is how they advance our basic knowledge. Studies asking whether consequences improve performance over and above that of antecedents alone and whether contingent pay adds to that of noncontingent pay are cases in point. Because the issues at stake—that of consequences and that of contingent consequences—are basic, these studies do not necessarily advance our knowledge as much as they confirm what we already know.

On the other hand, studies examining praise and feedback and those looking at individual and group feedback, for instance, have the potential to advance our knowledge. Issues such as what constitutes a social consequence and what is the best basis for aggregation can be addressed. Even higher level issues such as what constitutes a consequence, whether it be social or informational or delivered to an individual or a group, would also be welcome topics for research. In my leadership research (Komaki, 1998b), I have begun to expand the traditional definition of a consequence to include positive, negative, *and* neutral ones and to predict that effective leaders would provide a mix. Another set of issues goes beyond the necessity of providing contingent consequences to look at what supervisors can and should do to ensure that the consequences provided are related to performance and what occurs when the latter is *and* is not done.

While we heartily agree that 'it is often easier simply to show that techniques work than to simultaneously make important conceptual contributions' (Hayes, Rincover & Solnick, 1980, p. 284), we recommend more conceptually based research that would include discussions of higher level abstractions, conceptualizing new hypotheses, operationalizing the variables accordingly, and then testing out the hypotheses. Such an approach is more likely to result in data-based refinements, replacements, and better applications, as founders, Baer, Wolf and Risley (1968) envisioned over 30 years ago.

In short, criticisms about the effectiveness and generality of the ABA approach have been adequately addressed, whereas those concerned with soliciting workers' viewpoints and going beyond the technical to a more conceptual understanding are still in need of attention.

## Wish List

Poised at the entry to the twenty-first century, we propose several new directions. The first applies what we already know, while the second pushes ahead with what we would like to know.

*Applying what we already know*

*To document problems in performance and attitudes when relying on antecedents, the most common panacea in work settings.*   Since we know how to document on-the-job changes, we recommend using this knowledge to illustrate the effects of relying on antecedents. Why antecedents? Because the most common recommendation given when confronted with problems involving the work force is 'to inform or exhort, or both' (Mager & Pipe, 1984, p. 1), both of which are antecedents. As Daniels (1994) portrays in the following passage, most organizations attempt to motivate their employees by giving them antecedents and:

> by telling people what to do. . . . We send memos, have meetings, write policies, hold classes. . . . Interestingly, when these methods don't get the desired

response . . ., we tell the same people again, usually in the same ways. . . . We send new memos around (with bolder type, capital letters, and even exclamation marks) about old memos that were ignored. . . . If we train people about the importance of doing it 'right the first time, every time,' and they don't, we bring them in and we train them again. If we inspire them to reach for the heavens and they barely raise their hands, we make a more impassioned plea. (pp. 17–18)

Training is particularly prevalent. When injuries skyrocket, employees are scheduled for safety classes. When complaints of racial discrimination occur, the remedy offered is training in cultural sensitivity (Finkelstein, 1999). Unfortunately, consequences are rarely provided, the only thing being delivered is lip service.

Given the preponderance of antecedents, questions arise: Are there problems in relying on antecedents? What happens to morale and performance over the long term when only antecedents are used? Is it better when consequences are provided as well? If so, how much better is it? Alas, there is little evidence to answer these questions. Few studies have been done that assess what occurs over the long term in terms of both performance and morale. Experiments have been done addressing how consequences add to the effectiveness of antecedents. But few have used a between-group design to directly compare antecedents alone and antecedents and consequences.

The study which comes the closest is a laboratory study by Johnson (1975). He used a traditional control group design to directly compare antecedents and consequences, modeling the interventions after work settings in which employees have previous experience with reinforcement contingencies, some of which conflict with the antecedents given. He found that when only antecedents such as announcements were provided, performance improvements were 'relatively weak,' just as he surmised they would be in work settings where previous conditioning is opposed. He concluded that consequences were essential 'for stable performance change to occur' (p. 321). Although Johnson (1975) did not assess the subjects reactions, the results of the direct comparison suggest that relying on antecedents alone may not be the most prudent method, particularly when delivered in the context of conflicting reinforcement contingencies.

Our prediction is that antecedents might work in the short term, but that long-term decrements will be seen in both performance and attitudes. To test this hypothesis, we would like to see a study assessing employees' performance on the job that takes place over an extended time, reflects the reactions of workers, and uses a traditional control-group design. This recommendation takes a two-pronged approach which not only shows what occurs when providing positive reinforcement, but also demonstrates what occurs in its absence. Perhaps the results from such a study will help convince organizations to expend the additional resources needed to ensure that employees are not only told what to do, but that something happens when they do.

*To use tests of interrater reliability to help reduce employment discrimination.* Next, we recommend a series of checks and balances involving multiple raters to help address the prevalent problem of bias on the part of managers when evaluating employees (Komaki, 1998a). This test of interrater reliability, which involves coders independently recording and then checking their agreements and disagreements, is a standard for ABA investigators measuring performance.

Why bother? Unfortunately, managers do allow themselves to be influenced by factors other than appraisees' performance. In fact, a candid set of interviews with 60 upper-level executives vividly suggests that the unspeakable does happen: truthfulness is not always their foremost concern (Longenecker, Sims & Gioia, 1987). One executive admitted: 'There is really no getting around the fact that whenever I evaluate one of my people, I stop and think about the impact—the ramifications of my decisions on my relationship with the guy and his future here. I'd be stupid not to. Call it being politically-minded, or using managerial discretion, or fine-tuning the guy's ratings, but in the end I've got to live with him, and I'm not going to rate a guy without thinking about the fall-out' (p. 183). Furthermore, in court case after court case, employees successfully sought compensation, attesting to their charges that decisions can be influenced by appraisers' expectations about the appraisees' race, gender, or age rather than performance (e.g., *Roberts* v. *Texaco*, 1994; *Price Waterhouse* v. *Hopkins*, 1989). In fact, the workplace has been characterized as 'unquestionably the major civil rights battleground of the twenty-first century' (Roberts, 1998, back cover).

Although good agreement exists that bias is an insidious problem, it has found few truly workable and effective solutions (Eichenwald, 1996; Williams, 1997). After reviewing the litigation in the area of performance appraisal, Cascio and Bernardin (1981) described their reactions to 'reading the testimony of company officials in many of these cases . . . one gets the uneasy feeling that (a) top management was totally unaware of what kind of appraisal system was in effect at lower levels, or (b) the employer was well aware of the (illegal) appraisal system in use but was unaware of what was wrong with it' (p. 223). Despite these problems, employees rightfully contend that these appraisals affect the quality of decisions made about whom to promote, train, transfer, reward, or discipline.

What, if anything, can be done to minimize bias? Unfortunately, constructive alternatives are rarely offered and almost never evaluated. Hence, it makes it difficult to ensure that past inequities will not be needlessly repeated. In fact, an undocumented assumption exists that once evaluators are aware of biases they can avoid their pernicious effects. We would contend that this state is difficult to achieve when the appraisal instrument itself is faulty.

To mitigate these problems, we propose focusing on the appraiser rather than the appraisee and using the test of interrater reliability at three critical stages in the measurement process: (a) during the developmental stage, where the test provides natural springboards for ferreting out disagreements in the appraisal instrument and their bases; (b) during training, where raters have to obtain three consecutive, representative reliability scores of at least 90% or better, thus demonstrating that they can consistently use the appraisal instrument to make the proper distinctions across a variety of employees and situations; and (c) during the formal data collection period, where the scores act as a check to see if judgments are being consistently made across different employees over extended time periods.

Let us take an example of a classic case of gender discrimination. In the case of *Price Waterhouse* v. *Hopkins* (1989), substantial disagreements occurred among partners of an accounting firm with respect to what persons of a certain gender should and should not do, and because of different weights some partners placed on internal matters such as staff relationships and external matters such as procuring major contracts for the firm. It is enticing to speculate what might occur if the partners would use the test of interrater reliability as the basis for developing a new appraisal system: the partners could be trained until they passed the test of interrater reliability, and the same test could then be conducted periodically when the formal appraisals were made. Doing this would no doubt generate discussion about what constitutes performance worthy for promotion, as well as how to identify various acceptable combinations that could lead to more uniform evaluations on the next round.

While interrater reliability deals only with the appraisal instrument and the raters using it, it is at the very least a constructive alternative that puts in executives' hands an appraisal form that has been field tested to ferret out sources of disagreement. Furthermore, it ensures that trainees at least know what to look for, and it provides a check as to whether managers are using the same standards and are consistently applying them. Acknowledging that supervisors do play favorites, the president of Intel, Andy Grove (1991), suggests three safeguards. Besides the immediate supervisor, that person's boss should 'oversee and approve the written evaluation' (p. 116). The second check is to have someone from personnel approve the review. While this personnel representative 'probably can't judge the quality of highly technical endeavors, he is likely to catch signs of favoritism' (p. 116). Third, Grove (1983), recommends that 'the supervisor meets with his peers and, together as a group, they compare and rank all of their subordinates' (p. 116). While he agrees that 'no system is foolproof, especially one that is necessarily laden with human judgment' (pp. 116–117), Grove predicts that 'such checks and balances . . .' can indeed help to keep 'prejudice out of evaluations' (pp. 116–117), a worthy and necessary goal.

*Going beyond*

The above suggestions all have to do with the tried-and-true. The next set are concerned with what might be. Our first set of wishes focuses on the often neglected dependent variable.

*To accentuate the adequate assessment of the dependent variable.* The measurement of the dependent variable has always been an integral step in any ABA program. Traditionally, however, the independent variable (in this instance, the consequences for performance) has overshadowed it. As a result of an analysis comparing select studies in this review, we recommend paying more attention to the measurement of the dependent variable.

Using an inductive approach, we contrasted studies which did and did not show support for positive reinforcement. Of the four studies showing 'no support,' we found few common threads. Gaetani and Johnson (1983), for example, tried to decrease cash shortages in a retail beverage chain using a combination of data plotting, praise, and state lottery tickets; Haynes, Pine and Fitch (1982) endeavored to reduce the accidents of urban transit operators using a package of feedback and incentives; Johnson et al. (1991) attempted to enhance the performance of staff members of a housing cooperative using prompts, self-reports, and a combination of credits toward rent reductions and fines; and Komaki and Collins (1982) tried to promote preventive maintenance in the Marine Corps using both feedback and time-off. The subjects, settings, and dependent variables varied broadly, so we could not identify any one set of subjects, settings, or dependent variable that might be the culprit. The independent variables included both feedback and praise, both of which were used in the successful studies as well.

The only meaningful pattern we could discern between the studies that did and did not show support had to do with the dependent variable, specifically with the lack of responsiveness of the measure. For instance, in the Komaki and Collins (1982) experiment, preventive maintenance (PM) was originally measured during scheduled PM periods; the observers went on-site and directly sampled Marines as they worked. Despite the use of a potent consequence—time off with pay (shown in a previous military setting to be among the top-rated: Datel & Legters, 1971)—improvements were either short-lived or nonexistent (Figure 8.7). When the troops were questioned in an attempt to understand what went wrong, one persistent complaint that emerged was that, although they did do PM, it was not reflected in the way in which they were measured. PM was assessed during scheduled PM periods, but the troops were often ordered elsewhere (e.g., to get inoculation shots, to paint toolboxes) during those times. To ensure the responsiveness of the measure the next year, the dependent variable was redesigned (Komaki, 1998a). When the measures were changed to be more responsive to workers' efforts, performance dramatically improved even though the feedback consequence was not as potent as time off. What this suggested was that it was important to ensure that the measure of PM was under the control of the Marines.

An analysis of two other studies shows a similar trend, with dependent variables that were only partially under the control of workers. Realizing that accidents are sometimes not the fault of workers, management in a study by

Haynes, Pine and Fitch (1982) made a distinction between accidents that were avoidable and those that were unavoidable; it is important to note, however, that both the avoidable and unavoidable accidents were counted against the drivers earning them 3 and 1 point(s) respectively against their safety records. Similarly, in the Gaetani and Johnson (1983) study, there was some question as to whether the dependent variable was responsive to the managers because both cash and inventory shortages were included. The latter could have been due to customer theft, which is a variable largely out of the control of the managers. (Note: In the fourth study by Johnson et al. (1991), the questions raised were about the OCT criteria which did not take into consideration Miller's recommendation to ignore transition periods, rather than the dependent variable per se.)

On the basis of the above analyses, we propose that such factors as the responsiveness and frequency of the dependent variable may have a discernible impact on the success of our motivational programs. To assess whether this is true, we recommend conducting a series of experiments to ferret out these problems.

Another intriguing and related question would be to assess the trade-offs in the quality of the dependent and independent variables. Since we do not often have the luxury of maximizing both, we recommend empirically determining where we should best place our scarce resources. Our hypothesis is that a trade-off exists, but there are limits to how poorly targets can be measured. We predict that a potent consequence, such as time off, cannot compensate for a target that is poorly measured. On the other hand, we would expect that a higher quality measure would make up for a lower potency consequence such as feedback. These experiments would shed light on the measurement process as well as the interaction between the dependent and independent variables.

*To include as dependent variables negotiation and brainstorming-type tasks as well as execution-type tasks.*    Our next wish also casts a brighter, fuller light on the dependent variable. This time, however, the focus is on content. To date, virtually all of the dependent variables looked at in this review—99%—dealt with the execution of psycho-motor tasks. Such tasks, says McGrath, 'are very heavily represented in the workaday world and, against that base rate, are quite underrepresented in research on groups' (McGrath, 1984, p. 65).

While these dependent variables clearly fill a pressing need, if one looks at the context of an entire job, task-execution is only one aspect. Other questions which can be raised include: Who decides what tasks should be executed? How are the standards set? Such forward-looking companies as Hewlett Packard (HP) are starting to ask similar questions as they start to assess the strain of grueling hours and travel schedules on their employees. A sales manager at HP was shocked by a survey that found that 'more than 50 percent of the workers in her [sales] department had said they were "experiencing excessive pressure" on the job' (Kaufman, 1999, p. A1). She jumped at a chance to rethink workloads. Instead of only business goals, employees are urged to set personnel goals as well. This restructuring has had 'a noticeable effect on the work side of the equation,' with expectations being lowered about how much 'an employee can accomplish in a day' (p. C8). 'Still,' she counters, 'productivity has not suffered where it counts' (p. C8) and, in the 'drum-tight labor market' (p. C8) of the 90s, turnover remains low; her sales region still remains top and she proudly notes that 'out of a staff of 74, she lost only two people last year, and both of them were promoted within the company. Moreover, several staff members who received outside offers have stayed put, and one top performer who had been lured away by a start-up actually returned' (p. C8).

Rather than taking the task as a given, we would like to see researchers and, ultimately, workers question standards and their bases. To do this would require not just the execution of the task, but the first three types of tasks classified by McGrath (1984): those in which organizational members: (a) generate alternatives, coming up with plans or ideas about what to do; (b) choose among alternatives, solving problems or making decisions to use one tactic rather than another; and (c) negotiate under conditions in which there are conflicts of viewpoint and/or interest. For instance, a standard of 3000 missorts—defined as the ratio of the number of packages loaded correctly for every one package loaded incorrectly—had been set in a packaging company (Kortick & O'Brien, 1996). Legitimate questions could be raised, however, about the decision-making process used to determine whether the standard should be 3000 or 2800 or 3500 missorts. It is possible that critical elements of the task were not under workers' control: for example, packages can be mislabeled, addresses can be illegible or nonexistent, and information on the labels can be inconsistent. Assuming that these elements adversely influenced the ratio determining how supervisors or workers could best bring about a change in the standard would require skills in problem solving and negotiation which are sorely lacking in most ABA studies.

Enlarging the scope of the type of task so that workers learn how to negotiate and problem-solve as well as execute the tasks would enhance the generality of the tasks to which the approach can be applied. Furthermore, it would bode well for potentially longer-lasting and more humane endeavors.

*To extend boundaries of social consequences.* Our next set of wishes deals with the independent variable and the consequences provided. Social consequences in particular have been traditionally described in ABA experiments in ways that do not reflect the subtle ways that managers that we have observed interact. Typically, social consequences are portrayed as including commendations, compliments, criticism, reviews, and recognition for jobs well done. For example, winning teams were 'personally congratulated by the director of operations' (Haynes, Pine & Fitch, 1982). In another example, hospital supervisors made comments to staff members, saying such things as

'I'm pleased to see you interacting with clients, but I'm sure Mary [the client] is even more pleased' (Brown, Willis & Reid, 1981). While consequences like these do occur, many are not nearly so obvious. In observing managers in insurance firms and aboard racing boats over the past two decades, we ended up questioning whether a reinforcing/punishing dichotomy fully encompasses the breadth of consequences and fashioning a definition that included negative, positive, *and* neutral consequences (Komaki, 1998b). It was easy to see a supervisor named Charlie delivering positive consequences: 'Five hundred thirty-seven cases,' said Charlie when workers arrived the day after a successful shift. Then he would 'grin and thrust out his hand for a quick congratulatory shake, and move on' (Gellerman, 1976, p. 90). When workers did not quite meet his standards, he was likely to withhold his handshake and say something like, 'It wasn't too bad, but we can do better' (p. 90). We could easily classify as positive his hand-shaking and his comments: 'Good running last night. Five hundred thirty-seven cases.' But if we adhered strictly to a positive–negative classification, it was not immediately clear where to place the comment: 'It wasn't too bad, but we can do better.' While the first part of the statement—almost reassuring workers for trying—seemed too harsh to be simply categorized as a 'disciplining or punishing' event, the withholding of the handshake was far short of a congratulatory gesture. Comments and actions such as these were not atypical in the everyday interactions we witnessed.

Another issue relates to the fact that many leaders simply murmur 'okay' or 'hmn' to indicate that the follower acted appropriately—without further explanation. Sometimes an 'okay' means simply that they saw what the worker did, as in the case of a Marine Corps warrant officer who would sometimes simply say 'okay' or 'hmn' when a mechanic explained his actions. Occasionally, the officer described what the mechanic had done: 'So you've already tried that.' The question is whether these brief comments constitute consequences; for example, should the statement: 'So you've already tried that' count? We thought so. Although these comments are not distinctly positive or negative, we believed that there should be room in the definition for remarks such as these. To capture these less evaluative consequences, we revised and expanded upon the working definition to include consequences that are neutral and informational in character. Hence, performance consequences were defined as communicating an evaluation of or indicating knowledge of another's performance, where the indication can range from highly evaluative to neutral (Komaki, 1998b).

Another recommended broadening of social consequences is to consider them in context. Although we know that they do not occur in a vacuum, we rarely see these exchanges between bosses and workers reflected in our prescriptions. Recognizing the importance of these interactions, Sayles (1979) correctly identifies these exchanges as requiring 'skills involving extraordinary patience, endurance, continuous interaction, spontaneous compromises, and negotiation' (Sayles, 1979, p. 13).

While there is good agreement about the need to foster these give-and-take exchanges, it is not clear how to ensure that these high-quality exchanges take place. Most leadership research focuses on the leader. Few studies look at the interaction between the two. In searching for the answer to what leaders should do when interacting with their subordinates, we started to focus on the leader and follower and the process between them. In one study, we actually documented that a reciprocal interaction exists between the leader and the follower, with each influencing the other (Komaki & Citera, 1990). When the leader monitors (M) or gathers information about performance, then the follower talks about his or her own performance (OP), which, in turn, sets the stage for more discussion about performance. A set of interactions between a manager–follower pair was recorded as follows (where M = monitor, OP = subordinate own performance, and C = consequence). The manager began by asking: 'Can I see the itinerary you're preparing for me?' (M) and then looked over the itinerary (M). As the manager was nodding approvingly (C), the follower initiated a discussion of how she was performing: 'I have a list of all your meetings' (OP) to which the manager responded with a simple: 'Okay' (C).

While the manager in this dialogue went on to discuss some of the messages and meetings she would be having, most of the exchanges we recorded were even shorter than this one. How does one sustain these discussions? Alas, few exemplars exist. An exemplary model is provided by Wolf et al. (1995) who describe the interactions between a teaching parent and a subordinate. As shown in Table 8.14, the supervisor begins by expressing her affection for the subordinate and then acknowledging something that has been accomplished. At the same time, however, the supervisor does not neglect to point out what is being done wrong and demonstrates how and why to do it correctly. The interaction ends with the supervisor praising the subordinate. Interlaced throughout are probes encouraging the subordinate to participate in the conversation (e.g., 'Do you understand?'). Although a critical need exists for more models like this one, we can at least begin to impart how the leader and follower can have a fruitful dialogue conveying what needs to be done and what has been done, while at the same time conveying warmth and compassion. More work along these lines is highly recommended so that we can expand one of the most potentially potent reinforcers, that of social consequences.

*To pay attention to what and how informational consequences are provided.* We also would like to see more attention focused on informational consequences, in particular those factors that influence its effectiveness. While many writers talk about feedback in a general sense, scholars have identified specific dimensions or factors (Fairbank & Prue, 1982; Ilgen, Fisher & Taylor, 1979; Kluger & DeNisi, 1996). Among the most interesting are: (a) the task itself, particularly its complexity and novelty and how informational consequences may

**Table 8.14** Recommended interactions between supervisor and subordinate

| Recommended step | Example | Rationale |
|---|---|---|
| 1. Expression of affection | Supervisor smiles and says 'Hi. Are you having any problems?' | Indicates to the subordinate that the supervisor is pleased to see him/her, likes to interact with him/her, and is concerned about any problems the subordinate may be having |
| 2. Praise for what has been accomplished | 'Say, that report looks fine.' | Indicates to the subordinate that the supervisor is aware of what he/she has already accomplished |
| 3. Description of the inappropriate behavior | 'But you haven't gotten this filled out correctly. Here are some questions that you missed.' | Instructs the subordinate about what he/she did incorrectly or hasn't yet done |
| 4. Description of the appropriate behavior | 'So why don't you consult the manual to find the missing answers. Let me show you what I mean.' (The supervisor demonstrates). | Instructs the subordinate about what is expected. The task often should be broken into small steps. Demonstration may be needed in order to clarify the verbal instruction |
| 5. Rationale for the appropriate behavior | 'We want to make sure we fill every question out thoroughly. Otherwise, it makes it more difficult for the HR department to do their job.' | Instructs the subordinate why it is important that he/she engage in the behaviors, i.e., the potential future consequences for the organization |
| 6. Description of the present consequences | 'As soon as you finish filling out the missing information, you can take your lunch break.' | Instructs the subordinate about the immediate rewards for appropriate behavior |
| 7. Request for acknowledgement | 'Do you understand?' or 'Okay?' | Prompts the subordinate to ask any questions he/she may have. Also, provides feedback to the supervisor that the subordinate was attending to the instructions and understands them |
| 8. Practice | 'Now, why don't you try to locate the missing information.' | Gives the subordinate immediate feedback as to whether the appropriate behavior is in the subordinate's repertoire and he/she understands the instructions |
| 9. Feedback during the practice: praise and correction | 'That looks good. How about a little more detail on this question. That's right.' | Provides positive feedback for those behaviors the subordinate is performing correctly and provides further instruction and practice for the behaviors that are not yet appropriate |
| 10. Reward: praise | 'That is a fine job.' | Gives the subordinate immediate consequences for the appropriate behavior |

Note. Adapted from Wolf, Kirigin, Fixsen, Blase and Braukmann (1995).

need to be altered to take into consideration the nature of the task; (b) the deliverer of the feedback and their formal position within the organization—supervisory personnel, outside personnel, or peers or subordinates; (c) the way in which it is delivered: whether the deliverer of the feedback accompanies it with an evaluation of performance or even broader personality characteristics (e.g., self-esteem) of the worker; and/or (d) whether the deliverer provides cues identifying the standard and the discrepancy between the worker's performance and the standard. In an intriguing meta-analysis of feedback interventions (Kluger & DeNisi, 1996), accompanying feedback with praise was found to attenuate effects on performance, whereas referring to the standard was shown to augment effects. Researchers are encouraged to pursue these less traveled but potentially rich research directions about a highly used type of consequence, that of providing information to workers about their performance.

*To enhance the breadth and depth of our studies.*    Our last wish is to go beyond isolated targets or groups to encompass the organization as a whole. To do this, we recommend dramatically expanding the scope of our efforts, including but not limiting them to: (a) the personnel, looking upwards to include supervisors, the supervisors of the supervisors, and on up to the vice-presidents and the CEO as Methot, Williams, Cummings and Bradshaw (1996) have done; (b) the dependent variable, assessing both productivity and workers' viewpoints as Komaki, Collins and Penn (1982) and LaMere, et al. (1996) have done, and (c) the independent variable, ensuring that rewards indigenous to organizations such as promotions, raises, and job security are made contingent on the quality of performance. Furthermore, we would like to see researchers looking more in depth at: (a) the appraisal efforts of supervisory personnel to see not only how they gather information, but what information they gather; (b) the productivity indices and whether they are under workers' control; and (c) the tone or climate of the organization, such as whether a negative or positive reinforcement tone prevails.

Perhaps the study that comes the closest to this ideal is the one by Kortick and O'Brien (1996), which involved the vast majority of employees ($N = 110$) in an internationally renowned package delivery company. In this study, an internal competition, dubbed the 'world series of quality control,' was introduced. Each of the work teams was divided into leagues and divisions leading to playoffs and a world series. Two aspects important to the company—quality in sorting and loading packages—were assessed. 'For this company, speed and accuracy of package delivery are critical to company success. These outcomes are dependent on the quality of sorting and loading that takes place at their central loading facilities around the country' (p. 79). To increase quality, a combination of consequences was used. Informational consequences in the form of scores were posted weekly for all the teams to see; scoring points based on company quality control measures was a generalized consequence. Social consequences in the form of pizza and beer were also given weekly to the leading team. Each month, winning team members were given individual plaques and treated to dinner. As shown in Figure 8.2, the quality of sorting soared. Before (and after) the world series, performance hovered at or below 2200 packages. Only during the positive reinforcement phase did the company meet the standard of 3000. Company officials were so pleased with the results that they expanded the competition and instituted a regional competition between facilities in the entire Northeast region. Furthermore, some anecdotal comments indicated that employees enjoyed the competition. One employee from a winning facility was quoted as saying, 'I really eat up this competition between facilities. I think it generates a lot of pride in the job because it brings people together' (p. 91).

While this study included all the teams in the organization, incorporated meaningful company-wide indices, and used a variety of consequences that made a striking difference in the quality of employees' performance, we would not stop there. In addition, we would also like to see all employees' reactions to the intervention, a rethinking of the standard, the inclusion of indigenous reinforcers such as raises and promotions, and a focus on supervisory personnel and what they can and should do to maintain the productivity and well-being of employees in the functioning of the organization as a whole.

While we would not be so bold as to speak for founders Baer, Wolf and Risley (1968), the evidence from 126 studies spanning almost three decades indicates that their dream of promoting 'socially important behaviors' (p. 91) continues to be realized. As we stand on the threshold of the twenty-first century, we remain hopeful that our wishes concerning the tried and the true and the yet to be realized will be fulfilled, however, much remains to be done to realize their vision of 'a better state of society' (p. 91).

## ACKNOWLEDGMENTS

With many thanks to Jennifer Scharer and Josh Phillips for their typically unsung efforts behind the scenes, as well as the many investigators who allowed us to draw together such a cacophony of voices.

## REFERENCES

### Articles Referred to in the Text

Aamodt, M. (1996). *Applied Industrial/Organizational Psychology* (2nd edn.). Pacific Grove, CA: Brooks/Cole.

Alavosius, M. P. & Sulzer Azaroff, B. (1990). Acquisition and maintenance of health-care routines as a function of feedback density. *Journal of Applied Behavior Analysis*, 23(2), 151–162.

Anderson, D. C., Crowell, C. R., Doman, M. & Howard, G. S. (1988). Performance posting, goal setting, and activity-contingent praise as applied to a university hockey team. *Journal of Applied Psychology*, 73(1), 87–95.

Andrasik, F. (1979). Organizational behavior modification in business settings: A methodological and content review. *Journal of Organizational Behavior Management*, **2**, 85–102.

Anderson, D. C., Crowell, C. R., Sucec, J., Gilligan, K. D. & Wikoff, M. (1982). Behavior management of client contacts in a real estate brokerage: Getting agents to sell more. *Journal of Organizational Behavior Management*, **17**(1), 37–64.

Arvey, R. D. & Jones, A. P. (1985). The use of discipline in organizational settings: A framework for future research. *Research in Organizational Behavior*, **5**, 367–408.

Austin, J., Kessler, M. L., Riccobono, J. E., & Bailey, J. S. (1996). Using feedback and reinforcement to improve the performance and safety of a roofing crew. *Journal of Organizational Behavior Management*, **16**(2), 49–74.

Ayllon, T. & Azrin, N. (1968). *The Token Economy: A Motivational System for Therapy and Rehabilitation*. New York: Appleton-Century-Crofts.

Baer, D. M., Wolf, M. M. & Risley, T. R. (1968). Some current dimensions of applied behavior analysis. *Journal of Applied Behavior Analysis*, **1**, 91–97.

Balcazar, F. E., Shupert, M. K., Daniels, A. C., Mawhinney, T. C. & Hopkins, B. L. (1989). An objective review and analysis of ten years of publication in the *Journal of Organizational Behavior Management*. *Journal of Organizational Behavior Management*, **10**(1), 7–37.

Baron, R. A. (1988). Negative effects of destructive criticism: Impact on conflict, self-efficacy, and task performance. *Journal of Applied Psychology*, **73**, 200–206.

Becker, W. C., Madsen, C. H., Jr., Arnold, C. R. & Thomas, D. R. (1967). The contingent use of teacher attention and praise in reducing classroom behavior problems. *Journal of Special Education*, **1**(3), 287–307.

Bem, D. J. & Funder D. C. (1978). Predicting more of the people more of the time: Assessing the personality of situations. *Psychology Review*, **85**, 485–501.

Briscoe, R. V., Hoffman, D. B. & Bailey, J. S. (1975). Behavioral community psychology: Training a community board to problem solve. *Journal of Applied Behavior Analysis*, **8**(2), 157–168.

Brown, K. A. & Huber, V. L. (1992). Lowering floors and raising ceilings: A longitudinal assessment of the effects of an earnings-at-risk plan on pay performance. *Personnel Psychology*, **45**(2), 279–311.

Brown, K. M., Willis, B. S. & Reid, D. H (1981). Differential effects on supervisor verbal feedback and feedback plus approval on institutional performance. *Journal of Organizational Behavior Management*, **3**, 57–68.

Busk, P. L. & Marascuilo, L. A. (1988). Autocorrelation in single-subject research: A counter argument to the myth of no autocorrelation. *Behavioral Assessment*, **10**, 229–242.

Campbell, D. T. & Stanley, J. C. (1963). Experimental and quasi-experimental designs for research. In N. L. Gage (Ed.), *Handbook of Research on Teaching*. Chicago: Rand McNally.

Cascio, W. F. & Bernardin, H. J. (1981). Implications of performance appraisal litigation for personnel decisions. *Personnel Psychology*, **34**, 211–225.

Cherrington, D. J., Reitz, H. J. & Scott, W. E., Jr. (1971). Effects of contingent and noncontingent reward on the relationship between satisfaction and task performance. *Journal of Applied Psychology*, **55**(6), 531–536.

Chhokar, J. S. & Wallin, J. A. (1984). A field study of the effect of feedback frequency on performance. *Journal of Applied Psychology*, **69**, 524–530.

Cone, J. D. (1980). Template matching procedures for idiographic behavioral assessment. Paper presented at the meeting of the Association for Advancement of Behavior Therapy, New York.

Cooper, M. L., Thomson, C. L. & Baer, D. M. (1970). The experimental modification of teaching attending behavior. *Journal of Applied Behavior Analysis*, **3**(2), 153–157.

Daniels, A. C. (1989). *Performance Management: Improving Quality Productivity through Positive Reinforcement* (3rd ed). Tucker, GA: Performance Management.

Daniels, A. C. (1994). *Bringing Out the Best in People*. New York: McGraw-Hill.

Datel, W. E. & Legters, L. J. (1971). The psychology of the army recruit. *Journal of Biological Psychology*, **12**(2), 34–40.

Deluga, R. J. & Andrews, H. M. (1985/1986). A case study investigating the effects of a low-cost intervention to reduce three attendance behavior problems in a clerical training program. *Journal of Organizational Behavior Management*, **7**(3/4), 115–124.

DeProspero, A. & Cohen, S. (1979). Inconsistent visual analyses of intrasubject data. *Journal of Applied Behavior Analysis*, **12**(4), 573–579.

Diamante, T. (1993). The durability factor: A systems approach to management endurance. *Leadership and Organization Development Journal*, **13**(4), 14–19.

Diamante, T. & Giglio, L. A. (1992). The durability factor: A systems approach to managerial endurance. *Leadership and Organizational Development Journal*, **13**(4), 14–19.

Dillon, M. J., Kent, H. M. & Malott, R. W. (1980). A supervisory system for accomplishing long-range projects: An application to master's thesis research. *Journal of Organizational Behavior Management*, **2**(3), 213–228.

Eichenwald, K. (10 November 1996). The two faces of Texaco. *New York Times*, p. E2, F10–11.

Elizur, D. (1987). Effect of feedback on verbal and non-verbal courtesy in a bank setting. *Applied Psychology: An International Review*, **36**(2), 147–156.

Erez, M. (1977). Feedback: A necessary condition for the goal setting–performance relationship. *Journal of Applied Psychology*, **62**(5), 624–627.

Fairbank, J. A. & Prue, D. M. (1982). Developing performance feedback systems. In L. W. Frederiksen (Ed.), *Handbook of Organizational Behavior Management* (pp. 281–300). New York: Wiley.

Fellows, C. & Mawhinney, T. C. (1997). Improving telemarketers' performance in the short run using operant concepts. *Journal of Business and Psychology*, **11**(4), 411–424.

Finkelstein, K. E. (7 May 1999). Rookies told to serve, protect and respect, *New York Times*, p. B3.

Ford, J. E. (1981). A simple punishment procedure for controlling employee absenteeism. *Journal of Organizational Behavior Management*, **3**(2), 71–79.

Fox, D. K., Hopkins, B. L. & Anger, W. K. (1987). The long-term effects of a token economy on safety performance in open-pit mining. *Journal of Applied Behavior Analysis*, **20**(3), 215–224.

Frederikson, L. W. (1982). *Handbook of Organizational Behavior Management*. New York: Wiley.

Gaetani, J. J., Johnson, C. M. & Austin, J. T. (1983). Self-management by an owner of a small business: Reduction of tardiness. *Journal of Organizational Behavior Management*, **5**(1), 31–39.

Garson, B. E. & Stanwyck, D. J. (1997). Locus of control and incentive in self-managing teams. *Human Resource Development Quarterly*, **8**(3), 247–258.

Geller, E. S., Eason, S. L., Phillips, J. A. & Pierson, M. D. (1980). Interventions to improve sanitation during food preparation. *Journal of Organizational Behavior Management*, **2**(3), 229–240.

Gellerman, S. W. (1976, March–April). Supervision: Substance and style. *Harvard Business Review*, **21**, 89–99.

Gentile, J. R., Roden, A. H. & Klein, R. D. (1972). An analysis-of-variance model for the intrasubject replication design. *Journal of Applied Behavior Analysis*, **5**(2), 193–198.

Geoghegan, T. (1999). *Pursuing the Promise of American Life*. New York: Pantheon.

Gilchrist, J. A. & White, K. D. (1990). Policy development and satisfaction with merit pay: A field study in a university setting. *College Student Journal*, **24**(3), 249–254.

Gillat, A. & Sulzer-Azaroff, B. (1994). Promoting principles: Managerial involvement in instructional improvement. *Journal of Applied Behavior Analysis*, 27(1), 115–129.

Goltz, S. M., Citera, M., Jensen, M. & Favero, J. (1989). Individual feedback: Does it enhance effects of group feedback? *Journal of Organizational Behavior Management*, 10(2), 77–92.

Grove, A. S. (1983). Keeping favoritism and prejudice out of evaluations. In D. Asman (Ed.), *The Wall Street Journal on Management 2*. New York: Penguin.

Gupton, T. & LeBow, M. D. (1971). Behavior management in a large industrial firm. *Behavior Therapy*, 2, 78–82.

Hackman, J. R. & Morris, C. G. (1975). Group tasks, group interaction process, and group performance effectiveness: A review and proposed integration. In L. Berkowitz (Ed.), *Advances in Experimental Psychology*. New York: Academic Press.

Hackman, J. R. & Walton, R. E. (1986). Leading groups in organizations. In P. S. Goodman & Associates (Eds), *Designing Effective Work Groups* (pp. 72–119). San Francisco: Jossey-Bass.

Hammer, W. C. (1974). Reinforcement theory and contingency management in organizational settings. In H. L. Tosi & W. C. Hammer (Eds), *Organizational Behavior and Management: A Contingency Approach*. Chicago: St. Clair Press.

Harchik, A. E., Sherman, J. A., Sheldon, J. B. & Strouse, M. C. (1992). Ongoing consulation as a method of improving performance of staff members in a group home. *Journal of Applied Behavior Analysis*, 25(3), 599–610.

Hartmann, D. P. (1974). Forcing square pegs into round holes. Some comments on 'An analysis-of-variance models for the intrasubject replication design'. *Journal of Applied Behavior Analysis*, 7, 635–638.

Hayes, S. C., Rincover, A. & Solnick, J. V. (1980). The technical drift of applied behavior analysis. *Journal of Applied Behavior Analysis*, 13(2), 275–286.

Haynes, R. S., Pine, R. C. & Fitch, H. G. (1982). Reducing accident rates with organizational behavior modification. *Academy of Management Journal*, 25, 407–416.

Heward, W. L. (1978). Operant conditioning of a .300 hitter? The effects of reinforcement on the offensive efficiency of a barnstorming baseball team. *Behavior Modification*, 2, 25–40.

Hills, F. S., Scott, K. D., Markham, S. E. & Vest, M. J. (1987). Merit pay: Just or unjust desserts. *Personnel Administrator*, 32(8), 53–59.

Honig, W. K. (1966). *Operant Behavior: Areas of Research and Application*. New York: Appleton-Century-Crofts.

Hopkins, B. L., Conrad, R. J. & Smith, M. J. (1986). Effective and reliable behavioral control technology. *American Industrial Hygiene Association Journal*, 47(12), 785–791.

Hopkins, B. L. & Sears, J. (1982). Managing behavior for productivity. In L. W. Frederiksen (Ed.), *Handbook of Organizational Behavior Management*. New York: Wiley.

Houmanfar, R. & Hayes, L. J. (1998). Effects of feedback on task completion, time distribution and time allocation of graduate students. *Journal of Organizational Behavior Management*, 18(1), 69–91.

Huitema, B. E. (1988). Autocorrelation: 10 years of confusion. *Behavioral Assessment*, 10(3), 253–294.

Ilgen, D. R., Fisher, C. D. & Taylor, M. S. (1979). Consequences of individual feedback on behavior in organizations. *Journal of Applied Psychology*, 64, 349–371.

Johnson, G. A. (1975). The relative efficacy of stimulus versus reinforcement control for obtaining stable performance change. *Organizational Behavior and Human Performance*, 14, 321–341.

Johnson, M. D. & Fawcett, S. B. (1994). Courteous service: Its assessment and modification in a human service organization. *Journal of Applied Behavior Analysis*, 27, 145–152.

Muchinsky, P. (1997). *Psychology Applied to Work: An Introduction to Industrial and Organizational Psychology*. Pacific Grove, CA: Brooks/Cole.

Nasanen, M. & Saari, J. (1987). The effects of positive feedback on housekeeping and accidents at a shipyard. *Journal of Occupational Accidents*, 8, 237–250.

Neale, J. M. & Liebert, R. M. (1986). *Science and Behavior: An Introduction to Methods of Research*, 3rd edn. Englewood Cliffs, NJ: Prentice-Hall.

Nemeroff, W. F. & Cosentino, J. (1979). Utilizing feedback and goal setting to increase performance appraisal interviwer skills of managers. *Academy of Management Journal*, 22(3), 566–575.

Nord, W. R. (1969). Beyond the teaching machine: The neglected area of operant conditioning in the theory and practice of management. *Organizational Behavior and Human Performance*, 4, 375–401.

Nordstrom, R., Hall, R. V., Lorenzi, P. & Delquadri, J. (1988). Organizational behavior modification in the public sector: Three field experiments. *Journal of Organizational Behavior Management*, 9(2), 91–112.

O'Brien, R. M., Dickinson, A. M. & Rosow, M. (Eds) (1982). *Industrial Behavior Modification: A Learning-based Approach to Business Management*. New York: Pergamon.

O'Hara, K., Johnson, C. M. & Beehr, T. A. (1985). Organizational behavior management in the private sector: A review of empirical research and recommendations for further investigation. *Academy of Management Review*, 10, 848–864.

Panyan, M., Boozer, H., & Morris, N. (1970). Feedback to attendants as a reinforcer for applying operant techniques. *Journal of Applied Behavior Analysis*, 3(1), 1–4.

Parsons, M. B. & Reid, D. H. (1995). Training residential supervisors to provide feedback for maintaining staff teaching skills with people who have severe disabilities. *Journal of Applied Behavior Analysis*, 28(3), 317–322.

Pedalino, E. & Gamboa, V. U. (1974). Behavior modifications and absenteeism: Intervention in one industrial setting. *Journal of Applied Psychology*, 59, 694–698.

Pierce, C. H. & Risley, T. R. (1974). Improving job performance of neighborhood youth corps aides in an urban recreation program. *Journal of Applied Behavior Analysis*, 7(2), 207–215.

Podsakoff, P. M., Todor, W. D., Grover, R. A. & Huber, V. L. (1984). Situation modifiers of leader reward and punishment behaviors: Fact or fiction? *Organizational Behavior and Human Decision Processes*, 34(1), 21–63.

Pommer, D. A. & Streedbeck, D. (1974). Motivating staff performance in an operant learning program for children. *Journal of Applied Behavior Analysis*, 7, 217–221.

Porter, L. W. (1973). Turning work into nonwork: The rewarding environment. In M. D. Dunnette (Ed.), *Work and Non-work in the Year 2001* (pp. 113–133). Belmont, CA: Wadsworth.

Premack, D. (1965). Reinforcement theory. In D. Levine (Ed.), *Nebraska Symposium on Motivation*. Lincoln: University of Nebraska Press.

Price Waterhouse v. *Hopkins*, 490 U.S. 228 (1989).

Pritchard, R. D., Jones, S. D., Roth, P. L., Stuebing, K. K. & Ekeberg, E. (1988). Effects of group feedback, goal setting, and incentives on organizational productivity. *Journal of Applied Psychology*, 73, 337–358.

Pritchard, R. D., Leonard, D. W., Von Bergen, C. W. & Kirk, R. J. (1976). The effect of varying schedules of reinforcement on human task performance. *Organizational Behavior and Human Performance*, 16, 205–230.

Quilitch, H. R. (1975). A comparison of three staff-management procedures. *Journal of Applied Behavior Analysis*, 8, 59–66.

Reber, R. A. & Wallin, J. A. (1984). The effects of training, goal setting, and knowledge of results on safe behavior: A component analysis. *Academy of Management Journal*, 27(3), 544–560.

Redmon, W. K. (1992). Opportunities for applied behavior analysis in the total quality movement. *Journal of Applied Behavior Analysis*, 25, 545–550.

Reich, R. (7 March 1999). The secret lives of citizens. *New York Times*, p. B8.

Roberts, B. & White, J. E. (1998). *Roberts vs. Texaco: A True Story of Race and Corporate America*. New York: Avon.

Roberts, B., Chambers, S., Williams, J. L., Harris, M., Hester, B., & Shinault, V. vs. Texaco, Inc., 94 Civ. 2015 (1994).

Rudd, J. R. & Geller, E. S. (1985). A university-based incentive program to increase safety belt use: Toward cost-effective institutionalization. *Journal of Applied Behavior Analysis*, 18, 215–226.

Runkel, P. J., & McGrath, J. E. (1972). *Research on Human Behavior*. New York: Holt, Rinehart.

Saari, J. (1987). Management of housekeeping by feedback. *Ergonomics*, 30, 313–317.

Sayles, L. (1979). *Leadership: What Effective Managers Really Do . . . and How They Do It*. New York: McGraw-Hill.

Schay, B. W. (1988). Effects of performance-contingent pay on employee attitudes. *Public Personnel Management*, 17(2), 237–250.

Schliefer, L. M. & Amick, B. C. (1989). System response time and method of pay: Stress effects in computer-based tasks. *International Journal of Human Computer Interaction*, 1(1), 23–39.

Schliefer, L. M. & Okogbaa, O. G. (1990). System response time and method of pay: Cardiovascular stress effects in computer-based tasks. *Ergonomics*, 33(12), 1495–1509.

Schwartz, I. S. & Baer, D. M. (1991). Social validity assessments: Current practice state of the art? *Journal of Applied Behavior Analysis*, 24, 189–204.

Sharpley, C. F. & Alavasius, M. P. (1988). Autocorrelation in behavioral data: An alternative prospective. *Behavioral Assessment*, 10, 243–251.

Shook, G. L., Johnson, C. M. & Uhlman, W. F. (1978). The effect of response effort reduction, instructions, group and individual feedback, and reinforcement on staff performance. *Journal of Organizational Behavior Management*, 1(3), 206–215.

Sidman, M. (1960). *Tactics of Scientific Research: Evaluating Experimental Data in Psychology*. New York: Basic Books.

Siero, S., Boon, M., Kok, G. & Siero, F. (1989). Modification of driving behavior in a large transport organization: A field experiment. *Journal of Applied Psychology*, 74, 417–423.

Silva, D. B., Duncan, P. K. & Doudna, D. (1982). The effects of attendance-contingent feedback and praise on attendance and work efficiency. *Journal of Organizational Behavior Management*, 3(2), 11–44.

Skinner, B. F. (1974). *About Behaviorism*. New York: Vintage.

Stajkovic, A. D. & Luthans, F. (1997). A meta-analysis of the effects of organizational behavior modification on task performance, 1975–95. *Academy of Management Journal*, 40(5), 1122–1149.

Steers, R. M. & Porter, L. W. (1987). *Motivation and Work Behavior* (4th edn). New York: McGraw-Hill.

Stephens, T. A. & Burroughs, W. A. (1978). An application of operant conditioning to absenteeism in a hospital setting. *Journal of Applied Psychology*, 63(4), 518–521.

Stogdill, R. M. (1974). *Handbook of Leadership* (1st edn). New York: Free Press.

Suen, H. K. (1987). On the epistemology of autocorrelation in applied behavior analysis. *Behavioral Assessment*, 9, 113–124.

Suen, H. K. & Ary, D. (1987). Autocorrelation in applied behavior analysis: Myth or reality? *Behavioral Assessment*, 9, 125–130.

Sulzer-Azaroff, B. & de Santamaria, M. C. (1980). Industrial safety hazard reduction through performance feedback. *Journal of Applied Behavior Analysis*, 13(2), 287–295.

Thorensen, C. E. & Elashoff, J. D. (1974). 'An analysis-of-variance model for intra-subject replication design': Some additional comments. *Journal of Applied Behavior Analysis*, 7(4), 639–641.

Terpstra, D. E. (1981). Relationship between methodological rigor and reported outcomes in organizational development evaluation research. *Journal of Applied Psychology*, **66**, 541–543.

Ulrich, R., Stachnik, T. & Mabry, J. (Eds) (1966). *Control of Human Behavior*, Vol. 1. Glenview, IL: Scott, Foresman.

Ulrich, R., Stachnik, T. & Mabry, J. (Eds) (1970). *Control of Human Behavior*, Vol. 2. Glenview, IL: Scott, Foresman.

Ulrich, R., Stachnik, T. & Mabry, J. (Eds) (1974). *Control of Human Behavior*, Vol. 3. Glenview, IL: Scott, Foresman.

Webb, W. (1991). Resistant employees: Implications for EAP counselors. *Employee Assistance Quarterly*, 7(1), 9–18.

Welsh, D. H. B., Luthans, F. & Sommer, S. M. (1993). Organizational behavior modification goes to Russia: Replicating an experimental analysis across cultures and tasks. *Journal of Organizational Behavior Management*, **13**(2), 15–35.

Where Skinner's theories work, *Business Week* (1972, December), pp. 64–65.

Whyte, W. F. (1972). Skinnerian theory in organizations. *Psychology Today*, April, 67–68, 96, 98, 100.

Wikoff, M., Anderson, D. C. & Crowell, C. R. (1982). Behavior management in a factory setting: Increasing work efficency. *Journal of Organizational Behavior Management*, 4(1/2), 97–127.

Wilk, L. A. & Redmon, W. K. (1990). A daily-adjusted goal-setting and feedback procedure for improving productivity in a university admissions department. *Journal of Organizational Behavior Management*, 11(1), 55–75.

Williams, M. E. (Ed.) (1997). *Discrimination: Opposing Viewpoints* . San Diego, CA: Greenhaven Press.

Winett, R. A., Moore, J. F. & Anderson, E. S. (1991). Extending the concept of social validity: Behavior analysis for disease prevention and health promotion. *Journal of Applied Behavior Analysis* , **24**, 215–230.

Wisdom, B. & Patzig, D. (1987). Does your organization have the right climate for merit? *Public Personnel Management*, **16**, 127–133.

Wittkopp, C. J., Rowan, J. F. & Poling, A. (1990). Use of a feedback package to reduce machine set-up time in a manufacturing plant. *Journal of Organizational Behavior Management*, **11**(2), 7–22.

Wolf, M. M. (1978). Social validity: The case for subjective measurement or how applied behavior analysis is finding its heart. *Journal of Applied Behavior Analysis* , **11**, 203–214.

Wolf, M. M., Kirigin, K. A., Fixsen, D. L., Blase, K. A. & Braukman, C. J. (1995). The teaching–family model: A case study in data-based program development and refinement (and dragon wrestling). *Journal of Organizational Behavior Management*, **15**(1/2), 11–68.

Yukl, G. A. & Latham, G. P. (1975). Consequences of reinforcement schedules and incentive magnitudes for employee performance: Problems encountered in an industrial setting. *Journal of Applied Psychology*, **60**, 294–298.

Yukl, G., Latham, G. P. & Pursell, E. D. (1976). The effectiveness of performance incentives under continuous and variable ratio schedules of reinforcement. *Personnel Psychology*, **29**, 221–232.

Zohar, D. & Fussfeld, N. (1981). Modifying earplug wearing behavior by behavior modification techniques: An empirical evaluation. *Journal of Organizational Behavior Management*, **3**(2), 41–52.

Zohar, D., Cohen, A. & Azar, N. (1980). Promoting increased use of ear protectors in noise through information feedback. *Human Factors*, **22**(1), 69–79.

## Articles Referred to in the Tables

Abernathy, W. B., Duffy, E. M., & O'Brien, R. M. (1982). Multi-branch, multi-systems programs in banking: An organization-wide intervention. In R. M. O'Brien, A. M. Dickinson & M. P. Rosow (Eds), *Industrial Behavior Modification* (pp. 370–382). New York: Pergamon Press.

Alavosius, M. P. & Sulzer-Azaroff, B. (1986). The effects of performance feedback on the safety of client lifting and transfer. *Journal of Applied Behavior Analysis*, 19(3), 261–267.

Alavosius, M. P. & Sulzer-Azaroff, B. (1990). Acquisition and maintenance of health-care routines as a function of feedback density. *Journal of Applied Behavior Analysis*, 23(2), 151–162.

Allison, D. B., Silverstein, J. M. & Galante, V. (1992). Relative effectiveness and cost-effectiveness of cooperative, competitive and independent monetary incentive systems. *Journal of Organizational Behavior Mangement*, 13(1), 85–112.

Anderson, D. C., Crowell, C. R., Hantula, D. A. & Siroky, L. M. (1988). Task clarification and individual performance posting for improving cleaning in a student-managed university bar. *Journal of Organizational Behavior Management*, 9(2), 73–90.

Anderson, D. C., Crowell, C. R., Sucec, J., Gilligan, K. D. & Wikoff, M. (1982). Behavior management of client contacts in a real estate brokerage: Getting agents to sell more. *Journal of Organizational Behavior Management* 4(1–2), 67–95.

Arco, L. (1997). Improving program outcome with process-based feedback. *Journal of Organizational Behavior Management*, 17(1), 37–64.

Brand, D. D., Staelin, J. R., O'Brien, R. M. & Dickinson, A. M. (1982). Improving white collar productivity at HUD. In R. M. O'Brien, A. M. Dickinson & M. P. Rosow (Eds), *Industrial Behavior Modification: A Management Handbook* (pp. 307–334). New York: Pergamon Press.

Brown, M. G., Malott, R. W., Dillon, M. J. & Keeps, E. J. (1980). Improving customer service in a large department store through the use of training and feedback. *Journal of Organizational Behavior Management*, 2(4), 251–265.

Brown, N. & Redmon, W. K. (1989). The effects of a group reinforcement contingency on staff use of unscheduled sick leave. *Journal of Organizational Behavior Management*, 10(2), 3–17.

Brown, K. M., Willis, B. S. & Reid, D. H. (1981). Differential effects of supervisor verbal feedback and feedback plus approval on institutional staff performance. *Journal of Organizational Behavior Management*, 3(1), 57–68.

Burgio, L. D., Engel, B. T., Hawkins, A. M. & McCormick, K. A. (1990). A staff management system for maintaining improvements in continence with elderly nursing home residents. *Journal of Applied Behavior Analysis*, 23(1), 111–118.

Calpin, J. P., Edelstein, B. & Redmon, W. K. (1987). Performance feedback and goal setting to improve mental health center staff productivity. *Journal of Organizational Behavior Management*, 9(2), 35–58.

Carlson, J. G. & Hill, K. D. (1982). The effect of gaming on attendance and attitude. *Personnel Psychology*, 35, 63–73.

Carnine, D. W. & Fink, W. T. (1978). Increasing the rate of presentation and use of signals in elementary classrooms. *Journal of Applied Behavior Analysis*, 11(1), 35–46.

Carter, N., Holstrom, A., Simpanen, M. & Melin, L. (1988). Theft reduction in a grocery store through product identification and graphing of losses for employees. *Journal of Applied Behavior Analysis*, 21(4), 23–49.

Chhokar, J. S. & Wallin, J. A. (1984). A field study of the effect of feedback frequency on performance. *Journal of Applied Psychology*, 69, 524–530.

Cooper, M. L., Thomson, C. L. & Baer, D. M. (1970). The experimental modification of teaching attending behavior. *Journal of Applied Behavior Analysis*, 3(2), 153–157.

Cossairt, A., Hall, R. V. & Hopkins, B. L. (1973). The effects of experimenter's instructions, feedback, and praise on teacher praise and student attending behavior. *Journal of Applied Behavior Analysis*, **6**(1), 89–100.

Crowell, C. R., Anderson, D. C., Abel, D. M. & Sergio, J. P. (1988). Task clarification, performance feedback, and social praise: Procedures for improving the customer service of bank tellers. *Journal of Applied Behavior Analysis*, **21**(1), 65–71.

Deluga, R. J. & Andrews, H. M. (1985/1986). A case study investigating the effects of a low-cost intervention to reduce three attendance behavior problems in a clerical training program. *Journal of Organizational Behavior Management*, **7**(3/4), 115–124.

Dillon, M. J., Kent, H. M. & Malott, R. W. (1980). A supervisory system for accomplishing long-range projects: An application to master's thesis research. *Journal of Organizational Behavior Management*, **2**(3), 213–228.

Elizur, D. (1987). Effect of feedback on verbal and non-verbal courtesy in a bank setting. *Applied Psychology: An International Review*, **36**(2), 147–156.

Emmert, G. D. (1978). Measuring the impact of group performance feedback versus individual performance feedback in an industrial setting. *Journal of Organizational Behavior Management*, **1**(2), 134–141.

Evans, K. M., Kienast, P. & Mitchell, T. R. (1988). The effects of lottery incentive programs on performance. *Journal of Organizational Behavior Management*, **9**(2), 113–136.

Fellner, D. J. & Sulzer-Azaroff, B. (1984). Increasing industrial safety practices and conditions through posted feedback. *Journal of Safety Research*, **15**(1), 7–21.

Fellows, C. & Mawhinney, T. C. (1997). Improving telemarketers' performance in the short-run using operant concepts. *Journal of Business and Psychology*, **11**(4), 411–424.

Fleming, R. & Sulzer-Azaroff, B. (1992). Reciprocal peer management: Improving staff instruction in a vocational training program. *Journal of Applied Behavior Analysis*, **25**(3), 611–620.

Ford, J. E. (1981). A simple punishment procedure for controlling employee absenteeism. *Journal of Organizational Behavior Management*, **3**(2), 71–79.

Fox, D. K., Hopkins, B. L. & Anger, W. K. (1987). The long-term effects of a token economy on safety performance in open-pit mining. *Journal of Applied Behavior Analysis*, **20**(3), 215–224.

Fox, C. J. & Sulzer-Azaroff, B. (1987). Increasing completion of accident reports. *Journal of Safety Research*, **18**(2), 65–71.

Fox, C. J., & Sulzer-Azaroff, B. (1989). The effectiveness of two different sources of feedback on staff teaching of fire evacuation skills. *Journal of Organizational Behavior Management*, **10**(2), 19–36.

Frayne, C. A. & Latham, G. P. (1987). Application of social learning theory to employee self-management of attendance. *Journal of Applied Psychology*, **72**(3), 387–392.

Frederiksen, L. W., Richter, W. T., Jr., Johnson, R. P. & Solomon, L. J. (1981/1982). Specificity of performance feedback in a professional service delivery setting. *Journal of Organizational Behavior Management*, **3**(4), 41–53.

Frost, J. M., Hopkins, B. L. & Conrad, R. J. (1981). An analysis of the effects of feedback and reinforcement on machine-paced production. *Journal of Organizational Behavior Management*, **3**(2), 5–17.

Fulton, B. J. & Malott, R. W. (1981–82). The structured meeting system: A procedure for improving the completion of nonrecurring tasks. *Journal of Organizational Behavior Management*, **3**(4), 7–18.

Gaetani, J. J. & Johnson, C. M. (1983). The effect of data plotting, praise, and state lottery tickets on decreasing cash shortages in a retail beverage chain. *Journal of Organizational Behavior Management*, **5**(1), 5–15.

Gaetani, J. J., Johnson, C. M. & Austin, J. T. (1983). Self-management by an owner of a small business: Reduction of tardiness. *Journal of Organizational Behavior Management*, **5**(1), 31–39.

Geller, E. S., Eason, S. L., Phillips, J. A. & Pierson, M. D. (1980). Interventions to improve sanitation during food preparation. *Journal of Organizational Behavior Management*, **2**(3), 229–240.

George, J. T. & Hopkins, B. L. (1989). Multiple effects of performance-contingent pay for waitpersons. *Journal of Applied Behavior Analysis*, **22**(2), 131–141.

Gillat, A. & Sulzer-Azaroff, B. (1994). Promoting principles: Managerial involvement in instructional improvement. *Journal of Applied Behavior Analysis*, **27**(1), 115–129.

Godbey, C. L. & White, A. G. (1992). Increasing the accuracy of computerized summaries of court case activity. *Journal of Organizational Behavior Management*, **13**(1), 113–127.

Goltz, S. M., Citera, M., Jensen, M. & Favero, J. (1989). Individual feedback: Does it enhance effects of group feedback? *Journal of Organizational Behavior Management*, **10**(2), 77–92.

Gupton, T. & LeBow, M. D. (1971). Behavior management in a large industrial firm. *Behavior Therapy*, **2**, 78–82.

Harchik, A. E., Sherman, J. A., Sheldon, J. B. & Strouse, M. C. (1992). Ongoing consulation as a method of improving performance of staff members in a group home. *Journal of Applied Behavior Analysis*, **25**(3), 599–610.

Haynes, R. S., Pine, R. C. & Fitch, H. G. (1982). Reducing accident rates with organizational behavior modification. *Academy of Management Journal*, **25**(2), 407–416.

Henry, G. O. & Redmon, W. K. (1990). The effects of performance setback on the implementation of statistical process control (SPC) program. *Journal of Organizational Behavior Management*, **11**(2), 23–26.

Hermann, J. A., De Montes, A. I., Dominguez, B., Montes, F. & Hopkins, B. L. (1973). Effects of bonuses for punctuality on the tardiness of industrial workers. *Journal of Applied Behavior Analysis*, **6**, 563–570.

Heward, W. L. (1978). Operant conditioning of a .300 hitter? The effects of reinforcement on the offensive efficiency of a barnstorming baseball team. *Behavior Modification*, **2**, 25–40.

Hopkins, B. L., Conrad, R. J., Dangel, R. F., Fitch, H. G., Smith, M. J. & Anger, W. K. (1986a). Behavioral technology for reducing occupational exposure to styrene. *Journal of Applied Behavior Analysis* **19**(1), 3–11.

Hopkins, B. L., Conrad, R. J. & Smith, M. J. (1986b). Effective and reliable behavioral control technology. *American Industrial Hygiene Association Journal*, **47**(12), 785–791.

Houmanfar, R. & Hayes, L. J. (1998). Effects of feedback on task completion, time distribution and time allocation of graduate students. *Journal of Organizational Behavior Management*, **18**(1), 69–91.

Hundall, P. S. (1969). Knowledge of performance as an incentive in repetitive industrial work. *Journal of Applied Psychology*, **53**(3), 224–226.

Ingham, P. & Greer, R. D. (1992). Changes in student and teacher responses in observed and generalized settings as a function of supervisor observations. *Journal of Applied Behavior Analysis*, **25**(1), 153–164.

Iwata, B. A., Bailey, J. S., Brown, K. M., Foshee, T. J. & Alpern, M. (1976). A performance-based lottery to improve residential care and training by institutional staff. *Journal of Applied Behavior Analysis*, **9**(4), 417–431.

Johnson, M. D. & Fawcett, S. B. (1994). Courteous service: Its assessment and modification in a human service organization. *Journal of Applied Behavior Analysis*, **27**, 145–152.

Johnson, R. P. & Fredrikson, L. W. (1983). Process vs. outcome feedback and goal setting in a human service organization. *Journal of Organizational Behavior Management*, **5**(3/4), 37–56.

Johnson, C. M. & Masotti, R. M. (1990). Suggestive selling by waitstaff in family-style restaurants: An experiment and multi-setting observations. *Journal of Organizational Behavior Management*, **11**(1), 35–54.

Johnson, S. P., Welsh, T. M., Miller, L. K. & Altus, D. E. (1991). Participatory management: Maintaining staff performance in a university housing cooperative. *Journal of Applied Behavior Analysis*, **24**(1), 119–128.

Jones, H. H., Morris, E. K. & Barnard, J. D. (1985/1986). Increasing staff completion of civil commitment forms through instructions and graphed group performance feedback. *Journal of Organizational Behavior Management*, **7**(3/4), 29–43.

Kempen, R. W. & Hall, R. V. (1977). Reduction of industrial absenteeism: Results of a behavioral approach. *Journal of Organizational Behavior Management*, **1**(1), 1–21.

Komaki, J. L. (1994). Emergence of the operant model of effective supervision or how an operant conditioner got hooked on leadership. *Leadership and Organization Development Journal*, **25**, 27–32.

Komaki, J. L. (1998). When performance improvement is the goal: A new set of criteria for criteria. *Journal of Applied Behavior Analysis*, **31**, 263–280.

Komaki, J. & Barnett, F. T. (1977). A behavioral approach to coaching football: Improving the play execution of the offensive backfield on a youth football team. *Journal of Applied Behavior Analysis*, **10**, 657–664.

Komaki, J., Barwick, K. D. & Scott, L. R. (1978). A behavioral approach to occupational safety: Pinpointing and reinforcing safe performance in a food manufacturing plant. *Journal of Applied Psychology*, **63**(4), 434–445.

Komaki, J., Blood, M. R. & Holder, D. (1980). Fostering friendliness in a fast foods franchise. *Journal of Organizational Behavior Management*, **2**(3), 151–164.

Komaki, J. L., Collins, R. L. & Penn P. (1982). The role of performance antecedents and consequences in work motivation. *Journal of Applied Psychology*, **67**(3), 334–340.

Komaki, J. L., Collins, R. L. & Temlock, S. (1987). An alternative performance measurement approach: Applied operant measurement in the service sector. [Special Issue] *Applied Psychology: An International Review*, **36**(1), 71–89.

Komaki, J. L., Heinzmann, A. T. & Lawson L. (1980b). Effect of training and feedback: Component analysis of a behavioral safety program. *Journal of Applied Psychology*, **65**(3), 261–270.

Komaki, J., Waddell, W. M., & Pearce, M. G. (1977). The applied behavior analysis approach and individual employees: Improving performance in two small businesses. *Organizational Behavior & Human Performance*, **19**, 337–352.

Kortick, S. A. & O'Brien, R. M. (1996). The world series of quality control: A case study in the package delivery industry. *Journal of Organizational Behavior Management*, **16**(2), 77–93.

Kreitner, R. & Golab, M. (1978). Increasing the rate of salesperson telephone calls with a monetary refund. *Journal of Organizational Behavior Management*, **1**(3), 192–195.

Kreitner, R., Reif, W. E. & Morris, M. (1977). Measuring the impact of feedback on the performance of mental health technicians. *Journal of Organizational Behavior Management*, **1**(1), 105–109.

LaFleur, T. & Hyten, C. (1995). Improving the quality of hotel banquet staff performance. *Journal of Organizational Behavior Management*, **15**(1–2), 69–93.

Lamal, P. A. & Benfield, A. (1978). The effect of self-monitoring on job tardiness and percentage of time spent working. *Journal of Organizational Behavior Management*, **1**(2), 142–149.

LaMere, J. M., Dickinson, A. M., Henry, M. & Henry, G. (1996). Effects of a milticomponent monetary incentive program on the performance of truck drivers: A longitudinal study. *Behavior Modification*, **20**(4), 385–405.

Langeland, K. L., Johnson, C. M. & Mawhinney, T. C. (1998). Improving staff performance in a community mental health setting: Job analysis, training, goal setting, feedback, and years of data. *Journal of Organizational Behavior Management*, **18**(1), 21–43.

Lovett, S. B., Bosmajian, C. P., & Frederiksen, L. W. (1983). Monitoring professional service delivery: An organizational level intervention. *Behavior Therapy*, **14**, 170–177.

Luthans, F., Paul, R. & Baker, D. (1981). An experimental analysis of the impact of contingent reinforcement on salespersons' performance behavior. *Journal of Applied Psychology*, **66**(3), 314–323.

Luthans, F., Paul, R. & Taylor, L. (1985). The impact of contingent reinforcement on retail salespersons' performance behaviors: A replicated field experiment. *Journal of Organizational Behavior Management*, 7(1/2), 25–35.

Maher, C. A. (1982). Improving teacher instructional behavior: Evaluation of a time management training program. *Journal of Organizational Behavior Management*, **4**(3/4), 27–36.

Marholin, D., II & Gray, D. (1976). Effects of group response-cost procedures on cash shortages in a small business. *Journal of Applied Behavior Analysis*, **9**(1), 25–30.

McCarthy, M. (1978). Decreasing the incidence of 'high bobbins' in a textile spinning department through a group feedback procedure. *Journal of Organizational Behavior Management*, **1**(2), 150–154.

McGinsey, J. F., Greene, B. F., & Lutzker, J.R. (1995). Comptence in aspects of behavioral treatment and consultation: Implications for service delivery and graduate training. *Journal of Applied Behavior Analysis*, **28**(3), 301–315.

McKenzie, T. L. & Rushall, B. S. (1974). Effects of self-recording on attendance and performance in a competitive swimming training environment. *Journal of Applied Behavior Analysis*, 7(2), 199–206.

Methot, L. L., Williams, W. L., Cummings, A. & Bradshaw, B. (1996). Measuring the effects of a manager-supervisor training program through the generalized performance of managers, supervisors, front-line staff and clients in a human service setting. *Journal of Organizational Behavior Management*, **16**(2), 3–34.

Nasanen, M. & Saari, J. (1987). The effects of positive feedback on housekeeping and accidents at a shipyard. *Journal of Occupational Accidents*, **8**, 237–250.

Nemeroff, W. F. & Cosentino, J. (1979). Utilizing feedback and goal setting to increase performance appraisal interviwer skills of managers. *Academy of Management Journal*, **22**(3), 566–575.

Newby, T. J. & Robinson, P. W. (1983). Effects of grouped and individual feedback and reinforcement on retail employee performance. *Journal of Organizational Behavior Management*, **5**(2), 51–68.

Nordstrom, R., Hall, R. V., Lorenzi, P. & Delquadri, J. (1987). Organizational behavior modification in the public sector: Three field experiments. *Journal of Organizational Behavior Management*, **9**(1), 428–446.

Orpen, C. (1974). The effect of reward contingencies on the job satisfaction–task performance relationship: An industrial experiment. *Psychology*, **11**(3), 9–14.

Orpen, C. (1978). Effects of bonuses for attendance on the absenteeism of industrial workers. *Journal of Organizational Behavior Management*, **1**(2), 118–124.

Orpen, C. (1981). The effect of a behaviour modification programme on employee job attendance. *Mangement & Labour Studies*, 7(2), 73–76.

Panyan, M., Boozer, H., & Morris, N. (1970). Feedback to attendants as a reinforcer for applying operant techniques. *Journal of Applied Behavior Analysis*, 3(1), 1–4.

Parsons, M. B. & Reid, D. H. (1995). Training residential supervisors to provide feedback for maintaining staff teaching skills with people who have severe disabilities. *Journal of Applied Behavior Analysis*, **28**(3), 317–322.

Pedalino, E., & Gamboa, V. U. (1974). Behavior modifications and absenteeism: Intervention in one industrial setting. *Journal of Applied Psychology*, **59**, 694–698.

Pierce, C. H. & Risley, T. R. (1974). Improving job performance of neighborhood youth corps aides in an urban recreation program. *Journal of Applied Behavior Analysis*, 7(2), 207–215.

Pommer, D. A. & Streedbeck, D. (1974). Motivating staff performance in an operant learning program for children. *Journal of Applied Behavior Analysis*, 7(2), 217–221.

Prue, D. M., Krapfl, J. E., Noah, J. C., Cannon, S. & Maley, R. F. (1980). Managing the treatment activities of state hospital staff. *Journal of Organizational Behavior Management*, 2(3), 165–182.

Quilitch, H. R. (1978). Using a simple feedback procedure to reinforce the submission of written suggestions by mental health employees. *Journal of Organizational Behavior Management*, 1(2), 155–163.

Ralis, M. T. & O'Brien, R. M. (1986). Prompts, goal setting and feedback to increase suggestive selling. *Journal of Organizational Behavior Management*, 8(1), 5–18.

Reber, R. A. & Wallin, J. A. (1984). The effects of training, goal setting, and knowledge of results on safe behavior: A component analysis. *Academy of Management Journal*, 27(3), 544–560.

Reid, D. H., Schuh-Wear, C. L. & Brannon, M. E. (1978). Use of a group contingency to decrease staff absenteeism in a state institution. *Behavior Modification*, 2(2), 251–266.

Richman, G. S., Riordan, M. R., Reiss, M. L., Pyles, D. A. & Bailey, J. S. (1988). The effects of self-monitoring and supervisor feedback on staff performance in a residential setting. *Journal of Applied Behavior Analysis*, 21(4), 401–409.

Saari, J. (1987). Management of housekeeping by feedback. *Ergonomics*, 30, 313–317.

Seaman, J. E., Greene, B. F. & Watson-Perczel, M. (1986). A behavioral system for assessing and training cardiopulmonary resuscitation skills among emergency medical technicians. *Journal of Applied Behavior Analysis*, 19(2), 125–135.

Shoemaker, J. & Reid, D. H. (1980). Decreasing chronic absenteeism among institutional staff: Effects of a low-cost attendance program. *Journal of Organizational Behavior Management*, 2(4), 317–328.

Shook, G. L., Johnson, C. M. & Uhlman, W. F. (1978). The effect of response effort reduction, instructions, group and individual feedback, and reinforcement on staff performance. *Journal of Organizational Behavior Management*, 1(3), 206–215.

Silva, D. B., Duncan, P. K. & Doudna, D. (1982). The effects of attendance-contingent feedback and praise on attendance and work efficiency. *Journal of Organizational Behavior Management*, 3(2), 59–69.

Sulzer-Azaroff, B. (1978). Behavioral ecology and accident prevention. *Journal of Organizational Behavior Management*, 2(1), 11–44.

Sulzer-Azaroff, B., Loafman, B., Merante, R. J. & Hlavecek, A. C. (1990). Improving occupational safety in a large industrial plant: A systematic replication. *Journal of Organizational Behavior Management*, 11(1), 99–120.

Sulzer-Azaroff, B. & de Santamaria, M. C. (1980). Industrial safety hazard reduction through performance feedback. *Journal of Applied Behavior Analysis*, 13(2), 287–295.

Welch, S. J. & Holborn, S. W. (1988). Contingency contracting with delinquents: Effects of a brief training manual on staff contract negotiation and writing skills. *Journal of Applied Behavior Analysis*, 21(4), 357–368.

Welsh, D. H., Bernstein, D. J. & Luthans, F. (1992). Application of the Premack Principle of reinforcement to the quality performance of service employees. *Journal of Organizational Behavior Management*, 13(1), 9–32

Welsh, D. H., Luthans, F. & Sommer, S. M. (1993). Organizational behavior modification goes to Russia: Replicating an experimental analysis across cultures and tasks. *Journal of Organizational Behavior Management*, 13(2), 15–35.

Wikoff, M., Anderson, D.C. & Crowell, C. R. (1982). Behavior management in a factory setting: Increasing work efficiency. *Journal of Organizational Behavior Management*, 4(1/2), 97–127.

Wilk, L. A. & Redmon, W. K. (1990). A daily-adjusted goal-setting and feedback procedure for improving productivity in a university admissions department. *Journal of Organizational Behavior Management*, 11(1), 55–75.

Wilk, L. A. & Redmon, W. K. (1998). The effects of feedback and goal setting on the productivity and satisfaction of university admissions staff. *Journal of Organizational Behavior Management*, 18(1), 45–68.

Wittkopp, C. J., Rowan, J. F. & Poling, A. (1990). Use of a feedback package to reduce machine set-up time in a manufacturing plant. *Journal of Organizational Behavior Management*, 11(2), 7–22.

Zohar, D., Cohen, A. & Azar, N. (1980). Promoting increased use of ear protectors in noise through information feedback. *Human Factors*, 22(1), 69–79.

Zohar, D. & Fussfeld, N. (1981). Modifying earplug wearing behavior by behavior modification techniques: An empirical evaluation. *Journal of Organizational Behavior Management*, 3(2), 41–52.

# INDEX

*Index compiled by Mary Kirkness*

# International Review of Industrial and Organizational Psychology

# CONTENTS OF PREVIOUS VOLUMES

## VOLUME 11—1996

**Self-Esteem and Work,** Locke, McClear and Knight; **Job Design,** Oldham;
**Fairness in the Assessment Centre,** Baron and Janman; **Subgroup Differences
Associated with Different Measures of Some Common Job-Relevant
Constructs,** Schmitt, Clause and Pulakos; **Common Practices in Structural
Equation Modeling,** Kelloway; **Contextualism in Context,** Payne; **Employee
Involvement,** Cotton; **Part-time Employment,** Barling and Gallagher; **The
Interface Between Job and Off-Job Roles: Enhancement and Conflict,**
O'Driscoll

## VOLUME 10—1995

**The Application of Cognitive Constructs and Principles to the Instructional
Systems Model of Training: Implications for Needs Assessment, Design, and
Transfer,** Ford and Kraiger; **Determinants of Human Performance in
Organizational Settings,** Smith; **Personality and Industrial/Organizational
Psychology,** Schneider and Hough; **Managing Diversity: New Broom or Old
Hat?,** Kandola; **Unemployment: Its Psychological Costs,** Winefield; **VDUs in
the Workplace: Psychological Health Implications,** Bramwell and Cooper; **The
Organizational Implications of Teleworking,** Chapman, Sheehy, Heywood,
Dooley and Collins; **The Nature and Effects of Method Variance in
Organizational Research,** Spector and Brannick; **Developments in Eastern
Europe and Work and Organizational Psychology,** Roe

## VOLUME 9—1994

**Psychosocial Factors and the Physical Environment: Inter-Relations in the
Workplace,** Evans, Johnasson and Carrere; **Computer-Based Assessment,**
Bartram; **Applications of Meta-Analysis: 1987–1992,** Tett, Meyer and Roese, **The
Psychology of Strikes,** Bluen; **The Psychology of Strategic Management:
Emerging Themes of Diversity and Cognition,** Sparrow, **Industrial and
Organizational Psychology in Russia: The Concept of Human Functional
States and Applied Stress Research,** Leonova; **The Prevention of Violence at
Work: Application of a Cognitive Behavioural Theory,** Cox and Leather; **The
Psychology of Mergers and Acquisitions,** Hogan and Overmyer-Day; **Recent
Developments in Applied Creativity,** Kabanoff and Rossiter